W9-DED-939

Sundance to Sarajevo

Sundance to Sarajevo

Film Festivals and the World They Made

Kenneth Turan

UNIVERSITY OF CALIFORNIA PRESS

Berkeley Los Angeles London

University of California Press
Berkeley and Los Angeles, California

University of California Press, Ltd.
London, England

Library of Congress Cataloging-in-Publication Data

Turan, Kenneth.
Sundance to Sarajevo : film festivals and the world they made / Kenneth Turan.
p. cm.
ISBN 0-520-21867-1 (alk. paper)
1. Film festivals. I. Title.

PN1993.4 .T865 2002
791.43'079 — dc21 2001044418

Manufactured in Canada
10 09 08 07 06 05 04 03 02
10 9 8 7 6 5 4 3 2 1

The paper used in this publication meets the minimum requirements of ANSI/NISO Z39.48-1992 (R 1997) (*Permanence of Paper*). ⊗

To B, for everything, for always

CONTENTS

PART THREE:
FESTIVALS WITH AESTHETIC AGENDAS

PART FOUR:
THE POLITICS OF FESTIVALS

Acknowledgments

While a fiction writer can create on his or her own, a journalist, to paraphrase Tennessee Williams's especially apt line, is always depending on the kindness of strangers. And when a book has been in the works for as long as this one, close to a decade, that's an awful lot of thank yous.

I'd like to start with people who are hardly strangers, past and current staff at the *Los Angeles Times*, where earlier versions of many of these pieces appeared. Shelby Coffey III, Narda Zacchino, and John Lindsay made it possible for me to become the paper's film critic, and several levels of editors — Oscar Garza, Ann Hurley, Rich Nordwind, Kelly Scott, and Sherry Stern — supported my passion for watching films in distant lands. Francine Della Catena and Cindy Hively helped with selecting and procuring photographs, and *Calendar*'s fine copy editors, too numerous to mention, had the unenviable task of trying to keep errors out of my stories. I'd also like to thank the editors of *Smithsonian*, where a different version of the Pordenone chapter appeared, for believing that the silent film revival was worth a trip to Italy to investigate.

At each festival I went to, the staff and fellow journalists who helped me are too numerous to single out individually, but I could never have survived without their cheerful, selfless assistance. Where Sundance and Cannes are concerned, because I've attended for more than ten years in

a row, I'm going to break precedent and thank Sandra Sapperstein and R. J. Millard for the former and Catherine Verret and Christine Aimé for the latter. I also have nothing but gratitude for the owners and staffs of the Old Miners' Lodge in Park City, Utah, and the Hotel Splendid in Cannes, which have made me feel so at home that I look forward to staying at their establishments at least as much as to the festivals in question.

I'll always be grateful to James Clark at the University of California Press for immediately and wholeheartedly believing in this project, and to Eric Smoodin, who made the transition to finished book as smooth as possible. And of course my agent, Kathy Robbins, whose assistance with the contract was invaluable.

When film becomes your life, it's hard to have any other kind of life, and I would really be remiss if I didn't acknowledge the friends who put up with me while all this was going on. That also goes for my daughters, Whitney and Devin, who have enriched my life in unexpected ways. And to my wife Patty Williams, who also took many of the book's photographs, my thanks are too strong and complex to be safely entrusted to words.

Introduction

No one wants to speak against the Bible, but the sentiment found in Ecclesiastes famously insisting "to every thing there is a season, and a time to every purpose under heaven" in no way applies to the universe of film festivals.

Month in, month out, from the Flickfest International Outdoor Short Film Festival starting in early January in the Bondi Beach area of Sydney, Australia, through the Autrans Festival of Mountain and Adventure Films ending in mid-December in the high, thin air of southeast France, there is barely a day on the calendar where some film festival is not being celebrated in some exotic city somewhere in the world.

Haugesund, Norway, Oulu, Finland, and Umeå, Sweden, have festivals, as does Trencianske Teplice in the Slovak Republic, India's Thiruvananathapuram, Iran's Kish Island ("the Pearl of the Persian Gulf"), the Australian beach resort of Noosa, and the Italian city of Udine, which unexpectedly bills itself as "the world's largest showcase of popular East Asian cinema." There are nearly sixty Jewish film festivals in existence but only one QT event, in which director Quentin Tarantino annually takes over the Alamo Drafthouse Cinema in Austin, Texas, and shows favorite films to benefit the Austin Film Society. There is even an intentionally stateless movable feast called Transfest, which

facilitates "the simple idea of introducing film festivals which take place somewhere in the world, in another place."

Festivals have become such a growth industry that Missoula, Montana, has two and a petite but trendy town like Telluride, Colorado, now has three (MountainFilm Festival and IndieFest 2K in addition to the regular Telluride event). And, especially in Europe, various coordinating bodies have grown up to try and create order out of the impending chaos.

On the largest scale, the European Coordination of Film Festivals, created to remedy "the disparity of practises and some dangerous excesses and trends" of the continent's proliferating fests, listed 76 festivals when it began in 1995, a number that had more than doubled to 154 in twenty countries by 2000. On a different note, the existence of overlapping science-fiction-oriented events led to the birth of a European Fantasy Film Festivals Federation to, in its own words, "put an end to a grubby war and sign an armistice." This group joins festivals in Porto, Brussels, Luxembourg, Rome, Espoo, Stiges, Amsterdam, Lund, and San Sebastián to, among other things, annually present the Méliès d'Or (named after the great French imaginative director), a.k.a. The Grand Prize of European Fantasy Film.

Even with all these official bodies, no one seems to be exactly sure how many festivals there are in the world, not even books created specifically to keep track of them. *The Variety Guide to Film Festivals* by Steven Gaydos lists more than four hundred, while three other books (*International Film Festival Guide* by Shael Stolberg, *The Film Festival Guide* by Adam Langer, and *The Ultimate Film Festival Survival Guide* by Chris Gore) record over five hundred each.

Because, except for big names like Cannes and Sundance, there is less overlap in these listings than one might expect, it's possible that an outlandish-sounding *New York Times* estimate of more than a thousand fests around the world might not be as wild as it seems. That's enough for the festival circuit to have its own print publication ("*Iff*, the international film festival magazine") as well as a DVD periodical called *Film-Fest*,

which happily describes itself as "your exclusive all-access pass to the latest movies, the coolest parties, the hottest filmmakers and the brightest stars that travel the globe to celebrate the art of film."

Not surprisingly, film festivals are especially a growth area in the United States—so much so that critic David Thomson, in an arch list in *Movieline* magazine entitled "100 Questions We Honestly Want to Ask Hollywood" ("What is Tom Cruise going to do instead of aging?" "Why do they make the new James Bond films seem as if they were made in 1962?"), found space to wonder "Can anyone name five cities in America that do not now have film festivals?"

This proliferation is visible across the board. While New York, ever the cultural behemoth, hosts an estimated thirty festivals (the wildest being the New York Underground Film Festival, annually home to questionable items like *Home Brewer Serial Killer* and *Farley Mowat Ate My Brother*), North Carolina boasts thirteen, including something called the Hi Mom Film Festival in Chapel Hill.

It's one thing for just about every city within cheering distance of Los Angeles (Palm Beach, Malibu, Idyllwild, Temecula, San Luis Obispo, Santa Barbara, Santa Monica, Santa Clarita, the Silver Lake neighborhood proper, and the surfside trio of Newport Beach, Laguna Beach, and Hermosa Beach) to have a festival; it's another to witness a similar proliferation in the Midwest. Say hello to the Great Plains Film Festival in Lincoln, Nebraska, the Heartland Film Festival in Indianapolis, even the Hardacre Film Festival in wee Tipton, Iowa, set in the historic circa 1917 Deco-style Hardacre Theater and created, its promotional material would have you believe, to answer that age-old question, "Yes, but will it play in . . . Iowa?"

One result of this phenomenal growth is that films no one has heard of can take home heaps of honors. The yet-to-be-distributed and all-but-unseen *Wedding Cow* (formerly known as *Good Cows Are Hard to Find*) boasted in a press release of winning a full ten awards, including the Daedalos from IndieKINO, the International Independent Online Film Festival of Seoul, South Korea, and the Golden Unicorn from the

Europaïsches Filmfestival Alpinale in Bludenz, Austria. Garry Trudeau astutely gave a nod to this fest-mania in his "Doonesbury" comic strip by having B.D.'s actress wife Boopsie, the star of "Chugalug," "Beerblasters," and "Pompom Pam," be the subject of "The Barbara Ann Boopstein Film Festival," sponsored by the Aspen Ski Patrol and highlighted by, she is pleased to report, "a panel discussion of my film work! Led by Roger Ebert!"

Even a Boopstein festival doesn't seem out of place when you consider some of the stranger names on the festival circuit, events so outlandish they sound apocryphal even if they're not. What is one to make of items with names like the Takoma Tortured Artists Film Festival in Washington State; Eat My Shorts! Comedy Short Film Showcase in Montreal, Canada; Eat My Schlock! Home Grown Trash Film Festival in Brisbane, Australia; and Short Attention Span Film and Video Festival in San Francisco—not to mention another San Francisco event, the Brainwash Movie Festival, whose top prize is said to be the "Charles Manson Loose Eyeball" award?

The first movie event I was exposed to growing up in Brooklyn was the always serious New York Film Festival, which began in 1963 and included in its first five years classics like Roman Polanski's *Knife in the Water*; Milos Forman's *Loves of a Blonde*, Gillo Pontecorvo's *The Battle of Algiers*, Bernardo Bertolucci's *Before the Revolution*, and an explosion of films from Jean-Luc Godard: *Band à Part*, *Une Femme Est une Femme*, *Alphaville*, and *Masculine-Feminine*.

Not that I had the means to actually see all these films; it's the feeling of festivity and potential I remember from my younger days, the excitement of the full-page ad announcing the event's selections, written up in stirring prose, that appeared every year, one time only, in exactly the same format in the Sunday Arts and Leisure section of the *New York Times*. I felt, as I have not always felt since, the sense of a door opening into a world of culture and sophistication I had no idea existed, as well as the hope that there might be a place in there for me.

That feeling was only part of what I experienced in 1971 during my

first trip to a major world cinema event, representing the *Washington Post* at the Cannes Film Festival in the exotic (to me, at least) south of France. Mostly I was exhausted, deluged by more movies more often than I wanted to handle.

As naive as I was young, I confided these thoughts to the storied Italian director Luchino Visconti, one of the masters of cinema, who was doing interviews to promote his *Death in Venice*. "Isn't it a bit overwhelming?" I said to the great man, whose vibrant argyle socks I still remember. Visconti turned his hawklike, aristocratic face, features suitable for a fifteenth-century condotierre, to me in shock. "It is cinema, cinema, cinema, all the day long," he said, restating the obvious for my benefit. "I love it."

From that time to this, I have struggled to have Visconti's enthusiastic attitude toward festivals, but it has not been uniformly easy. Though they are often held in pleasant, diverting cities, too many theaters, too many deadliness, too large crowds, too much relentless hype, and too few memorable films can make these events more of an exasperating ordeal than might be imagined for a working reporter or critic.

Yet, paradoxically, it was the enormous number of cinematic celebrations overloading the world circuit that reinvigorated my interest in film festivals. I was intrigued by how many there were, how they styled themselves, and in what unexpected corners of the globe they appeared. I began acquiring brochures and pamphlets from events that caught my interest, and soon I had a collection serious enough, if not for a doctoral thesis, at least for some broad general observations.

Given that there are so many of them, the key thing these multiple festivals share is a need to differentiate themselves from each other. Sometimes the boast is straightforward, if a bit narrow, like Neuchâtel's claim to be "the only Swiss film festival devoted to the bizarre and the imagination," Toronto's Rendezvous with Madness and its focus on the myth and reality of mental illness, or the Rencontres Internationales Henri Langlois in Poitiers, France, which concentrates on film school projects, annually choosing some sixty examples from approximately

three thousand short- and medium-length works nominated by 140 schools.

Sometimes a festival's unifying concept is completely unexpected. The Golden Knight Slavonic Film Festival in the Ukrainian city of Kiev focuses on Slav brotherhood and Orthodox Christian values. Copenhagen's Night Film Festival annually sells 40,000 tickets despite screening all its films between midnight and 6 A.M. while, at the opposite end of the spectrum, Italy's International Giffoni Children's Film Festival recruits kids to discuss films with their directors and stars.

Occasionally the fit between subject and locale is so good that the synergy creates an international institution. Dinard, a town in France's Brittany, became so identified with its Festival of British Cinema that it placed a giant replica of the event's trophy, director Alfred Hitchcock with a bird on each shoulder, on the local boardwalk. And Cognac's devotion to thrillers and suspense films means that festival guests are politely fingerprinted in the town square and get served brandy and orange juice cocktails before screenings. In the United States, both Nantucket ("Where Screenwriters Inherit the Earth") and Austin ("King of the Screenplay Festivals") have made names for themselves by focusing on the underappreciated writer, with the Texas festival handing out what it calls "the coveted (and lethally heavy) Austin Film Festival Typewriter Award."

Perhaps the oddest corner of the festival universe is the one for films that other events have scoffed at. Roger Ebert uses the University of Illinois at Urbana-Champaign to host an Overlooked Film Festival, and one of the several festivals at home in Santa Monica is called "Dances with Films" (motto "No Politics. No Stars. No Sh*t"), which insists its entries must have no known actors, producers, or directors or, for that matter, no money from any known company.

Most refreshingly forthright of these events is Philadelphia's baldly named Reject Film Festival, with a VCR reject button for its logo and a frank parenthetical slogan: "As if a gathering of bitter, angry artists could be called a 'festival.'" Proud of the way it "enables filmmakers to tri-

umph in the face of rejection," it requires a dismissive letter from another event with its application and has become so popular, *Daily Variety* reports, that "the Reject Festival is not above rejection itself."

Besides coming up with surprising concepts, festivals can also set themselves apart by the nature of the prizes they give competitors. No two festivals hand out the same award, though after taking account of things like the Golden Raven (Brussels), the Golden Frog (Toruń, Poland), the Golden Calf (Utrecht), the Golden Olive (Kalamata, Greece), the Golden Orange (Antalya, Turkey), the Golden Bayard (Namur, France), the Golden Boomerang (Noosa), the Golden Alexander (Thessaloniki), and the Golden Anchor (Haifa), it does seem there is no object, either natural or man-made, that has not been gilded for presentation.

Perhaps tired of this particular gold rush, the Taos Talking Pictures Festival has gone in another direction with its top prize, the Taos Land Grant Award, which is nothing less than five acres of homestead property atop the Taos Mesa. The idea, the festival says, is "to plant media artists in the fertile soil of New Mexico" with the hope that a filmmaking community will take root and flower.

As to why so many festivals are flowering here and now, the reasons are severalfold, starting with the desire of the municipalities that host them to get their names before a wide public and attract visitors both during and after the celebration in question.

The key cause of festival proliferation, however, is a symbiotically linked trio of factors. Newly active independent and foreign-language filmmakers hunger for appreciative audiences, a need that dovetails nicely with audience members' yearning for alternatives to the standard Hollywood fare that dominates film screens not only in this country but also worldwide. And small distributors as well as national film industries locked into an unequal battle with the American juggernaut see these hungers as a not-to-be-missed opportunity to both earn money and promote their goods to the fullest extent.

For while movie fans have not lost their taste for the artistic and non-

commercial, theaters are not always willing to risk showing those films. "Of course there are too many festivals," Pierre-Henri Deleau, former head of Cannes's Directors Fortnight told *Daily Variety*. "People are going to them because theaters aren't doing their jobs to show films from the rest of the world."

Festivals have become, in effect, what Piers Handling, head of the powerful Toronto Film Festival, has called "an alternative distribution network. A lot of work only gets shown now at festivals. A lot of foreign-language film that would get distribution ten years ago doesn't get seen anymore." France has been especially assiduous in using festivals around the world to get its cinema seen, and it's impossible to imagine the current critical rage for Iranian films without the intense exposure these works have gotten at Cannes, New York, and elsewhere.

Even for those films that do get seen outside festivals, the event and its high-profile gathering of critics and journalists as well as the kind of intense partisans who create word of mouth mean festivals are also useful to distributors as an inexpensive marketing tool for about-to-be-released movies that can't afford to lavish tens of millions of dollars on print and television advertising.

"We'll play every regional festival we can," Tom Bernard of Sony Pictures Classics told the *New York Times*. "It's all about building buzz and creating awareness. Film festivals are an alternate p.r. universe. They save us millions." And earn millions as well. A key to the unprecedented success of Sony's *Crouching Tiger, Hidden Dragon* (four Oscars and more than $100 million at the box office, a U.S. record for a subtitled picture) was its shrewd use of film festival exposure, starting with a rapturous world premier at Cannes, a brief stop at Telluride, the opinion-makers' favorite, and then a bravura capturing of the coveted audience award at Toronto.

Given this ever-expanding universe of choice, how were the dozen or so festivals profiled in this collection selected? Some, like Cannes and Sundance, were obvious choices: besides the fact that I've been going to them for a decade and more, you can't hope to understand why and how

festivals function without considering the ins and outs of the biggest, brashest, and most influential of the bunch.

The other festivals investigated were not random selections. The ones I've focused on not only show films, but they also serve as picture windows onto a wider, more diverse world and cinema's place in it. Sometimes, as with Sarajevo and Havana, film is a vehicle for trying to understand the international political community's most vexing dilemmas. Sometimes, as with Burkina Faso's FESPACO and Pordenone's Giornate del Cinema Muto, it's a chance to examine the very nature of the cinematic experience. For different reasons and at different times, each of these festivals has made me feel the sense of excitement that lit up Luchino Visconti's face all those many years ago.

PART ONE

Festivals with Business Agendas

Cannes

What is this thing called Cannes?

Grueling, crowded, complicated, unforgiving, it's been likened by a survivor to "a fight in a brothel during a fire." A place where reputations are made and hearts are broken, fascinating and frustrating in equal parts, it has a love-hate relationship with Hollywood, yet gives out awards, including the Palme d'Or for best picture, that are the movie world's most coveted next to the Oscars. It's where Clint Eastwood might find himself watching – and enjoying – an Iranian film about baking bread, a place, novelist Irwin Shaw wrote, that attracted all of film: "the artists and pseudo-artists, the businessmen, the con men, the buyers and sellers, the peddlers, the whores, the pornographers, critics, hangers-on, the year's heroes, the year's failures." It's where you need a press pass to get your press pass, and where those passes come in five hierarchical (and color-coded) levels of importance. Its official name is Festival International du Film, the International Film Festival, as if there were only one, so it's no surprise that, more than anything else, Cannes is big.

Normally a city of 70,000, Cannes sees its population increase by 50 percent during the twelve days it functions as the stand-alone epicenter of the international film world. Producer David Puttnam calls it "one-

stop shopping," the place where business and creative types and the people who write about them congregate. "I'm quite enjoying it," Booker Prize–winning novelist A. S. Byatt told me on her first visit in 1995. "I'm a workaholic, and everyone here is too. It's a city full of them, frantically busy. Like the ant heap."

In a kind of self-fulfilling prophecy, then, everyone is here from everywhere because everyone else is here as well, and where else are you going to run into all those people? The French pornography industry schedules its annual Hot d'Or awards to coincide with the festival, and a group of more than a hundred French railway workers/cinema enthusiasts show up annually to award the wonderfully named Rail d'Or to a deserving film. To take advantage of all this, the festival has become the world's largest yearly media event, a round-the-clock cinematic billboard that in 1999 attracted 3,893 journalists, 221 TV crews, and 118 radio stations representing 81 countries all told. And then there are the films. Don't ask about the films.

For unlike most festivals, Cannes has a film market officially attached, where international buyers swoop in to view and possibly purchase the rights to something like six hundred films displayed in thousands of screenings in nearly thirty rooms. When you add in the nearly hundred films shown at the festival proper (which is actually more like three separate festivals competing against each other), what results is a cinematic triathlon so strenuous it even exhausts the man who put it together for twenty-three years, Gilles Jacob. When the festival is over, Jacob told me once, "I go home to Paris, and I talk to no one. Not my wife, not my children. No one."

But even saying all this doesn't truly capture Cannes, an experience *Variety*'s Timothy M. Gray once characterized as not only impossible to describe to someone who's never been there but also "nearly impossible to describe to someone who has been there." Because the halls of the headquarters Palais du Festival and the streets and beaches surrounding it are a circus with an infinite number of rings, anywhere you turn reveals something you can't quite believe you're seeing.

On a day chosen at random near the end of the 2000 festival, several large TVs in the Palais were broadcasting Brian De Palma's press conference, where the *Mission to Mars* director was seen lashing out at a questioner who had the temerity to ask about aspects of "*hommage*" in his work. "It's that word again," De Palma raged, literally pointing an accusatory finger at the unsuspecting miscreant. "It's been attached to me for forty years, and no one's been able to define it. What does it mean?"

Escaping De Palma and the Palais, you nearly get run over by a roller-skating young woman simultaneously turning in circles and selling newspapers: "*Nice-Matin, Nice-Matin*," she yells as the wheels grind. Turning away, you find your hand taken by a person in a giant Mickey Mouse costume who then pulls you within camera range of a man with a Polaroid who wants to be paid for the compromising photo of you and the Mouse he's about to take. Out of the corner of your eye you see a black-robed character, his face masked and hooded, nonchalantly walk by wearing a sandwich board advertising *Demonium*, a film few people have heard of and less care about.

You try and move away, but two women from something called Pop.com, a Web site whose ultimate purpose is as darkly mysterious as *Demonium*, hand you a red balloon and a lollipop. On the beach, a crowd is forming, silently watching as a kneeling young woman gets a tattoo etched onto her shoulder. Pause for a moment to watch and two people brush past, loaded down like Sherpas with dozens of heavy plastic sacks on their shoulders. Each sack turns out to be a press kit for a film called *Dead Babies*, including, for those who've always wanted one, a *Dead Babies* travel toothbrush.

With scenes like this all around, is it any wonder that the appearance of "bad boy Dennis Rodman" to promote a film called *Cutaway* at a party featuring "a laser show, go-go cages, ribaldry, revelry and European and U.S. DJs" causes hardly a ripple?

For many film people, a first trip to Cannes is kind of a grail, a culmination that tells you, whether you're a journalist with a computer or a filmmaker walking up the celebrated red carpet to the Palais du Festival

for an evening-dress only screening, that you've arrived. For me, paradoxically, it was a beginning, the first dizzying, tantalizing glimpse of a chaotic world I wanted to be part of but wasn't sure had room for me.

Cannes was celebrating its twenty-fifth festival when I first covered it in 1971 as a not-much-older reporter for the *Washington Post*. Though the event had strayed from its stated goal of being "a festival of cinematographic art, from which all extracinematic preoccupations would be excluded," it was even then a terribly exciting place to be.

Hardly any Americans made the trip in those days, and I was rewarded with a room in a smart hotel called the Gonnet located on the Boulevard de la Croisette, the city's trademark oceanfront promenade, filled even then with crowds and crowd-pleasing eccentrics, like the elderly gentleman who pounded a cowbell and exclaimed in French, "Always the same films, always the same circus. Pollution, mental and physical pollution. Nothing, nothing, nothing."

The old festival Palais was a classic white building, small but elegant, and patrolled by a vigilant cadre of tuxedoed guards determined to evict gate crashers. I got my first taste of how surreal Cannes can be as I watched a well-dressed French interloper being almost choked to death as he was literally dragged out of the Palais by a pair of tuxedos. Yet he didn't lack the presence of mind to insist, as loudly as that chokehold would allow, "Un peu de politesse, s'il vous plait" — a bit of politeness, if you don't mind.

Because U.S. reporters, even young ones, were a rare commodity, setting up interviews was easy and casual. I spent a rainy afternoon with Jack Nicholson, listening to him defend his directorial debut, *Drive, He Said*, which had been screened the night before to a wave of boos. And I talked to the great Italian director Luchino Visconti, who chuckled as he told me that his visa for an upcoming American visit didn't allow him to leave New York.

"I don't know why they think I'm dangerous — maybe they think I want to kill Nixon," he said puckishly. "I have no intention of doing any subversive actions. I don't want to kill Nixon, or even Mrs. Nixon. I just

want to see the rest of the country. Write this in Washington; perhaps the president will read it." I did; he didn't.

I didn't get back to Cannes until 1976, and the crowds had not abated. It was at a late-night debut of Nagisa Oshima's *In the Realm of the Senses*, whose lurid story of mutual sexual obsession leading to castration had created a ferocious want-to-see, that I got the closest I've ever been to being crushed against a wall by a surging, expectant overflow crowd. Even Oshima's images seemed tame after that.

That was also the year *Taxi Driver* won the Palme d'Or, and I watched, as surprised as he was, as youthful director Martin Scorcese got his first taste of how disconcertingly political European film journalism can be. Midway through the *Taxi Driver* press conference, a French journalist rose and referred to a scene between Robert De Niro's Travis Bickle and Jodie Foster's Iris where Travis talks about getting away from the city and spending some quiet time in the country.

"Mr. Scorcese," the journalist asked, "should we interpret that scene as Travis turning his back on bankrupt Western industrial capitalism and insisting on a more communal, socialist model for life in the future?" Scorcese looked truly, deeply baffled. "No," he said finally. "Travis just wants to spend some time in the country."

That festival also gave me an insight into the thought patterns of actors, even actors turned director. Roman Polanski was in attendance with *The Tenant*, adapted from a novel by Roland Topor, which tells the story of a man who takes over an apartment just vacated by a woman who has committed suicide and begins to feel his neighbors want him to end his life as well. Polanski played the lead in addition to directing, spending what felt like half the movie attempting suicide in drag by jumping out of an upper-story window, not succeeding, and then crawling back up the stairs, still in drag, to leap out all over again. And again.

"Mr. Polanski," I blurted out with what now seems like startling naïveté. "Why did you ever choose this film?" He looked at me with genuine surprise. "It's a great role for me, don't you think?" was his reply, and he meant it.

A bemused man with a rasping, infectious laugh that went along with an obvious streak of darkness, Polanski took advantage of the interview to tell a series of jokes to a receptive audience. My favorite concerned a man who came to a rabbi and asked, Polanski doing a fine Jewish accent, "Rabbi, I must know, am I going to heaven or hell?"

"The rabbi says, 'You come here on a Saturday to bother me about things like this?' But the man persists. 'It's become an obsession with me, rabbi. I haven't slept for three months; my wife wants to leave me; I must know.' 'All right,' says the rabbi. 'Come back next Saturday.'

"When the man comes back, the rabbi says, 'I prayed, I concentrated, I spoke with God, and I have an answer. First the good news. You're going to heaven; there's absolutely no doubt. Now the bad news. You're leaving Wednesday.' "

Don't misunderstand. It's not like this used to be some quiet little fishing village that regrettably got overrun by the glamoroids of the international film community. For more than 150 years, ever since Lord Brougham, a Lord Chancellor of England, was prevented by an outbreak of cholera from wintering in Nice in 1834 and spent his time here instead, Cannes has been a playground for the moneyed classes, home to regal hotels, chic restaurants, and pricey boutiques. Not for nothing is its sister city Beverly Hills.

And despite the French passion for cinema, there might never have been a festival here if it wasn't for the way the Italians under Mussolini and the Fascists ran the Venice Film Festival, founded in 1932. In 1937, Jean Renoir's *La Grande Illusion* was denied the top prize because of its pacifist sentiments, and the French decided if you wanted something done right you had to do it yourself.

The initial Cannes film festival (the city won out as the site after an intramural tussle with Biarritz on the Atlantic coast) was scheduled for the first three weeks of September 1939. Hollywood responded by sending over *The Wizard of Oz* and *Only Angels Have Wings* along with a "steamship of stars" including Mae West, Gary Cooper, Norma Shearer,

and George Raft. The Germans, however, chose September 1, 1939 to invade Poland, and after the opening night screening of *The Hunchback of Notre Dame*, the festival was canceled and didn't start up again until 1946.

According to the genial and informative *Hollywood on the Riviera: The Inside Story of the Cannes Film Festival* by Cari Beauchamp and Henri Behar, the ambiance of that first festival was not much different from today's. They quote an excerpt from a French newspaper about the 1946 event that could have been written last year: "Here the streets are so jammed that one would think one is still in Paris. The shops are full of stuff at astronomical prices and . . . on the Croisette it is a constant parade of cars. It's the rendezvous of stars and celebrities, a whole world, half naked and tanned to a perfect crisp."

Despite its advantages, Cannes started slowly, skipping 1948 and 1950 and only getting onto an annual basis in 1951. It was in 1954 that French starlet Simone Sylva dropped her bikini top and tried to embrace Robert Mitchum in front of a horde of photographers, resulting in the kind of international press coverage that secured the festival's reputation. It had no trouble holding the world's attention, one disapproving film historian writes, because it "early opted for glamour and sensationalism" by concentrating on "the erotic fantasies of naked flesh so readily associated with a Mediterranean seaside resort."

The rival sidebar event known as the International Critics Week was begun by influential French critic Georges Sadoul in 1962, but major change didn't come to Cannes until the pivotal year of 1968. In the face of a country in turmoil, with widespread antigovernment demonstrations and upward of 10 million people in the process of going out on strike, French directors like François Truffaut and Jean-Luc Godard pushed for and achieved the cancellation of Cannes at its midway point.

A tangible result of this upheaval was the founding in the following year of another independent sidebar event, the Quinzaine des Realisateurs, or Directors' Fortnight, which continues to compete with the official festival for films and has consistently shown edgier fare ranging

from Spike Lee's *She's Gotta Have It* to Todd Solondz's *Happiness*. The Quinzaine became such a threat to the festival that one of the first things Gilles Jacob did when he took over in 1978 was to start his own edgier, noncompetitive sidebar event called "Un Certain Regard."

By the time I returned to Cannes in 1992, even more had changed. The Gonnet, my first hotel, had been converted to luxury apartments, the old Palais had been torn down and replaced by the aggressively modern Noga Hilton, and a massive new Palais had replaced the chic casino next to the city's old port. Opened in 1983 at a cost of $60 million, the five-story Palais offers state-of-the-art projection in its two main theaters, the 2,400-seat Lumière and the 1,000-seat Debussy, and has so many hidden stairways, passages, and elevators I was still discovering new ones in the year 2000.

More and more, the festival had become a city within a city, taking over Cannes completely for the duration of the event. Flowers get planted two months before opening day so they'll look their best during the festival. Huge billboards on the Croisette display posters for films that are in the event as well as those that aren't but will be released later that year. A Planet Hollywood places the plaster handprints of Bruce Willis, Mel Gibson, and other stars next to a preexisting monument to Charles de Gaulle. The front of the august Carlton Hotel, a pricey survivor of the Belle Epoque, gets a different commercial makeover every year: once it featured a towering Godzilla, once a regrettably bigger than life Beavis and Butthead complete with the sentence "Huh-Huh, You Said Oui Oui," once a working Egyptian temple, including bandage-wrapped figures and life-size statues of the gods, to promote *The Mummy*. No wonder a French magazine headlined one year "Trop de Promo Tue le Cinéma," too much publicity is killing cinema.

Everywhere as well are the excesses only money and stardom can generate. Celebrity hotel guests, the *New York Times* reported, have been known to "require 150 hangers for their wardrobes and gallons of mineral water for their baths." The legendary Hôtel du Cap at Cap d'Antibes, where the German general staff luxuriated during the French occupation

and where I watched Burt Lancaster dive off the rocks for an ocean swim in 1971, insists that its superpricey rooms be paid for in cash in advance.

For people tired of living in hotels, vessels like a luxury barge ("be in the middle of the business, be far from the noise" for $8,500 per day for a royal suite) or the Octopussy ("world famous, 143 foot luxury megayacht" costing $15,000 per day or $80,000 per week) are available. And if a regular taxi from the Nice airport is just too pokey, there are helicopters and chauffeur-driven red BMW 1100 motorcycles to be rented as well.

For those looking for a way to combine ostentation with good works, the social event of the season is always the $1,000-a-plate Cinema Against AIDS AmFAR benefit at the nearby Moulin de Mougins restaurant. In 1995, benefit chairperson Sharon Stone started the evening with a personal and emotional appeal for more funds for research and ended it by snappily auctioning off model Naomi Campbell's navel ring for $20,000 to a Saudi Arabian prince. As the bizarre bidding went back and forth, a classic Hollywood type with more money than sense wondered aloud if Stone would throw in a pair of her panties. "Anyone who has $7.50," the actress replied in a bravura Cannes moment, "knows I don't wear any."

It was at a quiet breakfast on the pristine terrace of the Hôtel du Cap that Tim Robbins, exhausted after enduring a wild all-night party that had people screaming in the hallway outside his room, succinctly encapsulated the relentless duality that is finally the trademark of this unwieldy, difficult-to-categorize festival.

"Cannes is a very strange mixture of the art of film and total prostitution of film," he said. "One of the things I remember from my first year here in 1992 is walking into a room and meeting a great actor like Gérard Depardieu and then walking out and seeing this poster of a woman with large breasts holding a machine gun. The film wasn't made yet, but they already had a title and an ad concept."

This ability to somehow combine the yin and yang of the film business, to link at the same site the rarefied elite of the world's movie artists

and a brazen international marketplace where money is the only language spoken and sex and violence the most convertible currencies, is the logic-defying triumph of Cannes.

This is a festival where popcorn movies like the Sharon Stone–starring *Quick and the Dead* and *Torrente, the Dumb Arm of the Law* (advertised in its country of origin with the line "Just When You Thought Spanish Cinema Was Getting Better") share space with the work of demanding directors like Theo Angelopolous, Hou Hsiao-Hsien, and Abbas Kiarostami. Where festival head Jacob speaks with pride of attracting Madonna as well as cult director Manoel de Oliveira. Where within twenty-four hours in 1997 you could have a serious talk about the situation in Sarajevo with "Welcome to Sarajevo" director Michael Winterbottom and share a press lunch with Sylvester Stallone, who displayed an easy manner and surprising charm as he mordantly dissected past fiascoes like *Stop or My Mother Will Shoot*: "If it was a question of having my spleen removed with a tractor or watching it again, I'd say, 'Start up the engine.'"

Stallone also ridiculed the current crop of action films ("If you took the explosions out, 90 percent of them would not have endings; if someone stole the gasoline truck, it would be like an e.e. cummings poem at the end") and talked of looking forward to the gathering of all the previous Palme d'Or winners that was scheduled for later that week. "I'm gonna meet those people who won't work with me," he said, amused. "All in one room."

This uneasy but animated coexistence between the commercial and the artistic sometimes gets highlighted in a way no screenwriter could have concocted. Opening night of the 2000 festival, for instance, started with a casual screening of Ken Loach's *Bread and Roses*, an earnest film dealing with the urgent problems of labor organizers attempting to unionize impoverished, often illegal workers who make marginal livings cleaning the office towers of Los Angeles.

When that socially conscious picture was over, I hurried back to my room in the aptly named Hotel Splendid and changed from a T-shirt to

a tuxedo to attend the official opening night party for *Vatel*, a big-budget French film set amid the "it's good to be the king" splendor of the profligate seventeenth-century court of the Roi du Soleil himself, Louis XIV.

Once *Vatel*'s story of a celebrated chef and master of revels, played by Gérard Depardieu, had ended, the audience walked out the door of the Lumière theater and directly into the most elaborate, extravagant, and undoubtedly expensive re-creation of the film's world. The entire entrance hall of the Palais had been changed, via billowing red curtains, huge paintings, multiple candles, and artfully faked stone walls, into a vintage French chateau. And that was just the setting.

I joined the disbelieving guests in evening clothes and walked slowly down corridors that had become the physical duplicates of what had just been seen on screen. Actors dressed in period costumes brought *Vatel*'s kitchens to life: bread was kneaded, fruit was dipped in glazes, ice was sculpted, salamis and cheeses and an enormous fresh fish were displayed, and, adding just the right touch, a man rushed through the crowd clutching a goose.

At the dinner itself, white-coated waiters poured champagne from a stream of magnums as actors playing the king and his intimates ate on a stage. By the time tabletop fireworks ended the evening, the janitors of Los Angeles seemed to belong to another universe.

The key element ensuring that the bracing presence of the commercial remains integral to Cannes is the market, officially known as MIF, Marché International du Film. It started in 1959, apparently with one flimsy twenty-seat room jerry-built onto the roof of the old Palais. Now, with its own brand-new building, the 70,000-square-foot Espace Riviera, it attracts approximately 6,000 participants representing some 1,500 companies from more than seventy countries. Many Cannes regulars agree with Ethan Coen, the writer-producer half of the Coen brothers team, that without the market Cannes would be "a little too snooty."

Every year, festival regulars keep a watch for market films with titles that go beyond the preposterous. Standouts include *Biker Mice from Mars*, *Teenage Bonnie and Klepto Clyde* ("Desperate Kids, Bonded by Passion and Crime"), *Headless Body in Topless Bar*, *Kraa! The Sea Monster* (touted as the successor to *Zarkorr! The Invader*), and the always popular *Attack of the Giant Moussaka*. One year saw a wave of kickboxing films from Korea with titles like *Year of the King Boxer* and *Kickboxer from Hell* while comedies about sumo wrestlers never seem to go out of style: *Sumo Do, Sumo Don't* was offered in 1992, and in the year 2000 *Secret Society* showcased the story of an overweight housewife somehow becoming a sumo standout.

Having these films not only for sale but also available for viewing can be a refreshing change of pace, like a dish of palate-cleansing sorbet after a constant diet of heavier, more ponderous fare. I felt nothing but elation after experiencing Jerzy Hoffman's three-hour-and-three-minute *With Fire and Sword*, a Polish *Gone with the Wind* that came complete with a handsome hero, a deranged villain, and a beautiful princess with gold braids that reached almost to the ground. Other diversions included frequent male choral singing, bare-chested Cossacks pounding enormous drums, and a sidekick with the strength of ten who has taken a vow of chastity until he cuts off three heads with a single sword stroke. "I've gotten two many times," he says mournfully, "but never three." Only in the market.

The market is also the place where films that are little more than a concept and a title make themselves known in the hopes of raising enough money (via preselling foreign distribution rights) to actually shoot the film. In 1976, I was part of a contingent of revelers that was ferried out to a large cruise ship, where energetic waiters encouraged everyone to take part in the Greek party tradition of breaking plates. Hundreds of pieces of crockery dutifully made the ultimate sacrifice to help create interest in what turned out to be *The Greek Tycoon*.

Even as the market has grown more sophisticated, that kind of bombastic showmanship has not gone away. At the 2000 festival, the talk cen-

tered on a new film from resurgent mogul Menahem Golan ("the producer and director of *Delta Force*, $100 million in world box office"), who flooded the city with posters, flyers, and much-sought-after T-shirts for *Elian, the Gonzales-boy Story*, a.k.a. "the explosive, dramatic and human story that captured the world." Illustrated with an obviously faked photo re-creation of Elian's celebrated rescue at gunpoint, the film swore that it was "shooting now in a secret location." Everyone considered themselves warned.

This shameless carnival atmosphere is not for everyone, and it can be especially tiring for stars and directors who are dragooned into promoting new films. Frenetically shuttled from one-on-ones with key journalists to group situations to TV setups to still photo opportunities, prime interview targets can feel like valuable private railway cars being switched from track to track as they meet literally hundreds of media representatives. It's no wonder that by the time Chinese star Gong Li got to a group press lunch in 1993 to promote *Farewell My Concubine*, she was so hungry she ate all the rolls off the table and asked her interpreter if she could have some of her lunch as well.

Filmmakers also don't necessarily enjoy Cannes, because, unlike famously supportive festivals like Toronto and Telluride, it can be an unforgiving, high-risk, hostile place. Boos not infrequently clash with cheers after competition screenings, so much so that even as much of a Cannes partisan as head man Gilles Jacob has admitted "the commentators are merciless. There are festivals where you can send a film thinking that if it doesn't go down well, it may do OK in the long run. That's not possible at Cannes. Cannes is very violently for or against."

One form of dismay that is unique to Cannes is an activity I've come to call "thumping." The seats in the Palais snap back with a resounding sound when their occupants get up to leave, so when disgruntled viewers exit a screening before a film is finished, everyone knows about it. "There is something terrifying in the new Palais," is how a publicist quoted in their book described one unfortunate screening to authors

Beauchamp and Behar. "People were so bored they started leaving after an hour in droves. In packs. It went *clack clackclackclack clackclack clack*. You felt repeatedly stabbed in the back. Each clack was terrifying. And it's still terrifying. Those clacks remain engraved."

But no matter what they think about the dark and chaotic sides of the Cannes experience, even the unlikeliest filmmakers in the end are almost compelled to attend because it is so big, because so much worldwide publicity can be generated from here.

John Sayles and his producing partner Maggie Rienzi, called in one profile people who "will never be mistaken for the sort of couple who attract the paparazzi in Cannes," show up and, yes, attract photographers. "Being here is a job," explained Todd Solondz, who arrived with his genially twisted *Happiness*. "The picture doesn't sell itself, I have to sell it, especially since I don't exactly have a 'big opening weekend' kind of cast." Even Ken Loach, the dean of socially conscious British filmmakers, dons formal wear for the red-carpet premiers of his films. "There are bigger things to be rebellious about," Loach reminded me, "than black tie."

So it turns out, as with any big, glamorous party, that the people who are most upset about Cannes are those who can't get in. In recent years that has meant filmmakers from both Germany and Italy, two major film-producing nations that have had enormous trouble getting their pictures accepted into the official competition, the most prestigious part of Cannes.

The 2000 festival was the seventh year in a row that German filmmakers were shut out of the competition, and they were not happy about it. "We suffer when this happens," one German director told the *Hollywood Reporter*, which detailed that "since 1994, both Taiwan and China/Hong Kong have had four films each in competition; Denmark has had three; Iran, Greece and Japan have each had two; and Mexico, Belgium and Mali have each had one. During that time, Germany, which has the world's second-largest media industry and which has a newly booming feature film sector, has had none." The reason for the

snub, another director theorized, was the French belief that "France invented culture, and the Germans can't possibly participate."

Even more unhappy, and not at all unwilling to talk about it, were the Italians when they, too, were shut out of Cannes 2000. Veteran producer Dino DeLaurentiis was quoted as saying "These snotty Frenchmen make me laugh. In an international festival, it's ridiculous to exclude our cinema." Film director Ricky Tognazzi, retribution on his mind, said "For a year I will avoid eating French goat cheese." Christian De Sica, son of the great director Vittorio De Sica, added the coup de grace: "As if the French didn't also make a lot of stupid movies."

If there is one thing that is generally agreed about the official competition, it's that the selection process is baffling at best. Every Cannes veteran has his or her list of ridiculous films that were somehow let in, from the dim British comedy *Splitting Heirs* to the literally unreleasable Johnny Depp-directed *The Brave* to the even worse Steven Soderbergh *Schizopolis* (shown as an out-of-competition special event).

Even worse, if films with any kind of crowd-pleasing potential do get into the festival, they are often relegated to meaningless out-of-competition slots. Such was the fate of deservedly popular works like *Strictly Ballroom*, *Priscilla, Queen of the Desert*, *Trainspotting*, and *Crouching Tiger, Hidden Dragon*. This trend is so well known that comedy writer-director Francis Veber, the most widely popular French filmmaker of his generation (*The Tall Blond Man with One Black Shoe*, *La Chèvre*, *Les Compères*) genially told me that when he received a phone call from the festival announcing an official tribute to him in 1999, "I was so surprised I fell on my ass. Why the tribute now? Maybe they've seen my tests for cholesterol and sugar, and they think I will die soon."

The uncomfortable truth is that for a film festival that is the cynosure of all eyes, Cannes's taste, at least as far as the competition goes, is surprisingly narrow. France is the home of the auteur theory, which deifies directors at the expense of other creative parties, and Cannes overwhelmingly favors films by critically respectable auteurs who've been there before, a usual-suspects group of largely noncommercial film-

makers *Variety* categorizes as "heavyweight helmers." It's proved to be an increasingly unpopular philosophy.

"High Art pays low dividends at Cannes fest" was the headline on a much-talked-about 1999 piece by chief *Variety* film critic Todd McCarthy that placed the auteur theory in "an advanced state of decrepitude" and lamented that "the gulf between the sort of High Art films that many serious directors want to make (and that is generally sought by fests) and pictures that will hold some sort of interest for audiences is bigger than ever."

In the same vein, Maurice Huleu of *Nice-Matin* wondered if "this outpouring of work, of talent and creativity is predestined to satisfy only a few initiates." Talking of the 1997 decision, which split the Palme d'Or between rarefied films by Iran's Abbas Kiarostami and Japan's Shohei Immamura, Huleu emphasized that the jury "may have sacrificed other considerations in the name of art, but they also did a disservice to the Cannes Festival and to cinema."

Which brings us, inevitably, to Hollywood, that other center of the movie universe. It's the place that makes the movies the world hungers for, and though Cannes well knows the value of glamour and glitz, the festival in recent years has had great difficulty attracting top-drawer items from the bowels of the studio system. So Cannes 2000, for instance, settled for Brian De Palma's frigid *Mission to Mars* while even the most aesthetically rigorous French journalists and critics were wondering why *Gladiator* wasn't there in its stead.

There are reasons for this absence. Cannes, unlike Toronto, comes in the spring, the wrong time of year for the "quality" films studios would prefer to send to festivals. Cannes, as noted, can kill your picture, something studios don't want to risk with prospective blockbusters costing tens of millions of dollars. Cannes is expensive, especially when you factor in flying stars over in private jets. And, especially in recent years, the festival hierarchy has been unwilling to play the Hollywood game, to take trips to Los Angeles and do the kind of schmoozing and flattering of the powers that be that's necessary to overturn more rational considerations.

Also a factor is that the jury awards at Cannes can be so arbitrary and contrived, so governed by whim and geared toward advancing political and cultural agendas, that studio pictures rarely get what Hollywood considers a fair shake. For every year like 1993, when the Palme d'Or was wisely split between *The Piano* and *Farewell My Concubine*, there is a 1999, when the David Cronenberg–led jury horrified everyone except themselves by giving three major awards to the unwatchable *L'Humanité*. "David Cronenberg's decisions," one festival veteran said, "are scarier than his films." In 1992, the brilliant French-Canadian *Leolo* was shut out at least in part because its director, Jean-Claude Lauzon, made a provocative sexual remark to an American actress who was on the jury. "When I said it," the director recalled, "my producer was next to me and he turned gray." In an atmosphere like this, it's no wonder one of the best Hollywood films of the past decade, *L.A. Confidential*, made it into the competition and came home with nothing. Not exactly the kind of encouragment the studios are looking for.

Yet when a film hits here, when it wins a major award and touches a nerve in the audience, it really hits. Quentin Tarantino was genuinely shocked when his *Pulp Fiction* took the Palme in 1994 ("I don't make the kinds of movies that bring people together, I make the kinds of movies that split people apart"), but that moment was the engine of the film's enormous worldwide success. Steven Soderbergh had already won a prize at Sundance, but when he became the youngest person to win a Palme for *sex, lies and videotape*, he said the experience was "like being a Beatle for a week. It was so unexpected, like someone saying 'You've just won $10 million' and sticking a microphone in your face. I didn't know how to react, I don't know what I said." And then there was Roberto Benigni.

Benigni's *Life Is Beautiful* didn't win the Palme in 1998 (that went to Theo Angelopoulos's understandably forgotten *Eternity and a Day*); it took the runner-up Grand Prize, but it mattered not. A direct line could probably be traced from Benigni's effusive behavior that night, running on stage and passionately kissing jury president Martin Scorcese's feet,

to its eventual status as a triple Oscar winner and the then highest-grossing foreign-language film in U.S. history. That indelible image of Benigni in ecstasy will likely do as much for the status and mythology of Cannes as the earlier shot of Simone Sylva going topless with Robert Mitchum did for this festival of festivals so many years ago.

Sundance

He materialized all at once in a crowded room, his eyes wide and next door to desperate, his grip on my shoulder firm, even insistent. "See my film," he said, quiet but intense. "Change my life."

At any other film event in any other city, that moment with a young director might have seemed unreal, out of place, even threatening. But this was the Sundance Film Festival in Park City, Utah, the flagship of the burgeoning American independent film movement and a dream factory for the modern age, where, as Warner Baxter said to Ruby Keeler in *42nd Street*, "You're going out a youngster, but you've got to come back a star."

It happened to Kevin Smith after his *Clerks* debuted here in 1994: "When I came to Sundance, I was a wage slave. And then, twenty-four hours later, I had a filmmaking career." It happened to Ed Burns, now known as one of the stars of *Saving Private Ryan* and a director in his own right but then working as a grunt at "Entertainment Tonight" until *The Brothers McMullen* screened at Sundance: "Nothing has been the same since. The lights went down, the movie starts and the audience starts laughing. And then afterwards, agents, production companies, and distribution companies – right then and there – the bidding war begins."

It happened to Steven Soderbergh, whose unheralded *sex, lies and*

videotape took the audience award and went on to win the Palme d'Or at Cannes, gross $24 million, and create a directing career that blossomed with the Julia Roberts–starring *Erin Brockovich*. It happened on a bigger scale to the modest *Blair Witch Project*, which cost $100,000, sold for just over $1 million after a midnight screening, and ended up grossing $140 million and putting its formerly scruffy trio of filmmakers onto the covers of *Time* and *Newsweek* and into the carefully groomed center of a high-gloss ad for Dewar's scotch. Such is the power of Sundance.

That one particular festival held every January in a ski town thirty-something miles from Salt Lake City—a tourist-dependent hamlet "somehow both pristine and fake" (in critic David Denby's words) that likes to boast about having five hundred realtors and more chefs per capita than Paris, France—should have this kind of a transformative gift has been lost on absolutely no one.

While 250 films applied for the festival's dramatic competition in 1995, that number had more than tripled, to 849 films looking for but sixteen places, by the year 2000. Documentary entrants shot up from 220 in 1999 to 347 in 2000, a jump of 57 percent for the same sixteen spaces in just twelve months. The twenty-nine slots in World Cinema attracted 450 hopeful films, with directors who got in happy to make the trek from as far away as Bhutan and Tajikistan, two of the remoter parts of Asia. Perhaps most impressive was that but sixty short films were chosen from an almost terrifying 1,928 applicants.

"I meet people in so many walks of life and they're always grabbing a camera," says festival director Geoffrey Gilmore, both heartened and unnerved by that torrent of cinema. "People used to go to a garret and paint. Now it's 'I'm a filmmaker.'" Adds Steven Soderbergh, who ought to know, "making a movie has sort of crept up on being a rock star on the fantasy list for most people."

For a town with a population in the area of 6,000, the growth in attendance—it's now estimated that more than 20,000 show up annually—has been equally unnerving. The festival expanded from 15,750 seats sold in 1985 to 135,922 in 1999, an increase of almost 900 percent.

And that doesn't count the great numbers of people who take advantage of the area's ever-increasing supply of condominiums built for skiers to show up without tickets on the increasingly unlikely chance they will stumble onto some.

At the 2000 festival, for instance, people stood on the waiting list line for the world premier of *American Psycho* for four hours without getting in (they can count themselves lucky), and other ticketless individuals have been known to show up with sleeping bags at the festival's outdoor box office as early as a frigid 3:50 A.M. to wait for released tickets. As the crowds increase, it's closer to truth than hyperbole when master documentarian Errol Morris (*Fast, Cheap and Out of Control*, *The Thin Blue Line*) waspishly says he prepares for trips to the festival by "spending seventy-two hours in a meat locker with people I don't like, and all of them have cell phones."

If further proof is wanted of this festival's preeminence and influence, it can be found in the ever-growing number of competing/complementary events that take place in Park City at the same time as Sundance, attempting with some success to latch onto whatever individuals can't procure tickets and won't be bothered with standing on those interminable lines.

Very much first among equals among the alternatives is Slamdance, founded as a salon de refusés by four directors whose films were turned down by Sundance and who initially grandly called their event "Slamdance '95, Anarchy in Utah: The First Annual Guerrilla International Film Festival." Helped by the scorn of Sundance Institute president Robert Redford, who grumbled about "a festival that's attached itself to us in a parasitical way," Slamdance has grown into something of a venerable institution itself, with over 2,000 films applying for slots and road show versions traveling to New York, Los Angeles, Washington D.C., London, and even Cannes. Not bad for a fest that was, to quote Redford again, "born out of rejection."

Aside from Slamdance, some of the more prominent rivals include No Dance, "acclaimed as the world's first and only DVD-projected film

festival," and Slamdunk, which made a name for itself showing Nick Broomfield's *Kurt and Courtney* documentary amid the mounted heads at the local Elks Hall after Sundance canceled its screening due to threats of legal action. More amorphous but very much present are such entities as Lapdance, DigiDance, Dances with Films, and Son of Sam Dance, which turned out to be a Toyota van with a projector attached to its roof. Even author Ken Kesey got into the act, claiming tongue-in-cheek that he was "going to organize the Slim Chance Festival. You will have to have received a number of rejections to qualify."

Though it lasted only one year, Slumdance is one of the more fondly remembered alternatives. Set up in a 6,000-square-foot basement that was once a Mrs. Fields cookie factory, Slumdance was started by a hang-loose group who called themselves Slumdance Programming Vagrants and managed 150 submissions before opening night. As their press release headline nicely put it, "Slumdance Stuns Movie World by Existing."

The Slumdance gang literally outfitted their basement like a mock slum. You entered through a mission area that served free soup, past a Tent City (individual video areas designed like hobo housing) and entered the Lounge, the main screening area outfitted with projectors, couches, and sleeping bags. Around the corner and behind a curtain was a set of concrete steps leading nowhere in particular. Not surprisingly, it was dubbed the Stairway to Acquisitions.

Equally inventive were the mock festivals dreamed up by the local alternative newspaper, the *Park City Ear*. One year it was Sleazedance, "a combination of exhibitionism and porn," which planned to show features like *Jeremiah's Johnson* in "a lime-green Volkswagen Vanagon with tassels on the headlights." This gave way to Skindance, the name changed for "credibility," which highlighted *Anna Lands the King*, *Adult Toy Story* 2, and *The Talented Mr. Strip-Me*. With Sundance showing films like *American Pimp* and *Sex: The Annabel Chong Story*, there were days when you couldn't tell Skindance from the real thing.

What all this means is that Sundance has become more than just the

mother ship for the American independent movement, more than the premier showcase for films that don't march to Hollywood's drum. Because the festival and the independent scene grew up together, because they nurtured each other and made each other strong, Sundance has become America's preeminent film event and, says Lory Smith in his *Party in a Box* history of Sundance, "arguably one of the most influential film festivals in the world." This is a highly unlikely situation for a part of the world where ten feet of snow can accumulate in ten days and a town that had hardly any movie theaters and none within walking distance of each other. Though careful planning has allowed the festival to pretty much keep pace with its growing importance, it was happenstance more than anything else that put it in Park City in the first place.

If anything made this town a good match for the festival, it's a rambunctious history as what "Walking through Historic Park City" calls "one of the largest bonanza camps in the West," the source of enough silver, lead, and zinc to create the fortune of William Randolph Hearst's millionaire father George. At its zenith Park City boasted sixteen houses in its Red Light District as well as twenty-seven saloons, one of which was robbed by George "Butch Cassidy" Parker. And from 1926 on, it had its own movie theater, the Egyptian, apparently a replica of Warner's Egyptian in Pasadena and, to quote "Walking through" again, "one of only two Egyptian revival–style buildings in Utah."

Though I experienced a lot of Sundance history, I wasn't there at the beginning. As detailed in Smith's book, the festival started in 1978 in Salt Lake City and, though immediately interested in films made regionally outside the studio system, it had to go through several incarnations and numerous name changes — from the U.S. Film Festival to the Utah/U.S. Film Festival to the United States Film & Video Festival to the Sundance/United States Film Festival to Sundance — to get to where it is today.

It was director Sydney Pollack, or so the story goes, who suggested to the powers that be in 1980 that "you ought to move the festival to Park City and set it in the wintertime. You'd be the only film festival in the

world held in a ski resort during ski season, and Hollywood would beat down the door to attend."

Involved in the festival, almost from the beginning, was local resident Robert Redford, who had purchased land in the Wasatch Mountains as far back as 1969. Redford, related by marriage to Sterling Van Wagenen, the festival's first director, was chairman of its board of directors and the key figure in eventually having his cultural-minded, multidisciplinary arts organization, the Sundance Institute, take on the festival in 1985 and eventually change the name in 1991. Lory Smith, one of the festival's founders, claims in his book, "We were on the cusp of success whether Sundance had become involved or not," adding "Sundance seemed determined from the outset to rewrite the festival's history as well as its own — to make it seem as if they had rescued a small-time festival from obscurity." Still, it's undeniable, as Smith himself reports, that Sundance's involvement "catapulted the festival into the stratosphere of press and public attention," which is where I found it.

My first festival visit was in 1986, when I didn't know enough to bring a heavy coat, skiers still looked down their poles at outnumbered movie interlopers, and the state's beverage consumption laws, once almost Talmudic in complexity, had changed enough to allow the local Chamber of Commerce to boast that "Utah's newly revised liquor laws are almost normal now."

Though it had been in Park City for five years, the event itself still had some of the sleepy spirit that Errol Morris remembers from showing his pet-cemetery themed *Gates of Heaven* at the 1982 festival, only the second to be held in Park City. "There was a snowstorm, I was staying in a godforsaken condo and I only had a small idea where it was located," Morris remembers. "I had to hitchhike back there, and I was picked up by people who'd been in the theater and had hated the movie. They asked me what I thought, and since I had no alternative means of transportation, I said I, too, was extremely disappointed."

I didn't attend Sundance on a regular basis until the 1992 festival, by which time I'd acquired a reliable winter coat, and American audiences,

increasingly let down by the unadventurous, lowest-common-denominator nature of Hollywood production, were acquiring a taste for what Sundance was providing, films that the festival itself amusingly caricatured in a clever, albeit self-satisfied thirty-second spot that began every screening at the 1996 festival.

A project of an ad/film class at Pasadena's Art Center College of Design, the spot opened on a unusual assembly line, with impassive workers taking identical cans of film and pushing them through slots of the same size, again and again and again.

But wait. Here's a film that doesn't fit. Alarm bells go off, a crack emergency team appears and thrusts the oversized can into a yellow box marked "Sundance International Film Festival." "Where do they take it?" someone asks as the offending item disappears inside a departing truck. A coworker gives a laconic, one-word answer: "Utah."

Almost every year of its existence, Sundance has managed to discover at least one memorable dramatic film. Aside from the features already mentioned, debuts included *The Waterdance*, *In the Soup*, *Four Weddings and a Funeral* (its American premier), *The Usual Suspects*, *Living in Oblivion*, *Big Night*, *Ulee's Gold*, *Girlfight*, and *You Can Count on Me*. And that's only the dramatic features.

On the documentary side, things were even stronger, and Sundance soon got a deserved reputation for being the country's top nonfiction showcase. The momentum for *Hoop Dreams*, perhaps the best, most-influential documentary of the past decade, began here, as it did for *Crumb*, *Theremin*, *Fast, Cheap and Out of Control*, and *Unzipped*. When the Academy of Motion Picture Arts and Sciences changed its rules for becoming a documentary finalist in 2000, a rule partially inspired by *Hoop Dreams*'s previous exclusion, six of the twelve features selected had appeared at Sundance in 1999 and a seventh was set for a Slamdance premier.

Though the concept soon became a ruinous cliché, Sundance in fact often was the place where you could see talent early. Here was Ashley

Judd in *Ruby in Paradise*, her first major role, easily the friendliest person in town. Here was Quentin Tarantino in a Q&A session after the premier of *Reservoir Dogs* brazenly telling a viewer upset about the violence, "I don't have to justify it, I love it." And here was Trey Parker, in Sundance with the slashingly irreverent animated short *The Spirit of Christmas*, talking about improvising the obscene dialogue with codirector Matt Stone in his basement while his mom was making fudge upstairs. And there was this little series called *South Park* in the offing as well.

Because of what it stood for, Sundance became a prime spot to hear the war stories of filmmakers who were almost literally burning to get their projects completed, who talked about overcoming their difficulties with the kind of messianic zeal that *In the Soup* director Alexandre Rockwell had in mind when he said, "It's great to meet filmmakers who are as crazy as I am and as desperate to make their films." For example:

- Todd Solondz, whose *Welcome to the Dollhouse* won the Grand Jury Prize in 1996, reminisced about his first brush with fame, when his NYU short film *Schatt's Last Shot* created a fuss. When he told his then-agent he just wanted to meet some of these new people, she started crying on the phone, and when he was cornered by a trio from another agency, "one of them got down on his knees and begged. You read about things like this but it's true, it happens."

  Soon Solondz had simultaneous three-picture deals with two different studios who crazily bickered about the release order of these unmade films. "It turned out the only thing I liked about these deals was telling everyone I had them. I wasn't interested in any of the pictures that came my way, and none of my friends could sympathize: 'Poor Todd, he has these two three-picture deals.'" He ended up leaving the movie business for a job teaching English as a second language (a profession he wrote into his next feature, *Happiness*), and whenever anyone asked him about his previous life, "I said I'd been working as a computer programmer, which ended conversation right there."

- Writer-director Toni Kalem, whose *A Slipping-Down Life* portrayed a woman fixated on a rock singer, told an appropriately obsessive tale about how her film ended up in the 1999 festival. Herself an actress (she was Gianelli in *Private Benjamin* and has a part in *The Sopranos*), Kalem said she'd been interested in turning the Anne Tyler novel into a film for nearly two decades ("since I pilfered the book from Random House when I worked there as a secretary") and originally wanted to play the starring role herself.

  "Other people buy houses or buy cars, I had a 'Slipping-Down Life' habit," Kalem explained. "I took acting jobs just to pay for the option. I had horrible, horrible moments when I thought someone else would do it; I once took the red-eye to New York to save my option. Everyone said, 'Toni, you've done enough, let it go.' But I said, 'If I can't do it my way, I'll keep optioning it; I'll come up here in a walker if I have to.' "

- Marc Singer, the director of *Dark Days*, the most talked-about documentary in the 2000 festival and the winner of the audience award, the freedom of expression award, and half of the cinematography award, had a back story as strong and compelling as his on-screen material.

  More than five years in the making, *Dark Days* deals with the people who live in Manhattan's underground train tunnels. A former model, the British-born Singer not only lived underground with his subjects for two years, he used them as his entire crew. More an advocate for the homeless than a filmmaker, he conceived of *Dark Days* strictly as a way to earn money to get these people above ground and rented his first camera without even knowing how to load it. "I just wanted to get them out," he said simply. "They deserve better than that."

If Sundance had a turning point event in recent years, something that showed just how important a Park City debut could be for a project, it

came in 1996. That's when the Australian *Shine*, the Scott Hicks–directed film about pianist David Helfgott, a child prodigy who descended into madness, debuted as an out-of-competition world premier. It's not only that the film's first two screenings led to frenzied standing ovations; that was not unusual for Sundance. It's that everyone recognized that, as a throwback to the best kind of Hollywood movies, able to move a mass audience without insulting it, *Shine* was almost sure to be a multi-Oscar nominee. (It in fact got seven, including best picture, and won the best actor Oscar for star Geoffrey Rush.) More than that, it was deliriously up for grabs.

"I'm too old for this," one not-very-old acquisition executive said to me in the midst of the chaos that erupted around Hicks when the second screening ended. Other executives, however, were less ambivalent. Miramax's Harvey Weinstein, who'd maneuvered his company to preeminence in the independent world by not letting films like *Shine* escape him, thought he had a deal with Pandora, the company handling *Shine*'s overseas sale, but it was not to be.

Against considerable odds, Mark Ordesky of Fine Line Features spearheaded what he called an "in-the-condo, in-the-room, nobody-leaves-or-the-deal-is-off" negotiation to bag the film. Weinstein was beside himself, threatening to sue to get the North American rights and loudly and publicly berating Pandora's representative in a Park City restaurant. Miramax and its parent company Disney ended up with the rights in certain key overseas territories, but Robert Redford had the last word. "We do very simple things to provide entertainment here," he said at the festival's awards show. "We leave it to the snow and to Harvey Weinstein."

The much-publicized fuss over *Shine* put a spotlight on how and why Sundance, which had changed considerably over its short life, had metamorphosized. Ever since Redford's Sundance Institute had taken over the festival, the putative specter of the evil empire of Hollywood and the movie establishment had hung over the event. Every year, agents and development executives made the trek to Park City in greater and greater numbers, paying up to $5,000 for coveted Fast Passes to the

entire festival and prowling the occasionally snowy streets on a lonely mission to discover the Next New Thing. As veteran independent director Victor Nunez, a two-time winner of the Grand Jury Prize (*Gal Young 'Un* in 1979, *Ruby in Paradise* in 1993) put it, "Sundance has always been a two-edged sword. On the one hand, the recognition is wonderful. On the other, that sword has always pointed west, and festival success is the calling card to making it into the establishment world."

The more certain Sundance films broke through commercially, the more distribution companies came and bought without looking back, conveniently ignoring other Sundance films that had proved to be overhyped and overexpensive once they got down to sea level. Executives might take annual vows of abstinence, but no one remembered overpriced box office disappointments like *House of Yes*, *Slam*, *Hurricane Streets*, *Happy, Texas*, *The Castle*, and *The Spitfire Grill* when something hot and new appeared on the horizon.

All this fuss attracted the media and those who understood how to use it. "Sundance is actually an old Indian word that means publicity; few people know that," actor Eric Stoltz tartly informed *Us* magazine, and Sony Pictures Classics codirector Tom Bernard told the *New York Times* that "Sundance has the biggest concentration of press in the country. It's better than a junket. We get interviews and stories placed on our movies we couldn't get if we weren't at Sundance."

Both Robert Redford and Harvey Weinstein are masters at handling the media. When Weinstein announces his annual party, journalists rearrange their schedules so as not to miss it. In 1995, he hosted an event at the pricey Stein Erickson Lodge at which Redford himself, in effect Sundance's uncrowned king, decided to make a rare social appearance.

As soon as Redford arrived, Weinstein, shrewd as well as gracious as a host, brought him over to a table where critics and journalists from *Newsweek*, *Variety*, the *Los Angeles Times*, and the *New York Times* were sitting. Redford nodded to everyone, and, since there were no more chairs, immediately went down on one knee to have a more intimate chat with one of the most powerful critics there. Observing this tableau

was Weinstein, never without words or unwilling to use them. "So Bob," he said in a voice loud enough to make the actor blush, "that's how you get those good reviews."

Though it still believes passionately in championing striving young filmmakers, Sundance itself, not immune to all the success that surrounded it, has become established and institutionalized enough to have an annual budget of $8.5 million. With a fleet of Mercedes M-Class vans as "official vehicles" and a catalog as fat and glossy as an issue of *Architectural Digest*, Sundance increasingly exudes the prosperity and success that go with its place in the film universe.

The festival catalog is as weighty as it is in part because of advertising from the festival's 125 sponsors, carefully organized into categories called Leadership, Major, Supporting, Official, and Festival. Corporations that would do credit to a Super Bowl telecast (Mercedes-Benz, AT&T, Apple, Blockbuster) lined up with less likely suspects like the San Miguel, Agua Calienta, Pechanga, and Viejas California Indian tribes and the makers of Altoids, which gave away so many mints one year that, their intrepid publicist announced, "If all of the Altoids were dropped from a helicopter over the festival center of Park City at the same time, they would blanket the area to a depth of 2.37 inches." With a festival audience both young (57 percent are between eighteen and thirty-five) and well funded (38 percent earn over $100,000), is it any wonder that the institute has expanded operations to include the Sundance Catalogue, the Sundance Channel, and Sundance Theaters?

Though people could and did argue over whether all this was good or bad for the festival, the fact that it brought increasing numbers of visitors to town (enough, apparently, to have spent over $25 million, including lodging and transportation, during the 1999 event) was undeniable. Cell phone usage during the fest rose 550 percent over the town's normal rate, and restaurants were booked a month ahead of time, with one establishment demanding a $60 food minimum per person as the price of reserving a table.

Sundance tries hard to cope with this influx, training "crowd liaison"

personnel and fine-tuning the festival's different sections, their locations, even the event's invaluable but increasingly complex shuttle bus system. And, at the most basic level, this may be the only festival that regularly adds theaters in a Sisyphean attempt to keep pace with its audience.

Starting with the venerable Egyptian, a tiny triplex called the Holiday Village, and an assembly room in a hotel, Sundance added a 500-seat theater in the town's former high school (which now houses the local library), tacked on one more in a different hotel, and spearheaded local voter approval for the Eccles Theater, named after a local philanthropist, a 1,000-seat structure (which doubles as a performing arts complex when the festival is not in session) that opened in 1998 and promptly filled up.

Though some local residents (like the high school kids who agreed to carpool during the festival and rented their parking passes for $200 each, funds going to the fine arts department) try and make the best of these massive crowds, the relationship between the town and the festival that fills its streets to overflowing with "L.A.liens" is not always ideal. As "Sundance – at a glance," a brochure subtitled "An Unofficial, Personal, Native, Local, Insider's Survival Guide to the Sundance Film Festival," notes, the alleged financial boost notwithstanding, "it's no great boon to replace ski tourists who spend thousands on vacation with people who eat off grocery salad bars."

It's the local alternative papers that turn out to be hardest on the festival. "Get Your Black Leather Out, It's Time to Be Scene," headlined the *Salt Lake City Weekly*, recycling the worn cliché that visitors are all PIBS (People In Black) who slip and slide on icy streets in their stiletto heels and/or Gucci footwear. Typical was a column in Park City's *Mountain Times* headlined "The Festival We All Love to Hate," which noted that "During Sundance week Park City virtually reeks with a desperate need to be seen as somehow relevant and important in a town overflowing with relevant and important personages. . . . This is the place where people who fancy themselves power brokers come to broker their power; this is the place where outsiders try to become insiders, and where the insiders are as plentiful as the slush in the streets."

Yet for all this carping and borderline sniveling, for all the people (invariably New Yorkers) who insist Sundance has become a twin to Los Angeles, the core feeling of the festival, its fundamental nature, has remained surprisingly unchanged albeit a bit harder to find under all the accoutrements of success.

It's a shaggy, countercultural essence, defined by the filmmakers themselves: invariably youthful, inevitably walking the streets in packs, determinedly pasting posters to every available blank space and giving the place a summer-camp-in-winter ambiance. It's a feeling one filmmaker summarized by saying his work was "made entirely without adult supervision," a convivial vitality that British playwright David Hare, attending for the first time in 2000, noticed at once. "It seems a very big dating festival, with a lot of hip young people teeming with hormones, sexual spores," he said. A gray-haired attendee, whose name I never did get, put it another way when he saw me, a complete stranger, at the far end of a long hallway and immediately broke into a grin. The smile widened as we got closer and just as we were passing he whispered bemusedly in my ear, "Another old guy."

Personally I tend to love the spirit of the place: the filmmakers on the street handing out cards and hustling an audience for their work, the director I met one year wandering the halls of the Yarrow Hotel stopping strangers and asking for $8 million in completion funds. And of course those ever-present signs and posters, like one at a box office saying "Way Sold Out" and another thoughtfully advising ticket sellers to "avert misunderstanding by calm, poise, balance."

The posters for individual films, especially for shorts and fringe items desperate to attract an audience, can be cleverer than the pictures themselves. "No Stars! No Action! No Sex! In Color!" for something called *Trigger Happy* was a personal favorite in 1999, and 2000 saw a flyer for *Johnny Greyeyes* headlined "Who is crying now???" and explaining, "I have spent three years and all my money making this movie. All my friends hate me and my girlfriend left me. But you know what? It looks pretty good. Come and check it out."

One of the most memorable guerrilla campaigns was mounted in 1994 for an Estonian/Finnish coproduction called *Darkness in Tallinn*. It not only kept coming up with new wrinkles for its zany photocopied fliers ("Dare to Cast the First Estone" read one, "Starring Sly Estallone and Sharon Estone" another, "Everybody Must Get Estoned" a third); it also started its screenings with a live a cappella version of what the film's director and producer claimed to be the Estonian national anthem.

Similar events happen frequently in Sundance theaters, adding to the festival's off-center charm. When a screening of *Rhythm Thief* was delayed for technical reasons during the 1995 festival, director Matthew Harrison (who'd shot the thing in eleven days for $11,000) sang a chorus of "There's No Business Like Show Business" to keep the audience entertained. When the delay at another film reached an hour, the staff at the Egyptian theater took pity on the audience and handed out free sticks of Twizzlers red licorice. And Arthur Nakane, an L.A.-based one-man band and the subject of a short called *Secret Asian Man* showed up with all his instruments during the 2000 event and had people literally go-go dancing in the aisles of the tiny Holiday Village cinema. Believe me, this sort of thing doesn't happen at Cannes.

This kind of energy tends to be contagious. In 1994, for instance, a group of twenty-four exuberant students from a filmmaking program at Pacoima Junior High outside of Los Angeles came en masse as the festival's partial guests, supplied with free tickets by Sundance but having had to spend the entire year, in classic Judy Garland–Mickey Rooney fashion, raising money to pay their expenses.

"We sold hundreds of boxes of chocolates, blow pops, gummy bears, gummy worms, everything there is that's gummy, and if you counted each of the M&Ms we sold, it was in the millions," said student Josh Gray-Emmer. Was it worth it? "We've been at other festivals, but since we're kids, we don't always get a really good response," said fellow student Megwynn White. "But here we can go up to directors, say, 'Hi, we're students' and actually talk to them."

Also typical, in another way, was twenty-nine-year-old aspiring writer-

director Garry Dinnerman, a graduate of Georgia State's film school whose short, *Outside Looking In*, was turned down by the 1996 festival.

Nothing deterred, Dinnerman rented a corner room at the Treasure Mountain Inn on Main Street, hung a banner advertising his film from the balcony, and even projected a slide announcing screenings to be held in his room on the wall of a building across the street, next to a Mrs. Fields sign. He faxed notices of his intention to about two hundred potential viewers and spent much of his time in that hotel room (which had a prankish faked autographed photo of Robert Redford calling *Outside Looking In* "truly the best short film I've ever seen" on the door) waiting for an audience to arrive.

"If I could have somebody from Fine Line or Touchstone or an agent come by and look at it, I'll be happy," he said cheerfully. Only six people showed up the first day, but Dinnerman was undaunted. "The festival," he said, "is just getting started."

Given all of this, it is hard not to be taken by the Sundance Festival, and almost everyone is. Yet it's gotten harder and harder to return every year without noticing that the event has a core flaw, something that infrequent visitors don't notice and regulars shrug off, a flaw in, of all places, the dramatic competition. This is the section that gets the most filmmaker interest and the most publicity, yet it's also the one that Sundance regulars would count as the weakest and most disappointing.

Despite, or maybe because of, the festival's success, there has been an increasing disconnect between how large and prestigious it's gotten and a stubborn insistence on focusing this most celebrated event on films that seem almost perversely picked to conform to a narrow and outmoded aesthetic agenda, films that feel as if they're making the cut because they will never reach a wider audience.

Despite the number of successful films that have debuted at Sundance, it's difficult to escape the feeling that the competition selection process has an unmistakable anticommercial bias. This may sound noble and honorable, but in reality it's a counterproductive exercise in artistic elitism that does the independent movement no good at all.

What viewers often see is a string of earnest, well-meaning films that are as sensitive and artistic in intent as anyone could want, but have zero chance of pleasing audiences outside of a festival's rarefied atmosphere—and frequently not much of one even there. While no one outside the studio system would argue that just being commercial makes a film good, it's equally true, though by no means accepted at Sundance, that just being noncommercial doesn't automatically confer worthiness either. Yes, there are wonderful films there is no large audience for, and those have a place at the festival, but just because there's no audience for a given film doesn't make it by definition wonderful.

For many years, that dynamic was typified by Sundance's steadfast patronage of painfully self-absorbed films made by and about disaffected young people trying to make sense of their alienated lives. One year, in the weeks leading up to Sundance, I joined entertainment writer Gregg Kilday in a pre-festival Los Angeles screening of such an item, a film that was such a classically morose Sundance item about sullen teenagers confused about their sexuality that when the lights went up Gregg and I looked at each other, shook our heads, and just laughed. It was such a Sundance film, Gregg said, he'd reflexively reached under his seat for his parka when the credits started to roll.

This anticommercial bias has infected Sundance juries as well. The popular *The Brothers McMullen*, the Grand Jury Prize winner in 1995, was apparently a compromise choice after the jury split on other, more rarefied choices. Back in 1990, the jury gave its top prize to the formidably inaccessible *Chameleon Street*, giving a lesser award to a tremendous film that could have benefited from the buzz of being number one, Charles Burnett's *To Sleep with Anger*.

One way Sundance has managed to keep the competition safe for orphan films is by ghettoizing established independent directors in the Premiers section. But given that these directors are still at a disadvantage in the real movie world, no matter how heroic they seem in Park City, wouldn't it make sense to practice a form of cinematic triage and allow films that have a chance to succeed in megaplexes to benefit from the

imprimatur of being a Sundance winner and not focus so lovingly on those that are D.O.A.?

Sundance has also looked askance at other films with audience potential, either rejecting them outright or putting them in the less prestigious American Spectrum section. Wes Anderson's *Bottle Rocket* and Carl Franklin's *One False Move,* both independent landmarks, were rejected, and *Gods and Monsters,* good enough to earn an Oscar for best adapted screenplay, was deemed not strong enough for the competition and relegated to Spectrum.

Sundance has thrived because it has shown that there is a market for the best of these films; it has shown that Americans will flock to hand-crafted, non-machine-made independent cinema if it is well done. Commercial vitality is not an enemy or a danger sign; it's something to be embraced.

Similarly, supporting films whose potential audience is microscopic, worshiping their inevitable lack of success like a relic of the true cross, is both perversely holding onto something outmoded in the world Sundance has created and missing the chance to do more tangible good.

To its credit, Sundance seems to be trying to change. The 2000 event was, in terms of overall quality and the lack of hair-pulling fiascoes, the most successful festival in memory. The pleasantly schizophrenic interaction between the minions of Hollywood and the scruffy independent world shows no sign of disappearing and continues to prove the truth of the familiar dictum that what doesn't kill makes one stronger. And no matter what else changes, this festival can't help but remain the place where dreams come true. "It's in the nature of hope," director Allie Light said in 1994 after winning the Freedom of Expression award for her *Dialogues with Madwomen,* "that the more you put it down, the more it seems to rise like a wild dream." If you want to find a credo for Sundance, you couldn't do better than that.

ShoWest

LAS VEGAS — In a plaid shirt, loose-fitting pants, and nonchalant attitude, Adam Sandler was indistinguishable from the fans who've made him one of the most sought-after stars in America. "I'm not particularly smart," he mock-confessed to increasing laughter and applause. "I'm not particularly talented; I'm not particularly good looking. But I'm a multimillionaire because of you people. So thank you very much."

Welcome to ShoWest, as in show me the talent, show me a little respect, and, most of all, show me the money. Again and again at the awards banquet of an event that's been called everything from "the largest and most important gathering of motion picture professionals in the world" to simply "the greatest show on earth," the gratitude expressed by Sandler, named ShoWest Comedy Star of the Year, was echoed by some of the biggest movie stars around.

Here was Sean Connery, talking up his next film, *Entrapment*, and concluding with a heartfelt hope "that we'll make a lot of money." Here was Meg Ryan wryly confessing, "I've never been called 'bankable' in front of so many people." Here was Bobby Farrelly, half of *There's Something about Mary*'s Farrelly brothers, admitting, in a serious moment for him, "If it weren't for you people, Pete and I would be doing TV." And here was superpopular Will Smith, introduced by director Barry

Sonnenfeld as the "ShoWest Human Being of the Planet," topping the Farrellys with the deadpan tribute, "Without you, someone else would have had to buy the building and put movie theaters in there."

On one level, ShoWest, which had all these stars and more as its twenty-fifth anniversary guests, is simply a convention, a film festival if you like, for people who own movie theaters both in this country and overseas. Delegate registration is capped at 3,600, but when friends, family, and related personnel are added in, an estimated 10–12,000 people annually crowd Bally's hotel/casino complex in the center of the Las Vegas strip.

ShoWest is a place where awards are given, like the one that went to Charles D. Cretors, a fourth-generation popcorn man whose great-grandfather patented the process of popping corn in oil back in 1885. It's a place where trade announcements are made by the National Association of Theater Owners (NATO for short, and jokingly thanked a few years back by Leslie Nielsen for "the wonderful job you're doing in Bosnia"), which recently unveiled a new initiative to keep the audio level of coming attractions trailers down. And it's a place where speeches can lapse into boilerplate phraseology like "return on capital," "cash flow perspective," and the always popular "ancillary revenue streams." Unlike other festivals (no names, please), the people here are not frightened by the prospect of earning a little money.

ShoWest in fact has a language of its own, opaque to civilians. Theater owners are known as exhibitors ("'exhibitionists,' as we call them in England," Hugh Grant joked). Movie studios are never called studios, but are rather broken down into their component parts: production, the process of making films, and its more significant partner, distribution, the system of getting them into theaters. Moviegoers are often (no kidding) called guests, and as for the concession stand, it's inevitably referred to, with appropriate reverence, as "our profit center."

So calling ShoWest merely a convention is like calling *The Blair Witch Project* a satisfactory earner. ShoWest is the place where George Lucas, not known to be passionate about public speaking, came to give

exhibitors "a special big hug" for their efforts with the *Star Wars* reissue and to personally unveil the new coming attractions trailer for *The Phantom Menace*. It's the place that Miramax's Harvey Weinstein flew to from New York not to receive an award, not even to present an award, but just to present a presenter to the assembled multitudes. And the very last creative thing Stanley Kubrick did on this planet was to personally put together a thirty-second teaser for *Eyes Wide Shut*, his first film in more than a decade, specifically for the ShoWest crowd.

Though little known to the public, the four-day ShoWest extravaganza turns out to be in many ways the most fascinating, even the most significant dawn-to-dusk movie event in the country, drawing correspondents not only from expected sources like *Entertainment Weekly* and *Premier* but *Time*, *Newsweek*, and major newspapers as well. If you want to know what's happening in mainstream moviemaking and moviegoing today, this is the place to be. "If you're not here," a conventioneer told the *Hollywood Reporter* a few years back, "you're not in business."

A privileged look behind the scenes at the interlocking gears of the theatrical experience, ShoWest has increased in importance over twenty-five years in part because it's several events in one. One part is hard-core educational, a presentation of in-depth statistics, surveys, and information. One part is flashy, an energizing showcase where studios display what they hope theaters will be showing in the months ahead. Perhaps the most irresistible segment is the trade show, where more than 500 vendors pack booths with an eye toward selling every single thing you can think of that a movie theater might possibly want or need, and some, like the tiny ice cream pellets frozen to 40 degrees below zero and dubbed "Dippin' Dots," that it would be difficult to even imagine.

To come to ShoWest as more or less a civilian, as a once and future moviegoer, is to understand that in our lives inside theaters we've all been living a "Truman Show" experience without ever knowing it. Every casual decision we make, from what to see to what to eat, has been carefully observed, analyzed, and acted upon. As a top Nestle marketing official put it when discussing strong consumer feelings about high con-

cession prices, "I don't want to say they can be manipulated, but they can be affected."

ShoWest, obviously, hasn't always been this big, and it hasn't always been in Las Vegas either. It started with a 1974 meeting at Los Angeles International Airport between three key figures in West Coast theatrical distribution, Jerry Forman, Bob Selig, and B.V. Sturdivant. Differences of opinion with the national organization meant that California exhibitors were not then members of NATO and, remembers Forman, head of Pacific Theaters, "We were trying to establish a forum and a place to meet, to bring exhibition and distribution together in a little trade show where you could have a couple of lunches and just open an informal dialogue."

The first ShoWest (no one is sure anymore just who came up with the name) was held in San Diego in 1975. The attendance was roughly 200, there were barely more than a dozen booths at the trade show, the filmmaking companies who attended were mostly marginal entities like Brut Productions and Crown International, and the big news was the new Containment Screen for drive-in theaters, which for the first time did not deflect images out onto the highway. "That," said William Kartozian, later president of NATO, chuckling at the memory, "shows where we've come in twenty-five years."

If there is one key to how big ShoWest has become it was the decision, starting with the 1979 event, to move the proceedings to Las Vegas, a city where the airport looks like a casino and the casinos look like an Egyptian pyramid (Luxor), a medieval castle (Excalibur), even the Manhattan skyline (New York, New York). The whole city can be viewed as one big show, and the synergy between location and event couldn't have been more promising.

Like the movies, Las Vegas is about money and entertainment, about using dazzling fantasy to make you feel good about parting with your dollars. It's a place where everything conspires to make a mockery out of will power, where towering water fountains are choreographed to Frank Sinatra singing "Luck Be a Lady Tonight," and ads suggest that those in

a matrimonial frame of mind "have your wedding ceremony in our luxurious helicopter over Las Vegas. A unique and special way to begin your marriage."

Vegas is "the key to the whole event," said a top distribution executive, a potent energy source for the convention and a place, when all is said and done, where movie people feel right at home. "It's pretty glamorous, there's a whole exciting aura about Las Vegas," says Jean Gregory, who runs the Deluxe Outdoor Theaters in Clermont, Indiana. "If the convention was held somewhere else, there wouldn't be as many people attending." In 1989 the national organization finally got the message, and ShoWest, which had been run since its inception by NATO of California/Nevada, became the official convention of the entire exhibition industry as well.

Also attracted to Las Vegas were international exhibitors, theater owners in far-off places like Thailand and Brazil, who felt even more removed from the heart of the business than their counterparts on the outskirts of Indianapolis. They came from so many countries—more than forty were counted in 1999—that ShoWest set aside its first day just for them. And their problems.

Who knew, for instance, that video piracy is so out of control in Vietnam and Malaysia that the exhibition business has become close to impossible. Or that Russia, a nation of 170 million, "has virtually no modern screens." Or that Italy suffers in the summer from a lack of air-conditioned theaters, and that British exhibitors sometimes have show times dictated by bossy local governments.

ShoWest can't solve these difficulties, of course, but it can offer a forum to schmooze and complain and feel among friends. American exhibitors tend to patronize ShoWest for the same reasons; as a theater owner tartly put it to the *Hollywood Reporter*, "You're with your peers, the people you love and the people you hate."

There is an additional lure, of course, and that is the glamour, the chance to witness movie celebrity in the flesh, to experience what NATO's Kartozian calls "treating them to a bit of Hollywood in Las Vegas."

Does it work? You bet. "We like to see the stars of the films we run in person," says Daniel Van Orden, circuit general manager of the Fulton, Missouri–based B&B Theaters, which owns two dozen screens in that state and neighboring Kansas. "It makes for good talk in small towns."

The studios, ever solicitous, have tried to oblige, putting on elaborate luncheons and dinners where wave after wave of stars parade to the dais and smile at exhibitors and a slickly produced montage of coming attractions (known as a product reel) is screened. Warner Bros. has traditionally set the standard for these events, and its dais can groan under the accumulated celebrity of Clint Eastwood, Keanu Reeves, Will Smith, Salma Hayek, Hugh Grant, Jeanne Tripplehorn, Elizabeth Hurley, George Clooney, Cuba Gooding, Jr., Geoffrey Rush, and numerous others. They're all flown in on company jets in a hectic undertaking that *Premier* called "kamikaze publicity" and Tom Hanks characterized as "one of the great and goofy twenty-four hours you get to spend in the business."

But even though ShoWest picks up the tab for food at these events, providing that touch of glamour has proved expensive and difficult for studios. Those jets from around the world cost serious money, as does paying for a stop in production for whatever films the stars happen to be in at the moment. When all the expenses are added in, one of these afternoons can cost a studio one or even two million dollars.

So it's not surprising, especially in a world where the top ten movie circuits control 60 percent of America's theatrical gross, that the studios periodically chafe at the expense of the ShoWest experience and search for alternatives. In 1995, for instance, MGM/UA flew thirty-two top exhibition executives to Paris for a preview experience. Even Warners, one of ShoWest's most faithful supporters, now cites expense in its plan to do the Las Vegas event only every other year.

Given the expense and difficulty, why do the studios do it at all? In addition to intangible factors like inertia and the value of showing the flag to the industry, studios value the kind of instant feedback on upcoming product that only showing it to thousands of people who have a major stake in a film's success or failure can provide. The feeling was

unanimous — and accurate — after the New Line luncheon, for instance, that the new Mike Myers movie, *Austin Powers: The Spy Who Shagged Me*, was the likeliest success on that studio's roster, and Warner Bros. watchers had the same dead-on sense about *The Matrix* and the Tom Hanks–starring, Stephen King–based *Green Mile*.

But while these successes may have been expected, ShoWest sometimes provides the more valuable service of anointing unexpected films. "Studios might not even be sure themselves what they've got, and ShoWest showcases what might be sleeper product," explains Barry Reardon, Warners' highly respected former head of distribution. "All of a sudden, boom, an unheralded film like *Free Willy* can become a big hit here." Reardon put a more colorful spin on the same thought when he told a reporter a few years back, "A little picture can get kosher at ShoWest."

Also, as more and more of the mainstream media cover ShoWest, the event becomes a perfect opportunity to create valuable international publicity and put studio spin on a film. Which is just what Warners did by providing a small but provocative (and, as it turned out, misleading) glimpse of Kubrick's *Eyes Wide Shut*, characterized by *Daily Variety* as "an eye-opening teaser that features more explicit nude footage of Nicole Kidman than the entire Broadway run of *The Blue Room*."

As important as the information the clips provide, the ShoWest studio events, where executives are dutifully paraded onto the dais like members of the old Soviet Politburo, are useful in fostering a kind of intimacy and camaraderie between exhibitors and distributors, a celebratory "among ourselves" atmosphere capable of creating good feeling that can last through an entire year.

Watching Cuba Gooding, Jr., juggling pats of butter at the Warner Bros. luncheon, seeing Will Smith mock-shine cochairman Terry Semel's shoes (don't ask), hearing Smith unexpectedly extol the virtues of Tucks Medicated Comfort Pads ("I sure hope we did a tie-in with that company," Semel commented), and hearing George Clooney say that he and *Boogie Nights*'s Mark Wahlberg were "stopping at Planet Hollywood to drop off Mark's penis," exhibitors were certainly well on the way to being con-

vinced they were as much a part of the Warners family as Clint Eastwood, candidly introduced by Semel as "the reason we can pay the bills."

In case exhibitors don't get the underlying message that the studios think they're important, a lot of specific making nice and stroking of theater owners goes on at ShoWest. A few years ago, Julia Roberts, the biggest of female stars, assured the ShoWest crowd that her hair in *My Best Friend's Wedding* was "red and long and curly, just the way you like it." In 1999, Peter Cherin, president of News Corp., Twentieth Century Fox's parent corporation, showed up to call film "the greatest igniter of human emotions ever invented" and promise that "the movies will always remain the core priority of what we do." This mutual admiration society is authentic: both exhibition and distribution unwaveringly believe that a good film is a film that makes money, period, and this willingness to speak the same language when it comes to evaluating product is one both sides cherish.

Though it doesn't draw the big stars, even the informational/educational aspect of ShoWest can seem glamorous in the right hands. AC Nielsen EDI, for instance, enlivened the statistics in its new Movie*Views survey of national moviegoing habits by using colorful graphics and making the frequent moviegoers who drive the marketplace (the 18 percent of ticket buyers who account for 66 percent of the box office gross) sound like the stars of their own TV program about poundage-challenged individuals by calling them "The Heavies." Among the more daunting pieces of information revealed were that reviews were important to only 9 percent of all respondents (but 12 percent cent of The Heavies!) and that 82 percent of moviegoers had no clue as to which studio released *Titanic*.

Easily the most entertaining of the information providers was the venerable Jack Valenti, chairman of the Motion Picture Association of America, who made the annual state-of-the-industry presentation. At least as interesting as Valenti's news that production costs had stayed pretty much the same while marketing and distribution numbers had jumped a daunting 13 percent was the chairman's gift for stem-winding

oratorical flourishes. Looking as if he would have been just as comfortable wearing a toga on the floor of the Senate of Rome, the silver-haired Valenti made it sound natural to call high costs "that fiscal Godzilla slouching around movie budgets for so long, like a sullen, unwelcome Banquo's ghost." He enlivened things further with references to what happened when the Saracens invaded France in the eighth century, causing NATO's Kartozian to comment, "It's rare to get an account of the Saracen invasion from an eyewitness."

While theater owners seemed baffled by futurist Kevin R. Roche, who insisted that the line between entertainment and retail was blurring and that in the twenty-first century competition would not be over market share but over "capturing share of mind, share of time," they paid a lot more attention to seminars on two of the biggest issues facing them in the here-and-now, the explosion of the megaplex phenomenon, a.k.a. "megaplex mania," and the maturing of digital technology.

Roughly defined as a theater with from a dozen to thirty-something screens, the megaplex was virtually unheard of just a few years ago. Even the now-déclassé multiplex is a relatively new phenomenon, and it was as recently as the late 1950s that exhibitor Stanley Durwood, head of the AMC chain and considered the creator of the duplex, realized when he closed the balcony during the third week of "a crummy picture" he was running at the Roxy in Kansas City that "if I had another crummy picture upstairs, I could double the gross."

Today, the megaplex is where everyone wants to be: forty-one of the fifty top grossing theaters in America are megaplexes. They are enormous enterprises, as big as 150,000 square feet, utilizing 4,000 light bulbs to illuminate six-story lobby rotundas, and they seat 12–15,000 people on a given weekend day, between two and three million in a year. Yet they've also caused havoc in the exhibition sector, making non-megaplexes seem out of date years before their time, "siphoning customers from existing theaters," said Mike Campbell, head of Regal Cinemas, the nation's largest chain, in what proved to be an accurate warning, "like a huge vacuum cleaner and cannibalizing their business."

These behemoths can be daunting to run, with even veteran theater managers saying they were not prepared for what they saw. So in addition to informal discussions of these issues, ShoWest provided a nuts and bolts event called "Managing Top Grossing Megaplexes" laden with real-world specifics. "You have to know who touches the money," said one manager, detailing his own "triple-check system." Another talked of how disoriented customers may become because of a megaplex's size and described authorizing his staff to "take ownership" of anyone within their physical "zone of influence" and solve any problem within that space. Plus, you have to be smart with your concessions, said John King, Jr., general manager of the Winnetka 21 in Chatsworth, California, relating how an exclusive contract to serve Pink's hot dogs, the pride of Hollywood, led to 175,000 sold in the first year, a figure that drew appreciative gasps from the savvy crowd.

The other much discussed issue at ShoWest was the coming of digital technology and whether, as one speaker put it, "we will enter the new millennium embracing a 100-year-old technology or a new one." Two companies put on side-by-side comparisons of their digital images with Kodak film, and while the general consensus was that film still had the edge, it was a near thing. Later that same day, George Lucas stunned the crowd by announcing that *The Phantom Menace* would play in four theaters in a digital version and that he'd shoot the next *Star Wars* prequel exclusively with digital equipment. Said one exhibitor to the *Hollywood Reporter*, "The sound you heard during the *Star Wars* trailer was twenty guys from Kodak jumping off the roof of the hotel."

• • •

1 box Clark Miniatures
1 box Sour Patch assorted candy
1 box Hot Tamales ("Great Cinnamon Taste!")
    chewy cinnamon-flavored candies
1 box Nuclear Sqworms ("You'll Really Dig 'Em!")
    sour neon Gummi Worms

1 bag microwave popcorn from Packaging Concepts Inc., "Converters of Flexible Packaging"
1 bag Strips for Dips tortilla chips from Ricos, "Originators of Nachos in Concessions"
1 bag theater-style tortilla chips from Wyandot World Class Snacks
1 bag Starburst fruit chews
1 box BC's Candy-Coated Real Milk Chocolate Pieces from Banner Candy ("Banner Makes Movies Magic") to celebrate their 70th anniversary
1 sack Swiss-Miss French Vanilla Cappuccino ("Just Add Hot Water") instant coffee blend
1 bag Care Bears Gummi Bears ("Made with Real Fruit Juice")
1 bag Nestle Raisinets
1 package Star Punch artificially flavored strawberry licorice
1 package Funacho Zesty Cheese Sauce
1 package Ricos Nacho Cheese Dip ("Spiced Right! Good Hot–or Cold!")

—edible contents of concessions bag given to every ShoWest delegate

• • •

They call it simply "the trade show," but if there is a secret heart to the ShoWest experience, it lies in this sprawling, 541-booth extravaganza squeezed into a specially constructed 90,000-square-foot tent perched in Bally's backyard. It's a cradle-to-grave tour, in a manner of speaking, of the theater-going experience, from Wagner, the company that invented the slotted marquee letter in the 1920s to consultants like the Plotkin Group who help you hire the help ("Reduce employee theft and turnover! Identify honest, dependable, hardworking, capable employees!") to a seat refurbisher named Premier with the motto "We Do for Theater Seating What Tarantino Did for Travolta."

It's at the trade show that you can meet the legendary Frank Liberto

of Ricos Products of San Antonio, the genial man credited with originating what's known as "concession nachos," a Tex-Mex snack that he's introduced to twenty-three countries. Here, not unlike the open bazaar in Ouagadougou, Burkina Faso, hypnotic waves of committed salespeople call out beseechingly as you wander the aisles, and even the woman who hands out sacks emblazoned with the Coke logo insists "they're not empty, they're filled with air, absolutely essential for life."

Because theaters make a sizable part of their profits from the concession stand (most of the box office revenue goes back to the studios, especially in a film's busy opening weeks), it's this aspect of the theatrical experience that draws the most vendors and the most interest. Some half-a-dozen popcorn-related enterprises, for instance, including the makers of Popwise Popping Oil ("Your Popcorn's Ready for an Oil Change"), compete in this high-profile area, and if you want to understand how the Metric Weight Volume Tester (MWVT for short) measures all-important kernel expansion, this is the place to learn. Also on hand and prepared to talk up their products were salesmen for Jelly Bellys ("making 40 million of these beans a day keeps us busy"), Cookie Dough Bites ("people can't say no to cookie dough"), and Knott's Berry Farm Smoothies with names like Fiji Freeze and Strawberry Goes Bananas ("zero to awesome in twenty seconds.")

No one here is without a story, like Josh Schreider and Bryan Freeman of Bavarian Brothers Pretzel Bakery ("Twisted at Birth") in Van Nuys. No, they're not brothers, they're not even Bavarian, but they are passionate about pretzels. "We started this company on credit cards," Schreider says, his eyes hot with pretzel fervor. "We bought a pretzel-making machine from a junkyard owner who said it couldn't be made to work. I took it apart; there were thousands of pieces on the back room floor of a pizza parlor, and the owner bet me I couldn't put it together again." And today? "Over the past seven months, we've been doubling the number of theaters we're in every twenty-three days." Is this a great country, or what?

It's also, regrettably, a messy country, and ShoWest does not stint on

cleaning opportunities. Arnold Meltzer of Ampac Theater Cleaning Services talked of finding everything from underwear to sleeping people to an Uzi machine gun on the floors of theaters, while brothers Jaimy and Dameon Johnson of Inglewood demonstrated the Kwick Bag trash container, which fits conveniently under theater seats. And Kory Wright of Natural Solutions Cleaning Productions ("The Nation's Leading Producer of Human-Friendly, Building-Friendly, Environment-Friendly Conscious Cleaning Products") boasted, "If you drink this product, which employees will, it won't kill them."

A veteran of more than a dozen ShoWests is Robert Hotch, president of Modular Hardware, which specializes in toilet partitions, hardware, and accessories, and he, too, has a spiel: "Everyone who goes to movie theaters ends up in the bathroom. More people rate the movie theater by the condition of the bathroom than anything else."

This logic worked on a theater owner from the nation of Georgia that Hotch met at ShoWest a year or so back. "Not only did he order the partitions and hardware, we had to send him the paper and soap. He can't get it over there. Needless to say, the money was in the bank before we sent it, and in American dollars, not rubles."

All of this energetic selling can be exhausting, and the trade show also offered mini-massages ranging from the $5 Feel Good to the $30 Ultimate from a group called On-Site Stress Relief, Inc. But for this visitor, at least, there was something inescapably exhilarating about this kind of joyful cacophony. Movie theaters are where it all began, where everyone first fell in love with movies, simply but finally, and if that love still endures, what ShoWest has to offer is easy to embrace wholeheartedly. Somewhere in the world, it's show time every minute of every day, and what could be better than that?

PART TWO

Festivals with Geopolitical Agendas

FESPACO

OUAGADOUGOU, BURKINA FASO — The crowd, estimated at 40,000, pours through an honor guard of mounted camels and overflows the biggest stadium in the country. For the next three and a half hours a kaleidoscopic spectacle unfolds, made up of flowery political speeches in two languages, performances by celebrated musicians like Malhatini and the Mahotela Queens, a pantomime executed by five hundred schoolchidren, choreographed prancing by elaborately costumed horsemen, dazzling fireworks, even a ceremonial ribbon-cutting and release of multicolored balloons by the nation's president.

Is this any way to open a film festival? For FESPACO, the Festival Panafricaine du Cinéma de Ouagadougou, a spectacular occasion whose fourteenth edition took place in 1995, it is simply business as usual.

Held every other year at the end of February, FESPACO's celebration of African cinema (an event relatively unknown in this country despite visits by domestic celebrities like Alice Walker, Tracy Chapman, and John Singleton) is an extravaganza with few peers, a massive cultural happening that shreds preconceived notions of festivals as merely places where tickets are taken and movies are shown.

Yes, there are films. Hundreds of them from all across Africa and the African diaspora are available to be seen here, both on the big screen and

in a parallel video film market known as MICA, providing an unequaled opportunity to view the entire range of production from Algeria to South Africa and beyond.

The choicest films at FESPACO compete for the festival's equivalent of Cannes's Palme d'Or, the Etalon (Stallion) de Yennenga, named after the legendary horsewoman who is considered the progenitor of the country's predominant Mossi tribe. And all entries are hugely appreciated by the legendarily responsive African audiences, one of FESPACO's lures, crowds who pack the theaters and roar appreciatively at situations that strike home.

"In the United States, African films are shown in the context of museums and art cinema, so they tend to be received reverently, with deference and respect," explained Richard Peña, program director for the Film Society of Lincoln Center, director of the New York Film Festival, and a FESPACO visitor. "Here you can see how open and dialogic the relationship to film is. Godard said that cinema is what goes on between the screen and the audience, and it really goes on here. You are seeing a truly communal experience."

But more than for what it shows, FESPACO is noteworthy as a matter of enormous national pride for this striving West African country the size of Colorado. Called "desperately, and famously, poor" by one guide book, "not near the top of anyone's short list of travel destinations" by another, French West Africa's former Upper Volta, in a scenario that even Hollywood would reject as outlandish, has managed by a combination of passion and determination to turn itself into the undisputed capital of the African film world.

Ouaga, as the locals call this hot, dusty city of half a million, gives itself over body and soul to FESPACO, starting with releasing all its fifteen screens to the festival. These range from the spacious, air-conditioned Ciné Neerwaya (meaning "the beauty has come" in Moré, the primary local language), at 1,200 seats one of the biggest theaters in West Africa, to outdoor venues in the city's remoter locales that are more prosaically named ("Secteur 17," "Secteur 29") after the areas they're located in.

I arrived in the city, as most international visitors do, in the cooler nighttime. Though Ouaga has so little electrical illumination that a well-lit Elf gas station stood out like a spaceship, what was most noticeable during the drive into town from the airport was the conviviality of the street life, how many people were out and about. Also noticeable, not to say unavoidable, was the multiplicity of motorbikes, called Mobylettes after the most popular brand, whose taillights twinkled like fireflies in the pleasantly sultry night air.

Though the bikes, the city's most popular vehicle, are even more omnipresent during the day, Ouaga when the sun is out is in some ways a different story. Because Burkina is part of the edge-of-the-Sahara area known as the Sahel (from the Arabic word for shore), it is a famously hot and dusty place for much of the year, so dry it is rare to see a Westerner without a bottle of Lafi, the local mineral water.

Yet unlike neighboring Abidjan, the bustling capital of the Ivory Coast, Ouaga has the refreshing air of an overgrown village, with few billboards, no skyscrapers to speak of, and the ambiance of a city under construction that might never be finished. The streets are either completely nameless or grandly dedicated to heroes of liberation like Nelson Mandela, Che Guevara, and Kwame Nkruma. And just a ten-minute journey into the countryside brings you to traditional village compounds that look as they have for centuries.

Though Burkina is a poor country, it is an industrious one, with makeshift market stalls seen on many Ouaga streets. The intensity and variety of commercial life include a steady parade of women dressed in colorful print dresses balancing huge loads of everything from oranges to piles of mirrors on their heads. And bicycles do not just transport people, they convey towers of hay, massive water cisterns, sacks of coal, piles of ox skins, anything and everything you might not even imagine could be moved this way. Even my French-speaking driver would occasionally eye a particularly outrageous load and sigh, "Ah, Afrique."

At the same time, it is impossible to move through Ouaga without noticing the poverty, visible in everything from persistent child beggars

(often sent out by Islamic imams) to grim housing to the country's paper money, which has been worn to a remarkable thinness by repeated use. And the city's ever-present vultures, visible everywhere and often just perched on buildings to have a look around, do not make for a prosperous feeling.

Yet talking about Ouaga in terms of what it lacks gives a misleading impression of the city. For in line with the cliché of African travel that you go to the East for the wildlife and the West for the people, the Burkinabe are known for their wonderful spirit. Warm, lively, with an enviable self-assurance linked to a dignified sense of who they are, the citizens of Ouaga have no intention of being defined by their poverty and manage to turn almost every transaction with them into a restorative experience.

FESPACO makes itself felt locally in numerous ways. Those who can afford it wear clothing made from special FESPACO commemorative cloth, the national lottery has inaugurated a special "Millionaire" drawing to mark the festival, postage stamps have been issued to honor Gaston Kaboré and Idrissa Ouedraogo, the country's most celebrated living directors, and one visiting film critic unexpectedly found himself chatting about movies in a private audience with Burkina's president.

Several of the city's main streets, festooned with banners proclaiming uplifting slogans like "FESPACO: Pride of a Continent," are closed off and turned into a pedestrian shopping mall generically called Rue Marchande. There Ouaga's residents, benefiting from a government decree giving everyone half days off for the duration of the festival, jostle with tourists at crowded booths where merchants from all over Africa sell souvenirs, hand out free cigarettes and condoms (AIDS is a major problem here as in the rest of the continent), and distribute literature about buying fax machines and supporting the Intra-African Union for Human Rights.

There is also the city's Grand Marché, a reinforced concrete structure in the center of town that is one of West Africa's newest, and reportedly one of the cleanest and most manageable as well. Its sights and smells are

immediately overwhelming, with everything from slabs of salt ar of dried fish to gorgeous fabric and imported Chicago Bulls T-sh sale from innumerable tiny booths on several different levels.

If you slow down just to think about a purchase, or even if you don't, determined sellers importune you in French and occasionally English and don't hesitate to follow you to other booths, talking furiously. Once buying is a possibility, bargaining is essential: to agree to the first offered price is unthinkable, like rushing right to the table at a dinner party without first saying hello to your host. Bargaining has everything to do with ritual and tradition and almost nothing to do with gouging money out of the unwary, so much so that resident foreigners who gain a reputation for agreeing to the first offered price and refusing to bargain are considered undesirable customers. And should you indicate that your French is weak, the seller, even if he looks as if he had stepped out of the Arabian Nights, is sure to reach into his voluminous robes and come out with a pocket calculator to help things along.

For those without the inclination to shop, international exhibitions on the art of the Niger Valley and the image of Africa in Europe were available during the festival I attended. And devotees of nightlife who didn't plan on showing up for FESPACO's 8 A.M. press screenings could partake of the "Nuits Chaudes" or "Hot Nights" series of dance concerts that didn't even get started till around midnight.

As for the city's more conventional tourist attractions, they tended to be slighted during the festival. This proved especially true at the Musée National, located inside the Lycée Bogodogo on Avenue d'Oubritenga headed out of town, where I was the only visitor in an oppressively steamy building. None of this fazed Jean-Pierre Bikienga, the museum's guide, who took me on a passionate, detailed tour of the collection's masks and artifacts, delivered in a musical French that was pleasant to the ear and easy to understand.

My favorite item was a gris-gris sack confiscated by police after the arrest of a potent local sorcerer accused of using magic to kill his enemies. The sack had initially been hung on a branch of a blooming tree,

which proceeded to sicken and die within days. Afterward the sack had been left outside in the heat and rain for a year before it was considered safe to touch. It did look considerably the worse for wear, but the sinister air about it continued to be unmistakable.

Yet even all this does not tell the whole story of FESPACO. It doesn't explain why the festival draws thousands of journalists and participants from dozens of countries as distant as Japan, Romania, and Brazil as well as African luminaries who in 1995 ranged from Nigeria's Nobel Prize–winning novelist Wole Soyinka to the controversial South African political figure Winnie Mandela, then on her first state visit to West Africa.

Simply put, FESPACO has become the preeminent African cultural event of any kind. To stand in the lobby of the Hotel Independence, the festival's central meeting place, to admire the various styles of traditional dress and read the gazetteer of countries on passing name tags is to feel that the entire continent has somehow gathered in this one place. For the eight days it occupies, FESPACO is the focal point of Africa's consciousness, the place where this perennially neglected continent comes to examine itself. And as the medium chosen for this task, film assumes an importance that is rarely felt elsewhere.

"Our country is modest and underdeveloped, and people used to say that priority in development should be for agriculture and other things," says Filippe Sawadogo, at that time FESPACO's affably driven secretary general and the man who ran the festival for more than a decade. "Now we understand that no people can be developed without their own culture, that showing our own culture is a priority. If you know yourself in terms of identity, you can succeed."

The year 1995, celebrated worldwide as the centenary of cinema, seemed especially promising for Africa. Both the Toronto Film Festival and the British Film Institute used FESPACO as the occasion to announce major new African film series for later that year, and the general consensus was that, in Richard Peña's words, "African film feels vibrant at a time when so much of cinema is looking around at how to cut its losses.

A wonderful and intoxicating sense of pride hangs over the whole festival, you feel nothing but hope here."

Though the postcolonial history of African cinema is no more than thirty-something years old, the medium has always been one of enormous importance for this continent, partly because the reality that, in one director's words, "there are no illiterates in the world of cinema" makes it the ideal method for reaching the widest possible audience.

More than that, Africans feel an intense need to control the way both their own people and the world at large view the African experience. "Traditionally images have been used to dominate Africa, doing damage to the minds of colonized people, telling them they are less important," says Gaston Kaboré, the pioneering Burkinabe director whose *Wend Kuuni* is celebrated as the first black African picture to win a César for the best Francophone film. "But ever since we started making films, we have used cinema as a tool of liberation, liberating the individual in his mind. We need to describe our own reality by ourselves."

Though this is a feeling that echoes across the entire continent, there are other factors that divide African filmmakers, and none more sharply than the language issue. For reasons that are still debated, perhaps stemming from the French belief in culture as an end in itself versus an English desire to make all things utilitarian, the majority of the most successful and celebrated directors in Africa come from the Francophone countries of the West and the North.

As a result, FESPACO has in the past been viewed as a Francophone event, where it is the rare film that has English subtitles and eleven of the twelve winners of the Etalon through 1995 have come from countries where French is the predominant European language. But though the French continue to provide considerable assistance to West African filmmakers, the festival has taken increasing steps to make itself accessible to English speakers, and in 1995, with South Africa invited to attend for the first time, even more of an attempt at outreach in terms of simultaneous translation and bilingual printed material was made. "We are

not Francophone or Anglophone," said FESPACO's Sawadogo on opening night. "We are Africaphone."

For the filmmakers themselves, who come to the festival by the hundreds, these kinds of divisions seem less important than the rare chance to mingle with peers. Though admitting that "non-French speakers can tend to feel out of it," prominent Nigerian director Ola Balogun said that that drawback was far outweighed by "the unique opportunity to see other filmmakers. It's not like we are all living in one country; we are dispersed, with different schedules to cope with, so there are lots of reunions here."

Because of its importance, even the most celebrated African directors try not to miss the festival. The 1995 jury president, the celebrated seventy-one-year-old Ousmane Sembene, called "l'ainé des anciens (the elder of elders)," considers it a duty never to skip a festival, and Burkina's Idrissa Ouedraogo warmly calls FESPACO "my first mother, the place I made my first short film for."

In fact, FESPACO has gotten so big and successful that, in an unexpected parallel to the controversy that eternally swirls around America's Sundance Film Festival, participants argue about whether the event has gotten too large and too commercial, whether it has lost its Africanness, its sense of direction, the purity of its spirit.

"People grumble that as FESPACO has gotten bigger it has grown out of all proportion to the growth of African cinema," says June Givanni, the British Film Institute's chief African film programmer. "But it is a celebration, and I don't think those things are necessarily bad. The festival has the difficult task of balancing things, but you can still find the whole spectrum here, the edge and the passionate discussions with people not mincing words as well as the glitzy side."

What most African filmmakers wanted to talk about, however, was not FESPACO's flaws but the perennial allied difficulties of first raising money to make a film and then, something that turns out to be even more difficult, finding a way to get it shown on the African continent.

Because one of the great paradoxes of African filmmaking is that, in

Gaston Kaboré's words, "Our films are strangers in their own territories. It is easier to watch an African film in New York, Los Angeles, London or Paris than in Lesotho, Botswana, Nigeria or Kenya. If audiences are given the opportunity to see them, they are rushing to go, African audiences are keen to watch movies where their reality is reflected. But our films are made outside of an economic system, we do not have producers or distributors with financial and economic clout, so our movies do not have the ability to circulate."

NINETY PERCENT OF AFRICAN FILMS WILL NEVER BE SEEN BY AFRICANS THEMSELVES. So reads a flyer handed out by Daniel Cuxac, whose Ivory Coast–based DC Productions is one of the few companies attempting to put African films on video to increase their local availability. "After FESPACO the light will be off and we will find again the hard realities," he says. "After their films are shown in the festivals, the filmmakers stay in their houses, they don't know where to go." Language barriers, the expense of subtitles, the uncertainty of getting both money and films back from other countries all contribute to the problem.

One potential way out of these difficulties, at least for the most prominent directors, is to get financing from European entities like television networks, usually French but increasingly German, Dutch, and British as well. But taking this money, welcome as it is, can present its own set of problems.

"When you write a script to please European producers, you take their expectations into consideration; if you are spending ten million French francs, you are wondering what kind of box office results you will get in France," Gaston Kaboré explained to me. "Our films can become unbalanced, we are so weak we are turning like this and like that. The danger is forgetting your own people, your own fundamental vision, and presenting Africa only as Europe is prepared to receive it. The danger is we will lose our souls."

Four years later, Africa's Francophone filmmakers were, if anything, more concerned. Senegalese-born director Mama Keita told *Variety* in May 1999 that he was "really worried that the image we are seeing of

Africa in most films has virtually nothing to do with the reality of the individual countries.

"Even if you look at the French government funds, which are supposed to help develop African cinema," Keita added, "what happens is the cash goes to pay French technicians, French laboratories and French post-production facilities, who all work on African films. The money stays in France. Why do you think there are no post-production facilities worth speaking of in Francophone Africa?"

Besides lamenting requirements from funding companies that the film be shot in Africa—"that means you can't use the money if you are an African director who wants to do a film about the African experience in France"—Keita also noted that "many of the political regimes in Francophone Africa are not exactly democracies. You are not going to be allowed to shoot a film about what life is really like. That's why the African film today boils down to shots of naked kids running around mud-hut villages. That doesn't bother anybody."

One filmmaker who has made his peace with Europe to the point of dividing his time between homes in Ouaga and Paris is Idrissa Ouedraogo, a rising star of African cinema whose 1999 retrospective at the British Film Institute paid tribute to his "fierce determination to retain a poignant fidelity to the reality of the people, and his truly poetic rendering of the simplicity of the rural Burkinabe life." The director's first feature, *Yaaba,* won the International Critic's Prize at Cannes; his next, *Tilai,* took that festival's Special Jury Prize and won the Etalon at FESPACO, and his third, *Samba Traore*, was given the Silver Bear at Berlin.

A relaxed man with a kind of affable swagger about him, Idrissa, as everyone calls him, says he works out of Europe from simple necessity. "The gods don't love us here in Burkina; taking airplanes, making phone calls, everything is very difficult, very expensive," he says with a smile. "Here there are not so many opportunities to make films and to make contacts as in Europe."

Working in Europe, using non-African crews and non-African casts, has made Idrissa something of a controversial figure, an identity he eas-

ily shrugs off. "It is normal for people not to like me, because I can get financing outside of the traditional ways," he says. "All the people who speak about me, they can't do it. People speak about the imperialism of the American cinema. It is true, but there is a certain efficiency to American cinema that is a good thing, and we should try to have that as well."

More than anything, Idrissa wants his work to be seen not as African film but simply as film. "When I do some of these things, people say 'Stop, you are becoming white,' but I think cinema has no color. When I used French actors in one of my films, people wanted to kill me, they said, 'It is not African cinema.'

"But to me African cinema is a ghetto. When people think of African films, they want to see huts, they won't let Africans show something different. But Africa is not one country, it is a continent, and filmmakers are not alike, we are not the same. Even two American filmmakers do not have the same sensibility. Filmmaking is the personal thing you give to the world. You don't give your country or your continent, you give yourself."

While these issues get argued back and forth, the key underlying astonishment about FESPACO remains constant: how completely unlikely it is that this desperately poor country with a literacy rate of 18 percent, so underdeveloped that the UN's Human Development Report at one time ranked it 170th out of 173 countries, should have become the polished host of an event of this scale.

Some 80 to 90 percent of the Burkinabe toil as subsistence farmers, and one million others have moved to the neighboring Ivory Coast to find work. And, with life expectancy at forty-eight years, health is also a problem for residents, and for visitors as well. During the nineteenth century, West Africa was known as "the deadliest spot on earth," and even today buying medical evacuation insurance (it's not as expensive as it sounds) is strongly recommended for all tourists.

Prior to my own trip, having rashly requested what turned out to be dozens of pages of faxed warnings about malaria and other insect-borne

maladies from our government's Center for Disease Control and Prevention, I became obsessed with health, even getting into arcane discussions with wilderness supply store clerks about the relative advantages of spraying or washing clothes with the powerful insect repellent Permethrin. Things got so bad that when I boarded my Air Afrique flight from Paris to Ouaga and saw an elderly man with a portable oxygen supply, my first thought was to wonder why I'd neglected to bring one myself.

In truth, when the festival began in 1969 as a small, informal Week of African Cinema showing but twenty-three films, no one expected it to grow into what it has. But, says Gaston Kaboré, who besides directing has for more than a decade been the secretary general of FEPACI, the Pan-African Federation of Filmmakers, "a conjunction of many desires, events and phenomena" gradually transformed what had begun as little more than a gathering of friends.

The first event was a 1970 conflict between the government of what was then Upper Volta and the French companies in charge of film distribution and exhibition, which resulted in an unprecedented state decision to nationalize those functions.

"It was a revolutionary thing, nobody thought that cinema could interest a government to such a point," remembers Kaboré, a vibrant, thoughtful man. "Many countries sent secret missions to know how we did this. The French retaliated by deciding not to furnish films, and we sent people to French-speaking places like Belgium and Algeria to buy them. It was like a little war.

"Eventually the French were obliged to reestablish the relationship, but those events gave us a kind of image in the world, that of a little country that, despite being one of the poorest, was the most interested in cinema and culture. So many things came from that."

The next event giving FESPACO a boost on the world film scene was a military coup in Upper Volta in 1983 that brought a thirty-four-year-old army captain named Thomas Sankara to power. A committed, innovative Marxist revolutionary, Sankara turned the country upside down, striking out against corruption and making childhood health and

women's rights priorities. A charismatic populist, he sold off the government's fleet of official Mercedes, personally wrote a new national anthem, and changed the country's name to Burkina Faso, a combination of words in Moré and Dioula, the two dominant native languages, that together mean "land of honest, upright men."

Sankara saw the potential of FESPACO and embraced it wholeheartedly, and his reputation as a kind of African Che Guevara (he put slogans like "Fatherland or Death, We Shall Triumph," on everything from airport walls to tourist brochures) made attendance at the event attractive on a wider scale. His policies, however, alienated the country's traditional establishment (he for instance decreed that on one designated Saturday each month men had to do the family shopping) — and Sankara himself was overthrown and killed in another coup four years later, with his close friend and former corevolutionary Blaise Compaoré taking over as head of government, a position he still holds.

Though some African filmmakers have refused to return to FESPACO since Sankara's assassination, considering attendance a betrayal of the positive things he stood for, FEPACI's Kaboré has another point of view. Though "people from abroad thought Sankara created FESPACO, it was already established as a national concern when he came. He gave it a new impetus, brought a new vision, but cinema in Burkina does not belong to one government or one president. It is part of the patrimony of our country."

The phone rang promptly at 7 A.M. "The president will see you today," a cool voice said. "A car will pick you up outside your hotel at 10:30." They didn't have to tell me it would be a good idea to be ready on time.

Even before I left Los Angeles for FESPACO, the word had come from Burkina Faso that if I wanted an interview with Blaise Compaoré, "president of Faso, chief of state, president of the council of ministers," to give him his official title, it could be arranged. Since most film festivals won't even let you talk to the president of the jury, this was not an opportunity to be shrugged off.

In the years since he took control after that violent 1987 coup, Compaoré had gradually liberalized the political process, but when he ran for president in 1991, not surprisingly winning a seven-year term, the opposition parties boycotted the election, resulting in a voter turnout of only 25 percent. In 1998, he was once again returned to power.

Meeting me in the lobby of the Hotel Silmande was the owner of that cool voice, Naye Nell Diallo, a woman with a story that seemed straight out of a novel. Born in Alabama, she had worked for international organizations in Africa for ten years and then married one of President Compaoré's closest advisers, making her important enough to have been the first American ever to receive one of Burkina's highest national decorations, the Chevalier de l'Ordre National.

The president would be meeting us at his Camp David–style compound located about twenty minutes north of the capital at Zinaire, which means "that which has never been seen before" in Moré and is also the site of the village where Compaoré was born. "He relaxes here," Diallo explained. "In town, everybody tells him all the problems."

No signs, obviously, announced the compound, just a plain wire fence, a group of red and white painted concrete poles and a handful of lounging soldiers who casually approached our car. "I don't play with the military," Diallo said, rolling down the window and taking care to tell the soldiers who we were.

Surrounded by a large light brown wall over which green tile roofs were visible, the compound consisted of a main house and several smaller alcoves surrounding a swimming pool and a large open pavilion. The whole effect was tasteful but not opulent.

"This was donated to the president by his friends," Diallo said as we entered. "It will be eventually given to the country." Almost as an afterthought she added, "There is a lion around here somewhere, it was also given to the president," and sure enough, the unleashed animal could be seen pawing a nearby tree, with a handler hovering just behind. As we moved slowly toward the pool in the intense heat, the lion's presence made the entire situation seem only marginally more surreal.

Wearing black shoes, sharply creased black pants, and a white shirt worn outside, President Compaoré first played with the lion and then laughed when Diallo teased him that his staff says he's not the president when his shirt isn't tucked in. A handsome man with watchful eyes and a nice smile that he used only sparingly, the president gave serious answers to serious questions but relaxed more when the talk turned to film, revealing that thirteen years earlier he too had felt the restless urge to direct.

The result was a half-hour documentary on the National Commandos, a military group that he was then the leader of. "People consider them strange, like your Marines" he said in French, with Diallo translating. "So I made this to show they were real people." After he added that he has "many, many stories in his head for future films," Diallo suggested that he go to Hollywood and everyone laughed.

Asked if he'd seen many American films, the president smiled and, echoing the French cultural imperialism line, said, "Every film is American." It turned out he'd most recently screened, of all things, *Dirty Harry* with Clint Eastwood. The thought and the film seemed to amuse him. "It was in English, so I didn't understand everything, but it seemed a typical American film, with a lot of violence, a lot of action, and always a good car chase."

Asked if he'd seen anything from the current FESPACO, the president mentioned that *Guimba*, a film from neighboring Mali, had been brought out to the compound. "It's a good one," he said, which did not seem surprising, because, after all, who would want the responsibility of bringing out a film that was not good for the president to look at.

Guimba, in fact, was more than a good film, it was the popular winner of the Etalon de Yennenga that year, as well as many of the special jury prizes awarded by organizations as diverse as the European Union and Air Afrique. Directed by Cheick Oumar Sissoko, this gorgeously produced, bawdy costume drama about an evil sorcerer king, his mean-spirited, sexually active dwarf son, and the mother and daughter they want

to force into marriage, mixes magic, spectacle, political commentary, and raunchy comedy in a vivid, spirited way. *Variety* later called it "in a class by itself among African films" and it achieved a rare level of American success for films from the continent, gaining a nationwide theatrical as well as a video release in the United States.

As for Burkina Faso, what with hosting FESPACO (with funding coming from the state and more than fifteen international partners) and being the headquarters for FEPACI, the country has gradually increased its commitment to film, even passing legislation providing for an admission tax on non-African films to help finance domestic production. One of Africa's few film schools is located in Ouaga, the city has dedicated a large, Claes Oldenburg–type public monument of a camera and reels of film to African filmmakers, and one of the main events of 1995's FESPACO was the opening of the continent's only climate-controlled film archive and library.

And FESPACO itself is hardly prepared to rest on its accomplishments. Feeling that "it is a pity that if a film is finished ten days after FESPACO it has to wait two years" for a festival showing, Secretary General Sawadogo talked about turning the event into an annual occurrence. "This would dynamize our industry, and as you say in the West, life is too short to wait to do something. The highway of information is coming, and we have to be present at some stops. Africa has 750,000,000 inhabitants, and we must give our own images to the world."

Havana

Scratch a Cuban, uncover a paradox.

To spend time in the crumbling but still heartbreakingly beautiful city of Havana, to talk to Cuban filmmakers during the Festival of New Latin American Cinema, is to hear the same words repeated over and over: contradictory, paradoxical, inexplicable, miraculous. "It's more difficult to explain what happens in Cuba in rational terms than to live here," says prominent director Gerardo Chijona. "If you're going to go by common sense, forget it."

To examine this small island's film history is to discover how far from conventional expectations everything is. Isolated and beleaguered by an American economic blockade that is almost as old as its revolution, Cuba should never have been able to muster the resources to develop any kind of film industry or to play host to a prestigious international festival dedicated to the socially conscious Latin American cinema.

Yet, starting in the late 1960s, when Tomás Gutiérrez Alea's *Memories of Underdevelopment* and Humberto Solás's *Lucia* impressed international audiences with their skill and brio, Cuba rapidly established itself as a world cinematic force.

And along with the industry the festival in Havana grew in the 1980s into the biggest, most important showcase for Latin American films,

complete with Dionysian all-night parties that showcased the best in Cuban music. Helmut Newton shot the festival for *Vanity Fair*, Bob Rafelson slept in George Raft's celebrated circular bed at the Hotel Capri, Treat Williams flew in himself, Robert De Niro, and Christopher Walken in his private plane, and Cuban leader Fidel Castro took up so much of Jack Lemmon's time that the actor commented, "Anyone who can make me shut up for three hours has got to be extraordinary."

"During my years, cinema was born in the middle of the circus, the show was in the streets," says Pastor Vega, who ran the festival from its inception through 1990. "Everybody overseas thought that people were not happy here, that Cuba was a big jail. I decided to make a festival that was a film, theater, music, alcohol and sex festival, all together at the same time. In my opinion, that was cultural."

But all that was before what is known in Cuba as "the special period." Beginning in 1990 the tightening of the American blockade combined with the collapse of the Soviet bloc (which had accounted for 85 percent of Cuba's foreign trade as well as billions of dollars in foreign aid) to bring the island's economy to nearly a standstill.

The legalization of the American dollar as local currency in 1993 introduced a two-tier economic system to a society that had prided itself on its egalitarianism, making those without access to greenbacks feel like refugees in their own country and leading to too-true jokes with punch lines about bellboys making more money than brain surgeons. If Cuba had somehow managed to have a film industry and a festival before, surely this deepest of crises would bring everything to an end.

And Cuba's continuing economic miseries have made a difference in the relationship between its citizens and film. Estimates are that about half of Havana's movie theaters have been closed, victims of everything from persistent blackouts and weakened public transportation due to the lack of gasoline to projectors so ancient some are reportedly held together with string.

As a result, most Cuban moviegoing has transferred to television, especially a heavily watched Saturday night double bill that features hot

items from Hollywood like *Forrest Gump* and *Jurassic Park*, all conveniently bootlegged off satellite transmissions. Enrique Colina, whose film analysis program on Cuban TV has lasted twenty-seven years ("I will ask for the Guinness record, especially if there is money," he laughs), says that "if relations with the U.S. become normal, it will be a big problem for the mass audience, because we couldn't afford to show these films."

The special period has also affected Cuba's prestigious Three Worlds International Film and Television School, where Francis Ford Coppola is fondly remembered for the day he cooked 4,000 gnocchi and fed the entire student body. Fernando Birri, the venerated Argentine director who was a founder of the New Latin American cinema movement and the school's first director, came back to celebrate his seventieth birthday. "Cuba is changing and the school will, too," he somberly told the students at a cake-cutting party. "The revolution is like a flame that seems about to be extinguished but stays alive. The flame is different, but it does not go out."

Yet, with all these problems, the paradoxical truth is that Havana's film festival is not only surviving but, helped by the country's ever-expanding tourist industry (more than 600,000 non-U.S. tourists spent an estimated $850 million in 1994), is actually prospering compared to where it was a few years ago.

Despite competition from festivals in Cartagena, Colombia, and Guadalajara, Mexico, Havana is still the major player in this market. The seventeenth competition in 1995 attracted more than ninety features from a dozen Latin American and Caribbean countries, with the top prize, the Gran Premio Coral, going to *Miracle Alley*, the highest-grossing Mexican film of the year and an Oscar candidate.

Of course, much has changed. "Now," says Gerardo Chijona, "we are making a festival according to our times." Which means, Pastor Vega unhappily notes, "no parties, only seminars, something 'serious,' in quotes." Almost everyone pays their own way these days, and the festival has begun to sell advertising space on everything from billboards to

opening night tickets. Even Fidel Castro, far from schmoozing with Jack Lemmon, missed the event entirely. He was visible nightly on the TV news, however, visiting China and Vietnam, an exhausted presence in an overcoat being greeted by small children and giggling circus acrobats as he searched for tips on improving his country's economy.

As a concession to the Cuban population, the content of the festival has shifted markedly as well. Where in the 1980s the films shown were almost exclusively Latin American, now European, Asian, and even American films form a major presence. What audiences at more than twenty theaters in Havana and elsewhere in Cuba (the festival travels to half a dozen cities) may see has included *Pulp Fiction*, *Raise the Red Lantern*, *In the Name of the Father*, *Babette's Feast*, and dozens more. The reason: the country lacks the money to procure these films for regular theatrical runs, so if they were not brought in for the festival, Cuban audiences would not get to see them at all.

If all this sounds grim and somber, it shouldn't, because the passion and enthusiasm of the convivial Cuban population, the people the event is really intended for, make the Havana Festival just the opposite. Packs of lively fans crowd around the posted screening lists as if they were winning lottery numbers, and enormous throngs line up for hours in advance at major Havana theaters like the Yara and the Charlie Chaplin (the festival headquarters) and respond lustily to what's on screen.

It's difficult to think of another country where film is so important, has so transfixed an entire population from top to bottom. "Cubans," director Solás says flatly, "are the most cultured people in all Latin America." Moreover, adds veteran director Julio García Espinosa, "it's the only country in Latin America where people will stand in line to see Latin American films. Other audiences see that a film's in Spanish and they will not go."

Though Cuba was receptive to cinema even before 1959 (Solás remembers seeing such classics as *The Bicycle Thief* and *The Battleship Potemkin* by the time he was ten), there is no doubt that the Cuban Revolution raised the importance of film to a level never seen before. In

March 1959, less than three months after Castro's triumph, when other things were likely on his mind, the new regime's first cultural act was to create a state film organization, Instituto Cubano de Arte e Industria Cinematograficos, universally known by its initials as ICAIC.

Though propaganda and national self-image were reason enough to found ICAIC, Cuban filmmakers know, as critic Enrique Colina puts it, "all revolutions have family names, they depend on the people who make them." And if it wasn't for Alfredo Guevara, a courtly, cultured man usually seen with a sports jacket draped over his shoulders, the Cuban film industry might not exist at all.

Half a century ago, when Guevara was an undergraduate leader at Havana University, he took the advice of friends and sought out someone new on campus. "When I came back I said, and people remember my judgment, 'this student will either be the worst of gangsters or a new Jose Martí,'" the revered nineteenth-century Cuban patriotic leader.

The new student was Fidel Castro, and from then on Guevara's life intertwined passion for film and for the revolution. "I am who I am because Fidel is who he is," he says today. "If I hadn't met Fidel when I was so young, my path would have been different." Exiled in Mexico in the 1950s, he worked as a screenwriter and was Luis Buñuel's assistant on *Nazarin*. Always worshipful of Castro, he became one of the leader's most trusted assistants after the revolution, and he never forgot about film.

"Fidel knew I was obsessed with the idea of starting a film institute, we had talked about it a lot, but when I brought it up immediately after the revolution, he said, 'Don't think about that now,'" Guevara remembers. "But I think something was nagging at him, because a few months later he changed his mind and asked me to organize one."

Guevara became the first head of ICAIC, and his closeness to Castro immediately gave cinema considerable prestige. Also, since Guevara believed that ICAIC should be run by filmmakers and not bureaucrats, the institute gave Cuban writers and directors something unusual among state-run film systems: the ability to have give-and-take discussions about what can and cannot be filmed.

"Censorship is not organized in a bureaucratic sense, you have discussions and agreements," says Gutiérrez Alea, considered Cuba's master director both inside and outside the country. "In these thirty-five years that's the way it's been with me. No one has ever said, 'Do that.' I have made the films I wanted to make.

"When I went to Hollywood when *Strawberry and Chocolate* [which he codirected with Juan Carlos Tabio] was nominated for an Oscar, I said I would be happy to make films in America because they are seen everywhere, but I was afraid of the price I would have to pay. I am not sure I'd have the freedom I have in Cuba. That's the paradox."

Guevara eventually left ICAIC to be Cuba's delegate to UNESCO in Paris, but the crisis of the special period, which led to rumors that ICAIC would lose its independence and the film festival would go under, brought him back to run things again. "Fidel called me," Guevara reports, "and said, 'Come on, this is your problem,' and after all I am only a wink of Fidel." Coincidentally, Guevara also came back at a critical time for the philosophical direction of Cuban cinema. *Alice in Wondertown*, a satire on the Cuban leadership that won a Silver Bear at the Berlin Film Festival, was removed from local theaters after only four days of screenings, an unprecedented act that caused such a fuss that most Cuban filmmakers feel it helped pave the way for official toleration of the country's next controversial film, *Strawberry and Chocolate*.

While on the one hand, *Strawberry* is part of a Cuban tradition of irreverent comedies that mock the country's problems, it's difficult to overestimate the impact this film (Solás called it "extraordinarily audacious") had on Cubans, many of whom saw it numerous times despite long lines. Filled with inside references that only Cubans noticed, the picture not only treated homosexuality sympathetically for the first time, it also called passionately for tolerance of all differences of opinion. And it found a strong champion in Guevara, who even now speaks with feeling against the film's opponents, "those who think they are the most revolutionary but in fact are the most scared, the most conservative, the

Even all-business Cannes can look romantic in the right evening light. (Los Angeles Times photo by Al Seib)

John Malkovich deals with the media at a hectic Cannes press conference for Of Mice and Men. *(Photo by Patricia Williams)*

Few things symbolize Cannes as dramatically as beautiful women in gorgeous clothes: from left, actresses Claudia Schiffer, Andie MacDowell, and Gong Li get into the festival spirit. (Los Angeles Times photo by Al Seib)

Tim Robbins as a Hollywood prince of darkness in The Player *hovers over Cannes's bustling street life. (Photo by Patricia Williams)*

Miramax's Harvey Weinstein, always a presence at Cannes, doing one of the things he does best: holding court with journalists after the press premiere screening of Dogma. *(Los Angeles Times photo by Robert Gauthier)*

For ten days every January, the vintage ski resort town of Park City, Utah, gets completely taken over by the Sundance Film Festival. Only careful planning prevents the twenty thousand film people who descend on it from swamping both residents and skiers. (Los Angeles Times photo by Al Seib)

Geoffrey Gilmore, director of the Sundance Film Festival, displays some of the hundreds of films submitted for entry in the prestigious independent event. The numbers of submissions in all categories display dramatic annual increases. (Los Angeles Times photo by Ken Hively)

Director Karyn Kusama, whose debut Girlfight *shared the Grand Jury Prize at the 2000 Sundance, strikes a typical Park City pose. (Los Angeles Times photo by Al Seib)*

Flyers for films at Sundance cover every available Park City surface, the movable as well as the stationary kind. (Los Angeles Times photo by Robert Gauthier)

First-time film directors like Kaleo Quenzer of Memphis, Tennessee, try all kinds of stratagems to get their films noticed at Sundance. (Los Angeles Times photo by Al Seib)

Postcard advertising FESPACO, *the Festival Panafricaine du Cinéma de Ouagadougou. The gigantic sculpture representing reels and lenses stands in Ouagadougou's Place des Cinéastes Africains and is dedicated to the filmmakers of Africa.*

Filippe Sawadogo, FESPACO*'s secretary general for more than a decade. On his desk sits the festival's top award, the Etalon de Yennega. (Photo courtesy of* FESPACO*)*

Burkina Faso stamp issued to honor the 100th anniversary of cinema as well as Gaston Kaboré, one of that country's top directors, and his film Rabi.

Burkina Faso stamp issued to honor the 100th anniversary of cinema and Idrissa Ouedraogo, another of the country's top directors, and his film Tilai.

Banner advertising the Sarajevo festival and the location of one of its newest theaters, part of the rebuilding of the city after the war. (Photo by Kenneth Turan)

A bombed-out theater in downtown Sarajevo. (Photo by Kenneth Turan)

The Sarajevo festival's 2,500-seat outdoor theater, located on a former school playground and squeezed between apartment buildings. (Photo by Kenneth Turan)

Mirsad Purivatra, director of the Sarajevo Film Festival, in front of a poster for The Perfect Circle, *the first film shot in the city after the 1995 cease-fire. (Photo by Kenneth Turan)*

Seen at the Midnight Sun Film Festival in Sodankyla, Finland: Surely the only thoroughfare within hailing distance of the North Pole to be named after a cult-favorite American director. (Photo by Kenneth Turan)

Finnish director Mika Kaurismäki, one of the founders of the Midnight Sun Film Festival, with the two official festival Cadillacs. (Photo by Kenneth Turan)

Sodankyla's Mouth of Lapland theater, the "Grand Palais" of the Midnight Sun Film Festival, located next door to a driving school. (Photo by Kenneth Turan)

Reindeer snacks at midnight and after are a Midnight Sun tradition. Some people never go to bed during the whole five-day festival. (Photo by Kenneth Turan)

Local acrobats entertaining moviegoers waiting for a screening to begin outside the Midnight Sun Festival's largest venue, an Italian circus tent that seats roughly five hundred. (Photo by Kenneth Turan)

A banner for Le Giornate del Cinema Muto, the festival of silent film, outside the venerable Cinema Verdi, in Pordenone in northeastern Italy. (Photo by Patricia Williams)

Four of the founders of the Pordenone event fool around with the Buster Keaton–inspired silhouette that is the festival logo. From left: Lorenzo Codelli, Piera Patat, Paolo Cherci Usai, and Livio Jacob. (Photo by Patricia Williams)

Pierce Lyden at eighty-eight: The bad guy in numerous B westerns relaxes where many of his films were made, the breathtaking Alabama Hills, three hours from Los Angeles, now home to the Lone Pine Film Festival. (Los Angeles Times photo by Don Kelsen)

An expectant crowd waits patiently inside the Telluride Festival's showplace theater, the restored 1914 Sheridan Opera House. (Photo by Patricia Williams)

people who think that the revolution rests on a single card and are afraid if it's moved the whole house of cards will collapse."

Despite *Strawberry*'s success, some Cuban filmmakers continue to worry about the future of films that combine pointed looks at contemporary reality with a popular, comedic touch. They notice that Gutiérrez Alea and Tabio's follow-up film, *Guantanamera*, a gleeful dark farce that follows a coffin from one end of Cuba to the other, did not open the festival as might be expected for such prestigious filmmakers (though it did end up winning the second-place Coral).

Also remarked on was that Rolando Diaz's *Melodrama*, a raucous and crowd-pleasing sex comedy with a noticeable social message, was absent from the official catalog and screened only once at a nonprestigious morning slot. Is subtle repression at work here, the exercise of personal taste by the powerful Guevara, or a combination of both? The answer depends on whom you ask.

For most Cuban filmmakers, however, the more pressing problem is getting films made at all. Economic problems have cut down Cuba's annual production from a dozen or more features to three or four, and coproduction agreements with other countries ("Now you have to convince a person who's living in San Tropez," Solás half-jokes) are close to essential before a project can proceed. "A film is a mobile factory, it needs fuel," says director García Espinosa, who ended up shooting his last film, *Reina y Rey*, across the street from his house.

Things are so grim, in fact, it is surprising to see any film production at all. "It's another miracle, because most Latin American countries, even though they're not facing our situation, are not producing any films," says García Espinosa, who ran ICAIC when Guevara was in France. Given the credit are a tradition of fighting windmills plus the goad of hard times. "Man grows when faced with difficulties," says Guevara, and Gerardo Chijona quotes Tolstoy to the effect that "art is born in chains and dies in freedom."

Even if films do continue to get made, a larger worry for thoughtful Cubans is what the materialism and opportunism the special period is breeding will do to the soul of the country in general and young filmmakers in particular.

Though he admits that "there is a danger that Cuba will become like Italy, the most cynical country in the world," director Solás believes otherwise. "The day in which the U.S.S.R. was dismantled was the happiest in my life, for though we had material splendor there was a lot of spiritual poorness. Now it is my hope that there will be a new Utopia here. We have been through so much, from the excesses of commercialism through wrongly done socialism, we don't want to come to the end of the century feeling shame."

Still, it is difficult finally to dismiss the thoughts of Solás's comrade, Gutiérrez Alea. Universally known by his nickname of Titon, the then-sixty-seven-year-old director talks with difficulty (he was to die of cancer a year later), but everything he says resonates with thought and feeling.

"The revolution was very clear in the beginning, but now it is another system," he says. "It didn't work one hundred percent, it didn't work a big percent, but those who didn't have to fight for this don't understand how important it is. Those of us who were inside want to save the moral values and dignity the revolution brought to this country, but it's not easy."

Gutiérrez Alea pauses and is reminded of a line from his 1968 *Memories*, when his protagonist says, "This island is a trap. We're too small and too poor. It's an expensive dignity." The director nods. "Yes, it's a very expensive dignity," he says. "But we have to try to pay for it, that's what I think. Because if you lose your dignity, you lose everything."

Sarajevo

Shell them till they're on the edge of madness.
—Bosnian Serb commander Ratko Mladic,
ordering the bombing of Sarajevo

The poverty of life without dreams is too horrible to imagine:
it is the kind of madness which is the worst.
—poet Sylvia Plath, quoted in a press release
from the Sarajevo Film Festival

SARAJEVO, BOSNIA-HERZEGOVINA—Many things come to mind when this city's name is mentioned, but a film festival is not one of them.

This was the city that survived the longest siege of modern history, more than forty-six months of exhausting, terrifying shelling and sniping from the surrounding Serb-controlled hills that damaged or destroyed 60 percent of its buildings. Approximately ten thousand died, 150,000 fled, and those that remained did without much of what we like to consider essential.

Often there was no communication with the outside world, no electricity, no power but foot power, and the city became ironically known as one big Stairmaster. There was no water for bathing or grooming, so people would show visitors photographs of how they looked before the

war. There was no heat, so Aco Staka, the dean of Sarajevo film critics, a living encyclopedia of Yugoslav film who'd participated in festivals around the world, had to burn thirty-five years' worth of clippings to keep his family warm. And there was so little food during the siege that the average person lost close to twenty-five pounds.

In this formerly beleaguered location, once called "the world's biggest concentration camp" by a desperate Bosnian official, the notion of something as frivolous-sounding as a film festival, even nearly two years after the Dayton Accords was signed, seemed unlikely, anomalous, confusing. What was going on here?

While visits to more conventional festivals like Cannes or Sundance concentrate on rooting out what is new and different, the award-winners and trend-setters, Sarajevo promised a chance to examine the uses and purposes of film at ground zero, to get at the core of how the medium works and what it can mean to people no matter what their circumstances. Like the Hollywood director in Preston Sturges's classic 1941 *Sullivan's Travels* who takes to the road in an attempt to connect what he does with a larger reality, a visitor to Sarajevo could investigate the relevance of film in a setting considerably removed from the fleshpots of the studio system.

As Sullivan himself discovered, trips like this don't fit into tidy packages. On the one hand, film and the desire to see it turned out to be surprisingly central to the Sarajevo experience, not only in 1997 during the third year of the current festival—surely unique in its ability to offer a tour of the city's former front lines by the general who led their defense—but also during the worst days of the bombardment, when audiences literally put their lives at risk to go to the movies. "I was scared to death, running all the way with my cousin," said one woman about a clandestine expedition to see, of all things, *Basic Instinct*. "It was very dangerous, but we did it."

But the lesson of Sarajevo is more than the accurate but easy one that film can make the world whole. This is after all the Balkans, where nothing is straightforward and everything becomes politicized, where World

War I started after Gavrilo Princip, a Bosnian Serb seeking union with Serbia for his country, assassinated the heir to the Hapsburg throne. "You Americans are very lucky, you have a short history and a simple history," says filmmaker Srdjan Karanovic, the only Belgrade-based director to come to the Sarajevo Festival. "Here history is very complicated, there is conflict and remembrance from every period."

So while the Sarajevo Festival turned out to be a lively and exhilarating event, a miraculous breath of refreshing air experienced against overwhelming odds, film can only do so much in a city whose suffering has led to the removal of a Yugoslav monument to Princip (now seen as a Serb nationalist, not a liberator) and the wholesale changing of names of streets and buildings (the festival's headquarters hotel, once the Belgrade, is now the Bosnia) to fit new political realities. In front of the burnt-out shell of what was once Sarajevo's two-million-item library, deliberately targeted for destruction in an attempt to obliterate Bosnian culture, sits a plaque excoriating the "Serbian Criminals" responsible and ending with the stark peroration, "Do Not Forget. Remember and Warn!"

While the Sarajevo Festival in 1997 was noteworthy for films and filmmakers from Croatia, Slovenia, and Macedonia, three of Yugoslavia's former republics, no films came from Serbia. And the two movies from ex-Yugoslavia that have had the most impact on the world cinema scene, Emir Kusturica's Palme d'Or–winning *Underground* and Srdjan Dragojevic's festival hit *Pretty Village, Pretty Flame*, have not only not been widely seen here, they've been caught in a vortex of expectation-confounding survivor politics and generated anger and hostility that darkly oppose the acceptance they've received elsewhere.

Too much suffering and chaos has happened here for a tolerant, typically American, "let's forgive and forget" attitude to completely take hold, even among normally ecumenical filmmakers. More typical are the thoughts of director Ademir Kenovic, who stayed in Sarajevo during the war and whose *The Perfect Circle*, the first film shot in the city after the cease-fire, debuted at Cannes and opened the festival.

"I don't want to support in any way the stupid idea that what's needed

is 'shake hands you filmmakers from Belgrade, you filmmakers from Zagreb, you filmmakers from Sarajevo,' " he said bluntly. "Nothing will be made better by that, by establishing again the feeling that everything is okay. It's not about us shaking hands, it's about war criminals going to the Hague."

Once, when Yugoslavia was a country that didn't need the word "former" in front of it, Sarajevo was a charming, sophisticated locale that elicited comparisons to Paris and San Francisco, somewhere visitors felt, it was said, "the air was freer." Located at a cultural crossroads, "Western for the East and Oriental for the West," it was also the kind of place, a resident of another Yugoslav city remembered, where you'd wake up hung over and happy but couldn't remember why you felt that way.

While elsewhere in Yugoslavia's six republics and two autonomous provinces people paid attention to whether their neighbors were Muslim, Roman Catholic, or Eastern Orthodox, Sarajevo was different. Nominally Muslim, by all accounts it was an anomaly, a hummingbird of a city that shouldn't have existed but did, the kind of genuinely multicultural metropolis often paid lip service to but not often achieved. A place with passionate film buffs like Dzeilana Pecanin.

A reporter during the war for *Oslobodjenje*, the city's resolute daily newspaper, who now works for the Voice of America's Bosnia Service in Washington, D.C., Pecanin confesses to being "completely hooked on the movies. Other girls were getting married, but I was in love with Robert De Niro and nobody else was good enough. When *Raging Bull* opened, me and a colleague took shifts queuing up for tickets on an incredibly long line so we could see it opening night. Everybody was ready to queue for hours, in the rain or the snow, for a movie."

Then came the war, chronicled in books whose titles form a litany of despair: *Balkan Tragedy*, *Origins of a Catastrophe*, *The Impossible Country*, *Slaughterhouse*, *A Tradition Betrayed*, *The Tenth Circle of Hell*, *Yugoslavia's Bloody Collapse*, *Yugoslavian Inferno*, *Yugoslavia Dismembered*, and dozens more. A war that made a special target of Sarajevo.

"My belief is that it was the place that most embodied tolerance and multiculturalism and that's why it had to be destroyed," says writer-director Phil Alden Robinson (*Field of Dreams*, *Sneakers*), who visited four times during the height of the war and wanted to return in early 1998 to shoot his script for *Age of Aquarius*, about an international relief worker who has a relationship with a woman from the city.

"Before the war it was the one place where people got along, a combination of small town openness and warmth and big city sophistication; it was the best vision we have of ourselves," Robinson explains. He in fact became so taken with Sarajevo during his visits that "I dream about being back there, and they're the happiest dreams. It's a city that intoxicates you for the right and to be honest possibly the wrong reasons: for what it is, for what it represents, for being the moral crisis of our time."

To visit Sarajevo nearly two years after the peace accord was signed in Dayton is to experience a city balanced on the push-pull of then and now. Remarkably recovered from the destruction it experienced but not yet free of memories of the past and a sense that the future is not secure, it is simultaneously exhilarating and depressing, depending on your point of view.

While almost all of Sarajevo's downtown has been rebuilt, pockets of the city are bombed out and desolate. The streets are surely safer than many in America, but landmines remain in the hills. Signs for Calvin Klein and an upcoming U-2 concert compete for space with announcements about de-mining. The much-shelled Holiday Inn, press headquarters during the war, looks completely new, but the high-rise building that housed *Oslobodjenje* remains a gaunt, ruined scarecrow. Stores carry everything from Yves Roche cosmetics to bananas from Ecuador, but the German deutschmark is the country's currency of choice, and credit cards, as one travel magazine put it, "are useful only for putting under the leg of a rickety table."

Still, Sarajevo remains what Mirsad Purivatra, head of the Obala Art Center and the film festival's director, calls "this crazy but charismatic town," inhabited by an unstoppably gregarious people who jam innu-

merable cafés and enthusiastically promenade through a pedestrian mall in the old town as if each night of pleasure has to make up for all those months of enforced misery.

Purivatra's nine-day festival (which announced 1997 attendance of 45,000, almost double 1996's total) is a key factor in that renewed spirit, so important to local morale that the Bosnian government has issued a stamp in its honor. It shows the event's modest centerpiece and main site for showing films, a year-old 2,500-seat open-air theater, artfully shoehorned between buildings on an old school playground and complete with one of the biggest outdoor screens in Europe.

With financial backing from the city, UNICEF, the Soros Foundation, and private sponsors like fashion designer Agnes B., Renault, and Swissair, Purivatra and his programming director Philippe Bober put together a slate of sixty-five films from twenty-seven countries.

While many of these, well-traveled veterans of the festival circuit like *Guantanamera* from Cuba and Iran's *A Taste of Cherries*, were shown in the just-completed 200-seat indoor theater (also financed by international contributions), the spirit of the festival is most visible in its invariably sold-out outdoor screenings.

After French critics from *Le Monde* and elsewhere complained that the festival was becoming corrupted by Hollywood, the slate this time included European films as well as the first three features shot in Sarajevo: Kenovic's *The Perfect Circle* and Michael Winterbottom's *Welcome to Sarajevo*, both treated with deserved respect, and the unconvincing Spanish *Comanche Territory*, which was not. If audiences felt more than slightly surreal as they sat and watched wide-screen fictional representations of their former devastation, they were not about to let on.

Most of the open-air screenings, however, were of big-ticket blockbusters like the *Jurassic Park* sequel, *The Lost World*, *The English Patient*, *Batman & Robin*, and *Con Air* (whose John Malkovich was the only major star to attend). These were a considerable treat in a city without a viable film distribution system whose remaining functional theaters were showing well-out-of-date films like Paul Newman in *Nobody's Fool* and

Demi Moore in *The Juror*. The energy of people jazzed to be at the movies marked these packed outdoor screenings, and the cheering was loud when Haris Siladjdzic, Bosnia's prime minister, announced on opening night, "This is a very great occasion for Sarajevo. Those that wanted to kill the spirit of Sarajevo did not succeed."

Even though, says critic Aco Staka, Sarajevo's initial importance in film was as an exotic Eastern locale for European directors, "cheaper than going to Baghdad," the medium was always important in Yugoslavia because it was important to Marshal Josip Tito, the country's ruler for more than thirty-five years.

When the annual Yugoslavian national film festival was held in an enormous Roman amphitheater in Pula (now in Croatia), Tito was often found on a nearby island, and boats would shuttle key films out to him every night. "When the boat returned with the films," remembers Goran Markovic, director of the delightful *Tito and Me*, "the projectionist would tell us 'he laughed' or 'he stopped the projection.' Very often the films he loved became favorites at the festival."

While Yugoslavian directors like Dusan Makavejev (*WR: Mysteries of the Organism*) and Aleksander Petrovic (*I Even Met Happy Gypsies*) became international favorites, being a filmmaker in a restrictive socialist country was not easy. After Sarajevo-based director Bato Cengic directed two films in the early 1970s that poked impish fun at the system, the delightfully sly *Life of Shock Workers* and *The Role of My Family in the World Revolution* (which features a cake in the shape of Stalin's head that the family avidly devours), he wasn't allowed to direct for ten years. Cengic eventually turned his BMW, one of the city's first, into a taxi to make a living. "I was a proscribed director," he says today with pride. "I was the example for all Yugoslavia."

Then came the war, and the shelling, and everything changed. Some directors, like Emir Kusturica, left the city. Others, like *The Perfect Circle*'s Ademir Kenovic, stayed to bear witness. He founded a group called Saga to document what was happening around him, "the

absolutely different, horrible, outrageous, sometimes exquisite" things he saw, to record "the energy for life that was so strong it had to be documented." One of his projects, *Street under Siege*, a daily two-minute short about the inhabitants of the same block, ran for close to six months on the BBC and elsewhere around the world.

Because large movie theaters were obvious targets for shells and snipers and because electricity to run projectors couldn't be counted on, the only films seen during the war years were either on video or broadcast on television, both of which required loud, noisy portable generators to provide reliable power.

With bootleg cassette copies supplied by visiting journalists or international aid workers, Sarajevo TV stations would broadcast the same film dozens of times. Haris Pasovic, a successful theater director who recently completed the documentary *Greta Ferusic*, remembers, "It was not unusual to begin watching, have the electricity go off after fifteen minutes, and to continue in three months to watch again the same film. With *A Stranger among Us* (starring Melanie Griffith as an undercover policewoman in Brooklyn's Hasidic community), I needed three or four times over a year to complete the film."

"Sometimes you'd know a day in advance when it was the turn for your block to get electricity," says film buff Dzeilana Pecanin. "I'd go to the little video store by my house, and you can imagine, everything was outdated. I didn't mind, I'd take anything, especially if it was from before the war started. Watching it would completely take you back, you could completely escape from the horrors of reality for two hours."

Any kind of semi-organized public showings, however, took longer to get started, partly because, says Pasovic, "everyone felt 'this will stop next month.'" And, especially in the beginning of the war, Pecanin notes that "the shelling and sniping was so intense there was no way to go out, people hardly had the strength and courage to find food and water. All other, shall we say nice activities, completely died out."

Still, she says, "Many, many people, including myself, dreamed for

nights and nights, we wished to see just once more another good movie. It was really hard, many people missed it as much as bread." Adds director Bato Cengic, who tried not to skip even one of 1997's festival screenings, "If I'm seeing five movies a day now, you can understand what a thirst I had during the war for movies. If I'd meet some friends and they'd seen a movie, I'd beg them to tell me every detail of what it was like."

After the war's first six months, says festival director Purivatra, "everyone was getting more and more crazy, and going out was the only way to survive. It was like being in jail but worse, because even in jail there are new faces with cruel stories that could be interesting to hear. In Sarajevo, no one was coming in, and you heard the same stories from neighbors so often it was very possible you were going to one day kill your neighbor. Everyone tried to make some kind of trip out of reality, and everyone wanted to be part of a group."

To answer these needs Purivatra and his wife Izeta Gradevic, who had founded Obala as a theater group in 1984, began in 1992 to sporadically hold word-of-mouth screenings of donated tapes in a dark and claustrophobic basement room accessible only through a bombed-out hole in a surrounding wall. (The wall now borders the festival's open-air theater, and that hole has been only partially repaired as an unobtrusive memorial to those days.)

"It was a war cinema, one hundred seats and a video beam projector, but in spite of the war, in spite of the shelling, it was packed every night we had a showing," Purivatra remembers. "The audience reception of films was completely different here. Sharon Stone naked in *Basic Instinct*, no big comment. But there was a dinner scene in the film that got two minutes of applause."

Also different, and a feeling that in some cases has not changed, was the reaction to violence on-screen. "After my war experience, I really can't get excited, not at all, by films like *Die Hard* or *The Rock*," says critic Aco Staka's son Vladimir, an *Oslobodjenje* reporter during the war who now lives in Canada.

"Those films are dead for me. People don't kill or get killed that way, it's not that pretty, not that iconographic."

As the only Serbian director to attend the Sarajevo Festival, Srdjan Karanovic was besieged by questions at his press conference. What was going on in Belgrade, everyone wanted to know, who was working and what were they up to?

Karanovic rattled off half-a-dozen films currently being shot, but he did not mention *Black Cat White Cat*, the latest work by Emir Kusturica, the former Yugoslavia's most celebrated director, a native and former resident of Sarajevo who now divides his time between Belgrade and France. Asked later why he left Kusturica off his list, Karanovic got off a "you must be kidding" look before answering, "I didn't want to disturb them. They hate him here; they treat him like a traitor."

Just a few years ago, such a response would have been unthinkable. Kusturica was Sarajevo's favorite son and a bona fide national cultural hero: when his Oscar-nominated *When Father Was Away on Business* won the Palme d'Or at Cannes in 1985, Yugoslavia declared a national holiday.

In fact, each of Kusturica's first four works won a prize at Europe's top three festivals, an unprecedented record that makes him one of the continent's most admired filmmakers. His debut, *Do You Remember Dolly Bell?*, won a Golden Lion at Venice in 1981, *Time of the Gypsies* won Best Director at Cannes, the Johnny Depp–starring *Arizona Dreams* took a special jury prize at Berlin, and *Underground* won him a rare second Palme d'Or at Cannes in 1995.

There was no Yugoslavian national holiday in 1995 because by then a viable Yugoslavia no longer existed. The country had split into five separate nations that were creating Europe's bloodiest nightmare since World War II. Kusturica's politics and his film, which dealt with the breakup, became the subject of intense debate and fury not only in Sarajevo and Belgrade but also across Europe. It led to the director's public decision to quit filmmaking (he's since changed his mind) and to

turbulent, invariably hostile comments about him in his hometown. Probably nowhere in the world does the mention of a filmmaker's name elicit such an immediate and strong response from so many people as Kusturica's does here.

The reversal in this filmmaker's fortunes is a lesson in many things, from how deep the wounds of war can be to how puzzling yet intractable feelings of national identity and pride are and how central film has become to the expression of all of that. In fact, tell a film person from anywhere in the former Yugoslavia you have something complicated you want to discuss and before the questions can start, the reply comes, "It's about Kusturica, isn't it?"

Officially the country that still calls itself Yugoslavia (though it consists of only two of the former six republics, Serbia and Montenegro) is putting on a brave face. It regularly takes a booth in the international marketplace at Cannes and hands out a glossy booklet titled "Yugoslav Film: Culture of the Impossible." But to talk with directors from Belgrade, whether in person or on the phone, is to hear the voice of depression and despair.

They are as shocked as anyone, of course, at the carnage that has swept their country; "I never believed people could hate each other so much," says one director. "I never believed there could be hatred anywhere in the world like I've seen in this war." But even though they're aware that the world places the blame for the conflict almost unanimously on their country and on the ambitions of Yugoslavian president Slobodan Milosevic and Bosnian Serb leader Radovan Karadzic, it is impossible for most Serbs, who've viewed themselves as the downtrodden people in the region since they lost the battle of Kosovo Polje, the celebrated "Field of Black Birds," to the Turks in 1389, to see it the same way.

Even Karanovic, who says his presence in Sarajevo is testament to what he thinks, goes no further than "everyone is responsible, but the Serbian side is at least a bit more responsible." The causes were not religious or national, he says. "It was about robbery, as simple as that."

Echoing this is Srdjan Dragonjevic, director of *Pretty Village, Pretty Flame*, who says the conflict is "a new and primitive war for money, a kind of bloody capitalist revolution which established a new class of war rich."

Others, like *Tito and Me* director Goran Markovic, while bemoaning "this dirty war and this very big fascism in ex-Yugoslavia," see the conflict as a civil war (a claim that makes Sarajevans, who were attacked without provocation, apoplectic) and are troubled by Serbia's image in the world.

"It's not true that the whole Serbian nation are war criminals—you can't blame the whole nation for the people who made this war," Markovic says. "There were very, very brave people in Belgrade who were against this war. This simplification is very painful to me; I don't like this primitive view that Serbs are Indians, the Muslims are cowboys. It's a very complicated situation. You can believe me: even here we can't understand everything."

Sounding the most upbeat is *Pretty Village, Pretty Flame* director Dragojevic, but then again he is speaking from New York, where it's just been announced that he will codirect the upcoming *It's Me, the Hero* starring Harvey Keitel. This good fortune is the result of the worldwide reception of his film, which, though not immediately released in the United States, won awards at half-a-dozen festivals from São Paolo to Stockholm.

With scenes of Serbian soldiers looting and laying waste to Muslim villages, it was the first film to show Serbs in any kind of negative light and as such was a sensation in Belgrade and environs, with far and away the most admissions of any film of the year. "There were 5,000 people at the premier," reports Los Angeles–based actress Lisa Moncure, the only American in either the cast or the crew. "People were crying, there was something like a fifteen-minute standing ovation, it was an amazing experience for them to see the film. They were overwhelmed by it."

Given its willingness to show Serbs in a negative light, one might think that *Pretty Villages, Pretty Flames* would be embraced by Sarajevo, but that is not the case, and its reception illustrates the uncrossable bar-

riers a war at home can create. The film has been exhibited in small private screenings, but its share-the-blame philosophy has attracted hostility rather than acclaim from a city that was the victim of a brutal siege and never had an aggressive thought.

"I think it's disgusting, a very nasty film," says director Haris Pasovic, head of the first Sarajevo film festival. "Saying that Serbia was so provoked it went too far in self-defense is a popular Serb theory, but it mixes everything up." Adds Mirsad Purivatra, who runs the current festival, "The idea that everyone is guilty on some level is unacceptable to me as a human being. Defending yourself versus killing to make a bigger country and destroying all traces of another nation's culture are not on the same level. That cannot be considered as everyone is guilty."

The situation with Emir Kusterica and *Underground* is, if anything, even more complicated, as is his film, which was initially called *Once There Was a Country*. An unruly, audacious, unashamedly excessive requiem for a dying Yugoslavia, it is an impassioned and surreal look at the past half century of that nation's history through the lens of a conniving opportunist who keeps a group of people prisoner in a Belgrade basement by convincing them that the war with the Nazis is still going on.

Underground impressed even those in the audience at Cannes who considered the film's tone over the top and its three-hour-and-twelve-minute length (since trimmed for domestic distribution) unnecessary. Equally impressive was Kusturica's passion for Yugoslavia. "I had to do something about a country that I loved. I had a need to answer the question, 'What happened?'" the director said of his reasons for making *Underground*. He also expressed displeasure, referring to Bosnia, at "now having to find myself under another flag, another country, another anthem," which is where things get complicated.

For while what's known as "Yugonostalgia" is a not uncommon feeling, promoting the preservation of Yugoslavia came to be viewed within Sarajevo as a justification for Serbian aggression. Kusturica's coupling that with what could at best be called diffidence toward Bosnia at a time when it was under merciless attack did not go over well back home.

In addition, many of the subtexts of *Underground*, like its blaming the country's current problems on the policies of Marshal Tito instead of Serbian self-aggrandizement, were often interpreted as legitimizing the war. The more Kusturica thought, possibly naively, possibly with calculation, that he was refusing to take sides, stepping outside of politics by distancing himself from the Muslim nationalist party that ruled Bosnia, the more his actions placed him in the Serb camp. And his having shot the film partly in Belgrade with a bit of Serbian financing did not help the situation.

All this contributed to nearly a year of bitter intellectual trench warfare about the film fought in the pages of French political journals. One side saw it as "a rock, postmodern, over-the-top, hip, Americanized version of the most driveling and lying Serbian propaganda." Then, as Adam Gopnik reported in the *New Yorker*, the other side responded that "the subject of the film wasn't nationalism at all, but the consequences of Communism—that it wasn't a national myth of Serbia but a transnational allegory of the post–Cold War period." That in turn caused celebrated Austrian novelist Peter Handke, in an essay published in this country as "A Journey to the Rivers: Justice for Serbia," to take yet a third tack and defend *Underground* precisely for its Serbian point of view.

Then, perhaps not surprisingly, in the middle of all of this Kusturica announced in the French newspaper *Libération* that he was quitting filmmaking. "I don't know to what extent this will relieve my enemies," he said, "but I do know that my friends will understand to what extent my life will be less burdensome."

Speaking from Belgrade, where he described his new film *Black Cat White Cat* as "something much lighter, a genre piece, pure comedy," Kusturica says his decision to quit filmmaking was as much a product of exhaustion as anything else. "Each frame is like a question of life and death for me," he said. "So in the middle of every movie I'm definitely deciding to stop."

Still troubling to him is the criticism he received for *Underground*. "I made a movie that was really the most sincere expression of how I felt

about the past, that we were highly manipulated by politicians and the people who were leading us," he says. "I was doing all my best against propaganda and at the end I was accused of doing an Americanized version of Serbian propaganda. I felt in the middle of an Orwellian tragic comedy, I almost didn't find my way out of the 'Underground' story that was parallel to the *Underground* film."

Saying the reasons he left Sarajevo are "very personal," Kusturica is most troubled by the fact that his apartment (like the residences of many other people who left) has been confiscated by the state and given to a prominent writer. "In Sarajevo it's very profitable to scream slogans, to be against somebody who did not want to be involved so you can jump into his apartment and take all his belongings," he says. "Basically in the name of creating a multi-ethnic Bosnia they are looting our places."

To the people who remained in Sarajevo, it is the fact that Kusturica not only left but also did things like promote a Belgrade film festival while his birthplace was being bombed that caused the greatest anger against the director. "It's the 1940s—you don't give a concert with the Berlin Philharmonic. Everyone understands what is to be done when killers are killing people," says a furious filmmaker, and Dzeilana Pecanin, the film buff who moved to Washington, D.C., after the war, is even more direct. "I despise the person; I think he is the greatest jerk on earth. I don't care what he does, I don't think his movies deserve my eyes."

As to why Kusturica made the choices he did, there are as many opinions as people happy to offer them, though, given the suffering and death in the city, the willingness to give the director the benefit of any doubt is nonexistent. He's reviled as careerist, narcissistic, and vain, and, ironically given his insistence that he wanted to be outside of propaganda, his involvement in politics is cited by almost everyone as a cause of his plummeting esteem.

"Politics is fatal for cinema," says Aco Staka, the dean of Yugoslavian critics, speaking the words in English to accent their importance. Staka's son, former Sarajevo journalist Vladimir Staka, agrees but sees things in a wider perspective.

"The main reason is that people felt abandoned by him. He was the principal bearer of the Sarajevo spirit and he switched," the younger Staka says. "If there was a lot of irrational reaction against him, one should understand the irrational situation we were in. During the war people identified with the government that was struggling to keep as many people alive as possible, and he gave numerous statements that were critical of the regime. If you're an artist, you'll do anything, you'll sell your soul to the devil to get money to make movies. And now he bears a terrible mortgage in Sarajevo."

To Americans, who create the world's most popular films but look on the medium as a weekend diversion that can easily be done without, Sarajevo's kind of intense, almost heart-rending passion for film has to be unexpected, almost disconcerting. Some of it, Sarajevo residents say, is simply a heightened version of the love of film as (in Mirsad Purivatra's words) "the most alive medium in the world today" that cineastes everywhere share. But when you come to probe film's meaning in a city under siege, you hear different notions, expected ones like the need to escape and some that tend to go unspoken and unreflected on elsewhere.

Mentioned frequently was fear of cultural isolation, a determination not to be alone in the world. "Hunger is not the worst thing that can happen to a person," says director Bato Cengic. "As for death, I was ignoring it. If grenades went off, I didn't turn around. I was superior compared to death. But what made me unhappy and sad was that I didn't have communication with the civilized world. That was the worst part." Adds Dzeilana Pecanin, "In spite of all the hardships we never gave up on the things that made us human beings, not animals."

Linked with that was the way going to the movies was an act of defiance, a proof, says critic Staka, that the city and its residents were unapologetically alive. Seeing films also helped provide what was most denied Sarajevo's citizens, an ordinary feeling unnoticed during peacetime, the sense of simply being normal.

"You don't have to have everything fine to want to see movies," says

Haris Pasovic. "You see them because you want to connect, to communicate from your position on the other side of the moon, to check whether you still belong to the same reality as the rest of the world. The favorite question of journalists during my festival was 'Why a film festival during the war?' My answer was 'Why the war during a film festival?' It was the siege that was unusual, not the festival. It was like we didn't have a life before, like our natural state of mind and body was war."

Held for ten days in October 1993, in the teeth of the siege and the shelling, the Pasovic-run one-time-only Sarajevo International Film Festival symbolized the furious and foolhardy daring of those determined to watch films. Vladimir Staka remembers it as "crazy, something like a 'Mad Max' situation. People were shot and died on the way to the festival." It was also an event that completely embarrassed the UN, which found itself refusing, possibly on orders from the British government, to fly stars Vanessa Redgrave, Jeremy Irons, and Daniel Day Lewis into the city for the event. "So we had our scandal," says Pasovic ironically, "just like every big film festival."

Getting the films themselves in proved equally difficult, and the festival likely never would have happened if not for Mexican director Dana Rotbart, now the wife and then the companion of *Perfect Circle* director Ademir Kenovic.

"Since I had a Mexican passport and could get in and out of the siege, Haris asked if I could help him," she says. "I couldn't telephone from Sarajevo because we had access to a satellite phone for only five minutes every fifteen days. So I sent faxes to everyone I'd met in a year of traveling with my film. Then I took a plane to Paris and for a week or ten days called every possible person I knew or didn't know. It was totally nonprofessional, there were no contracts, I just was getting tapes, tapes, tapes."

Rotbart ended up with 170 cassettes, including documentaries, shorts, and cartoons, enough to fill seven large well-packed boxes weighing in the neighborhood of 150 pounds. Which presented a problem, for

the regulations on the UN military flight she had to take back allowed only 22 pounds of baggage per person.

"The soldier at the airport was very difficult. He told me the only way I was going to get those tapes on the plane was if I carried all the boxes myself in one trip. I put ropes on the boxes. It was extremely heavy, heavy, heavy, but I concentrated very hard and dragged them to the plane, where I made an impolite sign to the UN soldier." There was, however, a price to be paid. "I broke my back, literally, I dislocated two discs and I still can't pick up anything heavy." A small smile. "Maybe I should sue the UN and really get rich."

What started with Pasovic's determination "to see some new films" ended up with a staff of eighty. "We arranged with a tobacco factory to give us cigarettes, and a bakery donated extra flour and cooking oil, and everyone was paid with that," Pasovic remembers. Tickets were given away, more to control crowds than anything else, and when they appeared for sale on the black market, Pasovic knew the event would be a success. There was criticism about logistics, and even the director admits that wartime conditions meant the festival was "a bit chaotic, not always very well organized," with schedules so jumbled it was often impossible to know what was playing when. Still, Dzeilana Pecanin remembers crowds in front of theaters on opening day, "so excited and happy, just mesmerized by the chance to go into a real movie theater that nobody thought, 'I am standing right now in a street where any minute the Serbs can throw a shell and that's it.'"

Which is in fact what happened the second day. "The shelling was so intense and so strong it was too much," says Pecanin. "Absolutely I'm sure the Serbs knew how unhappy it made us. They just wanted to destroy any sign of humanity, any chance of us feeling like decent civilized human beings. I had a ticket to see Francis Ford Coppola's *Dracula*, and how strongly I can remember the feeling of pain in my chest. It was almost physical. I don't think I ever hated them so much."

Seeing films is not so difficult now, but the current festival, begun by Purivatra and Obala two years after Pasovic's event, remains essential for

the city's residents. Because they felt abandoned and disowned by the West during the war, says Vladimir Staka, "the main drive that people have is to feel that they are part of the scene," to reconnect with the culture of the larger world.

"They believed they were part of Europe, and they paid a terrible price for that perception," says director Phil Alden Robinson. "They're very angry that Europe does not embrace them; they still don't understand why we don't get it." The way the city's desire not be forgotten coincides with the West's guilt at having forgotten for as long as it did is the dynamic that makes the festival possible.

Allied to this ambition to regain the cosmopolitan status that film is the most direct route to, the festival's presence also speaks to deeper needs that most Sarajevans do not necessarily talk about. For nothing infuriates residents of this city more than the perception that, to paraphrase *Chinatown*, "It's the Balkans, Jake," that this is a place apart, a locale so riven by ancient hatreds as to be beyond saving.

For people here are intensely aware, as historian Maria Todorova has written in *Imagining the Balkans*, that that nominally geographic term has become "one of the most powerful pejorative designations in history, international relations, political science, and, nowadays, general intellectual discourse." To host a film festival, that preeminent symbol of the cross-pollination of modern culture, is a way of removing the stigma of the bloody Balkans, a way of reminding the world that this city fought a war because it believed it had earned a place in that cosmopolitan artistic cosmos.

In truth, the most powerful feeling generated by being in Sarajevo and attending the festival is the chilling one that if the apocalypse could visit a sophisticated city like this, it could happen anywhere. Almost as an aside, a Belgian director at the festival noted that film crews from the two ethnic halves of his country, the Flemish and the French, are never mixed, and he caused an uproar at home when he did so. Adds Phil Alden Robinson, "A Sarajevan asked me to imagine that the Ku Klux Klan completely controlled our government and media for two years

and sent out nothing but racist propaganda. Couldn't we have a race war in our country after that?" So if you choose to weep for the Balkans, it shouldn't be because they're unique, but because they're not.

Given how much Sarajevo has gone through to get to where it is, it would be unfair to leave on a pessimistic note, and, fortunately, it's not necessary to do so. Because a major part of 1997's festival was an extensive three-times-daily series of children's matinees of films like *The Lion King*, *The Little Princess*, and *Pocahontas*, which started when director Purivatra realized that the four-year siege meant that a generation of children hadn't had the opportunity to see movies on a big screen.

Held in conjunction with local schools, which bused the students to the thousand-seat Bosnian Cultural Center, these matinees were joyous and uplifting, a merry maelstrom of wall-to-wall children whose enthusiasm for the medium and for simply being alive went straight to the heart.

To see these small survivors, children who learned to sleep through shelling but were terrified when reconnected telephones started to ring after the war, literally bounce up and down in the purity of their anticipation and glee turned out to be as much of a privilege as this city provides. To witness the power of the unadulterated enjoyment film can provide, to experience the resilience of children, is to believe Sarajevo's permanent renewal is possible after all.

Midnight Sun

Finland is a law unto itself.
—Peter Cowie, Finnish Cinema

SODANKYLA, FINLAND—It's midnight not in Savannah's celebrated Garden of Good and Evil but in this distant Lapland village a hundred miles north of the Arctic Circle, a remote, mosquito-plagued time and place that, all things considered, might be even stranger.

It's not just the startling presence next to the town's high school of a genuine circus tent, vivid blue with yellow and red stripes and big enough to make the performers of Fellini's *La Strada* envious. A tent out of which into the breezy midnight air float the unmistakable tones of Ian McKellen's cultivated author in *Love and Death on Long Island* insisting to Jason Priestley's Hollywood hunk, "If Shakespeare were alive today he'd be doing something like *Hot Pants College*."

And it's not just the crowds fighting off swarms of mosquitoes celebrated enough to be on picture postcards ("It's Finland's national bird," someone says) while they line up for freshly cooked reindeer sausage on a street whose name you have to look at twice to believe: "Samuel Fullerin katu," surely the only thoroughfare within hailing distance of the North Pole to be named for a cult-favorite American director.

No, what makes all this especially strange is that even though clocks are striking midnight, a bright and cheerful sun is shining everywhere. Sun on the sign, on the circus tent, sun warming the wonderful Zen-like spareness of Sodankyla's wooden Lutheran church, built in 1689 and one of the oldest in the country, sun illuminating the large, muscular statue of a Lapp herder wrestling a reindeer, which sits on the town square. For this is one of those celebrated Scandinavian white nights, when, as the tourist brochures never tire of testifying, "the sun never slips below the horizon and a day lasts more than two months." If a celebration of cinema were to locate itself here and now, it could hardly be everyday, and no one has ever confused the Midnight Sun Film Festival with anything close to ordinary.

Held each year in mid-June (theoretically a week before the mosquito season starts, but, the local joke goes, the mosquitoes aren't always informed), this the world's most northerly film festival has also been called "the world's most impractical location," "one of the weirdest events in the film world," and, in its own literature, "something you have never even dreamt about . . . five days and nights during which life is far from being wasted with trivialities . . . the most informal and craziest festival in the world."

Despite, or perhaps because of all this, the Midnight Sun Festival, which recently celebrated its fourteenth year, has established quite an international reputation. In a world of carbon copy festivals, this event is unduplicatable, one of a kind, creating its own particular ambiance and spirit as it encourages its participants to get high on a quintessentially Finnish combination of cinema, summer sunlight, and, yes, strong spirits.

Though it has its share of new films, the Midnight Sun is better known for in-person tributes to some of the most celebrated and eclectic names in the history of film, including Michael Powell, Jacques Demy, Monte Hellman, Krzysztof Kieslowski, André de Toth, Roger Corman, Claude Chabrol, Stanley Donen, John Sayles, Terry Gilliam, and Wim Wenders. Its relaxed charms caused one British critic to call it

"the world's best film festival," and another, in a claim the Finns liked even better, insisted it was in fact "the second-best festival in the world."

The Finns favor that description because it fits with the easygoing, unruffled quality that the festival, which thinks of itself as "the anti-Cannes," takes pride in. Fiercely casual, with not a single necktie visible anywhere in town, the Midnight Sun Festival doesn't so much encourage as insist on low-key naturalness. "Our holy principle," says Peter von Bagh, Finland's best-known film writer and the festival's director, "is never to have any formalities."

Also, the Finns well know that as far as the rest of the world is concerned this is an unlikely country (not to mention neighborhood) for a major festival. Guidebooks tend to call Finland "Scandinavia's most culturally isolated and least understood country" and its language, part of the notorious Finno-Ugric family, "one of the world's strangest and most difficult." The country's population is small (5.1 million all in, with density in Lapland a spread-out five per square mile) and homogenous: non-Lutherans equal only 14 percent of the total and non-Finns make up a bit more than 1 percent of the 5.1 million, the lowest percentage in Europe.

And Finland's film culture, despite giving actionmeister Renny Harlin (*Die Hard 2*, *Cliffhanger*, *Deep Blue Sea*) to Hollywood, is one of the world's least celebrated. The British Film Institute's 1975 *Cinema in Finland*, the first English-language study of the subject, lamented "the aesthetic poverty of traditional Finnish cinema," and Peter Cowie's *Finnish Cinema* admitted that "for decades the cinema has been the ugly duckling of the arts in Finland." And this from the country's nominal champions.

The saving grace in all this is that, despite their reputation for Calvin Coolidge–type parsimoniousness with words, the Finns have a terrific albeit deadpan sense of humor. Take this gloss on early history from an official government tourist brochure: "When the ice went away the Finns arrived, and from that time until the 14th century they got by as best they could on a diet of clan warfare." Or this thought in a brochure about a new festival in Savonlinna in eastern Finland: "Had it been pos-

sible in the 16th century, Erik Axelsson Tott would have started a film festival in Savonlinna. The setting would have been perfect but, unfortunately, the times were not."

There is a similar droll quality to the Midnight Sun, a playful dada "let's do a festival in the middle of nowhere" spirit, says Mika Kaurismäki, one of the event's founders along with his brother Aki. In fact, Mika adds, just possibly seriously, "the original idea was to do a counterfestival in January, when it's dark all the time, to have open-air screenings in the freezing cold with films projected on screens made of snow." Maybe next year. . . .

To understand the Midnight Sun Festival, it helps to understand the Kaurismäki brothers, film directors both, who have jointly given Finland its most prominent place ever in the international film community. Though a smattering of Finnish films had achieved outside recognition over the years—*The White Reindeer* and *The Unknown Soldier* in the 1950s, *The Earth Is a Sinful Song* in the 1970s—the Kaurismäkis, especially younger brother Aki, one of the youngest filmmakers to have a Museum of Modern Art retrospective, raised the bar considerably.

Aki's *Drifting Clouds* was in the official competition at Cannes in 1996, and his silent *Juha* debuted at the New York Film Festival. Between them, the brothers have brought their striking blankly comic fusion of personal and Finnish sensibilities (including extensive use of the popular wacked-out rock band with foot-long pompadours, the Leningrad Cowboys) to both the Midnight Sun Festival and films that have played in something like sixty-five countries worldwide.

The brothers no longer live full-time in Helsinki (Aki has a home in Portugal, Mika in Rio), but they are still very much admired, and the way they've in a sense institutionalized the Finnish sense of humor has made them a presence either physical or spiritual at almost every festival. The night before 1999's event, it was Mika who organized a Helsinki treat for overseas guests, ferrying them to a dinner in the official festival cars, which, in a typical Kaurismäki touch, turn out to be vintage mint-condition Cadillacs, a black 1959 and a candy-apple red 1961.

The night ended at the brothers' one-of-a-kind Helsinki entertainment complex. This includes a coffee house, a pool hall decorated with stills from *The Hustler*, and a gorgeous two-screen art house called the Andorra, named after the tiny European country the brothers were once half-seriously thinking of emigrating to, and distinguished by a classic scene from Sergei Eisenstein's *Ivan the Terrible* reproduced not in marble but in cut linoleum on the lobby floor.

Right next door is another puckish Kaurismäki enterprise, the Moscow Bar. Determined, Mika insists, to be unpopular, the brothers (who have a production company called Sputnik) named the place in memory of "the totally unfashionable Soviet Union" and chose to feature what the USSR was known for, "expensive drinks and bad service." The Moscow, nevertheless, is always crowded. Maybe it's the hand-lettered sign behind the bar that reads, "In Lenin We Trust, Others Pay Cash." Or a photocopy on the wall of the actual Finnish declaration of independence from Mother Russia, signed in 1917 by Lenin, Stalin, and Trotsky and, with a flourish at a slightly later date, by Aki Kaurismäki.

It is possible, for those in a leisurely frame of mind, to take a special "festival train" from Helsinki to Lapland, a multi-hour trip that once featured pictures projected in 35 mm, advertised as "the world's only cinema on rails on the trains!" But a dispute with the state railway has temporarily derailed the movie projection, and I chose instead to join a group flying into Rovaniemi, a city right on the Arctic Circle with a street plan, suggested by celebrated Finnish architect Alvar Aalto, patterned after a pair of reindeer antlers. Rovaniemi is also the home of a thriving tourist attraction called Santa Claus Village, whose 700,000 letters received per annum encourages one Finnish guidebook to call it "the true home of Santa Claus, no matter what the Swedes or Norwegians may say."

Finland, the home of Nokia mobile phones, is considered the most wired nation on earth. From the air, however, with reindeer sausage sandwiches for the in-flight snack washed down by strong Lapin Kulta beer, the country presents a different face: many but by no means all of

its 187,888 lakes are visible, and trees are remarkably thick on the land. Forests are in fact said to cover three-quarters of the country's surface, giving the vistas a dense, verdant, almost pagan feeling.

Viewed from the ground, Lapland, the northern third of Finland, is a green and empty land, but a place whose clear air and great sense of space allows the spirit room to expand. A festival bus takes us the hundred miles to Sodankyla, a trip noticeable for its almost complete lack of cars and advertising signs: with hardly anyone on the roads, there's no one to try and sell to.

An overgrown town of some 11,000, Sodankyla, like most of Lapland, had to be rebuilt after World War II, when the retreating Germans torched just about everything, leading to mordant local jokes like "Vacation in Finland: Bring Matches." One of the things that was rebuilt was the movie house, located next to a driving school and called the Lapinsuu Teattrerissa, the Mouth of Lapland Theater. It's said to be the only such theater in all Lapland (Mika, in a joking reference to Cannes, calls it the "Grand Palais"), a key factor in the decision to locate the festival here. Inside its lobby it's the 1950s all over again, as vintage color-tinted photos of MGM stars like Clark Gable, Ava Gardner, Stewart Granger, and Elizabeth Taylor line the walls, unmoved for decades.

Screenings at the Midnight Sun also take place in two other venues, the local high school's gymnasium (with the basketball backboards neatly folded against the wall) and that enormous circus tent next door, purchased by the Kaurismäkis from Italy for the event's first year. Unlike the screens at most festivals, the three venues keep going close to twenty-four hours a day, with a sign at the box offices reminding the unwary that "the festival day changes at 9 A.M." In other words, films that start at 3:45, 5:45, and 8:30 on a Saturday morning are listed at the end of Friday's schedule. For no one's crazy enough to actually get up for these screenings; the sane thing to do, at least up here, is not to go to sleep in the first place.

Given that you can't show movies without darkness, the festival organizers are pleased with the genial conundrum of being in a locale where

the only place you can experience darkness is inside a movie theater. "It gives us our flavor," says Mika Kaurismäki, with fest director Peter von Bagh adding, "This dialogue with darkness and light is our very special circumstance, part of the subconscious effect of the festival."

Experiencing the white nights of the midnight sun was the key reason I'd wanted to visit this festival, but I'd recently seen *Insomnia,* an excellent Norwegian thriller directed by Erik Skjoldbjaerg and advertised as "introducing film blanc (film noir from the land of the midnight sun)," an experience that made me wonder if I'd made the right choice.

Insomnia stars Stellan Skårsgard as a Swedish detective investigating the murder of a seventeen-year-old high school student in Norwegian Lapland. One of his main obstacles turns out to be the pitiless twenty-four-hour sun, a terrifying, disorienting, invasive light that he can't seem to prevent from seeping into his room and destroying all possibility of sleep. The implacable light tortures and torments him with its unnatural perverseness, and there are moments when he all but collapses under its relentless pressure. What if all this happened to me? Would I start confessing to imaginary crimes, or even to real ones?

Fortunately, the midnight sun turned out to be not only benign in its effects but, with a knack for putting everyone in a festive mood, also quite wonderful to experience. A sun that never sets is frankly exhilarating and made me feel light-headed and giddy, in permanent high spirits. Nominally adult, I felt increasingly like a child who's getting away with something, who can't believe he's lucked into an unexpected, never-ending recess.

This isn't to say that the whole thing isn't formidably disorienting. It's not so much that you can't tell the difference between day and night, it's that you can't figure out why you should care, can't decide whether, except to deal with movie starting times, there's any point in ever looking at your watch. The situation is especially unsettling when you come out of a theater at 2 A.M. into that cheerful warm light and have such an instinctive expectation of darkness you feel as if you're expecting a stair that's no longer there.

What you don't feel like at all is sleeping. Though my room at the Scandinavian modern Hotel Sodankyla came with heavy curtains capable of blocking out even extra-strength sun, I was reluctant to give up on the light. I walked up and down Sodankyla's single main street, pretending to be Jussi Björling singing the great tenor aria "Nessun dorma" ("no one sleeps") from Puccini's *Turandot*, and, periodically forgetting what time it actually was, wondered why all the stores were closed. As opposed to sixteenth-century Europeans, who rioted when Pope Gregory's calendar reform robbed them of what they felt were ten days of their existence, I felt my lifespan was being added to, that to sleep would have been to squander a gift literally from the gods.

Most year-round residents of Lapland feel the same way. For them, the summer is a window of opportunity to live more fully, to sit in the sun eating ice cream (a national warm-weather mania) and feeling thunderstruck at all that light. It's also a time, because everyone feels in a celebratory mood, to do very little sleeping and a good deal of drinking.

While people here are already famous for take partying seriously ("Why Do the Finns Drink So Much?" is a chapter in one guidebook, and an estimated 10 percent of government revenue comes from the sale of alcohol at state-run Alko stores), the midnight sun accentuates the trend. Drinking is endemic but surprisingly low key; it's hard to think of another film festival where the people who run it pass around prescreening pints of Kosken Korvan, the extra-strong Finnish vodka that's been called "ideal for assessing the strength of your stomach lining." Try it, they say as they hand over the bottle, you'll like it, and, surprisingly enough, you do.

It's not only foreigners who are stunned by Lapland's endless light. The festival, which racks up close to 20,000 admissions, is attended almost exclusively by Finns from all over the country (last year two young girls from rural France arrived and caused a sensation), and they, too, have often never seen the true midnight sun. Olli Saarinen, for example, and his girlfriend Leena Tikkanen hitchhiked and drove ten hours from Imatra in eastern Finland to get here. "Is this something you

can see in Hollywood?" Olli asked her as they motored down the sunny main street in the wee hours of the morning. "It's really weird," Leena reported the next day. "I was really tired and waiting for the sun to go down so I could go to sleep, but the sun didn't go down at all."

Mostly young, mostly traveling with backpacks almost as tall as they are, the fans who call themselves "filmihullu," film mad, are the pride of the festival. They buy a twelve-admission card (which costs about $50) because, says Kristina Haataja, the festival's unflappable program manager, "if they feel, 'Okay, maybe I'll see one or two films,' they won't come in the first place."

Since Sodankyla has only two small hotels, most of the Midnight Sun audience – protected by omnipresent canisters of locally manufactured Johnson Off! mosquito repellent that look way too toxic for sale in the United States – spills over into several campgrounds in the area. With the movie theater and the high school offering some of the only public darkness for miles around, sleeping in your seat is a frequently taken option, as is dozing off curled up in your sleeping bag under the big blue circus tent. "When Paul Schrader showed his *Cat People* in the tent," recalls Mika Kourismaki, "he had what he called an ultimate festival experience: watching his film one morning with some people in sleeping bags making love on the ground."

Because this is a country that has only roughly 350 movie screens, one of the lures of the Midnight Sun Festival for Finnish audiences is the rare chance to see new foreign-language films in the eclectic "Pearls of New Cinema" section, which has included such diverse items as Erick Zonca's *The Dreamlife of Angels*, Shohei Imamura's *The Eel*, Bernardo Bertolucci's *Besieged*, and Hal Hartley's *Henry Fool*.

Often, these directors have come to Sodankyla with their films and have been inspired by the locale to do work of their own. Spain's Juan Carlos Medem thought up *Lovers of the Arctic Circle* after a Midnight Sun visit, and Mexican director Gabriel Retes, here with his wife and collaborator Lourdes Elizarrarás showing his deft and surprising comedy

Welcome, promised to make a film about an understandably frustrated midnight sun vampire.

Paradoxically, says program manager Haataja, because theaters in many Finnish cities "only show a few American big things," one reason Finns come to Sodankyla is to see the year's best of their own films. Nineteen ninety-nine boasted an unusually strong showing for homemade movies at local box offices ("Cool Finns — hot tickets," headlined *Moving Pictures*), and the Midnight Sun made a point of showing the country's top film, Olli Saarela's *Ambush*, which turned out to be an enjoyable, self-consciously heroic epic about a handsome young lieutenant and his platoon fighting behind enemy lines in the struggle against Russia at the end of World War II called the Continuation War. Imagine a Finnish *Saving Private Ryan*, and you'll be surprisingly close.

The Midnight Sun also provided a chance to see the loopy Finnish production that is the festival's signature film, a broad 1951 farce called *Rovaniemi Marketplace* whose cast was featured on the artwork for the first Midnight Sun Festival and has appeared on many of the posters since.

With accordion music by the locally beloved Esa Pakarinen punctuating the story of the Lapland misadventures — there really isn't a more appropriate word — of three bumpkins prospecting for gold, *Rovaniemi Marketplace* proved to be (at an 8:15 A.M. screening with its share of people sleeping and/or amiably sharing alcohol) one of those easy-going light comedies that's perfectly understandable without the assistance of subtitles.

According to the festival's program notes, this was "the first Finnish film where the heroes were ordinary poor wanderers, vagabonds and rascals, who later in the 50s dominated our film industry." "These comedies were part of our childhood, our Finnish heritage and tradition," says Mika Kaurismäki, while Peter von Bagh adds, with typical dryness, "It's a sacred film for me, but I'm a man of bad taste."

The one thing that can be said with assurance about *Rovaniemi Marketplace* is that it wouldn't get a similar place of pride at old-line events like Cannes, and it was a troubled frustration with that festival

and others like it that led directly to the creation of the Midnight Sun Festival.

"As young filmmakers, Aki and I would get invited to festivals in different parts of the world, and though that was always very exciting, in most cases we were really disappointed," Mika Kaurismäki explains. "They had very nice limousines, but they weren't Cadillacs. They put you in a nice room in a five-star hotel, but you had no contact with people. You'd know there were other filmmakers around but you'd never get to meet them. Once, in Toronto, security wouldn't even let me into my own party. I thought that would be the one place I wouldn't need an invitation."

Frustrated and thinking there must be a better way, the Kaurismäkis and fellow director Anssi Mänttäri came up with the idea to "do a festival in the middle of nowhere, where everyone would be in the same league and there wouldn't be any hierarchy." The brothers put in a quick call to some filmmaking friends ("We're doing this crazy festival, do you want to come?"), and the first year's guests were the impressive trio of Jonathan Demme, Bertrand Tavernier, and Sam Fuller, who grabbed Mika's arm so forcefully so many times that it was black-and-blue by the time the event ended.

Sitting in the bar attached to the Hotel Sodankyla, Mika Kourismäki, who met his wife, Finnish filmmaker Pia Tikka, in the Midnight Sun's "Grand Palais," knows some things have changed since 1986. "What's happening to me, I'm getting old," he mock grumbles. "Last night I went to sleep at 4 A.M., very early. During the first festival, I didn't sleep at all. For five days I only went to the movies."

Yet personal qualms notwithstanding, the director knows that the intensity of the Midnight Sun remains unchanged. "What makes this festival is our audience," he says. "They're very loyal and they make the atmosphere. They travel a day or whatever to get here, and they're coming to see movies. Thanks to the mosquitoes, everyone goes to the theaters. You can't escape the movies here." Attendees, Peter von Bagh

adds, are "the best asset of the festival, a totally fascinated audience, not at all cynical."

Also unchanged is the rare chance festival-goers have to examine the careers of featured filmmakers in retrospective tributes. The Greek-born Costa-Gavras was here, as was the great Italian director Francesco Rosi. Seven of each man's films were shown (usually but not invariably with Finnish subtitles), including Rosi's exceptional 1963 *Hands over the City*, a corrosive study of urban political corruption that features a dubbed Rod Steiger nevertheless giving one of the best, most gripping performances of his career.

Just as gratifying was that both men, as well as German actress Angela Winkler (*The Lost Honor of Katharina Blum*, *The Tin Drum*), settled in for frank and leisurely two-hour extended public conversations with von Bagh in the high school gymnasium that started each festival day at 10 A.M. Costa-Gavras, maker of political melodramas like *Z* and *State of Siege*, was especially fascinating, revealing that the first film he saw as a boy was documentary footage of Mussolini and his mistress being killed, their bodies dragged down an Italian street. When, talking of his boyhood familiarity with American westerns, Costa-Gavras asked, "Do you know Randolph Scott?" Von Bagh promptly replied, "I knew him better than my own father."

In addition to everything else, at one time the Midnight Sun Festival eclectically focused on both 3-D and silent films, but the 3-D part of the event was temporarily dropped this year. "We've shown the available repertory," says von Bagh. "Now there is a break, I don't even know why."

In part to make up for that loss, there were two innovative silent programs in 1999, including Walter Ruttman's 1927 German classic *Berlin – Symphony of a Great City*, accompanied by Finnish percussionist Jouni Kesti. But the film everyone wanted to see, the most anticipated event of the entire festival in fact, was *Juha*, a brand-new silent film directed by, of all people, Aki Kaurismäki.

Though the Finnish Film Foundation newsletter headlined "Aki

Goes Silent" in big letters when this project was announced, the younger Kaurismäki brother, whose characters are usually dour and who's often said, von Bagh reported, "words are polluting our movies," did not make a completely unexpected move in deciding to do a modern silent film. His choice of subject was also intriguing: *Juha* is based on a novel by Juhani Aho, one of Finland's classic writers, a book that's already been filmed three times, starting with a 1920 version by Mauritz Stiller, the director best known as Greta Garbo's mentor.

Expecting a crush, especially because the nine-piece ensemble providing the music, the Ansii Tikanmaki Film Orchestra, were Midnight Sun favorites, the festival put *Juha* in its largest venue, the big Italian circus tent that holds roughly five hundred. Still, people lined up in the sunlight more than an hour before the 8:30 P.M. starting time and waited genially through another hour's technical delay, entertained by teenage circus-type performers, including a young woman on stilts, a two-person tiger, and a contortionist.

Once it unspooled, *Juha*'s story of a happily married Finnish farm wife who gets lured to the big city by an evil procurer turned out to be a match for the director's style. A touching homage to silent techniques that was both sincere and amusing, *Juha*, typically, demanded simultaneously to be taken seriously and not seriously at all.

Before *Juha* started, Aki Kaurismäki, who'd missed the festival's first few days, stood up at the front of the tent to introduce his film. With the completely expressionless attitude he favors, Aki used English to welcome everyone to "the screening of a lousy movie." Pointing to the screen and the orchestra, he added, "If you look up, there's a movie. If you look down, there's music. I prefer you look down." The applause was thunderous. It was a Midnight Sun moment, for sure.

PART THREE

Festivals with Aesthetic Agendas

Pordenone

Silent films have magic. They've outwitted history.

Once the most potent worldwide entertainment medium, silent films were subjected to a cultural firestorm of numbing proportions when sound came in. The prints themselves, according to Kevin Brownlow, the author of the landmark book *The Parade's Gone By* and a reigning authority on silent film, endured "a record of destruction worthy of Attila the Hun: they have burned them, dumped them in the sea, hacked the reels with axes, or let them rot in vaults."

Even the estimated 20 percent of films made between 1895 and the late 1920s that survived this physical purge were treated with disdain both calculated and accidental by those who screened them. James Card, another silent authority, said these films were often shown in "seventh generation, pallid dupes of 16 mm prints run at the wrong speed on a small screen and without music."

Or else the poor survivors were chopped up and played for cheap laughs, sliced and diced to feed the hungry maw of television. This happened to such an extent that, again according to Brownlow, "an entire generation of viewers has contempt for them, a prejudice so tremendous that even the creators themselves became terribly apologetic. At times I almost had to bully these people into watching their films with me."

Mocked, reviled, long considered dead and buried, silent film is going through a revival that is as remarkable as it is unexpected as a new generation of viewers comes to appreciate Brownlow's celebrated dictum that "it's hard to understand the last reel if you haven't seen the first." In one memorable week in Los Angeles, for instance, I had a choice of four separate silent programs, ranging from the familiar *Gold Rush* to the rarely seen Danish *Atlantis* to a disturbing Lon Chaney double bill and the western *The Covered Wagon*, all complete with live musical accompaniment.

And that music is quite unlike the indifferent piano tinkling of the TV years. Local symphonies have found accompanying silent film to be among their most popular activities: when Washington's National played for F.W. Murnau's *Nosferatu* at Wolf Trap, 5,649 tickets were sold, and for the Indianapolis Symphony with *The Phantom of the Opera*, 6,404 paid to get in.

In addition, new groups have been formed specifically to accompany silents. The inventive Cambridge-based Alloy Orchestra played their rich percussive score to the German *Sylvester* at the 1993 Telluride Film Festival, and their dynamism galvanized an overflow audience into cheering as if they'd witnessed a Beatles reunion. Five years later, in 1998, I was so excited by how beautifully matched their driving sound was to the factory setting of Sergei Eisenstein's classic *Strike* that I stood for most of the performance.

This silent revival is not a phenomenon limited to festivals or major cities. According to the *"Live" Cinema Calendar*, a thick monthly compilation of silents performed with music, showings take place in sites as nonmetropolitan as Coos Bay, Oregon, Saginaw, Michigan, and Bar Harbor, Maine. "The common reaction," says Tom Murray, the calendar's compiler, "is 'My god, I had no idea there was so much going on.'"

And for those living outside the wide range of live shows, there has been an eruption of silent film on video and cable, where the Turner Classic Movies channel has instituted a Silent Sunday Nights feature. The Library of Congress has combined with the Smithsonian Institu-

tion to produce a six-cassette series, "The Origins of American Film," showcasing rare early works, and companies like Kino on Video and Milestone Film & Video have dozens of silents available, everything from the familiar antics of Buster Keaton to the beautifully photographed action of the little-seen Maurice Tourner–Clarence Brown *Last of the Mohicans*. "There was zero market demand for these films thirty-five years ago," says Kino's Don Krim, while Milestone's Dennis Doros adds, "The interest in this area and the quality of the videos available have all gone way up in the past ten years."

While several factors have contributed to this revival, everyone involved agrees that one of the critical elements in the rebirth of silent films has been an annual event held not in New York, Los Angeles, London, or Paris but rather in a little-known Italian provincial capital of 50,000, a city with no previous connection to silent film located forty-five miles northeast of Venice at the foot of the Alps.

Every October since 1982, "Le Giornate del Cinema Muto," literally "The Days of Silent Film," has attracted visitors from places as distant as Japan, China, Israel, and India, as well as from all of Europe, to the prosperous, energetic but nontourist town of Pordenone—a combination of event and locale so unexpected that it's been characterized as "like having a festival on Amish quilting in Oklahoma."

So unlike other film gatherings it doesn't even want to be called a festival, Pordenone has become the nonpareil event of the silent film year, a place where a week of enthusiastic viewing starting at 9 A.M. daily and inevitably ending well after midnight leaves participants feeling, as Milestone's Doros put it, "like I'd spend seven days in heaven." With encomiums like this the rule not the exception, an Italian pilgrimage was unavoidable if I wanted to understand why vintage silent films were making a celebrated resurgence.

Part of an underappreciated region of Italy known as the Friuli and inhabited by, one guidebook realistically claims, "the warmest and most hospitable of the Italians," Pordenone has both elegant shops located on the cobblestoned Corso Vittorio Emanuele and the kind of cozy and

welcoming restaurants you hate to leave. While the *New York Times* called the Friuli "home to one of the most refined food and wine cultures in the world," Pordenone, with but a handful of hotels within its limits, not only didn't rate any stars in the *Michelin Green Guide* to Italy, it was in fact dropped entirely from that magisterial volume in 1990.

Known a thousand years ago as Portus Naonis because of its function as a port on the River Noncello, Pordenone is now a manufacturing center, the home of Zanussi, Italy's biggest maker of appliances, considered to be the country's second largest industrial firm after Fiat.

Aside from the painting of sixteenth-century master and native son Giovanni Antonio de Sacchis, known to the world as "Il Pordenone," the closest the metropolis has gotten to any kind of fame is a backhanded mention in Ernest Hemingway's *A Farewell to Arms*. The great writer, who passed through the town as a World War I ambulance driver, was apparently not terribly impressed. He had a character dismiss it as "not much of a place" and in addition had his hero desert to Switzerland rather than retreat to its friendly confines. Not a ringing endorsement.

To its credit, however, Pordenone makes an excellent starting point for explorations of the rest of the Friuli, a region that has had three different capitals in its long history. Aquileia boasts a basilica with an enormous Roman mosaic floor, Udine a remarkable Venetian-style town square, and Cividale del Friuli the celebrated Tempietto Longobardo. This haunting, almost magical stucco relief of six maiden saints that sits on a high wall in a small temple by a rushing river has lost none of its mystery in the thousand years since the Lombards created it.

Back in Pordenone, with all screenings held at the creaky but endearing Teatro Verdi, a 1,200-seat opera theater dating from the early years of the century but given a 1950s remodeling replete with glass bricks and heavy curves, the Giornate traditionally elicits gasps of astonishment from the hundreds of visitors who gather for its pleasures.

The *Times* of London calls it "the annual miracle," and Edith Kramer, the current director of Berkeley's Pacific Film Archive, speaks for her fellow professionals, the people who already know the most

about silent film, by saying, "This is where we go back to school, where we learn and are enriched in our own field. It's a privilege to attend, intense, intimate, a very special week."

As surprising as the festival's success is the unlikely reason for its existence, a massive 1976 earthquake that devastated the entire Friuli region and practically leveled Gemona, hometown of a pair of married film buffs named Livio Jacob (now Pordenone's chairman) and Piera Patat.

Both students in Trieste, the couple had their interest in movies intensified by membership in a film society run by journalist Lorenzo Codelli. Through Codelli, they met the late Angelo R. Humouda, a legendary politically committed film archivist who until his death traveled throughout Italy in a green Volkswagen van jammed with silent films, early cartoons, and a projector, exhibiting his treasures to audiences that wouldn't ordinarily be exposed to them.

Strong regional partisans (Patat likes to wear a "Friulani Are Fabulous" button), the couple wanted to do something for their area, perhaps raise money to rebuild Gemona's destroyed movie theaters. They consulted with Humouda, who instead volunteered to bring his traveling silents to Gemona, which he did in 1977. And he offered some astute advice.

"He told us, 'with the little money you can raise, you won't ever be able to build a theater, but you can buy films,'" Patat remembers. "He introduced us to a world completely new to us, the world of American 16 mm distributors."

The couple began buying films, eventually founding an archive in Gemona called La Cineteca del Friuli. They became friendly with Paolo Cherci Usai, a colleague of Humouda's, and Piero Colussi and Andrea Crozzoli of Cinemazero, a film society with a theater in nearby Pordenone. In 1982, the group decided to put on a retrospective of the French silent comic Max Linder in Pordenone. Though the gathering didn't even have a name, and any thoughts of making it an annual event would have seemed preposterous, this was the first Pordenone Festival. There were only eight guests.

While the Pordenone committee (later joined by historian Davide Turconi and technical expert Carlo Montanaro and still later by critic David Robinson) was feeling its way, great changes were taking place in the silent film world. The most important was the international acclaim that greeted the 1980 screening of Kevin Brownlow's twenty-years-in-the-making reconstruction of Abel Gance's monumental *Napoleon*, accompanied by a specially written Carmine Coppola score.

"It filled Radio City Music Hall in New York for ten days," remembers Kino's Don Krim, still amazed. "It showed the possibility of what silent films could be to every theater owner, distributor, critic, and moviegoer." Anyone who experienced riding the huge wave of audience emotion when the multi-hour film reached its climax as the screen opened to three times its normal size and Bonaparte's revolutionary army marched into Italy counts it as one of their most intense moviegoing memories.

One of the things that *Napoleon*'s success demonstrated was the importance of being fanatical about showing silents in as authentic conditions as possible. In addition to procuring the best possible prints (especially important because the photographic quality of the originals couldn't be more different from the grainy, pathetic copies often seen today), this meant paying close attention to a pair of factors—projection speed and musical accompaniment—whose neglect had led directly to the way silents had dwindled in popularity.

For though there is a uniform sound projection speed of 24 frames per second, nothing of the kind exists for silent films, largely because they were shot by cinematographers who hand-cranked their cameras. They speeded up or slowed down the movement from film to film and even within films from 16 frames per second to 20-something per second as the action dictated.

Making things even more complicated is that footage was often supposed to be projected faster than it was shot, ensuring that stunts looked crisper and slapstick funnier. Speeds also varied with decades, and projecting D.W. Griffith's ambitious 1916 epic *Intolerance* at the late silent

speed of 24 frames per second instead of the intended 16 to 18 makes it play like comedy, while showing 1927's gently romantic *Sunrise* at 16 frames per second instead of the intended 24 has the unfortunate tendency, says Kevin Brownlow, "to put audiences to sleep."

Though modern silent projectionists don't generally change the tempo within films, they must have a knowledge of what the standard frames-per-second count was in each of the films they show plus the ability to work with today's breed of variable speed projectors. The aim remains what it was in 1911, when a practitioner wrote that the ideal projectionist is someone who "'renders' a film, if he is a real operator, exactly as does the musician render a piece of music, in that, within limits, the action of a scene being portrayed depends entirely on his judgment."

Music overall was a much more central element of presentation than modern audiences realize, accounting for what is generally conceded to be 50 percent of a given film's impact. The most prestigious films had specially composed music (Saint-Saëns wrote an early score) played by musicians with impressive credentials: according to one count, there were as many as five hundred orchestras working the biggest theaters, ranging in size from twenty-six to ninety players and coping with music of such complexity that the original score for D. W. Griffith's *Way Down East* contained 242 tempo changes. But no theater, no matter how humble, ever considered showing films without at least a piano player or organist, who, if he or she didn't have a full score or at least musical guidelines to work with, would be called upon to improvise on what was seen on screen.

"Most silent films were 80 percent emotional and 20 percent intellectual. That's not meant as a slap; it's the way they were constructed," said William Everson, one of the deans of silent film history. "The score minimized flaws, added punctuation and feeling, stretched the emotionalism and guided the audience into the right frame of mind. It's a major crime, absolutely deadly, to show these films without the proper accompaniment."

And, as Kevin Brownlow wrote, because "they were the movies until sound came in, calling them silent suggests they were lacking something"—many partisans wince whenever that term is used. James Card, in his appreciative memoir *Seductive Cinema*, goes so far as to refer to "speechless cinema" and "predialogue, so-called silent film," so deep is his passion for the art that is no more.

The rediscovery and reconstruction of *Napoleon* not only showed the commercial potential of correctly presented silent movies, it also symbolized the most surprising aspect of the art's revival. Pictures long thought to be lost forever, key works unseen for decades and written off as victims of nitrate film stock's inevitable physical disintegration, were turning up on a regular basis, uncovered in places ranging from an abandoned swimming pool in the Yukon to the basement of a Danish tavern where Peter the Great once spent the night.

One of the great Japanese silents, Teinosuke Kinugasa's 1926 *A Page of Madness*, the hallucinatory tale of an old man who works at the asylum where his wife is confined with the hope of freeing her, was found in a rice barrel in the garden of the director's country house. *The Last of the Duanes*, a celebrated Tom Mix western, was discovered under layers of bird excrement on the floor of a chicken farm building in a remote Czech village. And the actor James Mason came across many of Buster Keaton's personal 35 mm prints lying neglected in the garage of the comedian's former home.

Private collectors, a group so large that Pordenone's Paolo Cherci Usai calls them "a galaxy beyond our imagination," tend to be similarly reticent about their film holdings because possession of copyrighted films from an illegitimate source is illegal. And, as James Card notes dryly, "The FBI has not been shy about swooping down on private film collections and carrying them off." But other discoveries, paradoxically enough, began to come out of places that had legal rights to their films but didn't know exactly what they had.

Those would be state-run archives in far corners of the world, places like Australia and the former Czechoslovakia that had been terminal

points in studio distribution systems that were so lackadaisical about what they were shipping out they didn't think it was worth the return postage to have anything sent back.

But though these archives have prints in huge numbers (the National Film and Sound Archive of Australia recently returned more than 1,600 American films to this country), literally decades can go by before they get the money and the manpower to actually examine their holdings. "It's mind-boggling what it takes in terms of labor to look at entire films," says the PFA's Edith Kramer, and Kevin Brownlow adds, "Archives are ludicrously underfunded. If they'd take the budgets on about twelve of these TV movies they could save an entire era."

With all the ingredients for a silent film revival in place, from this continual rediscovery of important films to an understanding of how to present them, what was most needed was a spot to bring it all together—which is where Pordenone fortuitously entered the picture.

"I swear we had no idea it would ever be like this," says a harried Paolo Cherci Ursai, who is now curator of the prestigious George Eastman film archive in Rochester, New York, as well as a member of the Pordenone committee. "The first festival was a group of friends, not even a convention in the American sense. But as soon as we put this together, the speed with which people came was amazing, as if they were waiting for this to happen. It was the right thing at the right time—and in the right place. This wouldn't have become what it has in a big city like Paris; it would have been absorbed and disappeared in a hundred other things."

What Pordenone did from the start was display the field's best work to those who could best appreciate it, an essential task because, preservationists being human, there is not much impetus to do a great job of restoration if there is nowhere to take a bow. And since, explains Paolo Cherci Usai, "we put the spotlight on, if it makes a splash in Pordenone, it will make a splash everywhere." Both collectors and archives worldwide find themselves thinking, in Kevin Brownlow's words, "What can we dig up, what can we do for Pordenone this year?"

As a result, there is rarely an archive or private collector that can't be

prevailed upon to contribute prints; more than forty different sources were credited in 1994's program. This leads to both an unmatched completeness in the festival's retrospectives and the periodic appearance of one-of-a-kind rarities. Brownlow, for instance, is still talking about the 16 mm home movie footage an Italian tourist shot of Buster Keaton filming *The Cameraman* on the streets of New York that a collector brought to the Verdi screen one year.

Furthermore, says Paolo Cherci Usai, since Pordenone "refuses to obey the logic of the masterpiece," the festival also delights in showing "bad films that have slept on the shelves for eighty years, that no one dared to touch." Pordenone even has a section where unknown films are screened for audience identification: one year, remembers Lorenzo Codelli, the great Italian director Sergio Leone literally leapt out of his seat at the shock of recognizing an early film starring his own father, actor/director Vincenzo Leone.

Essential to Pordenone's success is the festival's most intangible quality: an unpretentious warmth that I felt from the moment I arrived. While most festivals pride themselves on scheduling more films than anyone could possibly see, making sleep difficult and meals impossible, Pordenone is a human-scale event, gracefully combining comprehensiveness with the conviviality of an intimate family.

Yes, this is a serious international gathering, but it retains a charming Mickey-and-Judy-putting-on-a-show energy, and it has enough respect for life's noncinematic pleasures to build in the kind of two-and-a-half-hour breaks for lunch and dinner that visitors to Italy will appreciate. And Pordenone itself turned out to be enough of a small town to encourage art students to compete in decorating local shop windows with displays incorporating the festival's Buster Keaton–inspired logo.

Holding the festival almost exclusively in one theater may seem like a small thing, but anyone who has spent frantic hours at other festivals first trying to figure out which of several conflicting films to see and then rushing around trying to get from one venue to another knows what bliss a single setting is. And because the Pordenone area's finite hotel space lim-

its the number of out-of-towners who can attend, lining up ahead of time to assure a decent seat, the bane of most festivals, is unheard of.

Run by the still-youthful zealots who were present at the creation and with its eager participants exuding an atmosphere of backpack academia ("a sort of Woodstock of silent cinema," said one bearded regular), Pordenone is completely in love with the purity of what is on the screen. There is no A list, no glitz, no glamour; "all the stars belonging to this world," someone said to me, "are dead." I did have a scare one morning, when I spotted a flock of limousines and video cameras at the Verdi, but they turned out to be drawn by a wedding in the hotel across the street, not a celebrity encounter.

"We're the same group of people. We've never forgotten the way the whole thing started, and we don't want to change," emphasizes Paolo Cherci Usai. "And though we're so different culturally and personally that our meetings can be like volcanoes exploding, no one wants to break the magic by leaving."

The collegial atmosphere at Pordenone is more than just pleasant, it makes what the festival does possible. For one of the characteristics that participants agree marks this gathering as unique is that it's the only place where all branches of the often-fractious silent film community declare a truce and fraternize with the enemy.

Arcane as it is, the silent film world is as rife with turf wars as any inner city neighborhood. Collectors scorn archivists as unduly cautious and conservative, while archivists return the favor by looking down on private enthusiasts as little more than freebooters who don't take proper care of their holdings. Even academics and archivists have their differences, the former angry at not being able to get the access they want and the latter upset because use inevitably damages their prints.

Pordenone, says Paolo Cherci Usai, is "the only place where you can meet everybody. Archivists, semiologists, the guy crazy for Louise Fazenda, they all want to come here, they're all equal here, with no sense of authority." And they are so determined to see every available frame that not even Pordenone's biggest public demonstration in more than

twenty years, part of a one-day nationwide general strike in 1994, could lure anyone out of the Verdi except me.

Because what archives and collectors bring to Pordenone is the newly found and the unexpected (often adding previously unknown or under-appreciated films like Frank Borzage's 1929 *Lucky Star*, the surprise hit of the 1990 event, to the list of accepted masterpieces), the festival has developed a reputation for what is called canon-busting, for shaking up everyone's ideas of what is significant and why. Pordenone, says historian David Shepard with appropriate drama (this is the movies, after all), "takes the chains off film bibles throughout the world. There are all kinds of films I had no idea were important until I saw them here."

The example at the top of everyone's list is Pordenone's 1989 exploration of prerevolutionary Russian cinema, specifically the films of director Evgenii Bauer. Unexpectedly sophisticated works that had not been seen outside their country of origin since 1917 and were thought destroyed, Bauer's productions were characterized by technical innovations, a subtle, Chekovian sense of character, and the dramatic use of light and shadow. "There was the exhilaration of discovery," wrote David Robinson in *Sight & Sound*, "a vision of marvellous vistas—but also an awesome sense of the vast interior that remains to be explored."

The uproar in 1994 was not quite so intense, but as always the festival was bookended by a pair of special screenings with full musical scores that were specially commissioned for the occasion. Opening night was *Lonesome*, a naturalistic late silent from 1928 directed by Paul Fejos and accompanied by a captivating score by the Alloy Orchestra, the crowd-pleasers from Telluride. A simple but enchanting Manhattan love story about a man and a woman (Glenn Tryon and Barbara Kent) who find each other during a raucous day at Coney Island only to nearly lose everything, it elicited sighs of satisfaction as it went up and down real roller-coasters as well as the emotional kind.

Closing night struck quite a different note. *The Unknown*, directed by the brooding Tod Browning in 1927, starred Lon Chaney as a circus performer who pretends to be armless and Joan Crawford as the ingenue

who likes him that way. It was so unnerving that even John Cale, who wrote and performed the ultramodern electronic score, was moved to call it "a fairly sick film, for want of a better word."

The biggest aural surprise was the intoxicating Indian music, a combination of vocals, percussion, and harmonium improvised on the spot by a pickup group of European-based Indian musicians for a selection of silents that had never left the subcontinent before. I found myself going to more Indian films than I'd planned on, just to hear the hypnotic instrumental interplay. The best of the lot was a stunning print of the 1928 *Shiraz*, an assured Oriental fantasy about the building of the Taj Mahal that featured everything from toothless soothsayers to execution by elephant's foot.

The festival's other main series featured Hollywood work that had never before been gathered together with such painstaking thoroughness, like the silent westerns of William Wyler, collected from eight sources scattered around the world and accompanied by rugged, indefatigable piano players who relieved each other at two-hour intervals. In a classic Pordenone touch, at the conclusion of the last Wyler shown, the spirited, sweeping *Hell's Heroes*, which has protagonist Charles Bickford crawling into a church as the congregation sings "Silent Night," a local Pordenone choir sneaked into the Verdi and sang several choruses of that hymn to great effect.

The films I looked forward to most were the elegant and sophisticated features from little-known, unaccountably forgotten director Monta Bell, who combined a sardonic sense of humor with surprising emotional subtlety and poignance. A typical moment, from *Lady of the Night*, had a hard-boiled Norma Shearer getting out of prison and casually checking her makeup in the shiny body of a passing hearse. It was hard not to be won over by the cool audacity of it all.

At the other end of the spectrum was the slapstick gang, well over a hundred comic shorts from obscure performers drawn together under the rubric "Forgotten Laughter: Unknown American Comedians." Most popular of these was the eccentric Jewish comic Max Davidson,

whose elaborate shrugs of resignation at increasingly ridiculous situations had audiences saluting him as Woody Allen's cinematic grandfather. His *Pass the Gravy* was voted Le Giornate's most popular comedy short, and had everyone in the Verdi truly convulsed.

Experiencing the total immersion of Pordenone, seeing these films as originally intended, makes inescapable the truth of what fans have continually maintained: silent film is a vivid world all its own. As historian William Everson insists, "This was not a shoddy little flickering art medium, not the primitive forerunner of anything. This deserves to be seen as a completely separate art, something unique and full blown."

Key to this view is to realize and accept that the absence of spoken dialogue is not a handicap to endure but a virtue to enjoy. For the hidden, unexpected pleasure of silent films is the way they seduce audiences into becoming, in the most modern way, full interactive participants in the movie experience. "You're not told what to think or feel," explains Michael Friend of the Academy of Motion Picture Arts and Sciences. "A kind of emotional space is produced which is open for you to enter, a space for reflection between the film and the music."

To understand what that means, it helps to recall one of the most famous scenes in silent film history, the moment in 1925's *The Phantom of the Opera* when Mary Philbin's mischievous Christine reaches around and removes the mask covering Lon Chaney's face. By virtue of a clever camera angle we see the Phantom's horrific visage before Christine does, in dreamy repose for an instant and then, unforgettably, in agony as the creature realizes that his dreams of acceptance and love are over. It is a moment of supreme emotion, one of the greatest the silent world has to offer, and because no speech is heard, nothing distracts or distances us from directly experiencing its shock. Because we are on our own, without words to guide or straitjacket us, we are in effect meeting the scene halfway, unavoidably filling it up with our own strong feelings.

Paradoxically underlining the difference between sound and silence was the 1994 festival's opening night screening of *Lonesome*, shown in a version to which some brief spoken inserts had been added once sound

became all the rage. The sophisticated emotions the dialogueless sequences evoked were shattered when the actors could actually be heard. For while sound particularizes, silence turns out to universalize, allowing the audience to share completely in the on-screen dream. No one spending time at Pordenone could fail to agree with Mary Pickford's famous statement: "It would have been more logical if silent pictures had grown out of the talking instead of the other way around."

If there is a downside to the story of Le Giornate de Cinema Muto it is that, like Italy itself, the festival always seems to be on the brink of falling victim to economic and logistical pressures. Though its roughly $400,000 annual cost is tiny (about as much, it has been said, as a single morning at the flashier Venice Film Festival), Pordenone has been more appreciated internationally than at home and never quite knows how or if it is going to cover its expenses. Its proximity to the nearby NATO base at Aviano has made hotel rooms perennially difficult to reserve. And the quasi-crumbling Teatro Verdi is always in danger of being closed for the kind of renovations that could take years to finish and possibly take the heart out of the proceedings.

(In 1999, when uncertainty about whether the Verdi would be restored or demolished and replaced by a new theater reached new heights, the Giornate moved less than ten miles down the road to the town of Sacile, "the Garden of Venice," located on a natural island formed by the river Livenza. Screenings were held in the 1911 Teatro Zancanaro, which fortuitously reopened in 1997 after renovations lasting nearly a decade.)

Pordenone, obviously, is not about to give up. For one thing, it means too much to its participants. One film historian told of a colleague who insisted on coming though he was close to death: "It was extraordinary, that visit, as if he just wanted to see Mecca before he died." It is no wonder then that Paolo Cherci Usai, speaking passionately for the entire committee, says, "It's a moral commitment, not a job. They will really have to kill us to kill the festival. They will have to walk on our corpses to cause us to disappear."

Lone Pine

Ask not what the world can do for you, says the self-sufficient Lone Pine Film Festival, show everyone what you've done for the world.

While the standard festival looks outward, offering itself as a place where movies from everywhere can find a home, the folks here turn that formula on its head, inviting visitors to celebrate what this tiny Eastern Sierra town three hours from Los Angeles has contributed to the universe of film.

In what has been called the most focused movie event in the world, the Lone Pine Film Festival, which began in 1990, concentrates exclusively on motion pictures shot in the harsh and craggy landscape of the unique Alabama Hills just outside of town. Even pretenders that were lensed only sixty miles away in Bishop are righteously excluded.

Named after a notable tree that was uprooted in a storm more than a hundred years ago, Lone Pine is known today as the gateway to Mount Whitney, the highest peak in the contiguous forty-eight states. That makes it attractive to so many European tourists that Jake's Saloon on Main Street has to have signs in three languages informing visitors of the state's liquor laws.

Isolated though it is (nearby Kirkwood advertises itself as the place where visitors "Rub Shoulders with No One"), Lone Pine is connected

to several strands of California history. Located in the heart of the Owens Valley, it had its water supply seized decades ago by impudent Los Angeles in an action (dramatized in Robert Towne's script for Roman Polanski's *Chinatown*) that still rankles locally. Also, the Manzanar War Relocation Center, where Japanese Americans were forcibly interned during World War II, is just up the road.

But as far as festival-goers are concerned, Lone Pine is celebrated for at least three hundred motion pictures that were shot here over a seventy-five-year period. These range from not-surprising efforts like *Bad Day at Black Rock* and *High Sierra* (which featured Humphrey Bogart careening down Whitney Portal Road just outside of town) to more unexpected titles.

Because of their singular topography and proximity to Hollywood, the Alabama Hills have stood in for everything from the Andes in the John Wayne–starring *Tycoon* to the wilds of Tibet in *The Shadow* and even another universe in *Star Trek V*. Most memorably, director George Stevens and company spent three months here shooting the classic *Gunga Din* in areas that look so much like the hill country of India's Northwest Frontier that Indian friends of star Douglas Fairbanks Jr. insisted they knew exactly where on the subcontinent it had been filmed.

More recently, commercials and videos have monopolized the landscape, with companies coming from as far away as Germany, Finland, and Japan and celebrities like Michael Jordan (for Gatorade) and Willie Nelson and Waylon Jennings (for Pizza Hut) getting comfortable in the scenery.

Mostly, however, they shot westerns in Lone Pine, westerns, westerns, and more westerns. And though some prestige items such as *How the West Was Won* and parts of the Mel Gibson–starring *Maverick* were lensed here, more often it was the sturdy and unpretentious B westerns that used the site, with cowboys such as Tom Mix, Hoot Gibson, Ken Maynard, and Tim Holt being invited to saddle up.

Both Robert Mitchum and Roy Rogers had their first starring roles in

Lone Pine, Gene Autry filmed sixteen pictures here, and William Boyd made thirty-two Hopalong Cassidy epics. Director Budd Boetticher shot several of his elegiac 1960s westerns starring Randolph Scott such as *The Tall T* and *Ride Lonesome* in the area, and it was the site of John Wayne's last filmed appearance, a 1978 commercial for California-based Great Western Savings & Loan.

Given all of this, no one should be surprised that Lone Pine has a distinctly western flavor to it. When I visited in 1995, the festival saluted Gene Autry, "America's Favorite Cowboy," but since Autry was too infirm to attend, the title of grand marshal of the Sunday afternoon parade went to a more unconventional choice. That was eighty-eight-year-old Pierce Lyden, a quintessential bad guy in black hat and pencil mustache who appeared in literally hundreds of B westerns and first worked in Lone Pine back in 1937.

More than knowing their B westerns backward and forward, festival-goers also know how to dress the part. When I walked onto the town's Main Street for the opening night party, I felt the eerie, anachronistic sensation that goes with hearing the surprisingly delicate but unmistakable jingle of spurs as dozens of revelers in full western gear wandered by, drinks in hand.

For one of Lone Pine's functions is to provide people who are not shy about confessing how major an impact western films have had on their lives the opportunity to do some serious dressing up. Joe "Hoppy" Sullivan, a district sales manager from Cicero, Indiana, spent years studying still photographs of Hopalong Cassidy with a magnifying glass and wears a beautiful costume that reflects that concern. And Ermal Williamson of Van Nuys, California, has an unexpected job description: he's a professional John Wayne impersonator who has even performed weddings as the Duke.

Visitors like these come to Lone Pine in such numbers they just about double the town's usual population of 2,000 and so strain the hotel room situation for miles around that Dave Holland, the festival's affable director says, "Where I'm at now is I need a bigger town."

Simultaneously bemused and proud of being the focus of this kind of worshipful attention, the residents of Lone Pine work to make the festival a city-wide event. Local businesses allow their windows to be painted with portraits of cowboy heroes and make room for photographs of Saturday matinee stars next to signs that read "Yes We Have Steer Manure." Both the VFW and the American Legion throw pancake breakfasts, the Lions Club provides a "Western Deep-Pit BBQ," and everyone lines Main Street for Sunday's hometown parade, complete with fire engines, dogs with bandanas, and the Inyo County Board of Supervisors.

Though the twenty-plus Lone Pine movies shown in 16 mm in the local high school auditorium are always a draw, the festival has other, equally down-home attractions. Veteran stunt man Loren James, who doubled for Steve McQueen for twenty-two years, shows his action reel, a panel discussion allows visitors to question visiting stars such as Peggy Stewart, "Queen of the Republic Westerns," and a dealers' area encourages purchase of hundreds of western videos and such oddities as an edible reproduction of Hopalong Cassidy's belt buckle—in either milk or dark chocolate.

Inevitably—and this is something that gives the Lone Pine event a haunting, indelible quality—what draws most festival-goers is exactly the same thing that brought all those movie companies to the area in the first place: the chance to wander around one of California's least-known and most extraordinary natural phenomena, the Alabama Hills.

Even though I'd seen them repeatedly on film, the actual sight of these enormous, grandiose boulders, stretched out in bewildering groupings like giant gumdrops randomly sprinkled over the landscape by a playful higher power, was genuinely breathtaking. These weathered granite rocks, once erroneously thought to be "the oldest hills in the world" and named by southern Civil War sympathizers after a Confederate battleship, give off an otherworldly aura, so much so that I felt almost frightened to be in their midst. My mind spun fantasy after fantasy, until it seemed plausible to view the outcroppings as somehow

huddled together for companionship, warmth, and understanding, like the outcast "Freaks" of Todd Browning's movie. If someone had told me these stones were once alive on another planet, or at the very least housed an H. P. Lovecraft–type alien, unknowable civilization, I wouldn't have doubted it.

The first Hollywood production to find its way to Lone Pine was a 1920 Fatty Arbuckle film called *The Roundup*. Film companies got to like it here partially because the local citizenry treated everyone like family, even building a hotel called the Dow (I stayed in the more modern annex) for their comfort. But mostly filmmakers returned again and again because of the wide variety of looks the Alabama Hills provided. Director Boetticher, a visitor so often "I should have been elected mayor long ago," spoke for his colleagues when he told a BBC interviewer, "The great thing about Lone Pine is that you don't need to go anywhere else. It looks like they built these mountains for the movies."

Equally enthusiastic about the locale are fans like the gentleman who flew in from Brazil one year and took a soon-to-be-legendary $300 cab ride directly from Los Angeles International Airport to the festival. Or people like Ian Whitcomb, author and entertainer and host of his own Los Angeles–area radio show, who'd watched Lone Pine movies as a boy in Britain and thought "maybe all of America looks like this."

Unable to track down the location once he came to the United States, Whitcomb stumbled on the hills, as many people do, on a drive back from the ski areas of Mammoth. "I suddenly realized I was in my dream," Whitcomb told me, wonder still in his voice. "I was in the America I'd always wanted to be in but never found. In fact, the whole of the dream the rest of the world got of America was contained in the Alabama Hills."

Since the hills are owned by the federal government and administered by the Department of Interior's Bureau of Land Management, they have the advantage of looking just as they did when all that filming took place. "Everything else has been mutilated," says Mike Johnson, a B western

fan who works for Lloyds of London in Toronto, shaking his head at the waste. "Only this location remains exactly as it was sixty years ago." Or, as festival director Dave Holland frequently explains, the hills are "a living museum."

Holland, a gregarious, still boyish man of middle years, is a former publicist and journalist who enjoys saying things like "I'll try not to blow smoke in your ear" and "There's no law against being friendly." He took over the festival, which was founded by Lone Pine resident Kerry Powell, in its second year. And because he is a self-described "location freak" who has been exploring the Alabama Hills for thirty years, he was instrumental in giving the event its unique character.

Location freaks, explains Holland, are people who "want to stand where their heroes stood, who think it's exciting to take a photo from a film and say, 'By god, that's the same rock, do you realize what happened here?' It sounds naive to want to relive a myth, but that's what it is."

For Holland, what that means first of all is keeping his eye on the scenery, not the plot, when he watches a vintage movie. Then, accompanied by batches of stills, he's tirelessly walked around the Alabamas, off and on for years with particular photos, examining the lines and contours of the rocks and hoping to match the picture to the location.

Having documented his findings in a book and video called, not surprisingly, *On Location in Lone Pine*, Holland was the driving force in setting up a range of tours of the Alabamas (there now are six different ones to choose from) that are the festival's most popular aspect. And at each stop on every tour, visitors get to see stills from the relevant movies attached to pedestals planted exactly where the original movie cameras stood. It gives you chills, it really does.

Going on tour with the contagiously enthusiastic Holland is invariably an energizing experience. He charges through the sagebrush, exclaiming, "Look at that!" while he points out, not for the first time, the small piles of rocks that anchored the famous *Gunga Din* suspension bridge. And when Holland introduces locales like the cucumber-shaped Gene Autry rock, used in everything from Autry's *Boots and Saddle* to

Lives of a Bengal Lancer, it is easy to feel with him when he says happily, "This is hallowed ground."

All this points to Lone Pine's unusual place in the film festival cosmos. Turning its back on today, it devotes itself to as mythic a genre as cinema history has. And unlike, say, the world of silents, westerns and adventure epics are films that festival-goers experienced firsthand while they were thriving, and most likely in the impressionable years of childhood. Being brought back to that world, being able to actually walk around in unforgettable scenery that seemed the very stuff of fantasy when first we saw it, is a heady experience indeed.

If there is anybody besides Holland who represents the spirit of Lone Pine it is parade grand marshal Pierce Lyden. Clear-eyed and good-humored at eighty-eight, he casually leaned against a hotel fence post while talking to me, speaking with easy grace and bemusement about a life both in and out of pictures that sounded as authentic and distant as if Buffalo Bill himself were standing next to me.

"I was born and raised in a sod house on a ranch in western Nebraska with no fences, no telephone, no electricity," Lyden remembers. "My dad bought horses for the cavalry, and I was handling cattle and breaking horses by the time I was eleven or twelve."

Determined to act, Lyden began on the stage but left it for Hollywood once the talkies came in. "Since I could do my own riding and stunt work, they didn't have to double me," he says. "The people who made the B westerns, we did a job, we went home, and we thought that was the end. We never thought they'd be remembered like they are today."

Going almost directly from Lone Pine to a western film festival in London, Pierce Lyden, who never got to wear a white hat, still can't quite believe all the attention that is being paid to his career. "The old bad man is the grand marshal," he says, shaking his head and smiling to himself. "They must be getting to the bottom of the barrel."

Telluride

More than twenty-two years ago, powered by the energy of youth, an innocent critic ventured out from the East Coast to a small festival in Colorado, then in just its third year. This is what he wrote:

"Telluride is the name whispered to you as you sit shivering from celluloid overdose in a café in Cannes. Go to Telluride, the voices say, only a few years old and already the most respected small film festival in the world. Telluride is different, the voices say, and for once the voices are right."

The words are mine, and when a considerably larger and more established Telluride recently celebrated its twenty-fifth anniversary with a gala five-day event (up from the usual four), the temptation to reexamine what London's *Sunday Times* has called "one of the US's most exclusive arts events" was hard to avoid.

Today's Telluride combines worthy new films, in-person tributes to cinema grandees, and exclusive showings of venerable rarities. Most people who make the trek to this remote western town seven hours from Denver experience varying degrees of ecstasy, praising the festival as artistically adventurous and iconoclastic. Even unlikely visitors like action director Renny Harlin told an audience he'd turned to producing

(he came with his debut, *Ramblin Rose*) because "I knew that as a director I'd never get invited to Telluride."

But Telluride was not always the way it appears now, and it doesn't necessarily call forth the same responses from all its visitors. Over its quarter-of-a-century lifespan the festival has made an almost personal journey from lionized darling to the focus of questions and doubts to its current position as a battle-scarred but still idealistic survivor in an increasingly commercialized world. "We live on such a tenuous edge between survival and extinction," says festival general manager Stella Pence, "that tiny factors become tidal waves." The ways Telluride has chosen to ride out those waves find echoes in my own varying levels of enthusiasm toward festivals in general and this singular one in particular.

The most obvious differences between Telluride then and Telluride now are, predictably, the surface ones, the inevitable results of celebrity, prosperity, and the passage of time. In 1976, you could buy a general festival ticket for $65 and an economy one for $35; today, a regular Telluride pass is $500, and the fast-selling patron passes run $2,500. The festival's first outlay was an almost invisible $8,300; today, it's $1.8 million, the size of the total annual budget for the local school system.

Instead of the one theater it began with, the restored 1914 Sheridan Opera House, the festival now has seven, five of which have to be built anew every year inside existing structures and then taken down. The theatrical building blocks, from seats to speakers, spend the off-season in rural Colorado inside large trailers with the festival's slogan "Show" painted on the sides.

Where food was once a catch-as-catch-can activity, Telluride, now with as many volunteers (close to five hundred) as it once had visitors, has to help out oversubscribed local restaurants by making extensive plans to supply its own people with an estimated 20,000 meals.

"The executive chef from the Putney Inn in Vermont brings in her staff and sets up an entire feeding operation," says Stella Pence. "She comes to town in early June, visits the local farmers to tell them what we

need, they plant and harvest it, and we give them the leftovers back as mulch. It's its own weird little cottage industry."

"Wouldn't it be nice to build a festival where the theaters were already there, a place where there would be restaurants?" Stella's husband, Bill Pence, one of the festival's permanent codirectors, wistfully adds. "This is not like the festivals at Sundance or Toronto, which get all kinds of resources from the town. We pay as we go, like a taxi."

As for the town itself, anyone who's slept through the past quarter century would hardly recognize anything about it except its celebrated location 8,750 feet high in the San Juan Mountains of southwestern Colorado, where the oxygen pressure is 40 percent lower than at sea level, smack at the end of a dead-end road leading into a spectacular box canyon.

Just about a ghost town when the festival started, with a population of only a few hundred, Telluride, especially after a nerve-racking small airport (the world's second-highest commercial facility) opened just outside town in 1985, has boomed into an example of what's alternately called the Aspenification or the Californication of the state. As one reporter tartly put it a few years ago, "A sleepy haven for aging hippies is now a boom town of condos, million-dollar houses and billion dollar ski resorts."

In 1976, the Telluride I wrote about was "a pleasant, if slightly unreal fantasy town, where 70 percent of the population is thirty-five or under, a live-in Disneyland for people who never want to go home anymore." A place where drug dealing was legendary and local phones had only four digits as late as 1989, Telluride now is overshadowed by Mountain Village, a big deal collection of costly trophy homes and ski resorts, located up the mountain a gondola ride away from downtown.

Where dirt and gravel roads were once the norm and entire city blocks could probably have been bought for $10,000, even Telluride's back streets have just been blacktopped because, says one bemused resident, "if you've got million dollar shacks, you've got to pave the alleys." In fact, snow-loving celebrities like Tom Cruise, Keith Carradine,

Sylvester Stallone, and Oprah Winfrey have places here, and Oliver Stone just sold his for an impressive $8 million.

Paralleling these changes and in some way reflecting them are the more important differences in how the festival has been perceived over time by the international film world. To understand those, it's helpful to start from the premise that the hothouse filmcentric universe Telluride creates over a Labor Day weekend has always been more a religion than anything as ordinary as a festival, complete with messianic believers and agnostic scoffers.

When Telluride began in 1973, Sundance did not exist, and neither did Toronto, currently the Bigfoot of North America's fall film events. Where well under a hundred festivals were then in business worldwide, now there are several times as many, including a number in Colorado. "The difference is huge," says codirector Bill Pence. "The whole thing's become an industry."

None of this was so much as a dream in the early 1970s, when the Pences ran the classics-oriented distributor Janus Films and, living in Ridgeway, Colorado, programmed two local opera houses, the Sheridan in nearby Telluride and the Wheeler in Aspen.

In 1972, the Pences and James Card, then curator of films at Eastman House in Rochester, New York, brought a pair of silent pictures to the Sheridan. "The town was filled with refugees from the '60s," remembers Stella Pence. "They gave us a wonderful reception. We were all so excited, we decided to do a festival there the next year, a one-time deal. We didn't start with any ideal. It was just, 'Let's have a party.' "

With a tribute to controversial German director Leni Riefenstahl attracting media attention, Telluride, with Card and Tom Luddy (then director of Berkeley's Pacific Film Archive) serving as codirectors with Bill Pence, was immediately successful. Luddy (now a producer whose credits include *Mishima*, *The Secret Garden*, and *My Family*), remains as a permanent codirector with Pence, but after Card and his successor and fellow silent film expert William Everson left, a system of using serious film buffs and scholars as one-year guest directors was instituted.

Judged by its often lurid past, Telluride was not a likely place for something as peaceful as a festival to flourish. Likely named after tellurium, a nonmetallic element often found combined with more prestigious ores, Telluride began as a mining town in the 1870s, and its mountains, which once yielded millions in gold, silver, copper, lead, and zinc, are still laced with enough miles of tunnels to extend from Los Angeles to San Francisco.

With a population reaching 5,000 and calling itself "The Town without a Belly Ache" because it was too prosperous to complain, Telluride, often a violent place, was the site of an 1889 escapade (the looting of the San Miguel National Bank of $24,580) by the man who went on to call himself Butch Cassidy. And in the closing years of the nineteenth century its mines were struck by the Western Federation of Miners, leading to what one source called "a miniature war" characterized by "the terrorization of the local population by armed guards and deputies and the dynamiting of company property."

By the early 1970s, the bloody past was largely forgotten and, benefiting from a close-to-innocent atmosphere Stella Pence accurately recalls as "spontaneous, loose, and easy," the film festival became a success. So much of one, in fact, that all kinds of other celebrations, including events devoted to hot air balloons, bluegrass, wine, mushrooms, and chamber music, have made the town the de facto festival capital of the Rockies, a place busy enough to decide to schedule a "Nothing Festival" where "nothing happens all over town for this annual nonevent."

Beginning with Riefenstahl, Gloria Swanson, and Francis Ford Coppola that first year, Telluride initially attracted fans because of its one-of-a-kind in-person tributes in the Sheridan Opera House, which over time came to include almost every old and new cinema notable imaginable, from Hal Roach, Karl Struss, and Ben Carre to Harriet Andersson, Clint Eastwood, and Pedro Almodovar.

Starting, Bill Pence remembers, in the festival's eighth year, when *My Dinner with André* had its world premier at Telluride, the festival also became known for showing important new work. Films like *El Norte*,

Stranger Than Paradise, *Paris, Texas*, *Blue Velvet*, and *Babette's Feast* all benefited from having either their world or their North American premiers at the festival. Some films, like Michael Moore's *Roger and Me*, even came unsolicited, arriving over the transom on the last day of the selection process.

Because filmmakers heard tales of Telluride's intimate ambiance, they often came to experience it for themselves, leading to memorable personal moments like eighty-one-year-old Cab Calloway dancing across the Opera House stage and the ninety-year-old French director Abel Gance watching from his hotel window as his epic silent film *Napoleon* was projected on an outdoor screen.

No matter what you thought about Telluride, those personal moments were always indelible. In 1977, it was electrifying for me to have the still-vibrant and gracious silent star Viola Dana speak after a screening of *Blue Jeans*, a film she'd made sixty years earlier, and to hear meticulous British director Michael Powell, celebrated for *The Red Shoes*, *Black Narcissus*, and *Thief of Baghdad*, break down after a screening of the silent *Scaramouche*, made by his master, director Rex Ingram.

Originally scheduled only to talk before the film, Powell was so overcome by seeing *Scaramouche* again after so many years that he rose afterward and told the audience, very slowly and quite emotionally, that "it was from Rex Ingram that I learned standards. It cost me a great deal, but it's been worth it."

Twenty years later, I was equally moved by a similar cross-generational moment when French director and critic Bertrand Tavernier (*Round Midnight*, *A Sunday in the Country*) introduced *Remous*, a daring 1934 film dealing with such subjects as impotence, voyeurism, and sexual desire by the little-known Edmond T. Greville.

Tavernier talked passionately of being one of four young French film buffs who'd befriended Greville in 1960, of coming to admire and appreciate his work ("even his flaws are daring"). Finally, when the director died "alone and penniless," it was Tavernier and his friends who paid for the destitute man's funeral. Of such moments are Telluride memories made.

Because it is so small and particular, Telluride has also become known for its idiosyncrasies, like the long, long lines outside theaters, which one must join to ensure getting a seat at most programs. Also, after a local newspaper made more of a fuss on the eve of an early festival about a celebrated actress canceling for health reasons than about who was actually coming, Telluride has been zealous (and largely successful) about trying to keep its selections a secret until the night before screening begins.

Experiencing all this, critic Howie Movshowitz wrote in the *Denver Post*, is "like taking an unrest cure at some remote, half-crazy and incredibly effective sanatorium. You get no sleep, your eyes wind up sinking into your cheekbones, the films start to run together and you can hardly remember your name. But you're healed."

While the festival was universally admired and envied in its early years, this kind of fragrant praise gradually became sprinkled with the doubts of naysayers. Though it continued to sell out without difficulty, Telluride was increasingly faulted for its exclusivity and claustrophobia, called precious and "almost snobbish." There were mutterings, then *Los Angeles Times* film critic Sheila Benson reported, that it had become "smug, self-congratulatory, elitist." Even as steadfast a fan as critic Movshowitz noted that Telluride had "flirted with big star syndrome for a while."

After being overwhelmed by the third and fourth Telluride festivals, I wasn't able to return until the tenth, and to my chagrin I found the thrill somewhat gone. The event seemed more emotionally uneven, alternating between celebration and self-satisfaction, and the increasing intensity of the experience was not always what I wanted. By the time everything ended, with hundreds of cinema zealots crammed into the tiny Montrose, Colorado, airport batting opinions back and forth like beachballs as they waited for planes to Denver and beyond, I found I had to retreat to the peace and solitude of the parking lot to maintain what was left of my sanity. I didn't come back for ten years.

The Pences and Tom Luddy, while noting that they can be viewed as

difficult ("We're not compromising, we don't make deals, maybe we can be a little bit too curt and honest," says Bill Pence), insist that at least from their point of view the festival's ambiance has never varied. And much of what has happened to Telluride could be attributed to the difficulties of an event gradually tripling in size as the town itself mushroomed as a ski resort and was able to accommodate increasing numbers of people. The idea that Telluride would ever be a place where a takeout spot called the Steaming Bean could sell more than 7,000 cups of coffee during the festival would have been inconceivable twenty-five years ago.

From a financial/logistical point of view, the Telluride festival has increasingly become what Bill Pence ruefully calls "a monster of its own creation." Perennially difficult and expensive to get to, Telluride is now so pricey a town that people who work in service jobs often have to live elsewhere, and the hotels, none of which existed when the festival started, now charge festival-goers what Stella Pence characterizes as "the highest of high season rates."

Festival prices, as noted, have also gone way up, a situation the Pences and Luddy agonize over, yet cannot help as long as the money from the sale of 1,300 tickets is needed to pay fully half of the event's cost. It's this desperate need for dollars to simply run the thing that has led to extensive and ever-increasing corporate sponsorship. The *Village Voice* journalist who was unnerved by the spectacle of a "Doc Martens' Southwestern Chili Chow Down" a few years back would marvel at the very visible support of Ralph Lauren and *Vanity Fair*, at a silent auction supervised by Sotheby's, and at a projected "Twenty-fifth Anniversary Special Theme Crossing" of the Queen Elizabeth II from New York to Southampton celebrating the festival.

The quest for funds is also behind the creation and persistence of high-end patron passes. Though their existence—and the right they confer to get admitted to theaters ahead of the milling crowds—have always blended awkwardly with Telluride's egalitarianism, the Pences defend these passes as essential to keeping the festival solvent and ticket prices for other attendees close to reasonable. "Patrons drive people

crazy by getting in early, but those people are essentially subsidizing everyone else's ticket," says Stella Pence. "That money means general admission tickets don't have to go up."

The way Telluride's at times controversial nature dovetailed with my own qualms about the event made me a bit wary when I returned to town for the first time in a decade in 1993 for the fest's twentieth anniversary. What I found then was still true at the twenty-fifth: Telluride was a festival whose stubborn spirit and refusal to bend had helped it weather its storm. It's not that those problems had disappeared, but rather that they felt less important in the overall scheme of things.

With new festivals willing to show anything that moves erupting almost daily, and with established events like Toronto and Sundance getting bigger and increasingly attuned to the rhythms of the commercial marketplace, Telluride's rigor, its sense of standards, and its unquestioned love of film seem increasingly of value even if they're not to everyone's taste.

Another trend in the film world that Telluride counteracts is the gradual disappearance of what Bill Pence calls "the great independent specialty houses, the art theaters. There is an audience, albeit small, for specialized films that do not find a showcase." From cities across the country, the vanguard of that audience makes its way to Telluride and is important for creating word of mouth for unheralded films. "We never wanted to be an exclusive club of film buffs," says codirector Luddy. "We want people to go back home turned on about something they hadn't known about before. We wanted the festival to have a ripple effect."

As for the event's resilience, says Luddy, "Partly it's a question of timing; most festivals are too long, they become an ordeal." And most festivals do without Telluride's centerpiece, the old-fashioned Main Street, a National Historic Landmark District, which everyone gravitates to. "It's a proximity I really like, there's still a sense that everyone's together in the same summer camp," says Bill Pence. "No one else has that particular hothouse environment, the town really does become the festival. You can't build that artificially; it's either there or it isn't."

Yet, ever mercurial, no sooner does the Telluride Film Festival seem to be set in its ways than the potential for change becomes irresistible. Just days after extolling the virtues of having the town's radioactive core as a base, codirector Pence announced that the next edition of the festival would for the first time include programming at a theater in Mountain Village, reachable only by that gondola. "For our first twenty-five years, we've been one kind of festival," Pence said. "Maybe in our twenty-sixth year we'll start to become a somewhat different kind of festival." If it didn't have that kind of attitude, it just wouldn't be Telluride.

PART FOUR

The Politics of Festivals

The Festival That Failed

We are like Cyrano. We know we cannot win, but we fight.
We are a loser, but a faithful loser.
—Daniel Toscan du Plantier,
president, Unifrance Film International

ACAPULCO—It's hot here, jungle hot. Hibiscus and bougainvillea are flourishing and the sultry air seems almost perfumed. I'm alone at Las Brisas, a celebrated pink and white honeymoon spot with private swimming pools and spectacular views, feeling, to paraphrase Raymond Chandler's been-around Philip Marlowe, as out of place as a tarantula on a piece of angelfood cake. But it doesn't matter. Like Marlowe, I'm on a case.

The death of a film festival is what I'm investigating. That's right, in this boom time for fests, with unprecedented numbers thriving and new contenders clutching at life every day, one of them up and died. At least that's what some people say.

Others, and there are always others, mutter darkly that it was hardly a natural death. Sometimes they even pull you aside, look furtively over their shoulders, and insist the festival didn't really die at all. It's still alive, they tell you nervously, living in Mexico under another name, taking advantage of the cinematic equivalent of a witness protection plan. I knew I'd have to check this one out. Personally.

First, though, I hit the books, poring over parts of the dusty archives of what used to be the Sarasota French Film Festival, which for seven years (1989–1995) was a November adornment of a Florida Gulf Coast resort town described by *Time* as "a spot so chic and pretty it might have been transported whole from the Côte d'Azur."

Its aim, said critic Molly Haskell, the festival's artistic director, was "to increase the presence and revenue of French film in America." "It enabled," *Le Monde* added with appropriate grandeur, "a minnow (the French cinema) to swim for a few moments in pike-infested waters (the American movie industry) and escape not only unharmed but reinvigorated." And now it was floating belly up like yesterday's tuna.

Sarasota was, by all reports, one hell of a party while it lasted. I scanned lists in French of local clubs and restaurants prepared for the more than a hundred film notables who were flown in annually from France. I read notes about the dozens of American journalists who also attended ("not a beach person" was the inside word on one scribe) and examined itineraries for the American stars who came as well; it was all strictly legit. And then there were all those elaborate festival meals: Chateaubriand Automne, Patés à la Chinoise, Tranche de Roquet au Saffron. Talk about a condemned man eating a hearty meal.

Just as my research was about to hit caloric overload, I got a tip. Go to Acapulco in November. Ask for something called the Festival de Ciné Français. See if anything about it looks familiar. The phone went dead and I booked my flight.

Once I arrived, it wasn't only the honeymoon atmosphere of the festival headquarters hotel that was unsettling. Though the setting was Mexican, a good deal of public advertising was in English; billboards reading "Tony Roma's Famous for Ribs," "Hooters," and a picture of Colonel Sanders with the message "Visita Kentucky Hoy" crowded the highway in from the airport.

At the modern, 1,400-seat Juan Ruíz de Alarcon theater in the city's downtown convention center, my linguistic troubles took a different turn. Here were fifteen French films showing over four days, all with

Spanish subtitles. Not completely at home in either of those languages, with not a word of English in sight, I felt overmatched and uncertain how to proceed, but I didn't want to give up. The very emotions, it turned out, that helped me break The Case of the Fugitive Film Festival wide open.

You don't have to be a detective, of course, hard-boiled or otherwise, to understand the flip side of my Acapulco situation: as disoriented as I felt dealing with French films with Spanish subtitles, that's how confused and left out foreign films feel when they attempt to penetrate what to them is the baffling English-speaking American market. With the non-English language share of the U.S. box office consistently below 1 percent, a truly anorexic level, it's a crisis that affects film industries worldwide.

But while all countries have this problem, only the French refuse to accept the situation as a given. To fully understand why the Sarasota Film Festival lived, died, and was reborn in Acapulco, it's necessary to explore the singular attitude the French have to their current and past film heritage, to appreciate a way of looking at motion pictures that is both closely allied to American attitudes and completely divorced from them.

How seriously the French were taking the problem became apparent several years ago when Daniel Toscan du Plantier convened an elaborate lunch for key American film journalists at the Cannes Film Festival. The energetic Toscan, as he is universally known, is a successful producer (*Cousin, Cousine*, Bergman's *Fanny and Alexander*, Fellini's *City of Women*, among others) who for more than a decade has been the president of Unifrance, the entity charged with promoting French film overseas.

There was a time, as everyone around the table knew, when French film needed little help in this country. During the 1960s heyday of the *Nouvelle Vague*, the French New Wave, Americans became passionate about the work of directors like François Truffaut, Jean-Luc Godard, Alain Resnais, Louis Malle, Eric Rohmer, and Claude Chabrol. If you

wanted to be considered film-literate or even just culturally sophisticated, these were pictures you had to see.

But while the French still have as many Best Foreign Language film nominations as any other country, plus the most Oscars, those days have vanished, not only for their pictures but also for all overseas product. Though there are periodic breakout films like *Cinema Paradiso*, *Life Is Beautiful*, and *Crouching Tiger, Hidden Dragon*, in general foreign films, as that anemic less than 1 percent of the market demonstrates, do not do the business or have the cachet that they once had. The audience was becoming so finite, Toscan joked, "that we've wondered, 'Why buy space for an ad in the *New York Times?* For the same money we could get a list of the people who go to our films and personally phone them all instead.'"

This situation is especially galling because of the powerful lock American films have on world markets in general, France included. More American films were released in France in 1997 than French-language films, and the United States captured a mammoth 55 percent of the French box office. In 1998, French films in France fell below 30 percent of the total audience, with only three French-made films listed among the top fifteen hits, a situation that the newspaper *Le Figaro* reported with a still from *Titanic* and the headline "Why French Cinema Is Sinking."

As discussed by the journalists around that lunch table in Cannes and revisited by Toscan in an extended interview during the Acapulco Festival, the reasons for the French fall from grace in the United States are numerous and interlocking. They range from broad societal changes like the ever-increasing competition for Americans' leisure time to specifics like the willingness of successful French directors (Luc Besson, Jean-Jacques Annaud, and, more recently, Mathieu Kassovitz) to forgo their native tongue and work on English-language projects. But all discussions inevitably come back to a trio of circumstances whose cumulative effect has been devastating.

(1) To put it as delicately as possibly, the core audience for French

films is aging into a time of life when moviegoing is not the passion it once was. "A coterie of middle-aged nostalgics" is how one writer unsympathetically described French film partisans, and Toscan himself once told the *Wall Street Journal* that "we need to go beyond that New York film type, the taxi driver wearing black reading Jean Renoir's biography in his spare time."

Though French director Bertrand Tavernier once complained about the inability of his country's films to break out of certain theaters and cities by claiming "we are kept on reservations like the Cherokee or the Navajo," those art houses and the elite press coverage that used to go with them are themselves an endangered species these days, making extended runs for foreign efforts increasingly problematic. "These films are not going to make it with the public based on thirty-second TV spots," says Michael Barker, cochairman of Sony Pictures Classics, one of the major distributors of French films in this country. "It hasn't happened before, and it won't happen now."

And while Toscan has characterized this situation by saying "French charm is obsolete," part of the difficulty is that the avatars of the latest generation of French directors, people like Arnaud Desplechin and Olivier Assayas, are influenced more by the astringent director Maurice Pialat (whose films like *A Nos Amours*, *Sous le Soleil de Satan*, and *Van Gogh* have never been popular in this country) than the empathetic Truffaut and are not very interested in being warm and cuddly. This theory is also Toscan's, who sums up by observing that "that special charm" is "no more the only definition of French cinema."

(2) As French cinema has changed, so has the new American movie audience, and for the worse. Most European audiences (except for the French, who, Toscan says, "are obsessed with original language, we have to be in the heart of authenticity") prefer to have their foreign films dubbed, but Americans have stubbornly and traditionally rejected that system. What is new is that these days, subtitles are getting just as rough a treatment.

"If you want to reach a large audience with a film, you cannot put sub-

titles on it," concedes Toscan, adding in mock exasperation, "Young people can read a computer screen, but for them the idea of reading a film is an impossible idea." One result is a frustrating situation where a Hollywood remake like *Three Men and a Baby* can earn approximately fifty times what the French original did in American business. No wonder critic Haskell, the former Sarasota artistic director, sums things up more in sorrow than anger, saying, "Americans have gotten spoiled and parochial."

(3) The audience that traditionally went to French films in the 1960s has been cannibalized by the explosive growth of the American independent movement. In decades past, to experience films that emphasized character, that were true to life and not mechanical and simplistic, to experience, in other words, an alternative to standard Hollywood product, foreign-language films were your only refuge.

But now, with independent film the hottest aspect of the American scene, audiences can get those same kinds of films without having to bother reading subtitles or hearing hollow dubbed voices. "Aside from artistic merit," adds Haskell, "in the days of the Production Code, French films had the merit of sensuality. The cachet of French cinema is that it was more adult, more sophisticated, more oo-la-la. It no longer is."

In the face of all these very substantial obstacles, other countries have to varying degrees given up on the possibility of their national cinemas making much of a dent in America's chauvinistic viewing habits. A trio of Italian cultural organizations recently started "Venezia a Hollywood," bringing five Italian films from the Venice Festival to Los Angeles, and the AFI in Washington hosts an annual European Union Film Showcase, but such efforts are few and far between, much to Toscan's discomfort. "It's my despair," he says, and he looks as though he means it.

The French, as Toscan noted, are different. Like Edmond Rostand's Cyrano de Bergerac, who persisted in loving the fair Roxanne though he knew she would never be his, the French have refused to give up on the prospects of their film industry, both at home and abroad. And that is, at least in part, because their attitude toward cinema is akin to our own.

"We have many things in common with the U.S., including taking film very seriously in terms of power," Toscan says. "We're the only countries where the presidents, both Bill Clinton and Jacques Chirac, think cinema is important enough to mention when they make state visits. We think the same; that's why we're fighting. The great empires think cinema is important. It's a kind of religion to both sides."

In addition, the French, who've made some of the world's greatest motion pictures in every decade of cinema's existence, feel, more self-consciously than Americans, that film is part of their heritage. "Cultural identity is a pretentious word in English, a heavy word, but it means something, and to French people film is one of the most important expressions of cultural identity," Toscan says. "It's not true in Italy, it's not true in Germany, it's not true in Mexico, but in France the heart of it, the best of it is the theatrical movie."

Not only, says Molly Haskell, do the French have "a sense of their own importance in movie history," they are "as moviegoers, scholars and appreciators generous in their attitude toward the rest of the world. So it's an offense to them that there's not any kind of reciprocity in the United States."

Jack Lang, France's former minister of culture and communications, echoed this sentiment when he told an interviewer, *à propos* France's determination to penetrate the U.S. market, "It's not so much a matter of making money. It's more a question of moral satisfaction. For a film to be shown in America amounts to a kind of international consecration for a foreign film maker." Added Toscan, when told by a U.S. trade representative that the film situation was the flip side of the cheese situation, that is, we eat theirs and they don't eat ours, "Our films are just as good as our cheese."

There are, obviously, elements of chauvinism in the French stance, what Haskell characterized as "a defiant attitude, a general irritation with American cinema as this kind of global juggernaut that's resented the same way they resented America going into Iraq." But along with that is the French feeling that more than being a nation-versus-nation

situation, their position represents standing up for a different kind of cinematic tradition, the personal, individualistic works that in France are known as *films d'auteur.*

"If it's either big Hollywood or little France, we are dead," says Toscan, facing facts. "We cannot fight against American power; China and India aside, the U.S. controls 75 to 80 percent of the world's market. It's not America and France, it's Hollywood and the rest of the world, including America. It's not a war, it's an attempt to survive by the rest of the world, including American independents, young American filmmakers who want to make small European films with no money. What we want to be are leaders of the alternative. What is good for cinema will surely be good for French cinema."

This is not just theoretical philosophizing. Because of that remarkable French consensus about the importance of films as part of national cultural identity, financing and taxation systems are in place that ensure ample funding for everything from modern theaters to the costs of production to the overseas activities of Unifrance.

Especially when compared to cultural funding in this country, where even traditional arts end up as beggars, the French largesse to film-related entities, which can amount to as much as $400 million per year (no, that's not a misprint) is more than impressive. It's not, Toscan explains, a line in the budget but rather a stream of revenue that flows from a series of stiff taxes, mostly on theatrical revenues. As a result, France supports close to two hundred film festivals and ranks behind only India and the United States in numbers of films made.

Also, because France, in Toscan's words, "chooses to defend cinema as culture against television as commerce," there are systems in place to ensure that the latter does not overrun the former. Television networks must invest 3 percent of their gross revenue in theatrical coproductions, and, even more against the American grain, network broadcasters aren't allowed to show films on Wednesday and Saturday nights, traditional French moviegoing evenings.

But, as people are wont to say in Los Angeles, there is money and

there is Hollywood money. In 1997, the average cost of a studio film was $53 million plus, while the average French film cost $6.2 million. In addition, the studios regularly spend more to simply promote their films than the entire budgets of French efforts, which is why the French, determined to have an impact, have turned to creating their own festivals.

"If we had $50 million to open a film, we would not be making festivals, that is something for the poor," is how Toscan puts it. To help open Hollywood-dominated markets to their films, the French have started and supported thriving festivals in several nations (including Japan, Australia, Brazil, Hungary, and the Czech Republic), and it was in this spirit that the Sarasota French Film Festival began. It was a question, Toscan says, of "organizing our survival."

The notion of placing a festival in Sarasota came, however, not from the French but from the Floridians, specifically from a veteran politician named Robert M. Johnson. A Republican who represented Sarasota in the Florida state senate, Bob Johnson was able to gather pledges from business interests as well as a financial commitment from the state legislature that ended up being worth $250,000 a year for the festival's first five years.

"Bob came to Paris with a delegation of eight old and rich ladies from Florida, and we were so surprised, no one wanted to receive them," Toscan remembers. "We'd never heard the name Sarasota, it meant nothing to us, but on the other hand in my life I'd never heard of public money in America being dedicated to cinema."

Once they got to know Sarasota and the Sarasotans, the French increasingly warmed to the idea of a festival in a wealthy beachfront community that was considered a cultural oasis and was home to a well-known art museum founded by circus magnate John Ringling.

"What we love is a nice place, a seaside to convince our film colleagues to come with us," Toscan explains. "Sarasota turned out to be a charming place, with charming people. There was a museum with great paintings, an opera house, and Ringling's son had been one of the husbands of Martine Carol. We said, 'Why don't we try?'"

The French also liked the idea of Sarasota because it offered a chance for them to display their films to potential distributors in the best possible way. "In New York, professionals look at movies in small rooms with three phones, the life of a movie is suspended on the caprice of a very few people," Toscan explained. "Here we would invite New York distributors and critics to see films in a real theater [the Asolo Center for the Performing Arts] with a real audience. Not specialists or film buffs, but nice people discovering movies they'd never heard of. Buyers are influenced by a good reception in a full theater. It's a better way to sell."

With the help of a luminary-heavy honorary committee (including Louis Malle, Douglas Fairbanks Jr., Norman Mailer, and Elie Wiesel, among others), the Sarasota festival became a reality in 1989, and at first everyone seemed to be happy.

Under artistic director Haskell, a self-described "passionate Francophile," the festival programmed the cream of French cinema, including eventual Oscar winners *Indochine* and *Burnt by the Sun* (a French coproduction). The *Miami Herald* generously proclaimed Sarasota "Florida's best pure film festival," the *New York Times* called it one of the world's up and coming events, and headlines like "19 Frenchies For Florida Fest" became common in newspapers nationwide.

The festival was also good for relations between France and Sarasota in particular ("une petite ville charmante," *France-Soir* gushed) and Florida in general. French flags appeared in windows of Sarasota shopping malls, the city achieved a name recognition in France exceeded only by Miami and Orlando among Florida metropolises, and, it was repeatedly reported, Tropicana products spiked upward in France after the festival's inauguration.

Increased orange juice sales, however, did not captivate all the people all the time, and the Sarasota Festival almost immediately faced obstacles. There were disputes about how many tickets were given away versus the number sold, run-ins with an irate local art house programmer who felt disrespected, and, perhaps inevitably, there were persistent cultural clashes.

The French were irked when *Sarasota Magazine* listed "Ten Commandments" for those wishing to become French ("marry and get yourself a mistress," "feel superior," "believe that Jerry Lewis is really, really funny"). And Sarasotans were not amused when a correspondent for *Le Figaro* wrote, "In Sarasota, only the pelicans—gorged and dirty—possess vitality."

The most long-lived and ultimately most damaging criticism had to do with the government money spent, money that, absent an American tradition of public funding for the arts, numerous local residents could not reconcile themselves to.

Molly Haskell, who remembers "a certain provincialism on the part of Sarasota," recalled comments that Senator Johnson had spent "$500,000 of Florida money so he could have lunch with Catherine Deneuve." And an irate local letter-to-the-editor writer demanded to know "what has happened to our sense of value? The French Film Festival is a pretense at high culture. . . . The dinners and receptions are aglitter in evening gowns and diamonds. Neither the films nor the receptions are of interest to the great majority of Floridians."

It was the charges against Johnson that most resonated with local voters. They surfaced in the 1992 Republican primary, when Johnson's opponent ridiculed the festival as a "pork barrel project." Johnson fought off that challenge, but despite his sixteen years in office, he was defeated in November by Democrat Jim Boczar, who made the festival the centerpiece of his campaign. Running, according to *Variety*, "on an austerity platform in this recession-hit region, his campaign oratory made frequent reference to the lavish festival as a boondoggle that cost Florida taxpayers $1 million."

With its main local champion vanquished, it was only a matter of time until the French pulled the plug on Sarasota, which, for a variety of reasons, they did in June 1996. The attacks on the festival in those political campaigns didn't endear the state to the French ("They were hostile, incredibly provincial in a bad sense," Toscan says), and the financial situation was also not promising. "It was a costly festival, we lost the sub-

sidy of Florida, there was no more support from anyone, and if we do not have private sponsorship, we must leave," Toscan explains. "We said, 'It is enough. We are fed up with Sarasota, we must find another place.'"

As Haskell points out, there was also another reason to leave Sarasota. The French, always looking to the future, were not completely happy with the audience they were getting. "It wasn't young enough," Haskell reports. "They wanted new, wider, younger audiences, and what they were getting were Francophiles, French professors, scholarly types and the national membership of the Alliance Française." Toscan agrees: "In a way we were glad to leave Florida. It was not a place for young people but for old ladies speaking about Truffaut."

Though the festival concept did not work in Sarasota, the French have by no means given up on the United States as a market for their films. Toscan has all kinds of schemes afoot, from hosting several smaller festivals to possibly supporting French films once they are released out of a special fund for prints and advertising. "The U.S. market is essential to us," he says, "but very difficult."

Neither have the French given up on the festival concept as the best way to get their films wider exposure and distribution around the world; given their zeal for the cinema, there is no way they could. Which is how the Sarasota French Film Festival moved south, took advantage of government subsidies, and became Acapulco's Festival de Ciné Français, which annually plays host to journalists, distributors, and exhibitors from Argentina, Brazil, Chile, Colombia, Cuba, Peru, Uruguay, and Venezuela (as well as, of course, Mexico), in sum a sizable potential market.

Things were not always this bright. When the French were considering Acapulco as a festival site, Toscan visited with director and cinephile Tavernier. "We went to a school classroom and asked 'have any of you heard of French cinema?' and the answer was 'no,'" he remembers. "In desperation, Bertrand asked if anyone had seen a French film, and a boy in the back raised his hand. 'My father spoke about a French film,' he said. 'It was called *Emmanuelle*.'"

Despite this unpromising beginning, Acapulco, where young people

in fact make up a healthy proportion of the audience, is turning into a genuine beachhead for French cinema. Congenitally upbeat, Toscan is delighted. The future here and elsewhere, if he has anything to do with it, will have a distinctly French accent.

"If you are on a street full of hamburger shops, you finally want to eat something else," Toscan sums up, brimming with passion. "If you hear there is an old lady who prepares *cassoulet* in a small apartment on the second floor, you will go there, you will seek her out. In a film world where there is too much noise, too much *Independence Day*, French cinema is *cassoulet* on the second floor."

I, the Jury

He was all eagerness and animation, this young man deep in conversation in a hotel lobby. "The aesthetics of these films are so different," he insisted to his friends, eyes hot with emotion. "I can't imagine being on the jury at this festival."

I had to smile as I walked past, not only because the speaker reminded me of myself a couple of decades back, but also because I happened to be one of the seven members of the jury at the twentieth Montreal World Film Festival. And in fact the state of affairs was as the young man imagined, a situation hard to visualize in the abstract that became more surprising, more exhausting, and more gratifying than almost any cinematic experience I could remember.

It was because the work of juries was so closed off and unknowable to outsiders that I'd been curious to participate for almost as long as I'd realized the position existed. My interest in juries as forces for good intensified after Cannes in 1993 when the chairman, French director Louis Malle, engineered the decision most people wanted but dared not dream of: a rare splitting of the Palme d'Or between Jane Campion's *The Piano* and Chen Kiage's *Farewell My Concubine*.

Understandably pleased with what he had accomplished, Malle came over to chat with a group of American journalists at the closing night

party. "I'm as proud of having done this," he said, satisfaction all over his face, "as anything in my career."

Of course, through the years I'd heard all kinds of other stories about how these panels operated, juicer tales that made jury life seem well suited for a series on the Fox Network. Rumors of backbiting, rivalries, and jealousy were everywhere, as were festivals where the films hadn't shown up, where jurors needed bodyguards or played tennis instead of seeing the movies, where a juror had insisted on taking her unruly cat to all the screenings, only to have it invariably escape and disrupt the theater.

Sometimes factionalism on juries had become so extreme that a film won because both sides detested it equally. Berlin before the Communists fell, with its wall dividing the city between the West and the Soviet bloc, had been a natural setting for divisiveness. One jury member remembered a Russian actress who announced, before a single film had been screened, that voting for anything from the United States or Canada was out of the question for her.

Especially good for trouble was the anarchic German director Rainer Werner Fassbinder. Once, in a particularly provocative mood, he determined what the worst film in the Berlin competition was and insisted it win the Golden Bear, reducing an American actress on the jury to tears of frustration and rage.

Perhaps my favorite jury tale came from Donald Ritchie, the doyen of Western writers on Japanese film, who described how you indicate preference in a country where expressing strong opinions is frowned on. "First everyone around the table mentions all the entries and agrees 'these are all good films.' On the second round, you do the same thing and, if there is a film you favor, you name it at the end and say 'this, this also is a good film.'"

Since the kind of jury experience I'd have would depend on my fellow panel members, all chosen by festival head Serge Losique, I was naturally curious as to who they were. The renowned French actress Jeanne Moreau was to be the chairman, to be joined by another award-winning

actress, Spain's Assumpta Serna, and a former critic, Guglielmo Biraghi from Italy, who'd also run both the Taormina and Venice festivals in his country.

Two members were directors: Cuba's Humberto Solás, whose *Lucia* was a classic of Latin American cinema, and Hungary's Judit Elek, whose *To Speak the Unspeakable—The Message of Elie Wiesel* had just been well received at Cannes. Finally there was French Canadian producer Denis Heroux, with films like *Atlantic City* and *Quest for Fire* to his credit.

It was an impressive group. Maybe even too impressive. Suddenly I realized I was the only native English speaker on the entire panel. How would we communicate, I wondered, and other worries, each more irrational than the last, soon followed.

Would I be faced with a cabal of aesthetic zealots whose taste would run to the obscure and unwatchable? Would I in reaction turn into the worst kind of American chauvinist, insisting on the plastic qualities of Sylvester Stallone's work? Would I get a late-night phone call from Jack Valenti, pleading with me to stand by the flag? Clearly this jury business might be more complicated than I thought.

Although Montreal is one of the world's larger film festivals, showing hundreds of films over its twelve-day span, only twenty-one of those would be in the official competition, and when I got a look at the list of titles, a completely different set of concerns made themselves known.

While the competition films came from sixteen countries (including Albania, India, Iran, Israel, Romania, Sweden, and South Korea), most of them were unknown to me, made by directors I was unfamiliar with, or both. What if the unthinkable happened and I couldn't find anything to get passionate about? Or what if everyone loved everything I hated, and vice versa? Would I be subject to cutting remarks in obscure languages? Or worse?

Once I arrived in Montreal and made my way through the hefty 400-page official program, I began to realize that the festival's international quality, both in and out of competition, was the essence of its identity. It is also critical to how the World Film Festival defines itself in relation to

its rival some three hundred miles down Highway 401, the Toronto International Film Festival.

Though their dates are close (Toronto began three days after Montreal ended) and they often try to snare the same films, the festivals say they don't really compete with each other, and while that sounds like a publicity nostrum, the claim contains a core of truth. Near as they are geographically, Montreal and Toronto can be seen as representing opposite poles of today's film world.

Toronto shows its share of obscure and worthwhile films, but its ethos, the reason for its success, is that it's the place to go if you want to be the first on your block to see what's going to be hot in the upcoming fall season. And as the movie business changed and it became clear that lucrative acquisition deals could be made on smaller pictures, Toronto became the North American equivalent of Cannes, the place where films are seen, the heat created, and the handshakes given.

Even French Canadian films made in the province of Quebec, like Robert Lepage's *Le Confessional* and Jean-Claude Lauzon's *Leolo*, films that should have been naturals for Montreal, premiered at Toronto's event for commercial reasons. As Piers Handling, director of the Toronto Festival, told *Maclean's*, the Canadian news magazine, his city is "friendly, safe and anglophone. The Americans don't feel like they are going to a foreign city, which is important to them."

Montreal, by contrast, exists to show films that not only won't get hot but also may in fact never be so much as seen elsewhere. Serge Losique, who founded the event, wrote in the program that "the Festival has become an obligatory dose of oxygen for those who are interested in what is being made in foreign cinemas." Says French actor Gérard Depardieu, who visited in 1995, "It's what I call Cinema Planet." For cinephiles like director Brian De Palma, who comes most years to sample the wide selection, no other festival can replace its breadth and noncommercial environment.

In some ways typical of Montreal fare (though paradoxically scheduled for Toronto as well), was something called *Seven Servants*, a hope-

lessly absurd film starring Anthony Quinn as a caftan-clad tycoon searching for meaning in his life. He pays a man $10,000 to put a finger in his ear and keep it there twenty-four hours a day for ten days. Then he pays another man to do the same for the other ear, a third man to do likewise for one nostril, a forth for the second. Most of the film consists of these five people moving in tandem across lawns and floors like some enormous crab. Really.

This international mix has been extremely popular with Montreal's citizens (annual attendance in the 400,000 range allows the event to call itself the largest publicly attended film festival in the Western world). More than that, it seems fair to speculate that on a psychological level the city probably had no choice but to host an event like this.

Montreal is a bilingual metropolis in the only Canadian province with a francophone majority, and its obsession with what the local French press calls "la crise linguistique" reaches a level of intensity difficult for outsiders to credit. So this city's festival could no more bend over backward to make English speakers feel at home than Toronto's could insist on Chinese subtitles for all its films.

Like many of the world's intractable crises, the battle between English and French in Montreal and Quebec has a long and complex history. Concerned that French is disappearing under the inexorable tide of worldwide English hegemony, the province's ruling Parti Québecois has pushed through a series of laws to redress the balance, like one that says all English commercial signs must be either half the size or half as numerous as their French counterparts.

(Sometimes this determination to protect national character can go to extreme lengths. In an episode the local press called "Matzogate," kosher for Passover products imported from the United States with English-only labels were pulled from Quebec shelves only two weeks before the holiday. When a compromise was reached between the government and the Jewish community, the *Gazette*, the city's only English-language newspaper, made "Passover Products Cleared" the four-column banner across the top of page one.)

Ever since a province-wide referendum on the possibility of independence for Quebec ended in almost a dead heat (everyone in the city knows the 50.6 percent "no" versus 49.4 percent "yes" figures), the situation has gotten, if possible, worse, with a new militancy on the part of English speakers leading to newspaper headlines about "the summer of the angry anglo."

One of the results of these internecine battles is a film festival that has been called more determinedly French than Cannes. When director Lina Wertmüller, admitting that her English was abominable and her French a disgrace, asked the audience which language she should use to introduce her film, all the voices boomed "française." Said one journalist, upset about the increasing number of French films shown without English subtitles, "I've been coming here for twenty years and the siege mentality gets worse and worse."

Aside from its determination to stay international and not become what scoffers call "a dog and pony show for Hollywood," what sets Montreal apart from Toronto and gives it a distinctive character is that it's the only Class A competitive film festival in North America recognized by the International Federation of Film Producers Association, putting it on a par with the European big four of Cannes, Berlin, Venice, and Moscow. Which is where we the jury rejoin the picture.

Their resumes notwithstanding, the jurors turned out to be a genial and good-humored bunch, constitutionally averse to taking themselves too seriously. On the average each member had been on half a dozen panels (Guglielmo Biraghi had been on that many in a single year), and it was a source of some amusement to find what one of them called "a jury virgin" in their midst.

The chairman, Jeanne Moreau, had previously headed juries in Cannes, Berlin, New Delhi, Avoriaz, and Monte Carlo. At once spontaneous, conscientious, and playful (novelist Nadine Gordimer, a fellow judge at Cannes, called her personality "an unlikely combination, at once imperious and lovable"), Moreau set an admirable tone for the proceedings. "Judging isn't protecting yourself from emotion," she said at a

press conference. "How can you approach a film coldly? You have to open up and be ready to receive. Cinema is the mirror of the world."

Judging soon settled into a soothing routine. Each morning the seven of us would rendezvous at the lovely circa 1912 Cinema Imperial for a double bill that began at nine and was broken in half by a coffee break at an adjoining festival office. Not only did we always sit in the same blocked off row, such was the force of habit that we ended up almost always occupying the same seats.

Because gossiping to outsiders about what we liked or disliked is understandably forbidden, being on a jury encourages a sense of removal from the rest of the festival. Not for us was dishing the hot films or keeping tabs on what everyone was saying, both critical to the life of a working journalist. Locked into a kind of monastic seclusion, we became dependent on each other for companionship and stimulation.

That traveling-in-a-bubble factor creates one of the most satisfying aspects of jury life, the sense of bonding among members that begins, probably in much the way it did for the O.J. Simpson jurors, in a camaraderie of misery.

For while it's a given of festival life that walking out on endless, pointless, and uninvolving films is not only permissible but also essential to maintain a semblance of mental health, if you are on a jury you absolutely, positively cannot leave. As we suffered together through films that were tedious beyond belief, we identified strongly with each other, not to mention a character in one competition film who screamed "Art takes sacrifice" as a group of prostitutes emptied chamber pots on his head. Sacrifice indeed.

Part of the reason journalists and audience members can leave but we couldn't is because what a jury does matters. Reviews and public cheers and hisses come and go, but awards last and often have a considerable impact on the success of the films in competition as well as the careers of people who make them.

This was something everyone in our group implicitly understood. We were serious, we were professional, and we worked so assiduously that

we may have been the first jury in Montreal history to spend considerably more time in meetings than at parties.

While some juries get together only once, to take a final vote, the seven of us met for hours-long sessions every other day. Because Moreau did not want anyone to experience frustration at being unheard, we discussed each film at length, thoroughly airing our likes and dislikes, pulling apart and dissecting what we loved as well as what we didn't.

Familiar with the acrimony that can attend similar discussions at critics' organizations, I was impressed by the intelligence and tolerance of the group and how willing everyone was to acknowledge flaws in their favorites and tolerate unfamiliar opinions. As jurors sipped cups of black coffee and talked through clouds of cigarette smoke about life, literature, the theater, and film, our meetings resembled those vivid Parisian cafe conversations that were a staple of the classic French New Wave films of the 1960s.

Enhancing that sensation was the fact that the discussions, excursions into both Spanish and English notwithstanding, were often in the language the jury as a whole was most comfortable in, which turned out to be French. Yes, everyone understood English and was happy enough to translate what I didn't understand, and, yes, this kind of immersion experience markedly improved my comprehension during the course of the festival. But still it was disheartening to represent American parochialism by being the only juror who wasn't bilingual at the very least.

When it came time for the jury's final meeting, the thoroughness of our previous sessions paid considerable dividends. Not only had we already eliminated many of the least worthy contenders, but also we'd gained a respect for each other's opinions that mitigated against the kind of going-down-with-the-ship fanaticism that had doomed other juries to deliberations that lasted till early in the morning.

Instead, within the space of a couple of hours, we very smoothly allocated the seven awards (plus two for shorts) within our power. Because none of the twenty-one features turned out to be a life-changing masterpiece that insisted on its preeminence, we were faced instead with the

task of distributing the awards in a sensible manner among the films that we felt were strongest.

The top prize, the augustly named Grand Prix of the Americas, went to a British film, *Different for Girls*, that convincingly brought the conventions of romantic comedy to the rarely seen world of transsexuals. The film had its problems, but the core relationship, impeccably acted by Steven Macintosh and Rupert Graves, was everything it should be.

In our most Solomonic move, we split the festival's runner-up award, the Special Grand Prix of the Jury, between two very different films. *Un Air de Famille*, directed by France's Cedric Klapisch, was a hilarious, perfectly pitched black comedy about a feuding family that also won the People's Choice Award as the festival's most popular film. It shared the jury prize with an elusive, elliptical, beautifully shot Japanese film called *Sleeping Man*, a small work that charmed us with its determination to be, as one jury member put it, "off-, off-, one hundred times off-Broadway."

That final meeting, and the satisfaction we all took in being as fair as we could, underlined what I came to appreciate most about jury service. It was the rare sense of being part of a community that believes in film, that cares deeply enough about the medium to put in the effort necessary to reward good work. So much of the film business, for actors, writers, directors, and producers as well as for critics, is frustrating and adversarial that having the opportunity to work closely together for the common good was more gratifying than I could have imagined.

Several hours after the public awards ceremony, as I was headed out for a late-night bagel run (Montreal has the world's best), I found myself alone in an elevator with of the filmmakers involved with *Sleeping Man*. He looked at me and gravely said, "Thank you. It is a great honor. We did not expect it."

Louis Malle, I think, would have understood how I felt.

Compositor: BookMatters, Berkeley
Text: 10/15 Adobe Janson
Display: Adobe Janson
Printer and Binder: Friesens

W9-COT-560

PASTORAL NOMADISM IN THE MARI KINGDOM (ca. 1830-1760 B.C.)

AMERICAN SCHOOLS OF ORIENTAL RESEARCH
DISSERTATION SERIES

edited by

David Noel Freedman

Number 3

PASTORAL NOMADISM IN THE MARI KINGDOM
(ca. 1830-1760 B.C.)

by

Victor Harold Matthews

PASTORAL NOMADISM IN THE MARI KINGDOM
(ca. 1830-1760 B.C.)

by

Victor Harold Matthews

Published by
American Schools of Oriental Research

Distributed by

American Schools of Oriental Research
126 Inman Street
Cambridge, MA 02139

PASTORAL NOMADISM IN THE MARI KINGDOM (ca. 1830-1760 B.C.)

by
Victor Harold Matthews

Cover design by Elizabeth Slote.

Library of Congress Cataloging in Publication Data

Matthews, Victor Harold.
Pastoral Nomadism in the Mari Kingdom (ca. 1830-1760 B.C.

(Dissertation series ; no. 3)
Originally presented as the author's thesis, Brandeis, 1977.
Bibliography: p. 000.
Includes index.
1. Mari, Syria—Civlization. 2. Nomads—Syria—Mari. I. Title. II. Series.
DS99.M3M37 1978 935'.02 78-16341
ISBN 0-89757-103-7

Printed in the United States of America

FOREWORD

I owe my initial interest in ancient Near Eastern Studies to Dr. James Moyer of Southwest Missouri State University, whose encouragement and continued friendship supported me throughout my work at Brandeis. I have benefitted from his suggestions in the reworking of the manuscript, and he encouraged me to publish my findings.

This study was undertaken at the suggestion of Dr. Dwight W. Young, who first introduced me to the letters of the Mari archive. He and I both felt that further work was needed on the historical anthropology of the Mari kingdom -- specifically, the pastoral nomadic tribes. He has made numerous suggestions which have aided in the completion of this present work. He has throughout my graduate studies given of himself as a friend and advisor.

I also wish to express my thanks to Dr. Helen Codere, the Dean of the Graduate School. Her suggestions in regard to the anthropological materials utilized in this study have been invaluable, and her scrupulous attention in reading the manuscript has added immeasurably to its readability.

I also owe a debt of gratitude to Dr. Ian Todd, whose suggestions on the origins of domestication and the archeological data used in sections of this work represent a large contribution.

The somewhat revised version of my dissertation which appears below contains many additions and suggestions graciously provided me by Professor Michael B. Rowton. He took time from his own work on this subject to scrupulously read through my manuscript and point out those areas which needed to be corrected or improved. I am deeply in his debt for this service and wish to express my thanks to him here. He has demonstrated his true stature as a scholar by aiding me in this manner despite the fact that we have never met.

Finally, I wish to express my real sense of appreciation and love for my wife Carol, who has spent many hours proofreading my manuscript and providing needed solace when the work was going slowly. Her patience and understanding have contributed in large part to the completion of this study.

TABLE OF CONTENTS

ABBREVIATIONS

AA	*American Anthropologist*
AfO	*Archiv für Orientforschung*
AGI	*Archivio Glottologico Italiano*
AHw.	W. von Soden. *Akkadisches Handworterbuch*
AJA	*American Journal of Archaeology*
AJBA	*Australian Journal of Biblical Archaeology*
Akk.	Akkadian
Am.An.	*American Antiquity*
A.N.E.T.	J. B. Pritchard. *Ancient Near Eastern Texts Relating to the Old Testament*, (3rd edition, with supplement). Princeton, N.J., 1969.
An.Or.	*Analecta Orientalia*
AOAT	*Alter Orient und Altes Testament*
AOS	*American Oriental Series*
AQ	*Anthropological Quarterly*
ARM	*Archives royales de Mari* (*TCL* 22-)
ARMT	*Archives royales de Mari* (texts in transliteration and translation)
Ar.Or.	*Archiv Orientální*
AS	*Assyriological Studies* (Chicago)
AZR	*Arid Zone Research*
BA	*Biblical Archeologist*
BARB	*Bulletin de l'accadêmie royale d'archêologie de Belgique*
BASOR	*Bulletin of the American Schools of Oriental Research*
Basseri	F. Barth. *A Tribe of the Khamseh Confederacy: The Basseri Nomads of South Persia.* Oslo, 1961.
Benj.	G. Dossin, "Benjaminites dans les textes de Mari," *Mélanges syriens offerts à M. René Dussaud, II.* Paris, 1939, 981-96. (text numbers are based on page number and placement on page, i.e., 985:a).
Bi.Or.	*Bibliotheca Orientalis* (Leiden)
BJRL	*Bulletin of the John Rylands Library*
BRM	Babylonian Records in the Library of J. P. Morgan

BZAW	*Beihefte Zeitschrift für die Alttestamentliche Wissenschaft*
CAD	*The Assyrian Dictionary of the Oriental Institute of the University of Chicago*
CAH²	*Cambridge Ancient History* (2nd edition)
CBQ	*Catholic Biblical Quarterly*
Ḫabiru	J. Bottéro. *Le problème des Ḫabiru à la 4e recontre assyriologique internationale*. Paris, 1954.
HUCA	*Hebrew Union College Annual*
IEJ	*Israel Exploration Journal*
ILR	*International Labour Review*
IOS	*Israel Oriental Studies*
ISSJ	*International Social Science Journal*
JANES	*Journal of the Ancient Near Eastern Society of Columbia University*
JAOS	*Journal of the American Oriental Society*
JBL	*Journal of Biblical Literature*
JCS	*Journal of Cuneiform Studies*
JESHO	*Journal of the Economic and Social History of the Orient*
JNES	*Journal of Near Eastern Studies*
JNSL	*Journal of Northwest Semitic Languages*
JRAI	*Journal of the Royal Anthropological Institute of Great Britain and Ireland*
JSS	*Journal of Semitic Studies*
Les nomades	J.-R. Kupper. *Les nomades en Mésopotamie au temps des rois de Mari*. Paris, 1957.
MEJ	*Middle Eastern Journal*
OA	*Oriens Antiquus*
OB	Old Babylonian
OLZ	*Orientalistische Literaturzeitung*
Or.	*Orientalia*
PAPS	*Proceedings of the American Philosophical Society*
PMAS	*Papers of the Michigan Academy of Science, Arts, and Letters*
PPS	*Proceedings of the Prehistoric Society*
RA	*Revue d'assyriologie et d'archéologie orientale*
RAI	*Rencontre assyriologique internationale*

RB	*Revue biblique*
RMSSJ	*Rocky Mountain Social Science Journal*
RSO	*Rivista degli studi orientali*
SAOC	*Studies in Ancient Oriental Civilization*
SIA	*Studia Instituti Anthropos*
Studies, Landsberger	*Studies in Honor of Benno Landsberger on his Seventy-Fifth Birthday* (*AS* 16)
SVT	*Supplement to Vetus Testamentum*
SWJA	*Southwestern Journal of Anthropology*
TCL	*Textes cunéiformes du Louvre*
TCM	*Textes cunéiformes de Mari*
TIM	*Texts in the Iraq Museum*
TGOS	*Transactions of the Glasgow University Oriental Society*
UF	*Ugarit Forschungen*
VS	*Vorderasiatische Schriftdenkmäler*, Berlin, Staatliche Museum
VT	*Vetus Testamentum*
WA	*World Archaeology*
WO	*Die Welt des Orients*
WZHB	*Wissenschaftliche Zeitschrift der Humboldt-Universität zu Berlin*
YBC	tablets in the *Babylonian Collection*, Yale University Library
ZA	*Zeitschrift für Assyriologie und verwandte Gebiete*
ZDMG	*Zeitschrift der deutschen morgenländischen Gesellschaft*

LIST OF SYMBOLS

Symbol	Meaning
<	comes from
>	becomes
-	separates syllables in transliteration
[ ]	indicates broken or uncertain readings in the transliteration
< >	indicates scribal omission in transliteration and in phonemic transcription
{ }	indicates scribal plusses in transliteration and in phonemic transcription
!	indicates an unusual or noteworthy reading of the cuneiform text

INTRODUCTION

The cuneiform texts produced in the northern Mesopotamian kingdom of Mari, which date from approximately 1830 to 1760 B.C., mention several tribal groups. There were both sedentary and pastoral nomadic members of these tribes. Despite the fact that the textual information concerning them offers an excellent addition to the social and cultural history of the Old Babylonian period, only a few historians[1] have studied them in depth. My examination will first set forth an outline of the main facets of the occupational existence of the ancient nomadic herdsmen of the Mari region. An attempt will then be made to establish the proper role played by all of the segments of the tribal population mentioned in the texts.

The majority of the published textual material from the Mari (Tell Harîrî) archive has come into general circulation since 1941. Of the nearly 20,000 clay tablets unearthed, approximately 1,700 have been hand-copied, transliterated, and translated in the *Archive royales de Mari*(hereafter *ARM*) series.[2] The team of French scholars in charge of the publication of the texts has also placed a number of these documents in journals and books. The texts describe economic, legal and administrative activities during the reigns of the kings Yaḫdun-Lim, Šamši-Addu (and his sons Yasmaḫ-Addu and Išme-Dagan), and Zimri-Lim.[3] They also include reports on the everyday happenings of the royal court and the activities of the local provincial functionaries. Among the dispatches from these officials there is evidence of close interaction between the various pastoral nomadic tribal groups and the state and local government.

The cuneiform tablets in the *ARM* series which specifically mention the members of the tribal units (primarily Yaminites, Ḫaneans, and Suteans) number about 200. Sixty additional documents have appeared in the other publication sources. This body of textual material will serve as the foundation for the statements on tribal customs, economic activities, and social contacts which will appear in the succeeding chapters. In addition to this, a number of anthropological studies will be

used to help clarify and explain the textual information.

Previous studies of the Mari period have dealt primarily with the urban civilization which produced the monumental remains and cuneiform documents.[4] This is only natural since the texts themselves perpetuate the point of view of the dominant culture. They exhibit the prejudices of their authors and must be assessed in that light. J. T. Luke, in his dissertation on the effects of urban politics on the pastoral tribes in the Mari kingdom, provides a clear warning about this situation. He notes that "any satisfactory historical estimate of the role of the tribal groups of the Mari period must attempt to penetrate that assessment (based on the values and designs of the urban ruling group's version)-- to continually test the claims made about the pastoralists and villagers by the authorities."[5] It is my intention in dealing with this material to test these claims by the government officials and to ascertain the actual position in the Mari kingdom of the pastoral nomadic tribal groups.

The search for water and pasture for their herds kept the pastoral nomads of the Mari kingdom for major portions of the year in the steppe and mountain regions on the frontier of the settled zone. Thus, their contact with the urban authority, based in Mari, was generally through lesser government officials. The members of the provincial bureaucracy dealt with most of the tribalists' concerns. They would at times ask advice from the government center or even refer a case which seemed to exceed their authority. On occasion the king took a personal interest in very delicate negotiations, or when it became necessary to compel the tribes to obey an order.[6] My discussion will point out and attempt to explain the reasons for the alliances which were made by the nomadic pastoralists with the Mari government. There will also be an examination of the tensions which surfaced as a result of the contacts between the urban and nomadic cultures.

The tribal groups are most often mentioned in the Mari texts in connection with a threat to the state or to the smooth administration of the provinces. They at times appear to be thought of by the officials in a collective sense. Still, there is some dialogue between members of the tribal community

(especially the tribal chiefs) and the government authorities. This supplies the most help in distinguishing the role of the tribes in Mari society. In order to further advance the process of clarifying the texts, it is my intention to merge this evidence from the cuneiform documents with analogous data on modern or near-modern pastoral nomadic groups.

Analogy does have its dangers and can only be used when there is a clear understanding of the social context as well as the differences made by time and the shifting environmental conditions of the region. Improper suggestions would strain the credibility of legitimate comparisons which an examiner might make. One study dealing with the use of analogy has recently been published by A.S. Gilbert, an anthropologist.[7] He suggests caution in its use when examining modern and prehistoric pastoral groups. His presentation demonstrates that the use of analogous material is often problematic because of the extreme changes which have occurred in technical knowledge and the resulting social changes in the course of the millennia.[8]

Gilbert points out that a sort of accordion effect is produced as new inventions and political changes are introduced. Further, it cannot be assumed that two different pastoral nomadic groups can be examined in the same light simply because they both happen to occupy roughly the same geographical area, with basically the same climatic conditions. The nomadic herdsmen would constantly be faced with pressures from their changing natural environment. They would also have to deal with political fluctuations as the urban authority in their region grew in strength or declined.[9] These conditions could push simple households, as well as entire tribal groups, into forced migratory detours or into social transformations.[10] Gilbert summarizes his argument with the axiom that "changes in society imply changes in the pastoral adaptation."[11]

This assessment of the usefulness of modern analogies in the reconstruction of the culture of prehistoric nomadic pastoralists is substantially correct. However, the evidence found in the reports of anthropologists and travelers prior to the First World War demonstrates that at least in tribal and political structure there is a very significant degree of simi-

larity between the sheep nomads of the 2nd millennium A.D. and those of the Mari period.[12]

In this century modern technical advances and machinery have begun to supplant herding methods which have been utilized for centuries.[13] In an effort to counterbalance this, I have gathered anthropological data on tribal groups which come from approximately the same geographical and social environment as the Mari tribes.[14] However, because tribal society has lost much of its cohesion in recent decades,[15] the concept of an integrated tribal society such as that which existed in the Mari period can not always be well documented through the use of modern anthropological studies. They can merely serve as one tool in our attempt to outline the probable character of the economic, social, and political situation in the Mari kingdom.

Both the members of the Mari tribes and their more recent counterparts comprised a well-defined and relatively numerous segment of the population. The cuneiform texts reveal that they too had to contend with the expansion of agricultural villages and the periodic shifts in political hegemony.[16] The nomadic pastoralists of the Mari kingdom, as well as the modern nomadic herding groups, were faced with periodic changes of political masters. These political changes sometimes resulted in suppression of the social practices, basic economic activities, and the traditional migratory patterns of the tribal groups.

It is not my intention, however, to attempt to make inflexible statements in defense of possible parallels between the Mari pastoral nomads and more modern tribal groups. The anthropological field studies which will be utilized in this study will provide a body of source material from which it will be possible to draw a basic outline of the occupational and social structures of the nomadic pastoralists of ancient Syria. The analogies which will be made are those which seem to bear directly on the textual evidence and contribute to its better understanding.

In order to arrive at a clear understanding of pastoral nomadism as an occupational specialization, it is necessary to investigate the total environment in which it is practiced. The

culture of pastoral people revolves around herding. Simple maintenance of their flocks and herds is of prime concern. Thus, whatever aids or threatens this task shapes most of their activities. Such factors as rainfall, water and grazing rights, and topographical and climatic conditions are always topics of concern and deliberation among pastoral people. The success or failure of their herding endeavors often depends upon their knowledge of their region and its resources.

One structural adaptation developed by pastoral nomadic groups, both ancient and modern, to deal with such factors is a smoothly functioning system of personnel interchange. This allows members of different tribal subsections to move freely from one herding unit to another without losing their former ties. The purpose of this system is primarily to help the pastoralists maintain the optimum herding size. It is influenced by both social and environmental controls.[17] Once it has become established among the tribal groups, an almost continuous movement of herding personnel and their families is initiated. These men and their families, who have been forced into the job market by economic setbacks (usually based on herd losses) are absorbed into more prosperous tribal sections or into the settled community.[18] Some of these surplus herdsmen may be hired by owners of larger flocks or by village pastoralists.[19]

Various circumstances at times combine which require pastoral nomads to establish economic ties with agricultural settlements or with the urban authority. The herders, because of their specialized economy, cannot provide all the food and manufactured goods which they may need or want. To obtain them they will either have to agree to mutual aid pacts with the villagers or resort to the use of force.[20]

Forceful means of obtaining these supplementary products can take the form of out and out raiding or, in some cases, the establishment of a regular collection of tribute from towns and villages for which they provide "protection services."[21] Both the peaceful and coercive courses of action may initiate changes in the tribal society. The development of social and economic ties can entice some of the tribal members (usually from the upper or lower economic levels)[22] to copy or join the seemingly more attractive and stable urban mode of living. This may re-

sult from a growing financial dependency or simply envy. On the other hand, the use of intimidation by the nomads eventually can lead the central government to take measures to limit their movements or even force them to become sedentarized.[23]

The activities and political dealings of the provincial governors mentioned in the texts provide some of the most important evidence on information exchange and decision making in the Mari kingdom.[24] These officials, known as *merhū*, were appointed by the king. No other member of the Mari bureaucracy had as much to do directly with the nomadic tribes. They were concerned primarily with the *nawûm* (defined by M. B. Rowton as "a nomadic group including the men, livestock, and camp")[25] and with the actions of the nomadic tribalists. Their role has been further clarified by a number of texts which have appeared recently in *ARMT* XIV.[26]

As a rule, nomadic pastoral tribes do not depend upon a single leader, but prefer to decide tribal policy by a vote of the council of elders. The tribal members chosen as *šībūtum*[27] apparently served in this capacity among the Mari tribes. F. Barth, one of the foremost anthropologists in the field of arid zone nomadic pastoralism, has suggested that among many tribes it is only when direct relations between nomadic and sedentary peoples occur that the channels of communication and administration devolve upon a chief or other tribal leader.[28] In the Mari letters the *sugāgum*,[29] tribal chief, served as a mediator and contact point between the government and the members of the tribal groups. However, his autonomy was not always absolute. As in the case of other leaders created or tolerated by the state, the *sugāgū* were at times exploited,punished, or eliminated when the costs of controlling them became exorbitant.[30]

The political climate was also an important force in determining the activities of the pastoral nomadic groups. During the period documented by the Mari texts, there were shifts of kingship, but a certain continuity was maintained in dealing with the provinces. It is possible to draw the conclusion from the texts that the tribes enjoyed somewhat more freedom of action during the Assyrian interregnum under Šamši-Addu than during the reign of Zimri-Lim. However, this was probably due to

the differing economies under the two dynasts.[31] Once the new regime became established, the basic administrative policy remained just about the same in respect to the tribes. The only major changes which the pastoralists had to contend with were the periodic transfers of the professional bureaucrats from one provincial outpost to the next.[32]

For the most part, the nomadic pastoralists were tolerated in the Mari kingdom. At times they were even courted by the government as a source of mercenary soldiers and gang labor. When there is a mention of friction in the texts between sedentary and nomadic groups, it is usually based upon conflicting economic interests or a disagreement over the extent to which the political powers of the Mari government should be exercised over the tribes. Both were members of what has been described as a dimorphic society[33] (i.e., one in which there is the double process of interaction between nomad and sedentary and between tribe and state). As such, they functioned as integral parts of the entire culture of the region. Their actions were based upon the mixed situation in which they lived.

Two other topics to be considered in the examination of the interaction of these two communities are the "process of sedentarization"[34] of the Mari tribal groups and the status of that group of people described as *ḫabirū*.[35] As part of this discussion, some attention also will be given to the theory of "withdrawal" and its applicability to the situation in the Mari kingdom. This concept of social behavior was first put forth by G. E. Mendenhall in his study of the Israelite "conquest" of the land of Canaan.[36] It was his contention that when the pressures and power of the existing political regime became too intolerable to a sizable percentage of the population, they would move to a point outside the political authority of the governing state. They would then renounce their obligations to that state and work to undermine the loyalties of the remainder of the population which it still controlled. Through the use of these subversive activities, they would eventually be able to siphon away the strength of the offending government. The final outcome would then be their own takeover of the region and its people.

Mendenhall's student, J. T. Luke, took up this theory in

more detail and applied it to portions of the Mari pastoral nomads and the *ḫabirū* elements of the population.[37] More recently, N. K. Gottwald has again expanded the hypothesis as it applies to the Israelite tribes of the conquest and settlement period.[38]

The basic elements of the theory of "withdrawal" have some validity for the discussion of the activities of the *ḫabirū*. They formed bands of uprooted and fugitive men and staged their raids from territories outside the control of the government.[39] However, I have some reservations about the limitations which Mendenhall has placed on the use of this concept. My main objection is that he rules out its applicability to those migrations which are compensatory in nature, lasting only short periods of time. Such movement may be necessary in order to obtain better grazing and may take the herders to areas outside the effective control of the government. In any case, the state would consider such unauthorized movement as "withdrawal."[40]

My reasons for undertaking this investigation of pastoral nomadism in the Mari kingdom are varied. Included among them is the lack of attention given to date to the pastoral nomads as members of a specialized occupational group. The basic ground work on the Mari period and the pastoral nomadic tribes in its vicinity has been done by J.-R. Kupper. Since his primary study, *Les nomades en Mésopotamie au temps des rois de Mari* (Paris, 1957), appeared, three dissertations have been written on the Mari kingdom. These studies by J. T. Luke, A. Marzal, and J. Sasson[41] have added to the general understanding of the texts and, to varying degrees, the pastoral nomadic tribes. However, none of them has made full use of the available anthropological and ecological materials.

Kupper does take into account, even emphasizes,[42] the environmental factors which influence the actions of the tribes. Unfortunately, he interprets them as evidence of the old maxim that the environment shapes them into raiders and natural adversaries of the settled zone--"le nomade est, par nature, un pillard; le razzou est pour lui une occupation normale."[43]

He sees them as instruments of change in the ancient Near East, serving to eliminate stagnant civilizations and founding new, vibrant ones in a continuous progression of nomadic incursive "waves." In Kupper's view, the demands of population and marginal aspects of their habitat forced them into these invasions. And, as they came into contact with the urban culture, they passed through various levels of sedentarization.[44] It is my opinion, however, that this set of explanations does not adequately grasp the importance of the occupational requirements of nomadic pastoralism. There are numerous other variables, including herding patterns and economics, involved in the movement of pastoralists. In addition, the sedentarization of portions of the tribal population and other adaptations made by the pastoral community in response to urban influences are more often based upon social and economic considerations than political goals.

Luke incorporates a small amount of anthropological data in his study of the Mari tribes.[45] However, he passes over many modern studies on nomadic pastoralism, including those of Fredrick Barth. Admittedly, much of the material I will be using for my study has been published since Luke wrote his dissertation. Still, there does not appear to be any conscious attempt on his part to provide an anthropological foundation to his examination of the Mari pastoral nomads.

Marzal, Luke, and Sasson, like Kupper, choose to read the documents from Mari from the point of view of their writers, the urban officials. It is my intention, however, to present the same material in the light of the needs and concerns of the nomadic tribal herdsmen. One model for this attempt has been outlined by M. B. Rowton in a series of articles which he has begun to publish in the last few years. He points out instances of "enclosed nomadism"[46] among both ancient and modern Near Eastern tribal groups. In this herding pattern, the pastoral units remain within the defined boundary of the central government's authority. Because of this it is possible for a more intimate relationship (a symbiotic society) to be established between the nomadic and sedentary elements of the population. Cultural sharing takes place between them but the occupational integrity of each is maintained. The herders are

recognized as a facet of the overall economy of the region.[47]

Rowton's statement that a definite need is present for a body of material to form a "comparative basis for discussion of the mountain peoples of the ancient Orient"[48] has provided me with the impetus to pursue this topic. In addition, his studies have demonstrated the worth and necessity of the inter-disciplinary methods which I will make use of in this study. There will be extensive use of both ancient historical records and contempory anthropological materials to ascertain the main factors to which the nomadic and sedentary communities found it necessary to respond. It is to be hoped that the picture outlined in the succeeding chapters will aid in the further understanding of the peoples of the Old Babylonian period in the Mari kingdom.

NOTES

INTRODUCTION

[1]Only two major studies have appeared to date: J.-R. Kupper, *Les nomades en Mésopotamie au temps des rois de Mari* (Paris, 1957) and J.T. Luke, *Pastoralism and Politics in the Mari Period: a Re-examination of the Character and Political Significance of the Major West Semitic Tribal Groups on the Middle Euphrates, ca. 1828-1758 B.C.* (University of Michigan, Ph.D. dissertation, 1965). Other works have dealt with the pastoral nomadic tribes in passing or as they relate to various other participants of the Mari population. See for instance A. Marzal, *The Organization of the Mari State* (University of Chicago, Ph.D. dissertation, 1969) and J. Sasson, *Northernmost Syria: a Survey of its Institutions Before the Fall of Mari (ca. 1757 B.C.)* (Brandeis University, Ph.D. dissertation, 1966).

[2]The use of the abbreviation *ARMT* signifies those volumes of transliterated, translated texts. Note that the most recently released volumes have been made part of the series *TCM (Textes cuneiformes de Mari)*. Thus, volume I of *TCM* equals *ARMT* XIV.

[3]The greatest mass of pertinent information comes from the time of Šamši-Addu and Zimri-Lim. Yasmaḫ-Addu is the son of Šamši-Addu and served as the Assyrian viceregent at Mari. He reigned only a short time after the death of his father. Yaḫdun-Lim, the father of Zimri-Lim, is known only from a foundation inscription and a victory stele, plus a few reminiscent mentions in letters from the time of his son.

[4]See for summaries of Mari history, G. E. Mendenhall, "Mari," *BA* 11 (1948), 2-19 and J.-R. Kupper, "Northern Mesopotamia and Syria," *CAH*[2], Vol. II/1 (Cambridge, 1973), 1-41. Recently, A. Parrot has published a new book dealing with the civilization at Mari, *Mari: capitale fabuleuse* (Paris, 1974). For studies on the political history of this period, see J. M. Munn-Rankin, "Diplomacy in Western Asia in the Early Second Millennium," *Iraq* 18 (1956), 68-110 and V. Korošec, "Les relations internationales d'apres les letters de Mari," *RAI* 15 (1967), 139-50. A great deal of attention also has been given to the texts from Mari dealing with prophecy and the possible parallels with biblical prophecy. Two good studies on this are H. B. Huffmon, "Prophecy in the Mari Letters," *BA* 31 (1968), 101-24 and W. L. Moran, "New Evidence from Mari on the History of Prophecy," *Biblica* 50 (1969), 15-56.

[5]Luke, J.T., *Pastoralism and Politics*, 102, n.118.

[6]The letters can be deceiving in this regard because it appears that these officials continually are depending upon the king for advice or sending men to him to interrogate personally. More likely, they are simply being good bureaucrats by giving

the king credit for all decisions. The men who were sent to Mari were passed probably from one court functionary to another. It is unlikely that many of them actually made their reports and petitions to the king in person.

[7]Gilbert, A. S., "Modern Nomads and Prehistoric Pastoralists: The Limits of Analogy," *JANES* 7 (1975), 54. His case studies primarily are concerned with the era of pastoralism previous to that evidenced at Mari and thus are not necessarily relevant in application to this study.

[8]Berque, J., "Introduction to Nomads and Nomadism in the Arid Zone," *International Social Science Journal* 11 (1959), 490-95, notes that great changes can be made by the pastoralists when they are faced with new technologies. Because they often find themselves caught in a squeeze between technological, economic, and political changes, the nomadic pastoralists must adapt quickly if they are to retain their identity. One way of doing this is to add new methods to their herding practices. Special arrangements may be made also with the sedentary community to help both cope with change.

[9]Note that these central authorities exercise differing levels of control, based upon their strength and ability to control the nomadic population. Cf. N. Swidler, "The Development of the Kalat Khanate" in *Perspectives on Nomadism*, eds. W. Irons and N. Dyson-Hudson (Leiden, 1972), 118 for an in depth discussion of this type of situation in Western Pakistan. J.-R. Kupper, "Le rôle des nomades dans l'histoire de la Mesopotamie ancienne," *JESHO* 2 (1959), 122, 126 provides a similar assessment of the political situation during the Mari period.

[10]Barth, F., "Capital, Investment, and the Social Structure of a Nomadic Group in South Persia" in *Capital, Saving and Credit in Peasant Societies*, eds. R. Firth and B. S. Yamey (London, 1963), 78-79. The social changes based on herding economics usually influence the process of sedentarization. Indeed, change of almost any kind can tip the delicate balance of economics for the pastoralists living in marginal regions.

[11]Gilbert, A. S., "Limits of Analogy," 54-55.

[12]For reference to these studies and a compilation of their findings, see M. B. Rowton, "Dimorphic Structure and the Tribal Elite," *Studia Instituti Anthropos* 28 (1976), 219-34 and "Enclosed Nomadism," *JESHO* 17 (1974), 1-16.

[13]Note in W. W. Swidler, "Adaptive Processes Regulating Nomad-Sedentary Interaction in the Middle East" in *The Desert and the Sown*, ed. C. Nelson (Berkeley, Calif., 1973), 36-38, the swift changes in the pattern of nomadic economic endeavors after the introduction of the diesel engine to aid irrigation in the northern valleys of eastern Baluchistan. Previous to this time, he notes on pp. 24-35, there were many similarities between these pastoral nomadic peoples and those who had inhabited the area for centuries.

[14]In order to maximize this, most of the material used here concerns the nomadic pastoral peoples in Afghanistan, West

Pakistan, and the primitive areas of Northern Iraq and Iran. All of these areas are similar in terrain and climate to that experienced by the Mari pastoral nomadic tribes. There are some conditions and practices in the tribal areas of Africa and North America which parallel the Mari situation. However, there are enough geographical and cultural differences between them to make their use problematic.

[15]Rowton has warned me in a recent communication that the impression should not be drawn from this that the anthropological material is confirmed in the Mari texts on a significant scale. Rather, what is confirmed is the picture we get over a period of ca. 1000 years prior to 1914 from the reports of travelers and historians.

[16]Marzal, A., *The Organization of the Mari State*, 29 suggests that a clue to this flux may be revealed in the shifting of such honorifics as *warad*, *abum*, and *aḫum* (slave, father, and brother respectively) among the writers of the texts.

[17]This is also a factor evidenced in the biblical material pertaining to the tribes of Israel. The large number of instances where an individual clan name appears in more than one tribal group can be explained by the process of fluidity. The genealogies in Gen 46:8-25, I Chronicles 1-8, and Num 26:5-62 supply sufficient information to justify this conclusion. Cf. Y. Aharoni, *The Land of the Bible, A Historical Geography* (Philadelphia, 1962), 221-27.

[18]Stauffer, T. R., "The Economics of Nomadism in Iran," *MEJ* 19 (1965), 293-94 points to a vicious cycle of overstocking and over grazing as a large factor in the impoverishment of small herd owners and their sedentarization. See also F. Barth, "Nomadism in the Mountain and Plateau areas of South West Asia" in *The Problems of the Arid Zone* (UNESCO, Arid Zone Research XVIII, 1962), 350.

[19]Modern studies mentioning the use of hired shepherds include R. N. Pehrson, *The Social Organization of the Marri Baluch*, ed. F. Barth (Chicago, 1966), 7-8 and F. Barth, "Capital," 71. For this practice during the Old Babylonian period, see J. N. Postgate, "Some Old Babylonian Shepherds and Their Flocks (with a contribution by S. Payne)", *JSS* 20 (1975), 9-10.

[20]Gellner, E., "Introduction: Approaches to Nomadism" in *The Desert and The Sown*, 7-8. He demonstrates that very often the application of the "means of coercion" and not the "means of production" is the most telling factor in interaction between the nomads and the villagers.

[21]Evidence of this "service" is found in W. Irons, "Variation in Political Stratification among the Yomut Turkmen," *AQ* 44 (1971), 150.

[22]See F. Barth, "Capital," 78-79 and T. R. Stauffer, "The Economics of Nomadism in Iran," 294.

[23]Bates, D. G., "The Role of the State in Peasant-Nomad

Mutualism," *AQ* 44 (1971), 122-23. Additional information on this pacification of raiding groups is given in W. Irons, "Livestock Raiding among Pastoralists: an Adaptive Interpretation," *Papers of the Michigan Academy of Sciences, Arts, and Letters* 50 (1965), 393-414.

[24]Marzal, A., "The Provincial Governor at Mari: His Title and Appointment," *JNES* 30 (1971), 196 and by the same author, "Two Officials Assisting the Provincial Governor at Mari," *Or.* 41 (1972), 359-77 provide a great deal of information on the government bureaucracy. In addition, he helps to define the hierarchy of this political system. An earlier study of the Mari government is J.-R. Kupper, "Un gouvernement provincial dans le royaume de Mari," *RA* 41 (1947), 149-83.

[25]See his discussion of *nawûm* (*nwh* in Hebrew) in "Enclosed Nomadism," *JESHO* 17 (1974), 18-26. The conclusions he draws are in part based upon the work of D. O. Edzard in "Altbabylonisch *nawûm*," *ZA* 53 (1959), 168-73.

[26]*ARMT* XIV (=*TCM* I) 53,80,81,86,98, and 121.

[27]See Klengel, H., "Zu dem *šībūtum* in altbabylonische Zeit," *Or.* 29 (1960), 357-75 for a complete presentation of the functions and actions of the *šībūtum* in *ARM* I-X.

[28]Barth, F., "Nomadism in the Mountain and Plateau areas," 349. Note also in W. Irons, "Variation in Political Stratification," 150-51 the discussion of the *saqlau* and L. E. Sweet, *Tell Toqaan: a Syrian Village* (Ann Arbor, 1960), 190-91, which reveals similar functions being performed by the village "muxtaar."

[29]For some attempts at finding the etymology of this word, see Fronzaroli, P., "L'ordinamento gentilizio semitico e i testi di Mari," *Archivio Glottologico Italiano* 45 (1960), 43-45 and by the same author, "*su-ga-gu-um* Sceicco," *La parola del passato* 14 (1959), 191-92. Recently, D. W. Young has suggested to me a possible parallel to *sugāgum* in Hebrew *šqq*.

[30]See *ARM* II 92:16-28, VI 32:13-16 and XIV 46:6-25 and F. Barth's statements in "A General Perspective on Nomad-Sedentary Relations in the Middle East" in *The Desert and the Sown*, 19-20. D. W. Young and this author also have a forthcoming article on this subject, "The *raison d'être* of the *sugāgum* in the Mari Kingdom," *Or.* 46 (1977), 122-26.

[31]The Assyrian economy was based in part upon trade and commerce. There was a large group of traveling merchants who depended upon the government to keep the trade routes open and free of raiders. Thus, the goodwill of the nomadic tribes was essential to free movement of commerce. Cf. L. L. Orlin, *Assyrian Colonies in Cappadocia* (The Hague, 1970), for a discussion of these traveling merchantmen.

[32]See A. Marzal, *The Organization of the Mari State*, for a discussion of this process and its effects on the tribal groups.

[33]Discussion of this social phenomenon of the integrated tribe by M. B. Rowton has appeared in "Enclosed Nomadism," 1-30. In "Dimorphic Structure and the Tribal Elite," 219ff., Rowton expands upon the model he had formulated to show that the process of integration between tribe and state is the prime political aspect of what he calls "enclosed nomadism." This form of pastoral nomadism is the result of the tribal enclaves becoming either partially or entirely enclosed within the sphere of urban settlement and influence.

[34]Kupper, J.-R., *Les nomads*, ix and "Le rôle des nomades," 122-24 outline several levels of sedentarization among the Mari pastoralists. These are represented by the "settled" Ḫaneans, the semicivilized Yaminites, and the untouched and "wild" Suteans. This model is a portion of his wave theory of continuous nomadic invasion into the settled community from the desert fringe. The shortcomings of his presentation will be dealt with later in this study.

[35]For previous discussions of the *ḫabirū* question, see J. Bottéro, *Le problème des Habiru à la 4e recontre assyriologique internationale* (Paris, 1954) and M. Greenberg, The *Ḫab/piru*, American Oriental Series 39 (New Haven, 1955) as well as M. Gray, "The Ḫabiru-Hebrew Problem in the Light of the Source Material Available at Present," *HUCA* 29 (1958), 135-202. Most recently, M. B. Rowton has published an article adding to the discussion--"Dimorphic Structure and the Problem of the ᶜApirû-ᶜIbrîm," *JNES* 35 (1976), 13-20.

[36]Mendenhall, G. E., "The Hebrew Conquest of Palestine," *BA* 25 (1962), 66-86. His most recent statement on the subject appears in "Migration Theories vs. Culture Change as an Explanation for Early Israel," *SBL Seminar Papers* (1976), 135-43.

[37]Luke, J. T., *Pastoralism and Politics*, 35-38 and 272-75.

[38]Gottwald, N. K., "Were the Early Israelites Pastoral Nomads?" in *Rhetorical Criticism: Essays in Honor of James Muilenberg*, eds. J. Jackson and M. Kessler (Pittsburg, 1974), 234. Y. Aharoni, "Nothing Early and Nothing Late: Re-writing Israel's Conquest," *BA* 39 (1976), 55-76 provides a radically different view to the theory of "withdrawal." He states that settlement patterns and fortification remains in the Negeb during the "conquest" period argue against any sort of actual conquest by the early Israelites. They settled in unpopulated or sparsely populated areas because they could not militarily compete with the Canaanites. The real takeover of Canaan did not take place until the time of the monarchy.

[39]See the discussion in M. B. Rowton, "The Topological Factor in the Ḫapiru Problem," *Landsberger Festschrift* (*AS* 16) (Chicago, 1967), 375-87.

[40]Mendenhall, G. E., "Conquest," 73. For instances of short term movement for political reasons or to escape military service by the tribal groups, see *ARM* III 12:16-26 and V 27.

[41]See also J. Sasson's monograph, *The Military Establish-*

ment at Mari (Rome, 1969).

[42]Kupper, J.-R. *Les nomades*, x-xiii and 260-61. Notice also his later restatement of these views on the Mari nomads in "Le rôle des nomades," 113-27 and in "Northern Mesopotamia and Syria," 24-28.

[43]Ibid., xi. This one-sided viewpoint depersonalizes the pastoralists and leaves little room for much study of their social context.

[44]Ibid., ix-xii.

[45]See, for instance, his use of H. Charles, *Tribus moutonnières du moyen Euphrates* (Damascus, 1939) and its discussion of the 'Agêdât in *Pastoralism and Politics*, 28-29.

[46]See note 33 above for an explanation of this term. Rowton's views are most recently expressed in "Enclosed Nomadism," 1-30. To date, five articles have appeared on this subject and several more are mentioned by him as being in press or near completion.

[47]In "Enclosed Nomadism," 3-5, Rowton suggests that "given the choice, most nomads would prefer enclosed nomadism as long as political conditions allowed them to retain a significant degree of autonomy."

[48]Rowton, M. B., "Urban Autonomy," 202. Much of the analogous information which he employs deals with tribes from Kurdistan and Luristan during the past 1000 years.

CHAPTER I

DEFINITION AND CHARACTER OF PASTORAL NOMADISM

Definitions Based on Resource Extraction

From the outset, it must be pointed out that pastoral nomadism, as an occupational specialization, is primarily dependent upon the ecologic situation of which it is a part. The pertinent points for study involve the specific aspects of adaptation by the pastoral nomadic groups to both physical and social factors in their environment. The degree of success they have in exploiting and in dealing with the social and economic circumstances of their region will determine their viability as a group.

The majority of the discussions concerned with pastoral nomadism touch upon the importance of these adaptations. A sampling of the definitions given in these studies for pastoral nomadism provides the following examples:

> . . . a technology involving the use of one or more domestic animals to the extent that the cultural system is primarily dependent upon these animals for exploiting the physical environment, and such that the exploitative techniques require year-round movement of the communities within a restricted territory.[1]

> It is a socio-economic mode of life based on intensive domestication of livestock which requires a regular movement of the animals and their breeders in a seasonal cycle dictated by the need for pasturage and water.[2]

> . . . a mode of life dependent primarily upon herding of animals and involving regular movement to new pasture lands which, from the agriculturalists' point of view, are marginal resources.[3]

Hunting and gathering. Each of these basic definitions[4] is centered around the use of animals, movement of men and herds, and the actions taken to provide for the physical needs of the herds. One further refinement in this attempt to establish exactly what is involved in a discussion of pastoral nomadism has been made by Philip Salzman. In his valuable study of multi-resource nomadism in Iranian Baluchistan, he chooses to define both pastoralism and nomadism separately. He then notes that one may complement the other.

> Nomadism is a kind of movement . . . as part of the cycle of food extraction. Pastoralism is management of food extraction from a particular type of resource, domesticated or semi-domesticated animals. Nomadism can be associated with several different types of resources, as in hunting and gathering, cultivation, labor sale, and of course pastoralism. Pastoralism can be associated with the entire range of movement, from none at all to continuous movement. Pastoral nomadism is one set of many combinations in which nomadism and pastoralism are involved.[5]

Thus, it can be seen that pastoral nomadism is only one option among many available to nomadic and/or pastoral people. While the nomadic herdsmen may spend the majority of this time engaged in basic animal husbandry and herd movement, it is also possible (even likely) that they will engage in an associative occupation or service.[6] The marginal areas they inhabit and the economic risks involved in pastoralism require the nomadic tribes to exploit all possible resources. Hunting, gathering, and simple (seasonal) agricultural activity are common place pursuits along the migration route.[7]

The tribal groups, which will be of interest to this study engage in these supplementary forms of food extraction as part of their general exploitation of the area. They are utilized, to the exclusion of all other activities, by only the most primitive nomadic groups. Once resource extraction becomes separated from simple hand-to-mouth existence and a particular nomadic specialization has been adopted, the group involved then becomes a factor in the total economy of the area. In fact, pastoral nomadism, as well as agricultural and commercial enterprises, can all be subsidiary endeavors complementing the economy of the nomadic group.[8]

Transhumance. The terms transhumant, seminomad, and full nomad are often used to designate the various types of migratory pastoral activity. Underlying these differentiations are the degree and nature of the ties which remain or have been forged with the settled community by the nomadic groups. Lawrence Krader has described transhumance as a particular tribal policy which maintains, as a matter of course, partial sedentary status and engages in agricultural activity.[9] A situation of this type implies a division of the labor force within the tribal group. While most of the tribe lives in villages and engages in farming for part or all or the year,

the remainder of the group (usually comprised of the able-bodied men) takes the herd to pasture.[10] P. Bohannan differentiates transhumance from nomadism by means of this migratory pattern. He points out that the transhumant follows a "cycle of movement (which is) an annual one and follows the seasons, rather than a longer one requiring several years in annual movement between village and cattle camp . . ."[11]

The particular herd management practices involved in transhumance[12] shape the social organization of the tribal group. The transhumants have a definite settlement pattern. During the spring and summer, the tribal dependents remain in the lowland villages and the shepherds direct their flocks to the highland plateaus in search of better grazing for their animals. They then return to the lowland settlements at the approach of winter. Once the grazing area has been chosen by the shepherds, they remain fairly stationary, unless the climatic conditions become unfavorable or the fodder is depleted.[13] In each case, however, the pastoral activity does not involve the main body of the tribe--only professional shepherds.[14]

Because transhumants are vulnerable to changes in the natural environment of their region and do not practice full-time nomadism, they leave themselves open to exploitation by the central government in their area.[15] The political forces tend to institutionalize, control, and at times protect the transhumants as an economic asset of the state. Since both agricultural and pastoral pursuits are being practiced effectively year round and no unrestrained or unauthorized movements occur with any great frequency, the government will promote transhumant activity by allowing its practitioners a certain latitude of action. This would be based upon the government's own self-interest since the movements of the shepherds tend to lessen the population congestion around the urban centers.[16] Moreover, the addition of herding and agricultural products, produced by transhumants, serves as a stimulus to the economy and prevents food shortages.[17]

Seminomadism. Seminomadism is another label applied to tribal people who engage in nomadic pastoralism. Like transhumance, it entails an intermixing of sedentary and nomadic living as well as the introduction of nonpastoral activities

into the tribal economy. In modern anthropological literature, seminomadism is used ordinarily to differentiate between sheep and goat-breeding pastoralists and what are termed "true pastoral nomads," the camel herders.[18] Attendant distinctions made between these two involve pattern and frequency of movement, type of dwelling (mud huts or buildings vs. tents and temporary shelters) and area of habitation (steppe and mountain, in distinction to desert environments).[19]

For purposes of this study, however, such distinctions are not possible since the camel had not as yet been domesticated to any large extent by the time of the Mari period.[20] The pastoralists of the Mari texts were primarily herders of sheep and goats. As a result of this, seminomadism, if it is to be given a separate designation, must be considered (like transhumance) as one of several pastoral alternatives or variants which could be utilized by the tribal peoples of the Mari kingdom.

The picture which seems to emerge from the texts is one in which several different pastoral options are used or adopted by the Mari tribes. Because of this, it is not possible to place them into standardized divisions or categories.[21] Members of the same tribe may be transhumants, seminomads, or fully sedentarized agriculturalists. The methods employed by individual groups in order to best exploit the natural resources of their area are the only criterion upon which they can be categorized. Nomadism serves as merely one of the adaptive tools upon which their economic success and cultural development is based.[22]

The fact that some members of the tribal groups are not completely or directly involved in the actual movement of animals is due in part to the need by the tribes for other sources of income. Another reason for this is the inability of the old and infirm to travel with the migrants. They can be allowed to die along the route or they can be set up along with other dependents, such as wives and children, in villages. This leaves them to raise supplementary food crops and to serve as liaison personnel between the nomadic community and the urban culture.[23]

Contact with a sedentary culture influences the tribal groups in many ways, including a certain degree of cultural as-

similation. This does not necessitate, however, any sort of step by step progression from pure-nomadism to a completely sedentary existence by the tribal units. Nor does every change in tribal structure result from the interchange of relations between nomad and sedentary.[24] Rather, occupational endeavors usually are designed to make use of all available resources which may strengthen the economic standing of the group. Borrowing from or adaptation to the urban culture is a part of this process.

In this study, the term pastoral nomads will be applied to all of the varied tribal groups who engage primarily in migratory herding for part or all of the year. They also may participate in such supplementary economic activities as agriculture, caravaneering, contract labor, or client services. However, they are to be considered subsidiary to the herding economy of the tribal group.

Development of Pastoral Nomadic Occupational Groups

Pastoralism was one adaptation adopted by early peoples as an aid to fuller utilization of their environment. It developed as a separate economic endeavor as the village setting became more stable and thus better able to support several forms of resource extraction.[25] With an established food source a reality, there would have been more time to engage in domestication projects.[26] These new domesticates opened new areas (namely the steppe and nonfarmable upland regions) for exploitation. They also served as a form of insurance against poor harvests and climatic changes.[27]

Domestication Processes. Nomadic pastoralism evolved from village herding as the size of the herds grew. Transhumance was probably the first measure employed by these early pastoralists. What appear to be their seasonal herding camps have been identified at Ali Kosh (Bus Mordeh phase) ca. 7000 B.C. and Hassuna Ia.[28] In later phases, these camps in turn became permanent settlements but the pattern of moving the herds in search of better pasture continued. It eventually became one of the prime causes of the cultural, as well as physical, separation of the pastoral nomadic groups from the settled community.[29]

W. Goldschmidt, noting this process, states that

cultural differences, "if they are to be explained at all, must be explained in terms of adaptation of human needs and capacities to the diverse ecological circumstances under which societies are to exist and which they must exploit with the techniques available to them."[30] Thus the cultural separation between pastoral nomads and sedentary agriculturalists is based upon the diversities of their occupational endeavors. The pastoralists move with their herds and are primarily concerned with grazing and animal husbandry. On the other hand, the farmers remain in one place and are preoccupied with the yearly yield from their fields.[31]

Once the nomadic pastoralists had established themselves as a separate occupational group, the formation of a social organization based more directly upon herd maintenance commenced. It should be noted that these herders never established a completely "natural" or self-sufficient culture. They still relied upon nonpastoral products as part of their diet and on goods which they could not manufacture themselves.[32] Their pastoral nomadic society, like the sedentary agricultural community, developed as a response to the circumstances of their environment. Their entire set of customs, rituals, institutions and social standards evolved in conformance with the dictates of their ecologic situation.[33]

Adaptation to the physical and social environment. It is often the case that forces from within the socio-cultural environment (i.e., village or urban population) determine the degree of cultural and economic adaptation made by the nomadic pastoral group. In this regard, Fredrick Barth suggests that a stable, symbiotic relationship between agricultural-urban communities and nomadic groups is possible if they exploit different ecologic niches. It may be that one will choose or be forced to submit to a subsidiary or tolerated position if they both happen to be utilizing the same niche.[34] In any case, he says, the distribution of these various groups is determined by the distribution of the ecologic niches. Further, the economic and political organization of each group is a factor in their ability first to exploit the area and second to coexist with each other.[35]

D. G. Bates refutes this as too limited a view, stating

that the most cogent aspects to consider are the result of the type of political response the members of the pastoral nomadic tribe make to the village communities and the central government.[36] He goes on to argue that ". . . it is incorrect to equate stable patterns of mutuality and close equivalent exchange with the non-competitive nature of cultural niches using a shared environment."[37] Basically, the degree of mutualism, in his view, which does develop between the nomadic and sedentary communities is based on the balance of power and not the different methods of exploitation.[38]

There is perhaps a difference of emphasis at the root of this disagreement. Barth does recognize political organization as a determining factor in the establishment of levels of cooperation and control between the groups. His model is applicable to the multileveled ecologic situation of the mountain and plateau regions of southwestern Asia and the Near East. In this area there are niches which can be utilized by different segments of the population exclusively or in symbiotic alliance. He, however, does not place (as Bates points out) quite as much emphasis as is deserving to outside political factors. The Mari texts demonstrate that the provincial villages and the tribal groups were quite often directed and controlled by the urban authority. Quite likely, these political and socio-economic influences were even more important to the cultural adaptation made by the nomadic pastoral group than the physio-biotic influences of their environment.[39]

In discussing the cultural adaptation made by pastoral nomads, W. Goldschmidt lists the following qualities, which are considered by him to make up the character of their occupational group:

> . . . a high degree of independence of action; a willingness to take changes; a readiness to act, and a capacity for action, self-containment and control, especially in the face of danger; bravery, fortitude and the ability to withstand pain and hardship; arrogance, sexuality, and a realistic appraisal of the world.[40]

In his opinion, the development of a sense and need for independence in the nomadic character is generated by two primary considerations. First, pastoral people must be free to travel about in as unrestrained a manner as possible. This is based on the requirements of herd maintenance (adequate water and

grazing). They may become identified with a general area, but their prime concern is the ability to move from one grazing zone in this region to another.[41]

Secondly, because of the unpredictable nature of their environment and herding in general, the pastoralists are to a large extent dependent on the outcome of their own decisions on the disposition of their animals.[42] As an independent businessman, the pastoral nomad has a responsibility to himself and to his individual migratory unit to maintain an equilibrium within the herds and produce a profit. The success of the herding group will be determined by his ability to make the correct decisions on migration routes (including stops and starts), ties with other groups, and the basic business of caring for the animals.[43]

Social Organization

The largest social unit among the nomadic pastoralists is the tribe. It is ideally conceived of as a collection of families, all descended from a common ancestor.[44] However, because of the marginality of the region in which the herders operate, this is essentially an unstable aggregation. Ecologic conditions serve to limit camp and herd size and cause fluctuations in the human and animal population from year to year.[45] Circumstances also may cause members of the migratory group to seek part-time employment in agricultural, marketing, or shepherding ventures.[46] Some pooling of labor and herd segments also may be employed for security and economic reasons. However, the burden of success or failure remains primarily on the individual herd owner's ability to deal with the seasonal changes, raids by other groups, political influences, or a combination of these and other variables.[47]

Tribal ties and affiliation. One counter-balancing factor to this dependence upon individual fortunes and the need for a continually fluid tribal society is the existence of an institutionalized social structure which traditionally ties the various groupings together.[48] The social instability which is caused by the formation of local migratory groups is offset to a degree by the conceptual stability provided by the idealization of the more inclusive social group, the tribe.[49] When the

migratory units are combined, in order to produce a subsidiary labor force or for reasons of protection, the reenforcement of tribal ties is affected. In addition, the hospitality system, which allows for the dissemination of information on pasturing conditions and the location of other groups, lessens the effects of fluidity in the pastoral nomadic community. It also strengthens the bonds of reciprocal aid among its membership.[50]

The social organization of pastoral nomadic groups begins with the family, which is the fundamental point of reliance for the individual. After this, usually based upon kinship or some ritualistic blood ties, the organized herding unit is of greatest importance. These groups range is size from the camp to the clan and section, and on up to an entire tribal community.[51] In fact, kinship is the principle glue in the social organization of nomadic peoples. And, the tribal genealogy is the most common basis for their model of societal structure.[52]

Kinship obligations among the migratory units. One such kinship tie is based upon marriage patterns. These may play a role in the practice of establishing social ties. This is due to the need by the nomadic herders for free access to water rights and pasturage. Since it is usually the case that these privileges are held traditionally by particular groups, it becomes very important (especially during the dry season) for the pastoralists to have as many kinship and marriage ties among the various groups in their area as possible. Obviously, the more ties a migratory unit has, the better chance it will have in obtaining sufficient grazing and water for its herds.[53]

The very presence of a diffuse network of social ties, (whether they be consanguineal, affinal, or extrakin[54]) combined with the very real physical mobility of the pastoral nomadic group, allows the herders to make the most of these arrangements.[55] B. Spooner points to the maintenance of a strong network of social ties (especially between distant, less competitive groups) as one part of their environmental adaptation. This permits them to become more competitive with other tribal groups as well as nonnomadic segments of the population.[56]

In line with a study of the nature of stateless societies, of which the pastoral nomadic tribe is one example, D. Easton has pointed out that the particular occasion facing them dic-

tates their decision on whether or not to form a connection with other parties. He states that "political relationships among the clans are activated for specific purposes and with respect to limited objectives or contingencies."[57] Philip Salzman adds to this that there are degrees of contingency within the political system. A society's response to these contingencies can be the determining factor in deciding "the extent of stability or instability of group parameters."[58]

Independence and tribal consciousness. The structure of pastoral nomadic society is an adaptation to the basic instability of their physical and economic environment. B. Spooner points to the resulting native model as a predictable cultural adaptation to a flexible ecologic situation.[59] When, however, the structuring of their society causes the tribal unit to become virtually isolated within a small and select contact group (or, as F. Barth defines it, ethnic group[60]), a basic distrust of everything outside the pastoral nomad's immediate association can develop.[61]

An example of the extent to which this distrust can actually go is presented in R. N. Pehrson's study of the Marri Baluch. These pastoral nomadic people have collectivized their segregationist social feelings into the concept which they term *taggi*, "deceit."[62] It reflects an institutionalized tribal paranoia which is embodied in the general consciousness as a complete distrust of the motives and honesty of every individual outside the immediate social grouping. It reaches the degree of placing suspicion upon all of one's neighbors, who, it is believed, must be planning the quick demise of every other tribal member. There is, as a result, a nearly complete failure among these people to develop any sort of binding agreement between persons and the larger corporate body. When collective activities are initiated, they invariably are narrow in scope and designed to accomplish a set of specific and usually short term objectives.[63]

Although this characteristic of distrust for outsiders and for long term collective activity by nomadic tribal sections is fairly common, it is not a culturally beneficial one. It usually is not allowed to reach the degree described in the case of the Marri Baluch because it tends to be counter-produc-

tive economically. However, isolation or "encapsulation" of particular nomadic tribal groups, within their cultural and physical environments, does occur as a result of a number of diverse circumstances. This is especially the case when the degree and importance of relations with the sedentary community and its political authorities increases.[64] When this occurs, it is usually based upon an interest on the part of the tribe or the state to integrate the tribal economy and social structure into the activities of the urban culture. This may be the result of a mutual agreement, based upon economic interests, or the decree of the sedentary authority, which had either conquered the tribes or held a large measure of control over their territory.[65]

The need for such contact between migratory herders and the settled population harkens back to the origins of the pastoral nomadic specialization. One of the events which was to eventually lead to the establishment of social and economic ties between them was the increased use of short-fallow cultivation. This had become necessary in the face of a rising population and the resulting increase in the demands for grain.[66] Over-cropping and the salinisation of the soil, which resulted from the intensified use of irrigation, caused the abandonment of many of the outlying farmlands.[67]

In order to combat the loss of these fields, herders were allowed to graze their animals in both the harvested and fallow fields. This supplied enrichment to the fields and prevented further exhaustion of the soil. It also insured winter grazing for the nomadic pastoralists.[68] Philip Smith and T. Cuyler Young, Jr. have pointed out that "this function of domesticated animals is so important that it is hard to postulate a widespread adoption of short-fallow cultivation without also assuming an increased emphasis on domesticated animals."[69] They also suggest in their discussion that the grazing of the animals in the fields helps to conserve moisture in the soil, which would otherwise be lost due to "accidental" growth, by trampling and eating the weeds.[70]

Relations with the sedentary community. One final feature of the pastoral nomadic character, which is of importance to study, is based upon the outward simplicity and economy to

expenditure of resources, as well as the patent dislike of civil control, which is the norm among these tribal groups.[71] These qualities do not necessarily have to stand in the way of the nomadic groups's social contacts with the settled community.[72] Still, pastoral nomads may consider their culture and occupation superior to a sedentary existence because of the advantages provided by their mobility. It allows them to escape unfavorable climatic conditions or social unrest and, in a sense, start fresh somewhere else. In addition, their herds are easily converted into working capital, while the sedentary farmer or craftsman is dependent on the vagaries of climate and the market place.[73] The fluid social organization of the nomadic pastoralists also aids them in taking advantage of new resources or in coping with changes in herding methods by familiarizing them with fluid situations.[74]

Despite the comparative ease with which the pastoral nomad may handle crisis and change in his environment, part of his social nature inhibits or at least slows the effects of change. These constraints are social and interactional, as well as cognitive. One basic stabilizer is found in the political organization of the nomadic group. Even stateless societies have an institutionalized authority structure and a value system from which this authority, be it an individual or a group, can draw power.[75] However, the local decision making body is constituted, its prime contribution to the tribal culture is the model of behavior it provides the individual members (both child and adult) in regard to authority structures within the total society.[76] Such a model may help to prepare the pastoral nomadic society for its dealings with the sedentary community. However, the heightening of the role of the tribal chief, as an intermediary between tribe and state, by the urban authority may require additional social adjustment (or rationization) on the part of the migratory group.[77]

The social situation which is found among the tribal groupings is the direct result of a process which balances the social and ecologic factors in their environment.[78] Institutionalization of their social and cultural norms is determined through this process which measures both stability and comparative rates of dividend. The simple fact is that "every

society . . . offers its members opportunities of succeeding in life by various criteria of success . . . ."[79] Pastoral nomads, because of their already marginal existence, are quick to test and sift out those opportunities which are most likely to fit in with their cultural scheme and aid their occupational endeavors. It can indeed be said with F. Barth that "the mechanics of change must be found in the world of efficient causes" for the pastoral nomad.[80]

It has been the intention of this preliminary discussion to provide an outline of the basic anthropological foundation for this entire study. The remainder of this examination will deal with the ancient epigraphic materials from Mari. Aside from attempting to place the pastoral nomadic and tribal peoples mentioned in these texts in their proper historical and social context, it will be the aim of this study to present an occupational analysis of these groups. The use of analogous anthropological data will make both of these goals possible.

NOTES

CHAPTER I

[1]Wilson, H. C., "An inquiry into the Nature of Plains Indian Cultural Development," *AA* 65 (1963), 363-64. He further subdivides the technological uses of the animals into three categories: the use of the animals for the production of material products, for mechanical power (draft animals), and the use of animals for a combination of both of these purposes.

[2]Gottwald, N. K., "Were the Early Israelites Pastoral Nomads?" in *Rhetorical Criticism: Essays in Honor of J. Muilenberg*, eds. J. Jackson and M. Kessler (Pittsburg, 1974), 226.

[3]Leshnik, L. S., "Pastoral Nomadism in the Archaeology of India and Pakistan," *World Archaeology* 4/2 (1972), 150. He goes on to say that the physical needs of their flocks are the main "motivating forces in the life of traditional pastoral nomads." Fodder can be also a factor in pasture selection since particular types prove themselves to be the most suitable for the type of animal which a group is herding.

[4]For additional statements defining nomadism, see R. Patai, "Nomadism: Middle Eastern and Central Asian," *SWJA* 7 (1951), 401 and L. Krader, "The Ecology of Nomadic Pastoralism," *International Social Science Journal* 11 (1959), 500 as well as D. Forde, *Habitat, Economy, and Society* (New York, 1934), 401. Forde provides a six-point division of the uses for domesticated animals.

[5]Salzman, P. C., "Multi-Resource Nomadism in Iranian Baluchistan" in *Perspectives on Nomadism*, eds. W. Irons and N. Dyson-Hudson (Leiden, 1972), 67. He notes that this separation of terms allows a more in depth examination of the reasons behind resource management, movement, and the establishment of cooperative arrangements.

[6]For a complete discussion of this itinerant occupational enterprise by pastoral nomads, see N. K. Gottwald, "Israelites?," 229-31. Note also the article by F. S. Frick on the nonpastoral, metal-working nomads in the Old Testament, "The Rechabites Reconsidered," *JBL* 90 (1971), 279-84.

[7]Salzman, P. C., "Movement and Resource Extraction Among Pastoral Nomads: The Case of the Shah Nawazi Baluch," *AQ* 44 (1971), 187, points out the various animal products available as well as those wild resources (gazelle, rabbit, wild onions and pistachio nuts) which can be obtained by the nomads. They often choose little-care crops, such as dates, to cultivate or they leave the actual agricultural duties to tenants or subject peoples. See, for a discussion of this, W. W. Swidler, "Adaptive Processes Regulating Nomad-Sedentary Interaction in the Middle East" in *The Desert and the Sown*, ed. C. Nelson (Berkeley, Calif., 1973), 33-34.

[8]Salzman, P. C., "Movement and Resource Extraction," 190. He adds the proviso that "pastoral does not necessarily entail nomadic and vice versa." See also N. Dyson-Hudson, "The Study of Nomads" in *Perspectives on Nomadism*, 17, who suggests that it is more relevant to study populations, "doing whatever mixture of things they do with whatever relative frequencies that they do them," than categories.

[9]Krader, L., "The Ecology of Nomadic Pastoralism," 500-1. D. L. Johnson, *The Nature of Nomadism*, Department of Geography Research Paper #118 (University of Chicago, 1969), 18, points out that the building of a village of permanent housing forms a nucleus of the society and although pastoral activities are one concern of the transhumant community, agriculture is nearly always the dominant interest of the village.

[10]Braudel, F., *The Mediterranean and the Mediterranean World in the Age of Philip II*, Vol. I (New York, 1972), 87-88. This movement was either to the plains or to the mountains depending upon the season.

[11]Bohannon, P., *Social Anthropology* (New York, 1963), 215.

[12]Johnson, D. L., *The Nature of Nomadism*, 19, notes that the true transhumant, as first described in studies of Alpine cultures, is a misnomer when it is applied to Near Eastern and North African pastoralism. However, N. K. Gottwald, "Israelites?," 235, disputes this, saying that it was especially in the Near East that the pastoral nomad's movements hinged upon the turn of the seasons. He expressed the opinion that the Near East itself demands such movement and even makes it inevitable "in the light of the alternating dry and wet seasons."

[13]Cohen, Y. A., "Adaptation and Evolution: an Introduction" in *Man in Adaptation: The Institutional Framework*, ed. Y. A. Cohen (Chicago, 1971), 8-9. The antiquity of the use of seasonal campsites seems to be authenticated by the remains at the site of Ali Kosh from ca. 6500 B.C. For the evidence on this, see J. Oates, "The Background and Development of Early Farming Communities in Mesopotamia and the Zagros," *Proceedings of the Prehistoric Society* 39 (1973), 154. Note also S. Bökönyi, "Zoological Evidence for Seasonal or Permanent Occupation of Prehistoric Settlements" in *Man, Settlement and Urbanism*, eds. P. J. Ucko, R. Tringham, and G. W. Dimbleby (Herefordshire, Eng., 1972), 121-26.

[14]Patai, R., "The Middle East as a Culture Area," *MEJ*, 6 (1952) 5. See also F. Braudel, *The Mediterranean*, 86, for a discussion of what he terms "normal" and "inverse" transhumanance and their separate effects upon the shepherds and the villagers.

[15]Barth, F., "General Perspective on Nomad-Sedentary Relations in the Middle East" in *The Desert and the Sown*, 17-18, makes the statement that the village peasant society is usually ground down by the elites and middlemen merchants. It is not as easy to control the nomadic groups, who have more

options in dealing with the urban authority. Still, the local elite of these tribes also is drawn into the urban system as it comes in competition with it and makes necessary accomodations.

[16]Braudel, F., *The Mediterranean*, 94. He notes in addition that the transhumant shepherds remain somewhat outside of society, a race apart. Cf. also T. C. Young, Jr., "Population Densities and Early Mesopotamian Urbanism" in *Man, Settlement, and Urbanism*, 829, on other methods of reducing population congestion, such as delayed marriage, contraception, and the forced migration of marginal members of the group.

[17]Ibid., 95. It was in fact shortages in the food supply which had necessitated the movement of a portion of the population into other regions of the district during parts of the year.

[18]Such a definition of nomadic types is made also by R. Patai, "Nomadism," 405 and Eugen Wirth, *Syrien: eine Geographische Landeskunde* (Darmstadt, 1971), 173.

[19]See M. Awad, "Settlement of Nomadic and Semi-Nomadic Tribal Groups in the Middle East," *International Labor Review* 79 (1959), 30-31, for a clear example of these two types of pastoral groups. His study on the Jawali of the western (Libyan) desert of Egypt pinpoints these differences between sheep and camel herders. A similar economic pattern, which relies on both sedentary agriculture and nomadic herding, is found in H. Charles, *Tribus moutonnières du moyen Euphrates* (Damascus, 1939). A summary of his study is given in J. T. Luke, *Pastoralism and Politics*, 28-29.

[20]Cf. below, pp. 67-68, n.7 for a presentation of the literature on the domestication of the camel in the Near East.

[21]This has been a common error in discussions of the Mari nomads and of the Old Testament patriarchs. One such study, which is guilty of fragmenting nomadic tribal peoples into categories based on one segment of their economy, is W. F. Albright, "Abram the Hebrew, a New Archaeological Interpretation," *BASOR* 163 (1961), 36-54. He posits that Abraham was a kind of merchant prince and leader of "ass-nomads." J. Van Seters, *Abraham in History and Tradition* (New Haven, Conn., 1975), 13-14 terms this theory an oversimplification if for no other reason than that asses (both historically and economically) were not used as commercial herding animals by pastoralists. Albright's explanation provides no more insight into the occupational life of the nomadic tribal herders of the Old Testament than do those who simply label them as seminomads and leave it at that. To truly understand them, it is necessary to explore all aspects of their economic and social life.

[22]See Salzman, P., "Movement and Resource Extraction," 197, for this interpretation of resource exploitation. A similar statement is made by B. Spooner in *The Cultural Ecology of Pastoral Nomads* (Philippines, 1973), 23.

[23]Cf. F. Barth, *Nomads of South Persia, The Basseri Tribe of the Khamseh Confederacy* (Oslo, 1961), 79-80. He notes that tribal elite and the wealthy tend to settle or are forced to settle in such villages. There, they serve as intermediaries (and sometimes as hostages) between the tribe and state. Thus, for example, in *ARM* VIII 11 two tribal segments of the clan of Awin apparently have divided, with some becoming sedentary and the remainder continuing a nomadic existence. The text shows, however, that both units still retain their sense of mutual tribal identity in that the elite from both segments participate in the consummation of the land transfer mentioned. The ritual which concludes the text also has all parties, including the government representative, participating as equals. A full presentation of this text is found below, p. 90.

[24]Bates, D. G., "The Role of the State in Peasant-Nomad Mutualism," *AQ* 44 (1971), 128, notes that while some changes are the result of political responses by the tribe to the urban authority, "many variations can also be correlated with the requirements of specific problems of herding and the economy."

[25]This would have occurred most likely in the areas of natural distribution of wild wheat and barley. K. W. Butzer, *Environment and Archeology*, 2nd edition (Chicago, 1971), 543-47 points to the Zagros mountains and the Taurus mountains of Southeastern Turkey as well as a large part of the Levant as the habitat of these wild grains (cf. his figure 88 on p.543). As J. R. Harlan, "A Wild Wheat Harvest in Turkey," *Archaeology* 20 (1967), 197-98 and K. V. Flannery, "Origins and Ecological Effects of Early Domestication in Iran and the Near East," in *The Domestication of Plants and Animals*, eds. P. J. Ucko and G. W. Dimbleby (Chicago, 1969), 80, have noted, the wild stands of grain would have attracted and encouraged settlement in their vicinity. Harlan even demonstrated that by the use of a primitive sickle (contra Butzer, *Environment*, 531-32) an adequate food supply could be obtained with only a few days labor. Further strengthening this is J. Oates, "Background and Development," 150-51. She points out that the huge storage problem involved in the harvesting of this grain and the task of having to transport it also promoted the establishment of village settlements. It, however, remained (p. 176) until "man attempted to extend the natural habitat" of these cereals that the actual cultivation and domestication of them began.

[26]Reed, C. A., "The Pattern of Animal Domestication in the Prehistoric Near East" in *The Domestication of Plants and Animals*, 367, declares that a settled village life, which had become dependent and supported by cereal grain and other storable food supplies, is a primary requirement for the earliest domestication of herding animals. J. F. Downs, "Domestication: an Examination of the Changing Social Relationships Between Man and Animals," *Kroeber Anthropological Society Papers* 22 (1960), 44, states that this early stage of animal domestication was one which was reached when at least a portion of a society's population could remain sedentary long enough to support those who were working with the captive animals. It is a simple fact that this has to continue until "domesticated

generations have been produced or the taming process is completed and the animals are controllable."

[27]Flannery, K. V., "Origins and Ecological Effects," 87, notes such a "banking" process in the herding of sheep and goats. They could be bartered for with agricultural produce in good years and then traded for seed grains and flour in bad years.

[28]Mellaart, J., *The Neolithic of the Near East* (New York, 1975), 70-71, discusses this type of seasonal sheep and goat-herding camp at Zawi Chemi ca. 8000 B.C. as well as at Ali Kosh. J. Oates, "Background and Development," 154, notes that sheep had been domesticated for some time prior to these early remains at Ali Kosh, thereby strengthening the argument for its use as a seasonal camp.

[29]Smith, P. E. L. and T. C. Young, Jr., "The Evolution of Early Agriculture and Culture in Greater Mesopotamia: a Trial Model" in *Population Growth: Anthropological Implications*, ed. B. Spooner (Cambridge, Mass., 1972), 33. They add that the lack of equilibrium in early societies was caused by man's over exploitive policies in respect to his environment. This necessitated greater investments in land use and new food supply sources. W. Herre, "The Science and History of Domestic Animals" in *Science in Archaeology*, eds. D. Brothwell and E. Higgs (London, 1969), 267-68, also points to this step toward domestication of animals as dependent upon the attainment of one cultural stage and a prerequisite for the next.

[30]Goldschmidt, W., *Comparative Functionalism: an Essay in Anthropological Theory* (Berkeley, Calif., 1966), 85.

[31]Cf. F. Barth, "Capital, Investment, and the Social Structure of a Nomadic Group in South Persia" in *Capital, Saving and Credit in Peasant Societies*, eds. F. Firth and B. S. Yamey (London, 1963), 70-71, for further discussion of this economic and social dichotomy, especially in regard to both fluid and constant capital.

[32]Spooner, B., "Toward a Generative Model of Nomadism," *AQ* 44 (1971), 201, adds that ". . .activities associated with acquiring them have figured largely in their annual cycle and division of labor."

[33]Berque, J., "Introduction to Nomads and Nomadism in the Arid Zone," *International Social Science Journal* 11/4 (1959), 488.

[34]Barth, F., "Ecologic Relationships of Ethnic Groups in Swat, North Pakistan," *AA* 58 (1956), 1088. His model is taken from a study of the Pathan society, which includes agriculturalists (Pathans), transhumants (Kohistanis), and nomads (Gujars). For another implementation of this model of symbiotic communities, see K. V. Flannery, "The Ecology of Early Food Production in Mesopotamia," *Science* 147 (1956), 1255. This article uses comparative material from the sites of Jarmo and Tepe Sarab. Recently, however, J. Mellaart in *The Neolithic of the Near*

East, 87-88, has taken away some of the effectiveness of his use of Tepe Sarab by showing that it was not used as a seasonal camp. S. Bökönyi, "Zoological Evidence for Seasonal or Permanent Occupation of Prehistoric Settlements," 122-23, provides corroboration of this finding.

[35]Ibid. Thus, an area can be divided and utilized according to the nature of the groups in it--whether they be agriculturalists, urban craftsmen, or pastoral nomads.

[36]Bates, D. G., "The Role of the State in Peasant-Nomad Mutualism," *AQ* 44 (1971), 127-29. He explains that the outside force embodied in the urban state can even influence the tribal migratory patterns and time table as well as their internal social organization. Such influences often depend upon the balance which is obtained between the tribes and the political authority.

[37]Ibid., 128. He adds on p. 127 that "sources of power from outside the immediate system are important in determining the local equilibrium which often results in the political dominance of one or the other of ethnically specialized modes of production."

[38]Ibid., 129-30. P. Salzman, "Introduction to Comparative Studies of Nomadism and Pastoralism," *AQ* 44 (1971), 106, agrees with this evaluation and states that social, political, and cultural factors are the prime adaptive factors for nomadic peoples.

[39]Salzman, P., "Political Organization Among Nomadic Peoples," *Proceedings of the American Philosophical Society* 111 (1967), 121-22, points to the importance of a dependable climate in the development of a beneficial coordination of activities between nomads and the villagers in their area. The ability to plan migration patterns and to know that there most likely will be sufficient pasture and water at the end of the move does much to promote interaction and to lessen friction. Conversely, the more unpredictable the climate, the more likelihood of a conflict to arise between the competing groups in the region. Still, it seems to me that this does not explain adequately the full set of forces which determine the political and social organization adopted by the nomadic groups. It would make little difference how much good pastureland existed in an area if the urban authority would not allow the pasturalists to reach it. An intermediary must be chosen or created who will prevent conflict and intransigence on the part of both the nomadic and urban communities. The final response and adaptation made by the nomadic pastoralists must be based on all of the factors which exist in their environment. However, it will be the most dominant, and long lasting, of these which will be the most influential.

[40]Goldschmidt, W., "Theory and Strategy in the Study of Cultural Adaptability," *AA* 67 (1965), 405.

[41]Goldschmidt, W., "The Dynamic Adaptation of Sebei Law" in *Man in Adaptation: the Institutional Framework*, ed. Y. A.

Cohen (Chicago, 1971), 121. This idea, which is necessary for agricultural activity, is based upon land use and tenure. It cannot apply to a migratory people except in the claims to pastureland and migration right of ways. J. Berque, "Introduction to Nomads and Nomadism," 485-86, remarks that herding often is dominated by political and strategic considerations in maintaining this freedom of movement and access to separate grazing areas.

[42]Goldschmidt, W., "Independence as an Element in Pastoral Social Systems," *AQ* 44 (1971), 136. Although the pastoral nomad's decisions may at times be based upon tradition or custom, he will not shackle himself to these when the welfare of the herd is at stake. If the flock would be better served by disregarding tribal custom on ecological or economic grounds, herdsmen very often will justify their actions by these practical factors while still avowing their tribal orthodoxy. In this regard, J. Chelhod presents the parodoxical definition of the nomad as ". . . un individualiste sans individualités, un traditionaliste sans tradition." His study appears in *Introduction à la sociologie de l'Islam* (Paris, 1958), 27.

[43]When larger herding units (tribes or subtribes) are involved, an ephemeral council of "elders" will weigh collectively the decisions to be made. See P. C. Salzman, "Movement and Resource Extraction," 191, for some of the variables which determine migration routes and resource exploitation.

[44]Patai, R., "The Middle East as a Culture Area," *Middle Eastern Journal* 6 (1952), 5.

[45]Swidler, W. W., "Some Demographic Factors Regulating the Formation of Flocks and Camps Among the Brahui of Baluchistan" in *Perspectives on Nomadism*, 70-73, notes that some of the movement between camps of family units is based upon affinal links, but of course, the changes in camp personnel are due in the main to the requirements and size of the flocks being herded.

[46]Salzman, P. C., "Movement and Resource Extraction," 191-92, describes tribesmen working in the grain and date harvests. He states that these modes of extraction developed partially in response to the elimination of raiding and extortion, on the part of the tribes, by the urban authority. B. Spooner, *Cultural Ecology*, 8, reiterates the necessity for this type of nonpastoral labor by the tribesmen, but he still thinks that "pastoralism always forms the primary ideological basis of nomadic cultural systems."

[47]Cf. Dyson-Hudson, R., "Pastoralism: Self-Image and Behavorial Reality" in *Perspectives on Nomadism*, 32-39, for a charting of these and related factors of animal husbandry and economics among the Karimojang of northeast Uganda. As W. Goldschmidt, "Sebei Law," 121, notes, there is of course a certain element of luck involved here too, but that is balanced by the individual skills of the pastoralist.

[48]Spooner, B., *Cultural Ecology*, 14-15. See also S. L. Pastner, "Camels, Sheep, and Nomad-Sedentary Contact: a Comment

on Rubel's Model," *Man* 6 (1971), 287. This finds its expression in intergroup obligations and the hospitality code.

[49]Ibid., 41. This is aided also by the concept of nomadic identity (i.e., identification with the occupation in much the same manner as the other economic groups collectively view themselves). Note also his statement in "Toward a Generative Model of Nomadism," 204, that the concept of tribal membership and cultural identity serve to tie together diverse and schismatic tribal elements.

[50]Swidler, W. W., "Some Demographic Factors," 72. He also notes that the ratio of animals to human population has a stake in the creation of the larger camping group.

[51]Johnson, D. L., *The Nature of Nomadism*, 162. He also demonstrates that local conditions, including the political situation, may circumvent the usefulness of some of the larger group sizes.

[52]Spooner, B., *Cultural Ecology*, 25. It is worth noting that the Old Testament is replete with genealogical lists. In fact, beside serving as a kind of literary glue, they are even used for the purpose of legitimizing kings and patriarchs. See, for instance, Genesis 10-11, Ruth 4 as well as Matthew 1 and Lk 3:23-28 in the New Testament. Regarding Mesopotamian genealogies and especially those nomadic chieftains claimed as ancestors by later dynasties, see J. J. Finkelstein, "The Genealogy of the Hammurapi Dynasty," *JCS* 20 (1966), 95-118 and A. Malamat, "King Lists of the Old Babylonian Period and Biblical Genealogies," *JAOS* 88 (1968), 163-73.

[53]Rubel, P. G., "Herd Composition and Social Structure: On Building Models of Nomadic Pastoral Societies," *Man* 4 (1969) 271. In some societies, she points out, the role of women in helping with the herding duties and as simple property is involved in the formation of these marriage patterns.

[54]Spooner, B., *Cultural Ecology*, 25, posits the axiom that when more complex native models are in operation, in addition to kinship ties, there will be established formal arrangements with extra-kin groups. The formation and reformation of subsistence groups and the actual position of the individual in respect to society as a whole may become more explicit through the sealing of these contracts and informal agreements. Certainly, their individual importance to the tribal economy will be defined better as a result of them.

[55]Pastner, S. L., "Camels, Sheep, and Nomad Social Organization," 285. This allows the pastoralists to better their lot by replenishing their herding stock or by gaining access to natural resources.

[56]Spooner, B., "Toward a Generative Model of Nomadism," 204-5, Cf. also P. C. Salzman, "Political Organization Among Nomadic Peoples," 122, for a discussion of climatic effects on competition and interaction between pastoral and nonpastoral elements of the population.

[57]Easton, D., "Political Anthropology," *Biennial Review of Anthropology* (Stanford University, 1959), 237. This is his defining statement of a contingent political system.

[58]Salzman, P. C., "Political Organization Among Nomadic Peoples," 120, n.4. He terms this a "more or less or not-at-all variable" and as such will allow for a bit more flexibility in social arrangements.

[59]Spooner, B., *Cultural Ecology*, 23-24. He suggests that there is a kind of dialectical relationship between the two aspects of tribal social organization, social groupings, and social status. He points to the use of rigid genealogical terms as an example of tribal reaction to the unpredictability of their environment.

[60]Barth, F., "Introduction" in *Ethnic Groups and Boundaries*, ed. F. Barth (Boston, 1969), 10-11. He defines the ethnic group as a biologically self-perpetuating population, which shares fundamental cultural values making up a field of communication and interaction of specifically identified members. They are categorized as distinguishable both by the members and nonmembers.

[61]Amiran, D. H. K. and Ben-Arieh, Y., "Sedentarization of Beduin in Israel," *IEJ* 13 (1963), 162. This study notes that tribes usually are enclosed in well-defined geographical areas too. Other tribes must obtain from them safe conduct or pay for protection when passing through their territory. Cf. also G. R. Fazel in *The Desert and the Sown*, 132, which suggests that eventually there may develop within these areas a truly segregated society. Only elements which are ethnically, linguistically, economically, and culturally similar remain in them.

[62]Pehrson, R. N., *The Social Organization of the Marri Baluch*, ed. F. Barth (Chicago, 1966), 104-5.

[63]Ibid., 105. A somewhat similar situation is described by G. R. Fazel, "Encapsulation of Nomadic Societies," 138, in his study of the Behmai and Taiyebi tribes of Iran. His examination shows that they are unable to form intertribal alliances because of internal rivalries, jealousies, and conflicts among their political leaders.

[64]Fazel, G. R., "Encapsulation of Nomadic Societies," 130, sets up three variables which account for the degree to which encapsulation of tribal structure is evidenced in the Middle East and specifically with his model, the Boyr Ahmad of southwestern Iran. These include ecologic circumstances, degree of integration with sedentary peoples in the national market economy, and the extent of political compatibility between tribe and state. D. Bates, "The Role of the State," 116, adds that security reasons may make it more feasible for the government "to reduce any region of shared co-exploitation to one where a simple ethnic specialization dominates to the exclusion or restriction of others."

[65]Bates, D., "The Role of the State," 122-23. M. B. Rowton, "Autonomy and Nomadism in the Western Asia," *Or.* 42 (1973), 254-55 and "Urban Autonomy in a Nomadic Environment," *JNES* 32 (1973), 204-11 also discusses the importance of the town in tribal territory. It serves as a link between tribe and state as well as a staging area for nomadic groups. Its population may include sedentarized members of the tribal elite, who serve as intermediaries and thereby promote a less friction-filled exchange of instructions and demands between the nomads and the government.

[66]Cf. Hole, F., Flannery, K.V., Neely, J. A., *Prehistory and Human Ecology of the Deh Luran Plain* (Ann Arbor, 1969), 367, for a study of this amplification of food production methods.

[67]Helbaek, H., "Plant Collecting, Dry Farming, and Irrigation Agriculture in Prehistoric Deh Luran" in *Prehistory and Human Ecology*, eds. F. Hole et. al., 421. See also J. Oates, "Background and Development of Early Farming," 174 and F. Hole, et. al., *Prehistory and Human Ecology*, 368-69 for discussion of population movement and the change in the food production cycle in response to the ecologic changes brought on by over-irrigation, over-cropping, and the salinization of the soil in many areas.

[68]For modern examples of these arrangements, see P. C. Salzman, "Movement and Resource Extraction Among Pastoral Nomads," 189 and R. M. Adams, *Land Behind Baghdad* (Chicago, 1965), 169, n.2.

[69]Smith, P. E. L. and T. C. Young, Jr., "The evolution of Early Agriculture," 40-41. In their description of the climate and geography of the northern Mesopotamian plain on p. 23, they state that the area has no natural depositing of alluvium as is the case in the south. As a result, there is no renewal of the fertility of the soil by this means. Thus, the depositing of animal excrement on the fields becomes doubly important.

[70]Ibid., 59, n.16. F. E. Zeuner, *A History of Domesticated Animals* (New York, 1963), 32-34 takes a much dimmer view of sheep grazing in fields. He says that they eat up the last vestiges of organic material, thereby depriving the soil of humus. Further, he argues that they trample the soil and their tracks aid erosion and the eventual reversion of the area from steppe to complete desert.

[71]Awad, M., "Settlement of Nomadic and Semi-Nomadic Tribal Groups in the Middle East," *ILR* 79 (1959), 32, notes that the chiefs of these tribes exercise little effective control until they are designated as mediators between the government and the tribes. W. G. Irons, "Variation in Political Stratification among the Yomut Turkmen," *AQ* 44 (1971), 148-53, describes just such channeling of government authority through a local tribal leader, the *saqlau*, "protector."

[72]Barth, F., "Nomadism in the Mountain and Plateau areas of South West Asia," *AZR* 18 (1962), 345, states that trade

agreements based upon the nomads' need for manufactured goods and the villagers for herding products strengthens these ties. Basically, the two can be thought of as "specialized occupational groups within a single economic system." They are adapted to each other's presence in this system, and they tend to exploit this situation to their mutual benefit when it is possible.

[73]Barth, F., "Capital, Investment and the Social Structure of the Nomadic Group," 70. The animals can be moved to ensure good grazing or they can be slaughtered and eaten or sold in order to sustain their owners. In addition, they are a quickly increasing, self-perpetuating source of income for the nomadic herdsmen.

[74]Spooner, B., "The Status of Nomadism as a Cultural Phenomenon in the Middle East" in *Perspectives on Nomadism*, 124 and 130. He explains on p. 124 that "a primary difference between nomads and peasants is that nomads inhabit and exploit a much larger and more varied environment."

[75]Cf. W. Goldschmidt, "Independence as an Element in Pastoral Social Systems," 140. Since these bodies are not absolute and generally are constituted as decision-makers and arbitors, they may be chosen in a number of different ways. Thus, among the Karimojong (cf. N. Dyson-Hudson, *Karimojong Politics* [Oxford, 1966], 174), a seniority system is used to designate these men and among the Yomut Turkmen (cf. W. Irons, "Variation in Political Stratification," 148-49), the head man is chosen by the households and can be removed at any time.

[76]LeVine, R. A., "The Internationalization of Political Values in Stateless Societies" in *Man in Adaptation: The Institutional Framework*, 297-98. The council of decision-makers can represent a region or an extended family. It proves in the study of stateless societies to be the only telling unit for study. This is because a study which takes a look at only the societal overview gives a false picture of egalitarianism. Such functions can continue even after the stateless society has been invested into the administration of a central authority.

[77]Irons, W., "Variation in Political Stratification," 150-51 points out that this role often fell to the best raider of the tribe. He already had acquired the respect of the tribal group. This may have helped to offset the effects of this heightened position of authority. See also F. Barth, *Nomads of South Persia*, 76-90, for a discussion of the powers of the chief and the utilization of an augmented chief in the political vacuum within the tribes by the Persian government.

[78]Barth, F., "On the Study of Social Change," *AA* 69 (1967), 668-69. He also notes in "Introduction," 11, that the changes which result from the circumstances and contacts with the sedentary community do not necessarily "lead to liquidation through change and acculturation."

[79]Mair, L., *Anthropology and Social Change* (London, 1969),

128. She adds that only the scale and technology of the society will serve to limit the variety and number of these chances for advancement by the group or individual.

[80] Barth, F., "On the Study of Social Change," 668.

CHAPTER II

THE ASPECTS OF HERDING AMONG THE PASTORAL NOMADS

The pastoral nomadic tribes mentioned in the Mari texts were shaped economically and socially by their natural environment. This chapter will deal with the ecological factors involved in maintaining their pastoral economy. A number of variables, including seasonal and climatic changes as well as grazing conditions, often decide whether the migratory group will prosper or fail. Of special importance to this discussion will be the examination of migration patterns and herding methods employed by the nomadic pastoralists. In addition, the political influences of the urban authority on the activities of the pastoralists will be examined.

Topography and Climate

It is necessary at the outset to define geographically the region utilized by the nomadic pastoral groups of the Mari kingdom. J.-R. Kupper points to the area of steppeland between the cultivated lands and the desert proper as their main grazing zone. This territory is distinguished by an annual rainfall of between 250mm. and 100mm. He sets its limits as the Euphrates river on the west, the area of Palmyra on the south, and the lands watered by the Balikh and Khabur rivers on the east.[1] Kupper describes this region as "le domaine des pasteurs par excellence."[2]

P. E. L. Smith and T. C. Young, Jr. have designated this region of ancient Syria as the "northern Mesopotamian plains." They describe it as the area bordered on the east by the Jebel Hamrin and on the north by the Taurus mountain range.[3] The heart of this area is that portion known as the Jezireh. It is a "fairly inhospitable country, deeply etched by wadis and marked by patches of marsh country, suitable primarily for exploitation by pastoralists."[4]

There are two distinct sections of this region which are utilized as grazing areas by the pastoral nomads. J. Sasson set the limits of these two zones using Kupper's geographical

model as a guide. He describes the first as beginning at the Jebel ed-Drūze and passing eastward of Homs. It then extends in a southerly direction below Aleppo and crosses the Euphrates River approximately at the midway point of its two bends.[5] The other section of pastoral territory passes in a parallel line to the first area. However, it then emerges slightly east of Damascus at a point just south of Deir-ez-Zôr.[6]

These two sections of the Syrian desert (today known as the Hamad) are the only regions which pastoral nomads could have used before the domestication of the camel.[7] The semiarid steppe land is only capable of sustaining small groups of cattle and sheep herders.[8] It should be noted, however, that there are no absolutely rigid geographical boundaries in this area. Seasonal fluctuations cause the zone to expand or contract from year to year.

Rainfall amount is the most important factor in determining the subdivisions of this geographical region. As Kupper has noted, the lines of demarcation are the 250mm. and 100mm. rainfall limits.[9] The first amount is the cutoff point for the reliable production of cultivated grains. The second marks the limit of the area which contains sufficient grazing for migratory herds. The only sections of the northern Mesopotamian plains which do not correspond to this generally arid pattern are the areas along the rim of the Jebel Sinjar, and between it and the Taurus mountain range. There are also lands suitable for dry farming along the eastern bank of the Tigris River and directly within the environs of Assyria proper.[10]

Tribal Territories Outlined

J. T. Luke has mapped out the migration patterns and grazing zones of the Mari pastoral nomads.[11] The idea that the movements of pastoral nomads are consciously thought out and patterned is not a new idea. M. von Oppenheim conclusively demonstrated in his voluminous study that the movements of the bedouin peoples of Syria and Mesopotamia were consistent and based on traditional routes.[12]

Luke's major contribution to this study of migratory patterns is his systematic mapping of the routes of each of the

Mari tribal groups. This allows him to identify the traditional areas of tribal activity. For instance, he places the Yaminites in the western section of the Mari kingdom. Their pasturelands lay north of a line "from the mouth of the Baliḫ River, in the west, to Qattunân in the east and south of a similar line from just above Carchemiš east to Ḫarrân and farther east to Chagar Bazar."[13] This region is spoken of in the Mari texts as the "Upper Country (*elenum*)."[14]

M. Birot has also defined the boundaries of the Yaminite tribal territory. He places it:

> tout le long de l'Euphrate (tout au moins en amont de Mari) jusqu'à Tuttul, puis de part et d'autre du fleuve, à l'est dans la vallée de Ḫabur autour de Sagarâtum et de Qattunân et jusqu'au-delà de la rive droite de cette rivière, c'est-à-dire dans l'Idamaras.[15]

Birot describes the region as a sort of patchwork of population centers with open territory and farm lands filling the spaces between the urban settlements.[16]

The cuneiform texts also provide information on the location of the Ḫanean grazing areas in this northern section of the kingdom. There was apparently a center of Ḫanean activity in the vicinity of the town of Kaḫat in the province of Idamaraṣ.[17] In *ARM* II 59:4-13 Kabia, a son of Zimri-Lim, reported to his father that the Ḫaneans were grazing their flocks in the pasturelands around Kaḫat. His report mentioned that the area had an abundance of water and pasturage.

Aspects of Animal Husbandry

The activities of the pastoral nomads were confined generally to specific areas. This was based partially on the different climatic zones in the region which were formed by varied rainfall amounts and changes in elevation. In addition, they had to compete with the agricultural communities for lands along the fringe of the marginal zone. Those areas which did become identified as tribal territories were held jealously by the tribes. In some cases, rights of passage through tribal areas may have been controlled by the tribal council.[18]

Grazing and water rights. One possible instance of the sectioning of pasturing areas among the tribal groups is found

in *ARM* VI 42:11-14, 18-19.

11 ša-ni-tam aš-šum ia-am-ḫ[u]-ú[19] na-wi-e-em
ša be-lí iq-bi-e-em-ma aš-pu-ru
mâru^{meš} ši-ip-ri-ia ša aš-pu-ru a-na ri-[i]š eq[lim]
^{I}Ka-a-la-an ú-ul ik-šu-du
18 na-wu-um i-na bi-r[i-i]t Nu-u[m]-ḫa-a
[ù Ia-mu-ut-b]a-[a]l i-ka-al

Translation: On another matter, in regard to the *nawûm* of the Yamaḫamum about which my lord has spoken to me and I have written, the messengers whom I sent have not (yet) reached Kalan . . . . The . . . . . *nawûm* is grazing bet[ween] Numḫa [and Yamutba]l.

Lines 11 to 14 confirm the fact that the *nawûm*[20] (in this case meaning "flocks") of a particular tribe was being investigated by order of the king of Mari. The other lines quoted contain the report made by the investigating agents. They had discovered that the flocks of this group were grazing in an area between the territories of the Numḫan and Yamutbalean tribes.[21] Unfortunately, there is a break in the text at this point and the result of this action is not known. However, the fact that the Mari administration felt compelled to investigate the matter leads one to speculate that it had some degree of importance. There may, for instance, have been the possibility of a major clash between the tribal groups over this infringement of grazing rights.[22]

There is evidence of the sharing of pasturing areas by tribal groups in the texts. This could have been based upon formal or informal agreements between them. In *ARM* II 90:7-11 the flocks of the Yaminites are said to be pasturing among those of an unknown group (quite possible the Ḫaneans). There is no mention of concern over this situation.

ša-ni-tam a-ḫa-ra-tim immerātum^{ḫa} na-wu-um
ša DUMU.MEŠ-Ia-mi-na a-na aḫ ^{nār}Purattim
[. . .]-ma it-ti immerāti^{ḫá} na-we-e-em
10 [ša Ḫa-na ?][23] ri-tam i-ka-la
mi-im-ma ḫi-ṭì-tum ú-ul i-ba-aš-ši

Translation: On another matter, the encampment of the Yaminites has crossed from the far side of the Euphrates to the near side. Their flocks are grazing

with the sheep of the[Ḫaneans(?)]. There have been no losses.

The final statement concerning their welfare may have had to do with the river crossing. However, it is just as likely that it was an assurance to Zimri-Lim from Kibri-Dagan, the provincial governor of Terqa, that there had been no confrontations between the two tribal groups.

There are also instances of the Mari government confirming the traditional claims of a tribal group to its territory. In *ARM* I 6:26-28, 36-37, and 41-43 this sort of decision is described in detail. The point in question had been whether the Ḫaneans could continue to use a particular group of fields.[24]

26 . . . Ḫa-na ša na-we-em
eqlētim^{ḫá} i-na a-aḫ ^{nār}Purattim
i-ṣa-ab-ba-tu-ú ú-ul i-ṣa-ba-tu-ú

Translation: . . . shall the Ḫaneans of the steppe encampments take possession of the fields on the bank of the Euphrates or not?

Precedent was then cited:

36 qu-tam ša u$_4$-um-šu awīlum ṣí-bi-is-sú-ma
pa-ni-im li-ki-il

Translation: As previously, each man shall retain what was formerly his.

Finally, the decision was spelled out specifically authorizing the use of the fields by the Ḫaneans.

41 . . . ù Ḫa-na [š]a na-we-em
[š]a i-na a-aḫ [^{n}]^{ār}Purattim eqlētim^{ḫá} ú-ki-il-lu
[i-n]a pa-ni-tam-ma eqlētim^{ḫá}li-ki-il-lu

Translation: . . . and the Ḫaneans of the steppe encampment, who held fields on the bank of the Euphrates, allow them to retain the fields which they had previously held.

Being constantly aware of pasturing conditions within the territorial holdings of the tribe always has been a necessity for pastoral nomads. They need to know according to the season what the supply of water and pasture would be in all of the possible grazing areas. The individual herder acquired an intimate knowledge of his region during his early years with

the migratory group. It constantly would be reenforced and revised as he traveled with the herds. The near encyclopedic gathering of environmental and occupational data by the pastoral nomads is one of the most essential adaptations they make in order to insure economic success. It represents an indispensible expenditure of time and energy.[25]

Sheep and goats physiologically require frequent access to water and pasturage.[26] Because of this, the nomadic pastoralists generally try to acquire grazing rights in as many sections of the tribal territory as possible. To do this they establish a network of affinal and other kinship ties with other tribal sections.[27] Information on the extension of kinship ties is not mentioned specifically in the Mari letters. However, the appearance of subtribes and clan groups (i.e., *gāyûm* and *ḫibrum*) in the texts makes this process a real possibility.

Development of breeding and herding group. Before going on it would be well at this point to present a brief reconstruction of the events which led to the creation of a separate occupational group of nomadic pastoralists. The actual development of pastoral nomads as a specialized occupational group began with the domestication of plants and animals. The domestication process began as men started to extend the natural habitat of the wild cereal grains into less productive areas. Previous to this there was probably harvesting of the wild grains (wheat and barley), which even today are found in stands as dense as cultivated fields.[28] As the practice of cultivation became more intensive, a "positive feedback" cycle was set in motion. F. Hole describes this cycle as a natural progression in which "the more wheat planted, the more mutants with touch rachis were selected for; the greater the yield, the more farmers survived; the greater the population, the more wheat had to be planted."[29] Once the human population had become fairly sedentary, it was then possible to begin the large scale domestication of sheep and goats. They could be fed on the domesticated annuals and would serve as a way of "banking" food surpluses in "live storage."[30]

The earliest remains of domesticated sheep (the most frequently mentioned animal in the Mari texts) have been found

at Zawi Chemi Shanidar in Iraq (ca. 9000 B.C.).[31] The domesticated goat appears at Ali Kosh and Jarmo ca. 7000 B.C., in Iran and at Ghar-i-Asp (Horse Cave) in northern Afghanistan ca. 8260 B.C.[32] The first domesticates were probably first and foremost a subsidiary food source. However, as additional animals were added to the village stock holdings, other animal products could have been selected for and added to the economy of the settlement.[33] M. L. Ryder has pointed out that there are a large number of genes which control fleece structure and weight. Careful selection and breeding would have been necessary to develop a woolier fleece. However, once this was accomplished, the seasonal migration of the herds would have carried the new characteristics to other herds using the grazing areas. Cross breeding then would have led to widespread development of the more desirable, woolier breeds.[34]

The ancient methods of sheep breeding eventually developed into a very specialized art. A lexical text of the series *ḪAR.ra=ḫubullû*, published by A. L. Oppenheim and L. F. Hartman,[35] lists just about every imaginable category for sheep and other domesticated animals. The listings range from "breeding sheep" (1.9 *rak-ka-bu*) to "sheep to be eaten at the festival of the gods" (1.37 *i-sí-*[*i*]*n i-lu*) to "sheep seized with a cutaneous disease" (1.45 *šá ga-ra-bí*) or "disease of the lungs" (1.46 *šá ḫa-še(!)-e*). There are white (1.98 *pi-ṣu-ú*) and black sheep (1.99 *ṣal-mu*), as well as brown (1.100 *sa-a-mu*), dapples (1.101 *bu-ru-ú*), yellow (1.102 *ár-qa*), and of course "plucked sheep" (1.67 *bu-qu-nu*). In all, there are 182 separate designations for sheep, 10 for ewes, 46 for goats, 21 for lambs, 17 for kids, 52 for oxen, 6 for sows, 13 for calves, and 28 for donkeys.

During the period from ca. 6000 to 4100 B.C. the population in both southern and northern Mesopotamia began to increase markedly as a result of improvement in dry-farming methods and the intensified use of irrigation.[36] This, plus the shortening of fallow periods, allowed (for a time) the maintenance of a large population and the colonization of a larger part of Greater Mesopotamia.[37] In addition to these population changes, the stabilization and utilization of six-row barley, a hardier, more salt-resistant cereal grain was

speeded up. This was due to the fact that the use of irrigation in regions which already had a precarious soil balance caused salinisation to become relatively widespread. Barley was cultivated in preference to other crops in order to combat this worsening condition and keep up production.[38] Following this phase of expansion (down to about 3750 B.C.), the strains placed upon the land began to manifest themselves. The widespread use of irrigation systems in marginal areas had exhausted the soil and many large tracts of former farmland in the southern plain and along the steppe had to be abandoned.[39] What emerged by the time of the Early Dynastic period was a series of walled and fortified city states in southern Mesopotamia with a buffer zone of uncultivated land between them.[40] Agricultural activity was intensified in regions less affected by the salinisation process while the most damaged areas were left open to the incursion of groups of pastoralists and their herds.[41]

Northern Mesopotamia did not experience the pressures for farmland and the subsequent need to reduce fallow periods to the same degree as in the south.[42] Because of this and the lack of forces to compel the population to move into walled towns, the pattern of dispersed villages and small towns persisted for some time.[43] R. M. Adams speculates that the larger number of small settlements which managed to perpetuate themselves in this area resulted from their adoption of a better ecologic balance between the farming and herding activities in their region.[44]

Migration patterns and grazing zones. Turning now to the cuneiform texts from the Mari archive, the researcher is faced with the fact that there is little actual information to be culled on the basic aspects of animal husbandry. Such important pastoral concerns as growth curves, gestation periods, fertility periods, calving intervals, and neonatal care[45] simply are not mentioned. The Mari officials do report on the movement of the royal flocks and herds in a few texts.[46] Perhaps more information on them will come to light in those texts to be published in future volumes.

The types of fodder upon which the flocks grazed are mentioned in the texts. The valleys in the hilly "Upper Country"

contained pasturing areas which provided the animals with grass and shrub vegetation.[47] When the pastoralists brought them down to the lower elevations in the arid season, the herds could find reeds and grasses along the river bank. There was also stubble in the freshly harvested fields which could be eaten.

An example of pastoral nomads pasturing their flocks in the territory of Ḫišamta and Terqa is found in *ARM* II 99:7-13. It is reported in this text that the Numḫan and Yamutbalian tribes had been grazing their animals along the banks of the Euphrates.[48]

Nu-um-ḫa-a^{ki} Ia-mu-ut-ba-al^{ki}
qa-du-um ṣé-eḫ-ri-im ṣé-ḫe-er-tim[49]
^{reš}wardi^{meš} amātim^{meš} alpi^{ḫá} ù imērūtim^{ḫá}
pa-na-am ù ba-ba-am ú-ul <i>-šu-ú
iš-tu še-em i-ga-ma-ru
ur-ba-tam ù a-pa-a-am ša a-aḫ ^{nār}Pu-ra-tim
[i-sa]-la-qú[50] . . . .

Translation: Numḫa and Yamutbal, with the male and female overseers(?), (and) the male and female servants (and) the cattle and donkeys are in a situation without recourse. After they have exhausted the barley they will have to cook cane and reeds from the banks of the Euphrates.

This statement may have been a deliberate exaggeration designed to portray the desperate plight of the tribesmen.

ARM III 12:10-11 appears to mention the use of fields by nomadic groups as grazing areas for their animals.

awīlū^{meš} Su-tu-[ú] 3 bi-ri eqlim i-na Pu-ra-tim
e-le-nu-um T[er]-qa^{ki} ša-ak-nu-ma

Translation: The Suteans are occupying 3 *bīrū* of fields beside the Euphrates, north of (lit. "above") T[er]qa.

There is a possibility that this tribal group was engaged in seasonal agricultural activity. However, it seems more likely that the Suteans in this text had contracted for the right to graze their flocks on the field stubble.

The necessity for arrangements of this type becomes quite evident in the light of the geographical realities of the northern Mesopotamian plain. In the region of the Mari kingdom

there is an almost complete lack of alluviation. This is due to the fact that both the Tigris and Euphrates Rivers at this point are in a "stage of down cutting and any irrigation involves the difficult task of artificially raising the water of the rivers above their banks."[51] The only way the soil could have been renewed in antiquity was through the depositing of animal droppings in the fields. Evidence is lacking, but there may have been traditional agreements made between individual tribes and villages in order to ensure the continuance of this mutually beneficial arrangement of pasturing on harvested fields.[52]

Feedlots may have also been used by the Mari pastoral nomads. Two technical terms were employed by the officials in their reports--*ḫaṣirātum* and *rubṣātim*, "camps" and "pens."[53] *ARMT* XIV 81:7-8 specifically names the town of Lasqum as the site of Ḫanean *ḫaṣirātum*.

. . . immerātum^{há} ša ^{awīl}Ḫa-na^{meš} XXXXX

i-ka-la ḫa-ṣí-ra-tum La-[à]s?-qa?-am ik-šu-da

Translation: . . . the sheep of the Ḫaneans . . . .

They have arrived at the camps at La[squm(?)].[54]

On another occasion, the flocks of the Ḫanean Yaminites[55] are said to have been installed already in their *ḫaṣirātum* and *rubṣātum*. The text (*Benj*. 989:c) describes an attack on these tribesmen by the forces of Zimri-Lim.

aš-šum ḫa-ṣí-ra-tim ù rubṣātim^{há} ša Ḫa-na-a DUMU.

MEŠ-Ia-mi-im

ma-ḫa-ṣí-im ù Ba-li-iḫ šu-bu-ri-im be-lí ú-wa-er

an-ni

Translation: You ordered me to force the camps and pens of the Ḫanean Yaminites to cross the Baliḫ . . . .

It may be that the pastoralists had entered an area which was not part of their territory or was politically unacceptable to the Mari administration.

Dissemination of herding information. In order to be well informed about the quality of the pasturage and water supply in their grazing areas, nomadic herders usually develop an information network. They employ an elaborate and institutionalized system of passing along the current data on pasturing

conditions.[56] This tribal grapevine keeps each herding unit informed of the environmental and social conditions in what S. Pastner has termed their "micro-pastoral orbit." He describes this as the area utilized by individual segments of the nomadic tribal groups.[57] Eventual decisions on direction, timing, and location will be based upon a synthesis of the information received through this system.[58]

The Mari texts, because of their urban centered perspective, do not report on these internal tribal communications. As a rule, only the final decisions on the movement of migratory groups are mentioned. There are examples, however, of the government itself dispensing information to various groups. Data was passed through channels to the district officials. And, at times, they were instructed to provide details to the tribal leaders, who would in turn pass them on to the nomadic herding units.

One instance of the dissemination of crucial herding information by the Mari government appears in *ARMT* XIV 86:31-40. In this case, the king was provided with information on the situation in the pastureland and was then asked to make the final decision on the movement of the flock to other pastures.

ù i-na Dūr^{ki}-Ia-aḫ-du-Li-[im]
a-na šu-lum sa-al-ḫi-i-im te-r[e-tim]
ú-še-pí-iš-ma te-re-tim
lu-pu-ta aš-pu-ur-ma
immerātim^{ḫá} ša i-na ḫa-am-qi-im
i-ka-la a-na qé-er-bé-tim
im-ḫa-ṣú-nim an-ni-tam l[a an-ni-tam]
be-lí li-iš-pu-ra-am-ma
immerātim^{ḫá} a-na aq-da-ma-ti[m]
lu-ša-bi-ra-am

Translation: And in Dūr-Yaḫdun-Lim, to determine the suitability of the water,[59] I have had por[tents] taken. However the portents were unfavorable. (Therefore) I sent word that the sheep which were pasturing in the river valley should be driven onto the plain. Now, let my lord send me his decision on whether [or

not] I should have the sheep taken across to the opposite shore.

ARM V 15:7-20 also contains a report on grazing conditions. The letter was a communication between Išhi-Addu, the king of Qatna, and Yasmaḫ-Addu, the Assyrian viceroy at Mari. Apparently, Yasmaḫ-Addu had requested permission to transfer some of his sheep to a grazing area in the vicinity of Qatna. Išhi-Addu consented to this arrangement, noting that the grasslands around Qatna were "most abundant."[60]

ARM X 48, while not dealing with nomadic pastoralists, does mention the passing of grazing information between Zimri-Lim and his sister, Niqḫatum.[61] She had requested previously that he entrust a portion of the royal flocks to her keeping. However, the king had demurred, saying that the weather was as yet too cold. He then promised that the animals would be sent when the winter season had passed. Now, in this text, she reminds him of his promise and renews her request. She points out that the winter weather had passed, and she is prepared to receive the royal flocks.

i-na-an-na a-nu-um-ma di-šu-um
immerātim ša na-da-nim
a-ḫi li-id-di-nam

Translation: Now is the time of full verdant growth.
My brother can (now) send (lit. "give") the sheep to me.

Movement of Herding Group

As has been noted above, the periodic migrations of pastoral peoples (when they are the owners of their livestock[62]) are based usually on the need to seek fresh grazing areas. They are not, however, random in nature. Either the exhaustion of grazing or the regular turning of the seasons can serve as the signal for the movement of the flock.[63] This movement is designed to meet specific tribal needs. Such is the case among the Yoruk tribesmen of Southeastern Turkey. For them, the limits of their movements are determined by their "habitat and the requirements of the flock."[64]

Because their migrations prevent the establishment of cultural ties to a particular country or nationality, the

pastoral nomads have developed an occupational ideal. They have incorporated into their traditions the idea that their way of life is the best possible way to exploit the land.[65] This concept is reenforced by their seasonal movements. The migration tends to revive occupational consciousness and re-establish tribal solidarity. The perpetuation of this ideal also serves to offset the devisive effects of the shifting of herding personnel between the various migratory units when there is a change in labor demands.[66]

Pastoral requirements for moving. In the Mari texts, the movements of the pastoral nomadic groups were based on two primary factors. The first was the fulfillment of basic animal husbandry requirements. The second involved their attempts to circumvent the political barriers and demands placed upon them by the officials of the state.[67] An example of the first migration variable is found in *ARM* II 102:9-16.

awīlū^{meš} ša ki-ma i-na Saga(!)-ra-tim^{ki}
wa-aš-bu e-li-iš-ma[68] pa-nu-šu-nu
ù immerāti^{ḫá}-šu-nu ša i-na la-as-k[i]-im
i-ka-la e-li-iš-ma ú-še-še-ru
Tr. ša ki-ma i-ša-al-lu
um-ma-a-mi ri-tum
ú-ul i-ba-aš-ši-ma
Rev. ù <e>-li-iš nu-še-še-[er]

Translation: The men who were living at Sagarātum have turned their faces toward the Upper Country only, and with their flocks which were grazing on *laskim*(?),[69] they have set out for the Upper Country. When he (the informant sent to investigate the situation by Yaqim-Addu) questioned them, they answered in this manner: "There is no pasture (here). Therefore, we are setting out for the Upper Country."

Despite the reluctance of the government to allow them to leave, the pastoralists felt compelled to move their animals to better pastures.

ARM II 90:5-12, which already has been cited above, enters into this discussion of pastoral migration. It describes the movement of the Yaminite flocks across the Euphrates to an area where they could graze with the sheep of the Ḫaneans.

For such an action as this to have taken place without violent consequences, there must have been some sort of arrangement made between the two tribes. The letter seems to point to this since it notes that there had been no problems in the grazing area.

One other tablet is worth mentioning in this discussion of the movement of tribal groups in the Mari kingdom. *ARM* V 27:25-27,36-37 reports that a group of Yaminites had crossed the Euphrates River into the land of Bisir.[70] This area, which has abundant winter pasturage, has been used for millennia by nomadic pastoral groups.[71] In the letter, Tarim-Šakim, a functionary of the court of Yasmaḫ-Addu, informed his lord that:

25 ù aš-šum DUMU.MEŠ-Ia-mi-na
ša a-na māt Bi-[s]i-ir i-bi-ru

---

36 wa-aḫ-ra-ku [ù a-na māt Bi-si-ir]
i-bi-ru . . . .

Translation: . . . and concerning the Yaminites, who (were planning) to cross over to the land of Bisir . . . . I arrived late [and into the land of Bisir] they had passed . . . .

Political aids and restraints on movement. There was at times an exchange of information between the government and the pastoral nomadic tribes. However, this was not particularly common. Often the bureaucracy acted to prevent the movements of the tribes.[72] Still, in *ARM* I 43:10'-12' appears one of these infrequent acts of assistance. Šamši-Addu instructs his son, Yasmaḫ-Addu, in this letter to pass on the following assurance of good will to the Yaminites:

10' i-na-aḫ a-na DUMU.MEŠ-Ia-mi-in ki-a-am q[í-b]í-[ma]
um-ma-mi aš-šum [i]-na ri-tim la i-ta-[a]b-t[u-qí-im][73]
a-na pu-ut ma-tim ku-ul-lim e-le-[e]

Translation: Now, to the Yaminites, [speak] in these terms: "So that from the pasturage there will not be a continual [cutting off], I have been up to the land to guarantee (this)."

It may be that brigands or some other obstruction to travel had been cleared away by the Assyrian king. Quite likely, the

government of Šamši-Addu policed the frontier to protect its own merchants and to promote the loyalty (or at least neutrality) of the Yaminites. The tribes produced goods useful to the economy and served as a buffer force in the grazing lands in the vicinity of Tuttul.[74]

On another occasion, Šamši-Addu passed instructions through Yasmaḫ-Addu to Yašub-El, the governor of Tuttul. He was requested to provide boats for the Rabbean tribesmen so that they could cross the Euphrates.[75]

awīlū^{meš} Ra-ab-ba-ia
ša i-na ma-a-at Ia-am-ḫa-ad^{ki} wa-aš-bu
iš-pu-ru-nim um-ma-a-m[i]
pa-ni-ne a-na e-bé-ri-im
ni-iš-ku-un-[m]a
^{iṣ}eleppētum^{há} a-na [e-bé-ri]-ni
ú-ul i-[ba-aš-še-e]
an-ni-tam iš-p[u-ru-nim]
awīlū^{meš} ú-ṣú-ú [
an-ni-iš a-na [
iš-ta-ak-nu
1^{àm} 2^{àm} uš-ta-la-X
ù ^{iṣ}eleppēt^{há} e-bé-ri-šu-nu
ú-ul i-ba-aš-še-e
i-na-an-[na] a-[n]a Ia-šu-ub-Ìl
[š]u-pu-u[r]-ma
^{iṣ}eleppētim^{h}[^{á}] [XXX] ia-[XX]-tim^{ki}
ù[
ša a-aḫ ^{nār}Purrattim^{ki}
li-iš-ku-ma[76]
ki-ma ma-aḫ-ru-u[m]-ma
ša i-il-la-[ku]
i-ib-ba-ra-X[
la i-ka-[al-la]

Translation: The Rabbeans who live in the land of Yamḫad wrote to me: "We have decided to cross the river, but there [are] no boats to make the [crossing.]" This is what they wr[ote to me.] The men are prepared (to cross?) . . . they want to (cross?) . . . . Once and then again they (tried to cross?), however, there were no boats for

> them to take passage on. Now, write to Yašub-El so that he will cause boats (to come upstream?) to the banks of the Euphrates. (Thus), as it has been previously, those who come will be able to cross [over] . . . (and) not be de[layed.]

The king probably was not providing this help to the tribesmen for purely altruistic reasons. H. Lewy has theorized that the Rabbeans wished to cross the river in order to join the army of Šamši-Addu. Naturally, the king would have welcomed this chance to strengthen his forces.[77] J. Sasson added to this assessment by suggesting that the aid extended to the Rabbeans had political motives. He points out that by helping these tribesmen Šamši-Addu could have embarrassed a rival dynast, Sumu-Epuḫ of Yamḫad.[78]

One other possible explanation for Šamši-Addu's actions may have been his desire to maintain good relations with the tribal community. He apparently felt it expedient to deal with them in a peaceful and cooperative manner whenever possible. In fact, the bulk of the textual evidence tends to show that he had fewer problems with the tribal groups in the Mari region than did his successor, Zimri-Lim.[79]

Šamši-Addu's policies also were based probably in part on economic considerations. He had attempted to reestablish a portion of the Old Assyrian Cappadocian trade.[80] Thus, it was very important that the caravan routes remain open to commercial traffic. In order to do this, alliances were made with a number of groups to prevent disruption from within the kingdom and from invading forces.[81] Another way to accomplish this aim was to establish good relations with the pastoral nomadic groups in the region. Agreements could have been made to prevent them from aggravating the defense problems of the kingdom. The tribal groups could have been given certain considerations in exchange for refraining from making raids on the caravans. Also they could have been contracted to provide protection against other tribal and nontribal raiding groups, such as the *ḫabirū*.[82]

Tribal Herding and Social Units

A discussion of the conceptual and physical aspects of the pastoral nomadic camp will conclude this chapter on herding. Like other important factors in the occupational existence of the pastoral nomads, "the camp, as a group, is an adaptive response to pastoral technology, mediating balances between pasture availability, the animal population and the human population throughout the year."[83]

nawûm. The most direct reference in the Mari texts to pastoral nomadic activity among the tribal groups is the use of the term *nawûm*. In many ways the *nawûm* of the Mari documents resembles the Brahui word for camp, *khalk*. The Brahui of the Kalat Khanate of West Pakistan use this word to denote both the physical entity (tents, animals, etc.) and the group of cooperating households of the camp.[84] This is a fairly good description of the basic meaning of *nawûm* in the Mari documents. However, there are some differences in meaning according to context.

Previous attempts to define *nawûm* have centered around either the more inclusive definition of "encampment" (i.e., "the group and its holdings including the traditional pasture lands"[85]) or the somewhat more limited meaning of "pastureland."[86] I believe, however, that the definition given to this term by D. O. Edzard[87] and M. B. Rowton[88] is more fitting when applied to the majority of its uses in the texts. They have shown that *nawûm* was employed by the Mari officials to denote a collective concept embodying the pastoralists themselves, their animals, and their camping area. The scribes did utilize it at times to connote a particular segment of the herding community or territory. However, in most contexts, the word *nawûm* was used to mean the total pastoral group and its surroundings.

Simple statements about the welfare of the migratory camps and the grazing areas were common notations in the reports of the district officials. For instance *ARM* II 33:21'-22' provides this terse assessment:

. . . na-wa-um ù TUR-Si-im-a-al[89]

[š]a-a-lim

Translation: The pastureland and the Sim'alites are fine.[90]

In the same manner, Kabia, the son of Zimri-Lim, reported to his father about the Ḫaneans in the vicinity of Kaḫat in *ARM* II 59:11-13.

> a-na na-we-e-em ša Ḫa-na
> ù a-na a-lim Ka-ḫa-at^{ki}
> šu-ul-mu-um

Translation: All things are well with the encampment of the Ḫaneans and with the city of Kaḫat.

More detailed accounts of the exact nature of the *nawûm* appear in *ARM* I 42:5-10, *Benj*. 988:a, and *Benj*. 992:b. The first of these texts deals with the conscription of Ḫanean tribesmen for a military expedition to be led by Yasmaḫ-Addu. Yarim-Addu, the recruiting officer, made this report:

> Ḫa-na^{meš} ša na-we-e-em ap-qí-id-ma
> 2 li-im ṣa-ba-am ša it-ti Ia-ás-ma-aḫ-^{il}Addu
> a-na ḫarranim i-la-ku ú-ki-in
> ù ṣa-bu-um sú-ú ka-lu-šu šu-mi-ša-am
> i-na tup-pí-im ša-ṭe$_4$-er an-ni-tam iš-pu-ra-am
> 2 li-im Ḫa-na^{meš} ša na-we-e-em ša it-ti-ka i-[i]l-la-ku

Translation: "I have inspected the Ḫaneans of the encampment and I have assigned[91] 2,000 men who are to go on the campaign with Yasmaḫ-Addu. All of these men are now listed on tablet(s)[92]." This is what he wrote to me. Two thousand Ḫaneans of the encampment[93] will be among those going with you . . . .

Another example of the use of *nawûm* to denote the migratory unit as a whole (including their grazing area) is found in *Benj*. 988:a. It was reported in this text that:

> 3 mētim^{tim} ṣa-ab DUMU.MEŠ-Ia-m[i-n]a
> a-na ša-ḫa-aṭ na-we-e-em ša aḫ ^{nār}Pu[rattim]
> it-ta-la-ak

Translation: Three hundred Yami[nites] have gone to raid the encampment on the bank of the Eu[phrates.][94]

As has been noted previously, this area along the Euphrates was one which commonly was used by the nomadic pastoralists as grazing land.[95] It is probable that the Yaminites mentioned

here planned to stage their raid against one of these pasturing groups.

Benj. 992:b provides a third use of *nawûm* for the collective pastoral body. In this case, it was reported that the Yamaḫameans, a subtribe of the Ḫaneans,[96] were frightened away from the pastureland by a series of attacks which Zimri-Lim had staged against the Yaminites in that area.[97]

šа-ni-tam aš-šum DUMU.MEŠ-Ia-am-ma-ḫa-ma-wi
ša be-lí iš-pu-ra-am iš-tu ūmim$^{\text{mi-im}}$
ša be-lí i-na na-we-e DUMU-MEŠ-Ia-mi-in
im-ḫa-ṣu it-ta-[al-k]u-nim
ma-am-ma i-na ḫa-al-ṣ[í]-ia
ú-ul i-ba-aš-ši
ḫa-al-ṣu-um ša-lim

Translation: On another matter, concerning the Yamaḫameans, about which my lord has written me--since the time that my lord attacked the encampment of the Yaminites, they (the Yamaḫameans) have l[eft]. There is not one of them in my district. The district is at peace.[99]

There were specific occasions when the writers of the Mari letters employed the term *nawûm* with the primary intent of sheep or flock. Even in these instances, however, the context allowed the scribe the flexibility to stretch also his meaning to include the pastureland and the herders. *ARM* III 15:10-15 provides such a usage of *nawûm*. This passage contains a warning sent to Zimri-Lim by his administrative assistant, Kibri-Dagan. It hints at the possibility of a potentially dangerous situation in his district.

i-nu-ma na-wu-ú-um
ša ^{awīl}Ḫa-na^{meš}
ag-da-ma-tam ša nārim
Rev. i-ka-lu[100]
na-ak-rum i-ma-aq-qu-út-ma
ḫi-ṭi$_4$-tum ib-ba-aš-ši

Translation: If the flocks of the Ḫaneans graze on the east bank of the river, the enemy will make a retaliatory attack and there will be trouble.

Another of these dual-natured usages of *nawûm* is found in

ARM II 45:7'-11'.

ù a-nu-um-ma re-ḫa-at bu-li-im ša ki-ma i-[ba-aš-šu-ú]
a-na ḫa-al-ṣí-im ša a-bi-ia aṭ-ṭa-a[r-dam]
a-bi a-na Me-ep-ti-im li-iš-pu-ur b[u]-lum [
a-na li-ib-bi na-wi-im ša a-bi-ia li-[
it-ti bu-lim ša a-bi-ia li-ku-la b[u(?)-

Translation: And concerning the remainder of the cattle, I have sent [them] to the district of my father. (Therefore my father should write to Meptim. The cattle into the midst of the herd (or perhaps pastureland?) of my father . . . . with the cattle of my father they will graze . .

M. B. Rowton, in discussing this text, points to the invasion of the kingdom by Silli-Sin, the king of Eshnunna, as the reason behind this transfer of animals. The cattle were moved to the relative safety of the royal pastureland (*ina libbi nawûm*) They would have been cared for there by the pastoral tribesmen employed by Zimri-Lim as shepherds.[101]

One additional use made of *nawûm* in the Mari texts was a geographical term. It was used to designate general areas of pastureland or nomadic pastoral activity in the kingdom.[102] *ARMT* XIV 92:17-22 contains an excellent example of this connotation. The text is a report on the seige of Aḫuna[103] and the subsequent desertion of the relief force when the situation began to look hopeless. Among the deserters was a group of Ḫaneans who took advantage of the unstable situation and renounced their obligations to the state.

ṣa-bu-um til-la-tum ka-lu-ši-na
a-na ma-ti-šu ip-ta-ṭà-ar
ù $^{aw\bar{i}l}$Ḫa-na$^{me\check{s}}$ iš-tu A-ḫu-na-a^{ki}
a-na na-wi-im-ma iṣ-ba-at
^{I}Ia-zi-bu-um qa-du-um ṣa-bi-im
i-na A-ḫu-na-a^{ki} i-zi-bu-nim

Translation: The relief troops have fled en masse to their lands and the Ḫaneans have taken the road from Aḫuna to the pastureland. Yazilum, with the soldiers in Aḫuna, they have abandoned.

Another text, *ARM* IV 7:8-11, also contains a usage of *nawûm* as a geographic designation. The letter is concerned

with the taking of a census in the district of Mari. Šamši-Addu instructs Yasmaḫ-Addu:

ù at-t[a] a-na te-bi-ib-tim[104]
a-a[ḫ]-k[a l]a ta-na-ad-[d]i
[a-na ša-]ap-li-it na-we-em al-kam
[ ] su-qá-qì ša a-aḫ ^{nār}Purattim

Translation: And do not be neg[ligent] in the taking of the census. Go [to the te]rritory below (i.e., downstream) the *nawûm* (encampment) . . . (meet with ?) the *sugāgū* of the banks of the Euphrates.

Apparently, it was felt that a meeting with the tribal officials, *sugāgū*, would facilitate the taking of the census.[105]

One final example of the use of *nawûm* to denote a specific locale appears in a text published by G. Dossin forty years ago.[106] This letter was written by Zimri-Lim to the *merḫum* of the Upper Country.[107] Lines 3-5 reveal what was probably a summary statement about the physical conditions of the district. This information was now being passed on to the other district administrators in a sort of government memo.[108]

i-na pa-ni-tim i-nu-ma a-na Ḫa-la-ab^{ki}
e-lu-ú aš-šum ṭe$_4$-e-em na-we-e-em
ša Kar-ka-mi-[iš^{ki}] ik-tu-[un]

Translation: Previously, when I went to Aleppo, the news concerning the pasturelands of (near or around) Carchemish was confirmed.

gāyûm. There are two other technical terms used for the social unit in the Mari texts. These are *gāyûm* and *ḫibrum*. At this point, I only wish to define and give clarifying evidence about these words. In subsequent chapters I will take them up again. They are especially important to the discussion of the effects of fluidity on the tribal groups.[109]

A. Malamat has defined *gāyûm* as "an ethno-geographic term for the pattern of settlement," which "as a rule, was the outgrowth of the common wanderings." He adds that in some cases it is used to designate a kind of military division.[110] The most common usage of *gāyûm*, however, is as a tribal section. Thus, in *ARM* IV 1:5-28 five men of the *gāyûm* of Yamaḫamum, a Ḫanean subgroup, were paid for serving in the military.[111]

Šamši-Addu instructed his son, Yasmaḫ-Addu, to have the *sugāgum* of the Yamaḫamum conduct the men to the same area where other members of their *gāyûm* already had been given fields.

^{I}Sa-ku-ra-nu
^{I}Ma-na-ta-nu
i-na Ḫa-ar-ra-tim^{ki} wa-aš-bu
^{I}Ga-i-la-lum
^{I}Za-zu-nu-um
^{I}Da-di-ia[112]
i-na A-ma-tim^{ki} wa-aš-bu
^{I}Ḫa-ti-ku ^{awīl}su-qá-aq-šu-nu
ga-ú-um Ya-ma-ḫa-m[u-X(?)]
5 awīlū^{meš} an-nu-tu[m]
ga-a-šu-nu i-zi-bu-m[a]
a-na ṣe-ri-ia
it-ta-al-ku-nim
ù an-na-nu-um aḫ-ḫu-šu-nu
še-em ù eqlam pa-aq-du
i-ša -ri-iš ap-lu
i-na-an-na a-nu-um-ma ^{awīl}su-qá-aq-šu-nu
aṭ-ṭà-ar-da-ak-kum
awīli^{meš}šu-nu-ti li-iṣ-ba-as-sú-nu-ti-ma
a-na qa-ti-šu pí-iq-dam-ma
a-na ṣe-ri-ia li-ir-du-ni-iš-šu-nu-ti-ma
i-ša-ri-iš li-pu-lu-šu-nu-ti
ù it-ti aḫ-ḫi-šu-nu
li-il-li-ku

Translation: Sakuranu, Manatanu--residents of Ḫarratim--(and) Gā'il-'ilum[113], Zazumun, Dadia--residents of Amātim--Ḫatiku is their *sugāgum*. (They belong to ?) the clan of Yamaḫamum. These five men abandoned their territory (and) came to me because their brothers had been entrusted with wheat and a field here (and) were satisfied. Now on this matter I have sent their *sugāgum* to you. These men should be taken and entrusted to his hand (so that) they may be brought to me. They should be given satisfaction and go with their brothers.

Again it is the case that Šamši-Addu is encouraging good relations with the tribal groups. His providing of land to these

five men not only paid a debt for services but also initiated them into the sedentary community. It is unlikely, that this was part of a general program of sedentarization. However, such rewarding of tribalists was probably a common tool employed by the government to gain better control over the nomadic pastoral groups.[114]

An appearance of the term *gāyûm* in a military context is found in *ARM* VI 28:6-8.

> . . . um-ma-a-mi ṣa-ba-am a-pa-qí-dam-ma
> ù a-tu-ur-ra-am šum-[m]a Ḫ[a-na]^{meš} KUD a-na KUD
> ù ga-iu-um a-n[a] g[a-ii-im ip-pa-qí-id][115]. . . .

Translation: I have inspected the troops and I have now returned. When the Ḫa[neans were inspected] section by section and clan by [clan] . . . .

The remainder of this report by Baḫdi-Lim deals with the problem encountered by the Ḫaneans and other allies in choosing a *rabi Amurru* ("general") to lead them.[116] In order to get the army on its way without further delay, he nominated a certain Zimri-Addu for the post.

ḫibrum. The second of these terms for social unit, *ḫibrum*, has been defined as "a group of families probably linked together by communal wanderings."[117] That is, of course, the standard definition for any tribal migratory unit. One occurrence of this word appeared recently in an article by G. Dossin.[118] It is included as part of the standard notification formula in this report sent by Itūr-Asdu to Zimri-Lim.

> [š]a-ni-tam ḫi-ib-ru-um
> [š]a Ḫa-am-mi-te-lu-ú
> ù Ia-pa-ḫu-um
> [1 ?] ME awīlū^{meš} Su-tu-[ú]
> iš-tu ma-ḫa-ar Si-ma-aḫ-la-n [e!-e]
> il-li-ku-ni[m]

Translation: On another matter, the clan of Ḫammitelu and of Yapaḫum (and) 100 (?) Suteans have come with Simaḫlānē.

It would appear that the individual *ḫibrum* were named for either the most important member of the unit (i.e., Ḫammitelu and Yapaḫum) or possibly an eponymous ancestor.[119]

All of the various aspects of Mari pastoral nomadism have not been discussed here. This is partially due to a lack of textual evidence for many of the basic factors involved in migratory herding. The various special and economic factors involved in camp formation and the effects of the interchange of ideas and cultures between the nomadic and sedentary communities, will be taken up in later chapters. To this point, the aim has been to establish the environmental problems faced by the pastoral nomadic groups. In the next chapter their adaptations to the society of which they were a part will be examined.

NOTES

CHAPTER II

[1]Kupper, J.-R., "Northern Mesopotamia and Syria," *CAH*[2], Vol. II/1 (Cambridge, 1973), 24. He provides a good map of this region in "Le rôle des nomades dans l'histoire de la Mesopotamie ancienne," *JESHO* 2 (1959), 114. M. B. Rowton recently has discussed the importance of this area which he calls the "dimorphic zone" in his article "Dimorphic Structure and Topology," *OA* 15 (1976), 20-21. He places this region between the 400mm. and 200mm. isohyets and states that within it ". . . a stable economic base could be achieved only by irrigation agriculture, where that was possible or else by means of symbiosis between rain agriculture and pastoral nomadism." His map on p. 31 shows that the area extends from the great bend of the Euphrates between Birecik and Meskene, and then all the way down to the region between Susa and Lagaš.

[2]Kupper, J.-R., *Les nomades en Mésopotamie au temps des rois de Mari* (Paris, 1957), ix. He describes this belt of steppe as the "source" of Semitic nomadism. J. T. Luke has presented adequately the various arguments for and against this theory in *Pastoralism and Politics in the Mari Period* (University of Michigan Ph.D. dissertation, 1965), 1-19. He also qualifies Kupper's geographic description on p. 18, saying that the zone separates the area known as the fertile crescent from the Nefud sector of the Arabian desert.

[3]Smith, P. E. L. and Young, T. C., Jr., "The Evolution of Early Agriculture and Culture in Greater Mesopotamia: a Trial Model" in *Population Growth: Anthropological Implications*, ed. B. Spooner (Cambridge, Mass., 1972), 23. See their map, with its five sectional divisions, of the fertile crescent on p. 22.

[4]Ibid. Detailed information and charts on topography, vegetation, and climate in this region are found in *The Bioclimatic Map of the Mediterranean Zone, Arid Zone Research* 21 (UNESCO, 1963).

[5]Sasson, J., *Northern Syria: a Survey of its Institutions Before the Fall of Mari (ca. 1757 B.C.)* (Brandeis University Ph.D. dissertation, 1966), 88.

[6]Ibid., 89.

[7]There has been a great deal of discussion over the years concerning when the domestication of the camel took place in the ancient Near East. Some of the more important contributions to the examination of this question are B. Bentjes, "Das Kamel im Alten Orient," *Klio* 38 (1960), 28-52 and the very thorough studies of R. Walz, "Zum Problem des Zeitpunkts der altweltlichen Cameliden," *ZDMG* 101 (1951), 29-51 and "Neue Untersuchungen zum Domestikationsproblem der altweltlichen Cameliden," *ZDMG* 104 (1954), 45-87, which give convincing evi-

dence that the type of camels used by the nomadic populations of the Near East today actually did not become sufficiently domesticated for commercial use until the 1st millennium B.C. Various other attempts to either prove or disprove this are documented in J. T. Luke, *Pastoralism and Politics*, 42, n.34. It is perhaps the article by J. P. Free, "Abraham's Camels," *JNES* 3 (1944), 187-94 which is most often quoted as an advocate of early domestication. This is because it was for a long time the only published disagreement with W. F. Albright's theory on the nature of the Old Testament Patriarchs' migratory practices. Albright's theory that they were "ass-nomads" (most recently presented in *The Biblical Period from Abraham to Ezra* [New York, 1963], 7 and in *Yahweh and the Gods of Canaan* [Garden City, N.Y., 1969], 64-73 and 179, which deal specifically with his proofs for the "late" domestication of the camel) has been discounted in recent publications--T. Thompson, *The Historicity of the Patriarchal Narratives* (Berlin,1974) and J. Van Seters, *Abraham in History and Tradition* (New Haven, Conn., 1975). This latter work, in my opinion, sums up the evidence on camel domestication by saying that it simply does not exist in any widespread degree until the 1st millennium B.C. (p. 17). In any event, there are no mentions of the camel in the Mari texts so far published, and therefore, the assumption used in this study, based on the arguments listed above and the lack of appearances by these animals, will be that they were not among the domesticated animals used by the Mari pastoral nomadic groups.

[8]Gottwald, N. K., "Were the Early Israelites Pastoral Nomads?" in *Rhetorical Criticism: Essays in Honor of James Muilenberg*, eds., J. Jackson and M. Kessler (Pittsburgh, 1974), 234.

[9]London, Meteorological Office, *Tables of Temperature, Relative Humidity, and Precipitation for the World* (London, 1966), 23-31 provide the following data on some of these cities: Deir-ez-Zor, elevation 699 ft., average yearly rainfall 6.2 in. (over an 8 yr. span); Esh Shām (Damascus), elevation 2362 ft., average yearly rainfall 8.6 in (over a 7 yr. span); Haleb (Aleppo), elevation 1280 ft., average yearly rainfall 15.5 in. (over a 10 yr. span). Mōsul, elevation 730 ft., average yearly rainfall 15.1 in. (over a 29 yr. span) appears on p. 34. In looking at this information, it should not be misinterpreted to mean that these figures reflect the actual situation for every year. There are fluctuations and years of complete drought. The usual seasonal rainfall range is ca. 3.5 in. in the winter at Aleppo and Mōsul and 1.6 in. in Deir-ez-Zor and Damascus and 0.1 in. in the summer months of June through September.

[10]Smith, P. E. L. and Young, T. C., Jr., "Greater Mesopotamia," 23. J. Oates, in "The Background and Development of Early Farming Communities in Mesopotamia and the Zagros," *Proceedings of the Prehistoric Society* 39 (1973), 147, places the boundary of rainfall sufficient for agriculture at 200mm. She points out that there has been no appreciable shift in this boundary (running across northern Mesopotamia from west to east and then turning southeast following the foothills of the Zagros) since 12,000 B.C. when temperature and precipitation gradually began to increase.

[11]Luke, J. T., *Pastoralism and Politics*, 69-75, for the Yaminites and 155-60 for the Ḫaneans.

[12]Oppenheim, M. F. von, *Die Beduinen*, I (Leipzig, 1939). See, for example, his documentation of the movement patterns of the Agêdât, whose movements between winter and summer pastures were within approximately the same area as the Mari pastoralists. F. Barth also examines these planned migrations by nomadic pastoralists in "Land Use Patterns of Migratory Tribes of South Persia," *Norsk Geografisk Tidsskrift* 17 (1960), 1-11. Still another look at this systematic migration routing is found in Pierre Oberling, *The Qashqā'i Nomads of Fārs* (The Hague, 1974), 15-16.

[13]Luke, J. T., *Pastoralism and Politics*, 70.

[14]See for example *ARM* II 92:15, 25 and III 67:5.

[15]Birot, M., "Les Lettres de Iasīm-Sumu," *Syria* 41 (1964), 49.

[16]Ibid. This would make for a clear division between urban and rural cultures. P. E. L. Smith, "Land-Use, Settlement Patterns, and Subsistence Agriculture: a Demographic Perspective" in *Man, Settlement, and Urbanism*, eds. P. J. Ucko, R. Tringham, and G. W. Dimbleby (Hertfordshire, England, 1972), 420, notes that this was unlike the settlement pattern in the south where the bulk of the population was concentrated in walled and fortified cities by the Early Dynastic Period.

[17]Rowton, M. B., "Enclosed Nomadism," *JESHO* 17 (1974), 27, gives a description of this small kin dom's relations with its nomadic population. J. T. Luke, *Pastoralism and Politics*, 177, n.87, locates this city, based on the evidence presented by W. Hallo in "The Road to Emar," *JCS* 18 (1964), 74, near Tell Barri, 40 km. from Tell Leilan.

[18]Cf. Barth, F., *A Tribe of the Khamseh Confederacy: The Basseri Nomads of South Persia* (Oslo, 1961), 5, in which the routes through these tribal areas on the way to pasturing zones were characterized by the pastoralists as the "tribal road" (*il-rah*).

[19]Luke, J. T., *Pastoralism and Politics*, 151, reads this tribal name as *Yamaḫamum*, thus making it possible for him to establish that a Ḫanean subgroup was engaged in grazing southeast of Mari, on the banks of the Tigris River near Kalan. M. B. Rowton, "Enclosed Nomadism," 20, takes it to be *Jamsa* and marks it as a case for a parallel between this text and *ARM* VIII 11, where a portion of the clan of *Awîn* appeared to be sedentary and another portion (which lived in the *nawûm*) was considered nomadic.

[20]This technical term will be discussed fully later in this chapter, pp. 59-63. In this particular text, the first mention has a meaning of "flocks or herders" and the second, by context, means "pastureland."

[21]Along with the political considerations in this official investigation, territorial infringement and tribal grazing rights may be part of the undercurrent of concern here and in *ARM* III 15:10-27. This second text deals with official policy on grazing areas. The Ḫaneans were to be allowed only to graze their flocks on one side of the Euphrates in order to avoid any confrontation with the "enemy" which lived across the river.

[22]Lambton, A. K. S., *Landlord and Peasant in Persia* (London, 1953), 284, describes just such a situation as this. In her study of the Persian nomadic groups, she notes that confrontations were the result of the following situation: "On the borders of the territory of two hostile tribal groups such as the Qashqā'i and the Khamseh disputes sometimes arise over the pastures and are usually decided by force majéure."

[23]The suggestion for this restoration came in a personal communication with D. W. Young.

[24]Luke, J. T., *Pastoralism and Politics*, 161 and 251, chooses to take this reference to mean that these agricultural areas were to be farmed by the Ḫaneans. However, it may be simply that the fields in which they were allowed to retain their rights were contracted as grazing area for their flocks. This would have been an aid to maintaining the fertility of the fields and would have provided good winter pasturage for the herders' animals.

[25]Spooner, B., *The Cultural Ecology of Pastoral Nomads* Philippines, 1973), 17.

[26]Mitchell, W. A., "Movement and Pastoral Nomadism: a Tentative Model," *Rocky Mountain Social Science Journal* 8 (1971), 70, sets the limit for sheep's watering spacings as four or five days in cold weather. This allows them to graze in a radius of 20 miles from the watering source. In warm weather, they require water everyday and can graze no more than 10 or 12 miles from a well or other water source.

[27]Pastner, S. L., "Camels, Sheep, and Nomad Social Organization: a Comment on Rubel's Model," *MAN* 6 (1971), 286.

[28]Oates, J., "Background and Development," *PPS* 39 (1973), 176, says that this advancement of the cultivated area by the middle of the 6th millennium reached lands which required farming techniques in order to get them to produce. Proof of the great stands of wild grain has been provided by J. R. Harlan and D. Zohary in "Distribution of Wild Wheats and Barley," *Science* 153 (1966), 1078. They actually made primative sickles and harvested in a few hours as much grain as a family could consume in a year.

[29]Hole, F., Flannery, K. V., and Neely, J. A., *Prehistory and Human Ecology of the Deh Luran Plain* (Ann Arbor, Mich., 1969), 367. They posit that this system of cultivation was continually amplified. Between 7000 and 6000 B.C., the amount of cultivated grain consumed by these early farmers grew from

less than 5% to almost 40%.

[30]Flannery, K. V., "Origins and Ecological Effects of Early Domestication in Iran and the Near East" in *The Domestication of Plants and Animals*, eds. P. J. Ucko and G. W. Dimbleby (Chicago, 1969), 87. C. A. Reed, "The Pattern of Animal Domestication in the Prehistoric Near East" in *The Domestication of Plants and Animals*, 367, considers a settled village life "a primary requirement for the earliest domestication of the ruminants and for pigs. . . ."

[31]Perkins, D., "Beginnings," *AJA* 77 (1973), 279, bases this identification on the percentage of juvenile sheep remains (50%). Such a high number implies a greater availability to these young animals than is common to hunters (who ordinarily kill only 25% of those 1 1/2 years of age or younger. In addition, the increase in the sheep population in an area characterized by flatlands (not a natural habitat for sheep) implies that many of these were domesticated. C. A. Reed, "Pattern of Animal Domestication," 371 and D. Perkins, "Beginnings," 280, both identify domesticated sheep at Çayönü in southeast Turkey ca. 7000 B.C. One method which recently has been put forward to determine domestication has been presented in I. M. Drew, D. Perkins, and P. Daly, "Prehistoric Domestication of Animals: Effects on Bone Structure," *Science* 171 (1971), 281-82. They present the findings of X-ray and spectrographic analysis of sheep remains from two Anatolian sites, Erbaba (5780 B.C.) and Suberde (6570 B.C.), as well as from the Northern Iraq site of Zawi Chemi. These tests showed definite developmental difference in bone structure between wild and domesticated sheep. One of these differences was the greater tendency of hydroxyapatite crystallites becoming aligned in the bone from domesticated animals. Another showed that the lacunae in wild bones were rounded while those of domesticates were more rectangular. In addition, wild specimens show a markedly slower transition between compacts and spongiosa as compared to the transition in domesticated animals. Should this method prove to be reliable, it would be of great benefit in the study of early domesticates.

[32]Berger, R. and Protsch, R., "The domestication of Plants and Animals in Europe and the Near East," *Or.* 42 (1973), 220, reports on the remains of domesticated goats at Ali Kosh and Jarmo based on the high percentage of juvenile remains as well as morphologic changes. J. Mellaart, *The Neolithic of the Near East* (New York, 1975), 71, identifies domesticated sheep and goats at Ghari-i-Asp. He points to a progression in which herding was followed by domestication on the edges of the Iranian plateau.

[33]Perkins, D., "Beginnings," 280. He theorizes that in most locales only one domesticate animal was developed originally. Then, as one or more domesticates were added to the village economy (ca. 6000 B.C.), they then became more than just a source of food. In fact, he states that ". . .with the beginning of agriculture, the pig, the most efficient meat producer, became an obvious choice for domestication."

[34]Ryder, M. L., "Changes in the Fleece of Sheep Following

Domestication (with a note on the coat of cattle)" in *The Domestication and Exploitation of Plants and Animals*, 500. On pp. 496-97 he refutes the suggestion in K. V. Flannery, "Origins and Ecological Effects of Early Domestication in Iran and the Near East" in *The Domestication and Exploitation of Plants and Animals*, 91-92, that the wooly coat on domesticated sheep developed in an evolutionary response to the movement of the sheep into a warmer climate. There is in fact evidence that the wool does act as a cooling device (tempering the sun's heat by as much as 40°C.) in K. Schmidt-Nielsen, *Desert Animals: Physiological Problems of Heat and Water* (Oxford, 1964), 96-98. However, Ryder states that ". . . wool is more likely to have been developed by man in a relatively cold evnironment, the insulation of the sheep against heat being a purely secondary and incidental feature of a fine-wooled fleece."

[35]Oppenheim, A. L. and Hartman, L. F., "The Domestic Animals of Ancient Mesopotamia According to the XIIIth Tablet of the Series *Har.ra=hubullū*," *JNES* 4 (1945), 156-65.

[36]Hole, F., et al., *Prehistory and Human Ecology*, 370. T. C. Young, Jr., "Population Densities and Early Mesopotamian Urbanism" in *Man, Settlement, and Urbanism*, eds. P. J. Ucko, R. Tringham, and G. W. Dimbleby (1972), 831, says that the population actually increased thirteen fold by the time of the Ubaid period, ca. 4500 B.C. There was an increase from 12 sites in Deh Luran during the Khazineh Phase to 102 sites in northern Kurdistan in the Susiana b period.

[37]Young, T. C., Jr., "Population Densities," 831. He uses E. Boserup, *The Conditions of Agricultural Growth* (Chicago), 39, which says that the introduction of irrigation tends to occur only after the fallow periods have been shortened due to the demands of population pressure.

[38]Hole, F., et al., *Prehistory and Human Ecology*, 363. They mark this as the beginning (between 5500 and 5000 B.C.) of the change from the old food producing pattern of wheat and goats to a barley-sheep complex which would characterize the region down through the Elamite period. As H. Helbaek has noted in "Plant Collecting, Dry Farming, and Irrigation Agriculture in Prehistoric Deh Luran" in *Prehistory and Human Ecology*, F. Hole et al., 421, the planting of barley only served to accelerate the salinisation process in marginal areas since six-row barley requires a higher water supply than wheat and irrigation would have had to be intensified to meet this need.

[39]Oates, J., "Prehistoric Settlement Patterns in Mesopotamia" in *Man, Settlement, and Urbanism*, 306. The irrigation systems proved too vulnerable to sabotage and could not provide adequate drainage because of the flatness of the land in Southern Mesopotamia. This is in contrast to earlier periods in this area. For instance Ali Kosh was simply abandonned after 1500 years of occupation (ca. 6000 B.C.) because the soil was depleted. The people had then just moved to an area a few miles away where the land had not been over-cropped and over-irrigated. Population pressures had not yet forced short fallowing and a shortage of farmlands.

[40]Adams, R. M., "The Study of Ancient Mesopotamian Settlement Patterns and the Problem of Urban Origins," *Sumer* 25 (1969), 116 and "Agriculture and Urban Life in Early Southwestern Iran," *Science* 136 (1962), 112. He notes in these articles that only two of 40 villages which previously had inhabited the 15 km. agricultural zone around Uruk remained by the time of the Early Dynastic period. F. Hole, et al., *Prehistory and Human Ecology*, 371, adds to Adams discussion that this population contraction was done for political and defensive reasons. He notes that the ecology of the region had necessitated the switch to fortified cities with buffer zones between them by 3500 B.C. The competition between the city states insured that the former settlement system of dispersed villages in southern Mesopotamia would not return.

[41]Ibid. He suggests that this change in human society created a "new ecological niche" to be utilized by the nomadic pastoralists.

[42]Smith, P. E. L., "Land-Use, Settlement Patterns, and Subsistence Agriculture" in *Man, Settlement, and Urbanism*, 420, points to the easy access to western land for emigrants from this northern region.

[43]Despite this, northern Mesopotamia did not escape the effects of the political shifts in the south following the end of the Ur III dynasty. See T. Jacobsen, "Salt and Silt in Ancient Mesopotamian Agriculture," *Science* 128 (1958), 1252-53, which suggests that the rise of Babylon at this time was based on the fact that it was located in an area which was less affected by the salinisation process. R. M. Adams, "Ancient Mesopotamian Settlement Patterns," 117-18, posits that many of the smaller settlements in the northern region were organized into corporate peasant (or even tribal) communities. This may have been one way for them to compete with larger urban authorities. Cf. G. E. Mendenhall, "Social Organization in Early Israel" in *The Mighty Acts of God*, eds. F. M. Cross, W. E. Lomke, and P. D. Miller, Jr. (New York, 1976), 132-51 for a discussion of peasant reactions and strategies toward urban states.

[44]Adams, R. M., "Ancient Mesopotamian Settlement Patterns," 118. Already in the 6th millennium there were groups of nomadic herdsmen or transhumants who had a working economic relationship with the settled villagers. Cf., for instance, J. Oates, "Prehistorical Settlement Patterns," 301-2. There is some question whether campsite settlements such as Hassuna Ia represented the seasonal stopping places for village transhumants from permanent sites such as Yarim Tepe (50 miles west of Mōsul) or whether there were distinct nomadic occupational groups contemporary with the permanent settlements. The answer is clouded by the difficulty of the evidence. S. Böyönyi, in "Zoological Evidence for Seasonal or Permanent Occupation of Prehistoric Settlements" in *Man, Settlement, and Urbanism*, 123-25, notes that it is possible to determine the age of animals killed at the site by calculating the calving season of the region and by examining the dentition. However, making judgments about whether the site was occupied for a part or

all of the year on the evidence of these remains is merely conjectural. Such factors as the size of the sample, the killing and dying period, local taste, the fodder situation, and disease must be contended with in making any determinations.

[45]Dyson-Hudson, W., "The Study of Nomads" in *Perspectives on Nomadism*, eds. W. Iron and N. Dyson-Hudson (Leiden, 1972), 24, provides a detailed discussion of these variables.

[46]Mention is made of the movement of royal herds in *ARM* II 45:7'-11', V 15:7-20, and G. Dossin, "Les archives épistolaires du palais de Mari," *Syria* 19 (1938), 124.

[47]Johnson, D. L., *The Nature of Nomadism*, Department of Geography Research Paper #118 (University of Chicago, 1969), 54. This pasturage is to be found in a range from 1200 to 2500 m. above sea-level. *ARMT* XIV 86:31-40 describes sheep pasturing in this type of valley. K. V. Flannery, "Origins and Ecological Effects of Early Domestication," 88, lists some of the small annual legumes which eventually became fodder for the grazing herds. Originally, the clover-like legumes as *Medicago* (wild alfalfa), *Astragalus* (spring milk vetch), and *Trigonella* (plant of the pea family related to *fenugreek*), as well as oat grass (*Avena*), Bermuda grass (*Cynodon*), and Canary grass (*Phalaris*) served as a source of food for early gatherers. However, by 6000 B.C. they had been relegated to the status of weeds and only were allowed to grow in uncultivated areas.

[48]Other examples of grazing on the banks of the Euphrates are *ARM* II 90:5-12 and III 15:10-27. This practice also is found on the Ḫabur River in *ARMT* XIV 22:9-11.

[49]MacDonald, J., "The Role and Status of the *Suḫārū* in the Mari Correspondence," *JAOS* 96 (1976), 66-76, theorizes that the *ṣeḫrum* and *ṣeḫertum* (both singular) may be the overseers of the *wardū* and *amātum* (both plural).

[50]This restoration and subsequent translation are based upon a suggestion made to me by M. B. Rowton. It may be that both the animals and the pastoralists lived off the gleanings from the fields.

[51]Smith, P. E. L. and Young, T. C., Jr., "Greater Mesopotamia," 23.

[52]See Sweet, L. E., *Tell Toqaan: a Syrian Village* (Ann Arbor, Mich., 1960), 99, where field grazing rights are said to be contracted to particular herding groups by the farmers.

[53]Weippert, M., *The Settlement of the Israelite Tribes in Palestine* (Naperville, Ill., 1971), 115-16 translates these terms as "stockyards and cattle pens." He notes that there is a correspondence between the Amorite word *ḫaṣirātum* and the Hebrew word *ḥ*ᵃ*ṣērōt* which appears in Gen 25:16 and in Isa 42:11. Van Seters, in *Abraham*, 18, notes that the manner of life of the Ishmaelites in Gen 25:16 and their use of *ḥ*ᵉ*ṣirim* is contrasted also by the biblical writer with that of Israel's direct ancestors in Gen 16:12 and 21:20-21.

[54]MacDonald, J., "The Identification of *Bazaḫātu* in the Mari Letters," *RA* 69 (1975), 142, makes the point that this report given by the *bazaḫātu* shows that these officials were also in charge of preventing any breach in the grazing rights. Could it be the case that the flocks were driven to places like *Lasqum* according to some sort of strict formula and that the *bazaḫātu* were charged with preventing side trips or movement out of the prescribed order?

[55]There has been a certain amount of debate on this dual tribal name. I. J. Gelb, " The Early History of the West Semitic Peoples," *JCS* 15 (1961), 37 and Weippert, *Settlement*, 115-16, n.59, both state that the name Ḫanean, as used here, may be simply a secondary appellative for "nomads" or "bedouin." On the other hand, H. Klengel, "Benjaminiten un Hanäer," *Wissenschaftliche Zeitschrift der Humboldt-Universität zu Berlin* 8 (1958/9), 212, states that it is used to designate those Yaminites who have settled or are living in Ḫana. J. T. Luke, *Pastoralism and Politics*, 153, tends to agree with him on the grounds that tribal affiliation is often very fluid. Whether this affiliation resulted from simple residency in Ḫanean areas or through marriage ties or other means is unknown. However, when one considers that other double appellations, such as *Ḫana Ia-ma-ḫa-mu-um* (*ARM* V 81:9), do appear elsewhere, it seems to be that affiliation is the key to its explanation.

[56]For example, see B. Spooner, *Cultural Ecology*, 17, for a use of this system by tribal peoples. It becomes institutionalized to the extent of becoming a part of the kinship and hospitality system within the tribes.

[57]Pastner, S., "Ideological Aspect of Nomad-Sedentary Contact: a Case from Southern Baluchistan," *Anthropological Quarterly* 44 (1971), 180, terms the combination of tribal territories (ca. 1000 sq. miles) as a macropastoral orbit. He describes this as a bounded entity in social as well as geographical terms.

[58]Salzman, P. C., "Movement and Resource Extraction Among Pastoral Nomads: The Case of the Shah Nawazi Baluch," *AQ* 44 (1971), 194.

[59]For *salḫum*, see W. von Soden, *AHw*, 1015, where it is translated "befluchlet."

[60]See Dossin, G., "Le royaume de Qatna au XVIIIe siè̀le avant notre ère d'après les 'Archives royales de Mari'," *Bulletin de l'academie royale d'archéologie de Belgique* 5 (1954), 422, for a complete treatment of this text and of the political relations of the area around Qatna.

[61]This text originally was published by G. Dossin in "Les archives épistolaries du Palais de Mari," *Syria* 19 (1938), 124. For a recent treatment, see W. Römer, *Frauenbriefe über Religion, Politik und Privatleben in Mari, AOAT* 12 (1971), 87.

[62]Rowton, M. B., "Autonomy and Nomadism in Western Asia," *Orientalia* 42 (1973), 251-52. Hired herders may be members of

pastoral nomadic tribes. However, when they are employed to work as shepherds of flocks not their own, they enter another category and do not figure into the discussion of the activities of the tribal groups.

[63]Cf. Leshnik, L. S., "Pastoralism in the Archaeology of India and Pakistan," *World Archaeology* 4/2 (1972), 150, for an example of this type of movement pattern in India. The movements in this region are based primarily on the seasonal rainfall pattern.

[64]Bates, D. G., "Differential Access to Pasture in a Nomadic Society: The Yoruk of Southeastern Turkey" in *Perspectives on Nomadism*, eds. W. Irons and N. Dyson-Hudson, 58-59. Economic status also can be a factor among the Yoruk in the order of migration. The poorer members of the tribe are forced to shear their sheep before leaving their winter quarters in order to pay their accumulated debts. As a result, they cannot risk moving at the start of the spring season for summer pasture in the mountains. This is because the sheared sheep cannot survive the cold of early spring in the mountains. When they are able to depart, the grazing along the way already has been depleted by the herds of the wealthier pastoralists who had left before them.

[65]Spooner, B., "Towards a Generative Model of Nomadism," *AQ* 44 (1971), 204-5. The migratory group generally retains its tribal affiliation and basic nomadic identity despite the political and population pressures placed upon them.

[66]Rowton, M. B., "Enclosed Nomadism," 27-28, shows that the revitalization is the result of the release from political influence when the tribes migrate to areas of less or no actual urban control.

[67]A full discussion of the effects of tribal fluidity appear below, pp. 107-14.

[68]Moran, W. L., "Review: M. Weippert, *Die Landnahme der israelitischen Stämme in der neueren wissenschaftlichen Diskussion*," *CBQ* 30 (1968), 644-45, translates *elišma* "to the Upper Country only." The *-ma* ending serves to throw into prominence the element to which it is attached.

[69]For a description of *laskum* as a type of pastureland, see D. O. Edzard, "Altbabylonisch *nawûm*," *ZA* 53 (1959), 170, n.8. *CAD* "L", 108, defines it tentatively as a West Semitic word for pasture.

[70]This had been a major staging area for the Amorite tribes for hundreds of years. A. Haldar, *Who Were the Amorites?* (Leiden, 1971), 13-15, cites the numerous ties in cuneiform literature between the nomads and the vicinity of Mt. Bisir. T. L. Thompson, *The Historicity of the Patriarchal Narratives*, 83, concurs in this assessment and equates the reference *a-na mat Bi*[*s*]*i-ir* with Jebel Bishri.

[71]Luke, J. T., *Pastoralism and Politics*, 100, n.106. He also makes the point, using information from H. Charles,

Tribus moutonnières de Euphrates (Damascus, 1939), 116 ff., that this area is still important to the economy of modern pastoralists.

[72]In most texts, especially those from the reign of Zimri-Lim, the state tried to limit the movement of the nomadic groups. This was probably the practice since it would have been easier for the administration to keep tabs on the pastoralists if they were kept within definite boundaries. See, for instance, *ARM* II 92:16-28; 98:4'-10'; 102:5-27;V 27:25-27, 36-37.

[73]This restoration is based upon W. von Soden, "Zu den politischen Korrespondenzen des Archivs von Mari," *Orientalia* 21 (1952), 80. He also treats this Ntn form in *AHw*, 115, and translates it as "abgeschnitten."

[74]Cf. Klengel, H., *Geschichte Syriens im 2. Jahrtausend v.u. Z., Teil 1-Nordsyrien* (Berlin, 1965), 115, for another discussion of this text and the region around Tuttul.

[75]*ARM* IV 6:5-28.

[76]This reading is based upon W. von Soden, "Neue Bände der *Archives royales de Mari*," *Orientalia* 22 (1953), 203, and is translated there "er möge 'setzen' (škn) und." See also A. L. Oppenheim, "The Archives of the Palace of Mari, II," *JNES* 13 (1954), 142, where the meaning "to travel up stream" is given to *šaqum*. He notes that this meaning is also attested in the Old Babylonian letter *VS* 16, 186:9.

[77]Lewy, H., "Šubat-Šamaš and Tuttul," *Orientalia* 27 (1958), 10, n.2. These men may have been defecting from the Yamḫadian army. If so, they carried with them valuable military information.

[78]Sasson, J., *Northernmost Syria*, 89-90.

[79]There is one exception to this picture. *Benj*. 986:a mentions a conspiracy by the Yaminites and kings of Zalmaqum to raid one of Šamši-Addu's towns on the Euphrates named Dêr.

[80]Cf. L. L. Orlin, *Assyrian Colonies in Cappadocia*. (The Hague, 1970), 212-13 and 246, for excavation results and pottery from *karum* Kanis, level Ib, which lasted for ca. 30 years during the reign of Šamši-Addu and his son Išme-Dagan. The level below this (Level II) was destroyed sometime between 1848 and 1826. Level Ib was destroyed in turn between 1775 and 1755 after the death of Šamši-Addu when the Old Hittite kingdom under Pithana rose to prominence.

[81]Larsen, M. T., *The Old Assyrian City State and its Colonies* (Copenhagen, 1976), 88-89, documents an alliance which was made between Šamši-Addu and Kuwari, the king of Šušarra (in the Rania Plain). This pact provided the Assyrian empire with an eastern outpost in exchange for military aid. It was somewhat one-sided, however, since Kuwari became in fact a vassal of the Assyrians. See J. Laessøe, "IM 62100: A Letter from Tell Shemshara," *AS* 16 (1965), 189-96. This text provides

evidence of Šamši-Addu's campaigns along his borders which precipitated the above treaty agreement. The military campaign was designed to forestall further incursions by the Gutian tribes from the north. For a discussion of the geographic boundaries of the Assyrian trading system, see J. Lewy, "Old Assyrian Caravan Roads in the Valley of the Habur and the Euphrates and in Northern Syria," *Orientalia* 21 (1952), 293-306, 393-425 and "Studies in the Historic Geography of the Ancient Near East," *Orientalia* 21 (1952), 1-12, 266-92, 394-495. Information on comparable commercial activities during the Old Babylonian period is found in W. F. Leemans, *The Old Babylonian Merchant* (Leiden, 1950) and *Foreign Trade in the Old Babylonian Period* (Leiden, 1960).

[82]See below, pp. 159-62, for my discussion of these non-affiliated segments of the ancient society. *Ḫabiru* 25:21-24 and 26:20-30 are reports which mention raiding by these people.

[83]Swidler, W. W., "Adaptive Processes Regulating Nomad-Sedentary Interaction in the Middle East" in *The Desert and the Sown: Nomads in the Wider Society*, ed. C. Nelson (Berkeley, Calif., 1973), 30-31.

[84]Swidler, W. W., "Some Demographic Factors Regulating the Formation of Flocks and Camps Among the Brahui of Baluchistan" in *Perspectives on Nomadism*, eds. W. Irons and N. Dyson-Hudson (1972), 71.

[85]Malamat, A., "Mari and the Bible," *JAOS* 82 (1962), 146. M. Delcor, "Quelques cas de survivances du vocabulaire nomade en Hebreu Biblique," *VT* 25 (1975), 319, envisions a sort of evolution of the meaning of *naweh:* "paturage, campement, demeure." In the same article, pp. 317-18, some biblical quotations of *naweh,* Isa 65:10, Ezek 25:5, 2 Sam 7:8, and Isa 33:20 are defined as "pasturage." Eventually, however, the connotation expanded to include "the end of a journey and the place of stable habitation."

[86]Luke, J. T., *Pastoralism and Politics*, 100, n. 107, argues against Malamat's ("Mari and the Bible," 146) interpretation, saying that the meaning "encampment" is only a derived one. He contends that "when tribal groups are referred to in the Mari texts as being in the *nawûm*, it simply means that they were not pasturing flocks; they were in the pasture-land,"

[87]Edzard, D. O., "Altbabylonisch *nawûm*," *ZA* 53 (1959), 168-73.

[88]Rowton, M. B., "Autonomy," 253. He considers that in Babylonia proper there is a different usage. There, it denotes the "countryside between the cities, including settlements, villages and livestock." He also discusses this in "Enclosed Nomadism," 18.

[89]There has been a certain amount of speculation about this little-mentioned tribal group (*ARM* I 60; II 13, 37; IX 15: XIII 144; *Benj*. 991:b). They generally are assigned a mediocre position among the tribes. C. F. Jean, "Lettres de Mari:

transcription et traduction," *JCS* 1 (1947), 152, n.12, suggests that they were the etymological counterparts of the Yaminites (i.e., "sons of the south," Yaminites, and "sons of the north," Simalites). A. Finet, in "Iawi-ilâ, roi de Talḫayûm," *Syria* 41 (1964), 142, later theorized that the term was a synonym for another nebulous group in the ancient Near East, the *ḫabiru*. W. F. Albright concurred with this identification in *Yahweh and the Gods of Canaan*, 79. One other suggestion was made by J. J. Finkelstein in "The Genealogy of the Hammurapi Dynasty," *JCS* 20 (1966), 117, n.86. He describes the name as an artificial coinage used to designate tribes which were known more commonly under their specific names. Until more information comes to light, however, a final conclusion on this matter is impossible.

[90]*ARM* II 37:25 also provides this same formulaic statement. It is possible that this compound expression refers to the totality of the tribal group and its holdings. It may in fact be a hendiadys, as D. W. Young has suggested to me.

[91]For this translation, compare *CAD* "K," 116a: *kiṣrātim lu-ki-in* in *ARM* II 31:11'.

[92]There are too many Ḫaneans being enlisted for one tablet to record them all. The use of a singular form here is merely idiomatic. English requires the plural translation.

[93]Rowton, M. B., "Enclosed Nomadism," 19, takes this to be a recruitment from a single Hanean *nawûm*. However, it seems more likely to me, due to the rather large number of men (2000) involved, that more than one or perhaps even all of the migratory units in the area were being drained of manpower. Otherwise, it would have been too great a burden for one tribal group to bear economically.

[94]Ibid., 21, compares this text with *TIM* II 38:11-14: "(500 men) are planning to commit a crime against the *nawûm*."

[95]See *ARM I* 83:34-39; II 99:7-13 and III 15:10-27 for this type of activity.

[96]Luke, J. T., presents evidence for this identification in *Pastoralism and Politics*, 150.

[97]It is evident that the king had not ravished only the grasslands (burnt-earth policy?) but also had inflicted severe damages and losses upon the camps and flocks of the Yaminites in this district of Sagarātum.

[98]Cf. Gelb, I. J., "Wa=aw, iw, uw in Cuneiform Writing," *JNES* 20 (1961), 194-96, for a discussion of this reading.

[99]The district mentioned here was that around the city of Sagarātum, and the author of this report was probably the governor of that district, Yaqim-Addu. *ARMT* XIV contains the bulk of the correspondence from and to this governor of Sagarātum.

[100]Rowton, M. B., "Enclosed Nomadism," 18-19, posits that

the phrase *nawûm ikkal* is an idiom marking the connotation "livestock" for *nawûm*. See *ARM* II 35:7-11, 19-20 and 59:4-13 where the use of this phrase supports the argument that *nawûm* is used with a double meaning of flocks and tribesmen.

[101]Ibid., 25, translates this phrase, "... now I have sent the rest of the livestock to my father's district. Let them go in among the *nawûm* of my father and graze with the livestock of my father." A very broken text, *ARMT* XIV 121:39-42, also has *nawûm* used in this very flexible manner.

[102]This is perhaps comparable to the use of *elenum*, "Upper Country," as a general geographic term of reference.

[103]The siege had been placed upon Aḫuna by the forces of Yarim-Lim of Yamḫad. The report on conditions there was being relayed to Zimri-Lim by Yaqim-Addu, the governor of Sagarātum. He had received the news from a Suḫean and a Ḫanean, who apparently had fled the scene of the fighting. For a detailed study of the textual information on Yarim-Lim, see S. Smith, "Yarim-Lim of Yamḫad," *RSO* 32 (1957), 155-84.

[104]Cf. below, pp. 147-49 and 171, n.83, for a discussion of *tēbibtum*, "census," in the Mari texts.

[105]Other texts which serve as examples of this connotation for *nawûm* of steppe or pastureland are *ARM* II 27:3-6; 98:4'-10'; VIII 11:1-3, 9-11, 20-31; and *ARMT* XIV 86:17-23. For the office of *sugāgum*, see below pp. 139-53.

[106]Dossin, G., "Iamḫad et Qatanum," *RA* 36 (1939), 49.

[107]Dossin cites another article by himself, "Les archives épistolaires du palais de Mari," *Syria* 19 (1938), 111, as proof of this official's place in the Mari bureaucracy. See below, pp. 136-39, for my discussion of his function in relation to the Mari tribal groups.

[108]Dossin, G., "Iamḫad et Qatanum," 49, n.4, suggests that this news was about a raid made on the *nawûm*. A. Marzal, "The Provincial Governor at Mari: His Title and Appointment," *JNES* 30 (1971), 199, takes note of the fact that it seemed to be standard bureaucratic practice for officials, such as Kiḫilum here, who resided in the Upper Country region to be kept informed of events in other districts of the kingdom, including the western area around Aleppo and Carchemish.

[109]See below, pp. 107-9.

[110]Malamat, A., "Aspects of Tribal Societies in Mari and Israel" in *La civilisation de Mari*. XVe Rencontre Assyriologique internationale (Paris, 1967), 133-34. See also E. A. Speiser, "'People' and 'Nation' of Israel," *JBL* 79 (1960), 157-63 for the equation *gāw/yûm*=Hebrew *gōy*. For the use of *gōy* in the theme of the Patriarchal narratives, see Van Seters, *Abraham*, 17-18.

[111]Sassoon, J., *The Military Establishment at Mari* (Rome, 1969), 47, theorizes that these men were deserters from foreign

armies. Šamši-Addu had enticed them to join his forces by promising them rewards and, as in this text, land grants. J. T. Luke, *Pastoralism and Politics*, 145-46 used this context to strengthen his meaning of "military unit" for *gāyûm* over the more commonly held "tribe or territory." Very likely, it is simply another multipurpose term like *nawûm*.

[112]Falkenstein, A., "Review: *Archives royales de Mari*, IV, V, VI," *Bi.Or*. 13 (1956), 27, reads this rather than *[I]iš-di-ia*, based on J. J. Stamm, *Die akkadische Namengebung*, *MVAG* XLIV, (1939), 242, *BRM* III 60:3. He also points to *ARM* XV, 143 *da-di-ḫadu-un*. J.-R. Kupper, *Les nomades*, 73, n.2, cites *ARM* II 61:3 and III 45:12 for *Da-di-ḫa-du-un*.

[113]For this reading, see H. Huffmon, *Amorite Personal Names in the Mari Texts* (Baltimore, 1965), 179. He also suggests the reading **Ga-'il-'ilum*, a genitive compound name.

[114]Asad, T., "The Beduin as a Military Force: Notes on Some Aspects," *The Desert and the Sown*, ed. C. Nelson (1973), 65-66, mentions rewards given to beduin members of the Arab armies during the early Islamic conquests. He notes that it is usually surplus (i.e., poor) men or rich (idle) men who take up military activity for either a livelihood or to reenforce their power.

[115]See A. Falkenstein, *Bi.Or*. 13, 31, for this restoration.

[116]Cf. A. Marzal, "Two Officials Assisting the Provincial Governor at Mari," *Orientalia* 41 (1972), 376, for a discussion of this military title. There is also a treatment of this military commander in J. Sasson, *The Military Establishment at Mari*, 12.

[117]Sasson, J., *Northernmost Syria*, 54. See also A. Malamat, "Mari and the Bible," 143-46 and J. Bottero, *ARMT* VII (Paris, 1957), 223-24, paragraphs 42-43.

[118]Dossin, G., "*Adaššum* et *Kirḫum* dans des textes de Mari," *RA* 66 (1972), 118, Tx. A.2801:14-19. Another occurrence of this term appears in *ARM* VIII 11:21 and will be dealt with in the next chapter, p. 90.

[119]It is common for migratory clans to name subgroups and even whole tribes for a supposed common ancestor and to trace their own ancestry from him. For this practice, see F. Barth, *Basseri*, 50-51 and T. Ashkenazi, "La tribu arabe: ses éléments," *Anthropos* 41-44 (1946-49), 667-68.

CHAPTER III

THE SOCIAL AND ECONOMIC ASPECTS OF A SYMBIOTIC COMMUNITY

Pastoral nomadic tribes do not exist in a social vacuum. It is necessary for these migratory herding groups to establish, at least to some degree, a symbiotic relationship with the sedentary community. This aids both segments of the population to exploit more fully the environmental situation of their region. This chapter will deal with the economic and social arrangements established between the settled and nomadic elements of the Mari Kingdom. Of prime interest to this study will be the effects which these agreements had on both the pastoral and urban cultures. The degree of economic interdependence and cultural assimilation between the two groups also will be central themes in the discussion. In addition, the political factors which contributed to the development of the symbiotic character of the Mari society will be examined in depth.

Occupational Specialization and Resource Exploitation

As has been noted previously in this study, there seems to have been a separation of occupational concerns as the domestication of plants and animals became more intensified and sophisticated.[1] The eventual adaptation toward nomadic pastoralism was based upon both the environmental conditions and the physical needs of the animals herded. This development toward or into pastoral nomadism may have occurred at any of several levels of technological progression.[2] However, once a definite separation of occupational emphasis had taken place, the differences between the objectives and economic priorities of the agriculturalists and herdsmen would have begun to mount. Still, there was never a complete break between them.[3] Primarily, it was the constant need to search for new pasturage for their flocks which tended to progressively drive the herdsmen away from the agricultural areas and into their nomadic way of life.[4]

Occupational diversification allowed early communities in the Near East to exploit more fully their physical environment

while maintaining or expanding their population.[5] One means of aiding in the better utilization of the resources of the area was the establishment of symbiotic arrangements between the various occupational groups.[6] It was in fact the diverse and at times unpredictable nature of the region which necessitated the creation of varying patterns of resource extraction. Cooperation among the elements of the population was one way in which these people reacted to the economic and physical realities of their area.[7] Thus, seasonal labor and surplus pastoral products (meat, breeding stock, wool) could have been exchanged in the villages for manufactured goods and nonpastoral services which were not naturally available to the tribal group.[8]

Dimorphic society. The social and economic state which existed during the period of the kingdom of Mari reflected a symbiosis between the sedentary and nomadic elements of the population. M. Rowton has defined a situation of this type as a dimorphic society; that is, one in which there was a double process of interaction between nomad and sedentary and between tribe and state.[9] This society, as he describes it, was marked by an autonomous chiefdom, centered on one village within the defined tribal territory. It was from this locus that the decrees of the local government were broadcast to the mixed population of tribal and nontribal elements.[10]

Enclosed nomadism. There were several environmental factors in the area occupied by the various tribal groups of the Mari kingdom's population which served to heighten intercourse among its members. Agricultural and pastoral lands in this part of northern Mesopotamia tended to border on or even merge with each other along the steppe and in the inland mountain ranges. Moreover, the majority of the grazing areas utilized by the pastoral groups were "enclosed" within the territory controlled by the sovereign dimorphic state of Mari.[11] Seasonal migration by the herding groups was thus an almost constant concern to the Mari administration. There was a continual flow of reports from the provincial officials to the court at Mari describing the movements and activities of the tribes.[12] The measures which both the state and the pastoral groups took in order to lessen the degree of friction between

themselves made them more aware of the concerns of each other's culture. The nature of the total society became a reflection of this constant interaction between tribe and state.[13]

Rowton chose to call the type of situation created by a dimorphic society "enclosed nomadism." He explains that "dimorphic structure has its roots, not only in the physical environment, but also in two apparently contradictory motives, mutual hostility and mutual need."[14] In fact, the fabric of dimorphic existence provided a stability to an otherwise hostile environment.[15] Unlike the "external nomads,"[16] the pastoralists of the Mari period never absented themselves from contact with the sedentary community for any great length of time. Their migration routes and entire geographic orientation were encompassed within the dimorphic society of which they were a part.[17]

Aspects of Interdependence and the Diversification of Tribal Groups

F. Barth has noted in his study of the Basseri of southern Persia that ordinarily pastoral nomadic groups do not take up a prolonged program of farming within their territories or along the migration route.[18] They will not, however, disdain agricultural activity when need or advantageous situations arise.[19] Quite often, when such an agricultural program is initiated, the nomadic tribalists will choose either quick-producing varieties of grain or crops which require little or no care, such as dates.[20]

Agricultural practices. Agriculture, when performed by these normally nomadic peoples, does tend to build a kind of affinity and accultured understanding of the values of the sedentary population. Beyond this, however, it serves the pastoralist as a more reliable source of extra income when government pressures make raiding and profiteering too dangerous.[21] In fact, it is not uncommon to see both activities, pastoralism and agriculture, being alternatively engaged in by the members of a tribal group. This may be the result of ecologic necessity and the dictates of their economic system.[22]

Actual instances of agricultural activity by the Mari pastoral nomads are fairly numerous and generally reflect the

ability of these people to adapt to the ecologic and political situation of their region. In this regard, G. Dossin noted that it was often the case that "il se trouvent être ainsi à l'occasion des semi-nomades, qui pratiquent l'agriculture une partie de l'année et mènent la vie pastorale le reste du temps."[23] Usually this seasonal agriculture would take place in fields located in the areas of summer pasturing. In some instances, semi-permanent settlements may have been built for the housing of women and old men who would work the fields since they no longer could travel with the flocks.[24]

Among the examples pointing to agricultural activity by the Mari tribal groups is a letter sent to Zimri-Lim in which it was reported that the grain of the Yaminites had been threshed.[25] Still another mention of Yaminite grain is found in *Benj*. 989:b. In this text the fields they were said to be using were on the banks of the Euphrates.

There are several texts which deal with the distribution of fields to tribal members. *ARM* IV 1:5-28 speaks of satisfying the claims of some men of the Yamaḫamu subtribe. They were recommended to receive grain and a field in the same manner as some of their fellows had previously. Presumably, this award was payment for some service performed for the state and/or to placate a heretofore rebellious tribal group. In another letter, *ARM* V 88:5-9,[26] there is mention of a decision made on the disposition of some fields belonging to the Ḫaneans. One final text in this vein is *ARM* I 6.[27] Apparently, this document reflects the fact that a group of Ḫaneans had for a number of years made use of some fields on the banks of the Euphrates River.

The most straightforward evidence of agricultural work by members of a tribal group in the Mari archive is *ARMT* XIII 39. This letter, which has been exhaustively discussed in an article by J. T. Luke,[28] deals with the seemingly common practice by the Mari government of supplying plows and other farm supplies in exchange for a portion of the harvest. More than likely this investment was made by the urban authorities for the dual purpose of acquiring grain to feed the cities and providing impetus to the natural process of sedentarization among portions of the tribal groups.[29]

ARMT XIII 39 contains a couched warning sent to Zimri-Lim to try to prevent an apparent miscalculation on the date of releasing the loaned agricultural equipment and its return to the hands of the state's officials. Its author, Yasīm-Sumû was attempting to convince the king (although he was careful not to criticize the royal decision and even managed to place a certain amount of the responsibility upon his superior, the district governor, Baḫdi-Lim) that it would be judicious to allow the planting season to pass before taking the projected action. Otherwise, he explained that the investment made by the government would be lost according to the specifications of the contract made with the Yaminites.

aš-šum eqel er-ṣ[e-e]t [DUM]U.MEŠ-[Ia-mi-na]
5 tup-pí be-lí-[ia] [i]k-[š]u-[dam]
um-ma-a-mi ki-ma ka-ša-d[i-ia]
eqel er-ṣe-et DUMU.MEŠ-[Ia-mi-na]
ú-wa-aš-ša-[x]-[ar][30]
la-ma tup-pí be-lí-[i]a-ma i!-ka-aš-[ša-dam]
10 ^{iṣ}epinnātum^{ḫá} i-na eqel é-kál-lim šamaššammam ša ki-ma ḫu-ur-ru-pí-im
ú-ḫa-ar-ri-pa ù iš-tu tup-pí be-lí-ia ik-šu-dam
i-na eqel DUMU.MEŠ-Ia-mi-na šamaššammam ša ki-ma e-re-ši-im
e-ri-iš

. . . . šum-ma er-ṣe-et
DUMU.MEŠ-ia-mi-na be-lí ú-wa-aš-ša-ru
^{iṣ}epinnātum^{ḫá} an-ni-ta-an i-re-qa
iš-tu ša-at-tum it-ta-a[l]-la-ku
10' be-lí i-ka-aš-ša-dam-ma a-ia-nu-um
mi-li-ik-ši-na im-ma-al-li-ik
iš-tu i-na-an-na a-na IT[U]2 KAM si-ma-an
ze-ri-im ša-at-tum it-ta-la-ak
be-lí tup-pa-am a-na Ba-aḫ-di-Li-im
15' li-da-an-ni-na-am-ma ^{iṣ}epinnāt^{ḫá} ḫa-al-ṣ[í-im?]
li-ma-al-li-[X-m]a? ^{iṣ}epinnātim^{ḫá} ši-na-ti
la re-qí-im {X} be-lí[li]-š[e-p]í-[i]š

22' be-lí ú-wa-aš-ša-ru
é-kál-lum i-na ma-na-ḫa-ti-šu[31]
i-teg-el-li-i

Translation: The letter of my lord concerning the field(s) in the territory of the [Yaminites] has [reached me] with its statement, "When I arrive I will set [free] the field(s) in the territory of the [Yamin]ites." (However) before the letter of my lord reach[ed me,] the plows in the field of the palace had plowed early for the sesame, all being prepared for early planting, and (then) when the letter of my lord arrived here, the sesame had been planted in the Yaminite field(s), which had already been prepared for planting . . . . Now, if my lord releases the territory of the Yaminites, these plows will be idle. If my lord arrives here after the season (for planting) has passed, in what manner will their use then be determined? From now until two months (from now) is the optimum time for seeding after which the (planting) season will have passed. May my lord give firm instructions to Baḫdi-Lim. Order him to put the plows of his district to full use so that they will not be standing idle. [Let this be] my lord's course of action ! . . . (For) if my lord sets the territory (of the Yaminites) free, the palace will forfeit its expenditure of work and outlay.

Luke suggests that the Yaminites, in making the arrangements with the government (embodied in the term *mānaḫtu*), were allowing others to do their farming for them.[32] This makes sense if one follows the reasoning that the tribal groups would not have wanted to do their own farming if it was not necessary. However, it may be that this was simply an instance in which a shared system of labor was utilized to take better advantage of the available manpower and equipment in the district.

This latter possibility is strengthened by the evidence given in *ARMT* XIV 80:4-10. In this document there is also mention of the use of government help by the tribalists in completing the plowing. The Ḫanean villages involved apparently contracted for the use of a team of oxen. No specific use for these animals is mentioned, but it is most likely that it was to do the plowing of their fields.

aš-šum ^{awīl}Ḫa-na^{meš} be-lí iš-pu-ra-am
um-ma-a-mi a-[n]a du-ul-[l]i alphi^{ḫá}
^{awīl}Ḫa-na^{meš} i-na a-[l]a-ni-$^{\text{ki.ḫá}}$ ka-li

i-nu-ma iš-tu Ter-qa^{ki}
ma-ḫa-ar be-lí-ia a[t-t]a-al-kam
2 awilē a-{X}-[l]i?-š[a-am]?
mu-še-ṣ[í]-i

Translation: Concerning the Ḫaneans about which my lord has written me in this manner: "In exchange for the service of oxen, the Ḫaneans are to remain in the villages." When I left the presence of my lord and departed from Terqa, I went and designated two men in [each village] (who would be responsible) for the enrollment.

It would appear that the tribes allowed or asked the government to help with the plowing and planting. This was probably based on the fact that a nomadic group would not have wished to burden itself with plows and oxen when they could be put only to occasional use. With the borrowed agricultural equipment, they could then bring in a crop which would sustain them and serve as repayment to the state for its investment. It should be noted, however, that in *ARMT* XIV 80 the loan repayment was made in manpower. Men from each village using the oxen were to be conscripted for service to the government in some capacity.

Another possible cause for the involvment of the Mari tribes in the agricultural process may be based upon the development of an integrated[33] social system. This would have resulted from the settlement of a portion of a tribe or clan while the remainder continued to practice full-time pastoral nomadic activities. The reasons behind this are varied, based on economic and social stresses, and will be dealt with at more length later in this section.

Since it is stated that the Ḫaneans in *ARMT* XIV 80 were to be instructed to remain in their villages (at least until a number of them had been conscripted for government service) it is possible that there was a portion of the tribal members who normally were nomadic as well as a segment which was primarily sedentary. Certainly, the team of oxen would have been of more use to agricultural villages than to pastoral nomads.

Integrated tribal groups. It may be that this act of cooperation was based upon obligations stemming from a system of extended kinship ties between the two tribal segments or at

least nominal recognition of their heritage by both.[34] One indication of the fact that the village dwellers were descendants of nomads is found in their continued use of tribal social structure.[35] There is evidence of this type of integrated society in the Mari documents too. One explicit example[36] of it appears in *ARM* VIII 11. This legal document mentions that both the nomadic and sedentary segments of the "house of Awin," a Rabbean clan, were involved in the apportionment of a section of the tribal property.

1 1 me-at 50 iku eqlum
ša bi-ši-tum
ša bīt A-wi-in
5 māru^{meš} A-wi-in wa-aš-bu-ut
10 Ap-pa-an^{ki} . . . .
20 8 māru^{meš} A-wi-in
ḫ̮i-ib-ru-um[37] ša na-wi-im
awīlu^{meš} an-nu!-tu-um
māru^{meš} A-wi-in
25 ^{I}Ia-ri-im-^{il}Addu
a-ḫ̮a-šu-[n]u eqlam in-ḫ̮i-lu[38]
ba-qi-ra-an i-ba-qa-ru
10 ma.na kù.babbar ì.lá.e
sar^{meš} ^{il}Šamši^{ši} ^{il}Addu ù[ ]
30 ù A-wi-in [R]a-[a]b-bi
i-k[u]-lu

Translation: 150 Acres of land, which is the property of the "house of Awin" . . . 5 sons of Awin, who live in Appan . . . 8 sons of Awin, of the families of the encampment . . . these men, sons of Awin, have apportioned as a field to Yarim-Addu, their brother. Ten minas has been set as payment against reclamation. The "herbs"[39] of Šamši-Addu and of [ ] and of Awin, the Rabbean, have been eaten by them.

Thus it appears that legal matters were still collectively engaged in by the various groups within the tribe whether they were actually economic partners or not. The ties of tribal affiliation are apparently quite long lasting.

Grazing of flocks in harvested fields. Aside from actually engaging in agricultural pursuits, the pastoral nomads of

the Mari region also performed a symbiotic function which aided both the farming community and themselves. This involved the grazing of flocks on the stubble left in harvested fields. Through this practice the herders could obtain needed pasture while they remained in close proximity to settled areas. It also supplied the agriculturalists with certain amounts of invaluable natural enrichment for their fields in the form of animal dung.[40] In fact, this cooperative venture seems to have been a common undertaking wherever herdsmen and farmers existed together in the ancient and modern Near Eastern area.[41]

Two cuneiform texts in particular from the Mari archive reflect clear examples of this procedure of herds grazing on field stubble. *ARM* II 99:7-13 is a report made to Zimri-Lim by a provincial official named Ašqudum. He was relating his concern over the plight of the herds of the Numḫan and Yamutbalian tribes. He reports that (lines 11-13) *iš-tu še-em i-ga-ma-ru/ ur-ba-tam ù a-pa-a-am ša a-aḫ* ^{nār}*Pu-ra-tim/ [i-sa]-la-qú*, "After they have exhausted the barley, they will have to cook cane and reeds from the banks of the Euphrates." In this instance there was not enough left in the harvested fields for either the flocks or their shepherds. This may have been due to a miscalculation on Ašqudum's part.[42]

The other example of animals pasturing in harvested fields appears in *ARMT* XIV 22:4-11.

aš-šum lātim^{há} i-na pé-e ša le-et[43] Ḫa-bu-ur
a-ka-lim te-re-tim šu-pu-ši-im
ù ba-za-ḫa-tim du-un-nu-ni-im
be-lí iš-pu-ra-am
ki-ma na-aš-pa-ar-ti be-lí-ia te-re-tim
ú-še-pí-iš šum-ma lātum^{há}
i-na pé-e ša Ḫa-bu-ur i-ka-la
b[e-lí^{aw}]^{īl} rabi Amurrim li-wa-e-er-ma

Translation: Concerning the cattle grazing on the stubble on the banks of the Ḫabur, the taking of omens and reenforcing of the *bazaḫātum*, (about which) my lord wrote me, I have had omens taken according to the instructions of my lord. (However) if the cattle are to graze on the stubble of the Ḫabur, my lord should appoint a *rabi Amurru*.

It would seem that the governor of Sagarātum, Yaqim-Addu, was responding to orders sent to him by the king and now he was adding some suggestions of his own on these matters.

Apparently, it was sometimes necessary for an overseer to be appointed in order to keep the grazing herds within their assigned pasturing zones. J. MacDonald recently has suggested that this was the reason for the order to strengthen the *bazaḫātum* forces (line 6) in the district.[44] However, Yaqim-Addu's suggestion that a *rabi Amurru* be designated seems to overshadow the possible responsibilities of the *bazaḫātum*. This one official would have been in charge of organizing and keeping the members of the pastoral groups of the district in line.

This role is made especially evident when the remainder of *ARMT* XIV 22 is taken into account. In lines 24-25 there is mention of a planned rounding up of unattached[45] men to work on a proposed dam project. The implication is that the *rabi Amurru* was to be in charge of this conscription process as well as the projected construction work.[46] During this process it is likely that he enlisted a number of the pastoralists in compensation for their use of the grazing areas along the Ḫabur River.

The *rabi Amurru* may have employed the services of the *bazaḫātum* to aid in organizing the manpower roundup and the policing of the pastoralists. Nevertheless, it would have been his responsibility to see to it that the instructions passed to him by the governor were carried out.

Economic Contacts Between Nomad and Sedentary

The contacts made between pastoralists and villagers also encourage an assimilation of cultural values as well as a certain amount of barter and trade. When the nomads camp near a village and graze their flocks in its fields and in the surrounding vicinity, they have ample opportunity to see some of the products of settled life and to develop a desire to acquire them for themselves. Thus, they may exchange their surplus pastoral products for such basic necessities as fresh vegetables, grain, and clothing as well as for objects of village craftsmanship, including new pottery, forged weapons, and

jewelry.[47] Each community thus becomes even further dependent upon the other as the village dwellers and the urban authorities find that the trading of goods and services with the nomadic pastoralists is advantageous. For instance, it may not be uncommon for the urbanites to rely upon the herding groups for breeding stock, transport of village animals, military personnel, and contract labor.[48]

Coping with the physical and economic realities of herding is also a factor in the establishment of contacts between nomadic pastoralists and village agriculturalists. The need to limit camp and herd size periodically requires the herdsmen to engage in various forms of hired labor in and around the sedentary communities.[49] This involves the breaking up of families and clans for at least portions of the year.[50]

Corvée or contract labor. As a rule there are a number of members of the tribal community who are temporarily out of work. In some cases this surplus population can be forced out of the migratory life altogether. This may occur when their personal herds are reduced to a number which economically can no longer sustain them and their families.[51] When this situation arises, these people will either have to turn to farming, as has been the case (although perhaps not for this particular reason) in some of the texts mentioned above,[52] or hire themselves out as laborers or specialists of some kind.[53]

The seeming availability of laborers among the tribal groups in the Mari texts may be explained by one or several of the situations mentioned above. However, it may be that they simply had no choice in the matter. The urban government did have the capacity to exercise force in conscripting tribal members for military duty. However, fluctuating political circumstances sometimes prevented the Mari government from maintaining constant control over the tribal groups.[54]

Turning to the cuneiform material which deals with the use of tribal members in labor projects for the state, *ARMT* XIII 30:5-12 provides a good example. This document lists a number of men, in several categories, who apparently had been conscripted to help with the sheep shearing.

[XX]X $^{\text{awīl.meš}}$Ḫa-nu-ú ša Ma-ri^{ki} ù Ṣú-up-ri-im^{ki}
[X]X ^{awīl}na-si-ḫu[55]

30 ^{awīl}Li-li-ba-ra-iú
24 awīlū ša te-me-ni
22 awīlū ša nu-ba-lim
5 ^{awīl}Nu-úr-ru-ga-iú
46^{awīl}wattāru^{meš} [56]
[naph]ar 2 ME 26 awīlū^{meš} ba-qí-mu[57]

Translation: [X] Ḫaneans of Mari and Ṣuprim, deserters, 30 Lillibareans, 24 men of the foundation, 22 men of the chair, 5 men of Nurrugum, 46 replacements--in total, 226 shearers.

Most likely, this conglomeration of men was thrown together as part of a general job pool of laborers, who were called to service when seasonal or other necessary work projects called for their services.

Another such gathering of laborers appears in *ARM* III 6: 5-9. In this case, the corvée force was collected to help with the clearing of a canal channel.

^{awīl}ṣa-ba-am e-pé-[i]š-tam [ša] ḫa-[a]l-ṣ[í-i]m
ù māri^{meš} Ter-qa^{ki} a-na ši-pí-ir nār[im]
ša Ma-ri^{ki} ú-ka-am-m[i]-ìs
i-na ^{awīl}ṣa-bi-[i]m ša a-[l]a-ni [XXX]
mu-ut-ta-tum ú-u[l] i[l-l]i-k[u]-nim

Translation: I have gathered working men of the district and the men of Terqa for labor on the canal of Mari. Among the men of the villages . . . half have not come.

The unreliability of the tribalists[58] in showing up for such projects and in performing other services was apparently fairly common and was reflected in many of the reports of this period.

Another text in which the attempts to conscript members of a nomadic pastoral group worked out in a less than successful manner was published by A. Finet in 1959.[59] In this case, Ḫaneans had been offered a ration of 100 *qa* of barley in return for helping with the sowing of the wheat crop. However, they refused this offer, apparently thinking the wage too small, and departed the area.[60]

There is even an example of the pastoralists, through their spokesman, replying in a defiant manner to the royal summons to work on the corvée and to aid with the harvest.

ARM III 38:15-26[61] provides a tangible illustration of the type of independent spirit which tended to characterize the pastoral nomad and which could not be completely submerged by subordination to urban authorities.

a-na a-la-ni ša DUMU.MEŠ-Ia-mi-na
aš-pu-ur-ma
LÚ su-ga-gu-um ša Du-um-te-ti^{ki}
ki-a-am i-pu-la-an-ni
um-ma-a-mi LÚ na-ak-rum[62]
l[e]-el-li-kam-ma
i-na a-li-ni-ma
li-it-ba-la-an-ni-ti
an-ni-tam i-pu-ul
ù qa-tam-ma i-na e-ṣé-di-im
i-na a-la-ni ša DUMU.MEŠ-Ia-mi-na
ma-am-ma-an ú-ul ú-še-zi-ba-an-ni

Translation: I wrote to the villages of the Yaminites (and) the *sugāgum*[63] of Dumteti answered me in this manner: "Let the enemy come and carry us off from our villages!" This is what he answered. Likewise, no one from the villages of the Yaminites helped me with the reaping.

For the Yaminites and their *sugāgum* to have so blatantly ignored the call[64] to serve on the corvée, they must have been operating from a strategically strong position (perhaps based upon alliances).[65]

Military service. One other form of employment for the nomadic tribalists was in the military service. They were, among other things, enlisted[66] to form the nucleus of the campaign armies, border defense posts, and palace gate sentinel stations. *ARMT* XIII 33 provides one of the best examples of concrete evidence for Mari tribal members serving in the armed forces. It is a request by the troop commander for supplies to feed his charges. As is perhaps the case with most armies, (lines 13-14) *ṣa-bu-um bi-ri ṣí-di-tam/ [ú-u]l ma-ḫi-ir*, "the troops are hungry, having not received (their) journey provisions." J. Sasson goes as far as to suggest that these Ḫanean troops may have even had to wander into the palace in search of provisions.[67]

A classic example of the mismanaging of supplies and the

lack of coordination between the segments of the Mari alliance is presented in a letter published by C.-F. Jean.[68] This text seems to show the extremes to which bureaucratic infighting can go in disrupting supply lines. Again it was the Ḫanean troops[69] who got the short end of the deal when lack of communication between the rival kings of the Mari region held up the shipment of wool which had been promised to them.

a-na mi-nim be-el-ka a-na A-ri-še-ni
[iš]-ta-na-pa-ar ù a-ia-si-im
[l]a iš-pu-ra-am aš-šum an-ni-tim
ši-pa-a-tam a-na ^{awīl}Ḫani^{meš}
Rev. ú-ul i-na-di-in . . . .

Translation: Why has your lord continually written to Ariš̌eni and has not written to me? Because of this, the wool will not be sent to the Ḫanean (troops).

Here, the king of Sinamu refused to allow the wool to be sent by his former vassal, Arišeni, because Zimri-Lim had not written directly to him. Obviously, the king of Sinamu did not wish to lose face over this matter.

Simple citation of tribal members as personnel in the Mari armies or on royal campaigns is fairly common in the texts. *ARM* II 5:5-12 describes the dispatching of 100 Ḫanean troops to Qatanum to join the previously assembled forces of Sumu-niḫum. This latter group of men had been gathered for some time and were simply awaiting the order to move out on campaign. On another occasion, documented in *ARM* II 22:19-20, 150 Ḫaneans and 50 Suḫeans were said to be among the expeditionary force sent to Šabazim by Ḫammurabi of Babylon.[70]

At times these tribal contingents seem to perform in a most acceptable and obedient manner. This may be the case in *ARM* IV 78:28'-31' where the broken condition of the text prevents any more than the supposition that Išme-Dagan is praising his Ḫanean troops for valorous conduct against the forces of Ešnunna and the Turukkeans. *ARM* II 118:10-21 also provides a positive note about the Ḫanean troops presently assigned to Baḫdi-Addu.[71]

ša-ni-tam i-na ḫarranātim^{meš} ka-li-ši-[n]a
uz$_4$-na-am ša-ak-na-ku-ma

Tr. ia-ga-a-tum ma-da-a
i-na-an-na i-na ḫarrānim an-ni-tim
uz$_4$-na-am aš-ku-un-ma
ia-ga-tum[72] ù mi-im-[ma]
Rev. ú-ul i-ba-aš-[ši]
ṣú-ḫu-um-ma me-lu-lu-um-[ma]
ki-ma i-na bitāti^{ta-ti}-šu-nu wa-aš-bu
li-ib-ba-šu-nu ṭà-ab
ša ṣi-ir-mi-im-ma e-pé-eš
ka-ak-ki-i ù da-ak na-ak-ri-im-ma

Translation: In addition, in all expeditions which I have observed there were many gripes; but in this expedition, I have observed no worries or anything of that sort happening. There is only laughter and joking. They are as happy as if they were in their own homes (tents!). Their hearts yearn only for fighting and killing the enemy.

Obviously, this description of his troops by Baḫdi-Addu reflected well on him and his command. However, life in an army camp, whether ancient or modern, is seldom filled with such congeniality. If this was not just an attempt by Baḫdi-Addu to gain favor for himself, it speaks highly of his ability as a commander.

The Ḫaneans and other tribal members of the military service were not always considered model soldiers by their commanders. They often were discovered to be missing from the ranks at crucial times or just when the spirit struck them. *ARM* VI 30:13-18 is a follow-up report on the Yaminite troops, which had been enrolled at Dīr. They had been instructed to meet Baḫdi-Lim elsewhere to serve as replacements on an expeditionary force.

[i-na-an-n]a [ṣ]a-ba-am i-na re-[eš eqlim][73]
[ap]-qí-id-ma ṣa-bu-um mi-ṭ[ì]
[DUMU].MEŠ-Ia-mi-na ša i-na [Di-ir^{ki}]
[l]a i-ti-q[ú m]i-im-ma mi-ṭ[ì-tam ir-šu]
ma-li ša a-[na] be-lí-ia aš-pu-ra-[am]
ú-ul ik-šu-du-nim pa-ṭe$_4$-ru

Translation: Now, the troops at the staging point I have taken in charge. Of the unsatisfactorally small number of

Yaminite troops, who were in Dīr, still fewer have made it (here). This is the situation I have written to my lord. They have not arrived; (they) have deserted!

Apparently, the charms of military life, at this point, were not sufficiently attractive to the Yaminites for them to obey the command to assemble for the projected campaign.

On another occasion, the desertion of palace slaves led Yaqim-Addu to speak somewhat disparagingly about his district's defense force. He exclaims that he is so short-handed--having only the 100 Ḫaneans previously sent him--that he cannot spare anyone to join in the pursuit of the slaves. *ARMT* XIV 121:5-12:

i-na pa-ni-tim i-nu-ma be-lí a-na Sa-ga-r[a-tim^{ki}]
il-li-ku ma!-ḫa-ar be-lí-ia aš-ku-un-[ma]
1 ME ^{awīl}Ḫa-na^{meš} be-lí ú-te-er-ra-am-m[a]
ḫa-al-ṣa-am ú-ša-al-lim i-na-an-na ša LÚ.M[EŠ?]
e-zi-ib-ma(sic) wardi^{meš}é-kál-lim mu-un-[na-ab-ti][74]
ilum^{lum} a i-di-in li-ib-ba-šu-ú-ma
ṣa-bu-um ka-aṣ-rum[75] {x} ša na-aḫ-ra-ra-a[m]
wa-ar-ki-šu-nu a-ṭà-ar<-ra>-du ú-ul i-ba-aš-š[i]

Translation: Previously, when my lord came to Sagarātum, I appeared before my lord and my lord apportioned 100 Ḫaneans to me (for) the protection of my district. Now, as for . . . the slaves of the palace in flight--"(Certainly) this will not please the God!" There are no reinforcements which I can send to aid in their pursuit.

It seems apparent that Yaqim-Addu did not believe that 100 Ḫaneans would be sufficient to defend and police his district.

One possible reason for the rather low esteem given to the tribal members of the army may have been the large number of deserters. This may have been based on the feeling among the tribalists that to remain a part of an organized military force would destroy their identity as nomadic pastoralists.[76] In addition, their service commitment may have been based on purely economic necessity. They may have been unable to retain the necessary herding capital to remain a part of the pastoral economic pattern and so were eliminated from the migratory group. The occupation provided by their relationship with the state would tend to build some ties to the sedentary community.

However, it also could allow them in some cases to obtain enough capital to rejoin the herding group.[77]

In many of the texts this situation was tolerated (or expected) by the government authorities. *ARMT* XIV 82:5-22 details the extent to which the state was willing to play along with the soldiers drawn from the tribal groups. In it Yaqim-Addu recommended that a juggler be sent to them for their entertainment and that the Ḫanean deserters not be pursued. He explained that there had been some unrest over this latter stipulation and that there had even been some veiled threats by the Ḫanean troop spokesman, Mebišum. This individual had explained to Yaqim-Addu that the Ḫaneans would be (line 22) *ma-di-iš i-ḫa-ad-du*, "very happy" if the deserters were allowed to go unmolested. Presumably, there is the unspoken threat of disruptions and delay of the campaign against Ešnunna if this is not agreed to. It would certainly seem that these tribal soldiers were needed or they could not have gotten away with such brash demands.

Another text provides a quite different opinion of the value of the Ḫanean troops. In *ARM* I 134:5-17 the commander of these troops speaks as if he wished that they had deserted. Having given up on them as soldiers, he is now sending them back to his lord and requesting that real troops be sent to him this time. However, perhaps for political reasons, he does not totally disown these Ḫanean troops:

Z[I. MU]NU$_x$ qa-[ta]-a[t] [awī]li^{meš} Ḫa-ni-i
aḫ-ḫi-šu-nu
li-im-ta-ḫa-ru[78]

Translation: Let them continue to receive the provisions[79] (in accordance with) the share of their Ḫanean kinsmen.

One of the more drastic methods employed by an official of the Mari government in order to get the pastoral groups to submit to the royal instructions sent to them is vividly portrayed in *ARM* II 48:5-24. The initial problem began when the Ḫaneans, who had just returned from their pasturage areas in the steppe, settled themselves in their villages[80] and then ignored every summons sent to them by Baḫdi-Lim to assemble for enlistment. That administrator then proposed to Zimri-Lim that this plan of action be carried out to get them to quit

procrastinating:

^{awīl}be-el ar-nim i-na ne-<pa>-ri-im li-du-ku-m[a]
qa-qa-as-sú li-ik-ki-su-ma
ù bi-ri-it a-la-ni-e
a-di Ḫu-ut-nim^{ki} ù Ap-pa-an^{ki}
li-sa-ḫi-ru aš-šum ṣa-bu-um i-pa-al-la-aḫ-ma[81]
[ar-ḫ]i-iš i-pa-aḫ-ḫu-ra-am
a-na ṭe$_4$-em ḫa-ma-ṭì-im
[ša] be-lí ú-wa-e-ra-an-ni
[a]r-ḫi-iš ge-er-ra-am
[a]-ṭà-ar-ra-du

Translation: . . . let someone execute a criminal who is in prison. Let his head be cut off and have it paraded among the villages as far as Ḫutnim and Appan. The troops will be frightened and will quickly assemble, so that I may quickly send out an expedition in accordance with the order for hastening which my lord sent to me.

Guard duty was another military activity for which the Mari pastoral nomads and tribal members were impressed into service. In *ARM* II 1:10-25 400 Ḫanean troops were to be favored with a transfer from their regular duties to serve on the special forces in charge of guarding the palace gate. In this particular case, it would be unlikely that the designated troops would desert enroute. This is because half of them were going to be "reliably" provisioned from the palace stores and the rest (presumably from semi- or totally sedentarized tribal families)[82] were to reside with their families when off duty.[83]

ARM II 39:67-71 also describes the assignment of tribal soldiers to the defense of a gateway. Due to the urgent nature of the situation, however, Yasim-El had portents taken to see if they would be the correct troops to entrust with the defense of that vulnerable point in the fortress of Karana.[84]

. . . .a-na-[k]u ù Me-er-rum ni-iš-ta-al-ma 1 me ṣa-ba-am Su-ḫa-am
ù I[a-]q[í-i]m[-Li-im[85]]a-[l]i-ik pa-ni-šu-nu[86] te-re-tim a-na šu-lum ṣa-bi-im še-te
e-pu-úš-ma a-na te-re-tim ša-al-ma-tim aṭ-ru-sú-nu-ti
[ki-ma t]e-r[e]-tim ṣa-bu-um it-ti Id-di-ia-tim a-bu-

ul Ka-ra-na[ki]

[i-na-ṣ]a-ar a-na ma-[ṣ]a-ar-ti a-bu-lim a-ḫu-um ú-ul na-di

Translation: . . . . Merrum and I made consultations concerning the 100 Suḫean soldiers and their commander, Yaqim-Lim. I made consultations on whether the omen(s) were salutary (in regard to) these soldiers. After the omens proved favorable, I dispatched them. According to the oracle, they are to guard the gate of Karana with Iddiatim. The guarding of the gate is not to be neglected.

In addition to the organized military bodies, various groups of the Mari nomads also served as escorts and body guards for important officials and messengers. Thus, in a text published by G. Dossin[87] this type of employment is engaged in by 50 Numḫeans and 150 Babylonians, who were said to be accompanying the king of Kurda, Simaḫlānē, on a journey to Mari.

A similar service role did not turn out too well for some Ḫanean mercenaries in *ARM* II 123:15-24. This report described a raid perpetrated upon a caravan which had a horse and 10 donkeys burdened with juniper wood.[88] In the course of the fighting, two Ḫaneans, as well as several other members of the caravan's personnel, were killed. Most of those who were slain had been in the vanguard of the company with the *ṣuḫārū*.[89]

As far as finding evidence in the Mari documents of the type of itinerant "nomadic specialists," which N. Gottwald describes in connection with the ancient Israelites,[90] there is not much to go on beyond the practice of hired shepherding. However, J. T. Luke may have provided an anticipatory instance of this in suggesting that the weaving and garment making described in *ARM* III 70:5'-11' was done by Yaminite specialists and not for them.[91]

Herding contracts. The one outside employment activity which was familiar to the pastoral nomads of the Mari region was herding. Thus, they often hired themselves out on contract as shepherds for village and palace herds. This may have been the result of the fact that upon occasion herd size and the composition of the family herding groups dictated the hiring or hiring out of surplus manpower to either help bolster or reduce the herding force.[92] The need to obtain additional herd control may have necessitated the circumstances upon which

ARM II 90:5-11 is based. This letter notes that the Yaminites had brought their flocks over the Euphrates and apparently had moved them into the area also occupied by the pasturing flocks of the Ḫaneans(?).

The seal of approval placed upon this apparent cooperative arrangement is the statement in line 11, [*mi-im-ma ḫi-ṭi*]*-tum ú-ul i-ba-aš-ši*, "There have been no losses." J. J. Finkelstein has posited that this statement may have been a formula similar to those used in other Old Babylonian herding contracts. He suggests that this legal idiom may have had the connotation that the shepherds (the Ḫaneans?) would be held in legal obligation for the flocks while they were in their custody.[93] One reason for the Yaminites entrusting their flocks to an area which also was occupied by another group may have been based on a need for additional herding personnel. Also, they may have desired to cross-breed their animals.

Actual movement of herds or flocks for other parties by the nomadic pastoral groups is mentioned explicitly[94] in two texts from the Mari archive. *ARM* V 81:5-12 recounts that a group of Ḫaneans and their flocks accompanied those of the king. Eleven other shepherds were also traveling with them for their mutual service and protection.[95]

immerātum^{ḫá} ša Ḫa-na^{meš} ù mu-uš-ke-nim
ša a-aḫ Pu-ra-at-tim
a-na na-ḫa-li i-te-bi-ir
11 ^{awīl}nāqidū NÍG.ŠU ^{d}Šamaš-mu-ša-lim
ù Ḫa-na^{meš} Ia-ma-ḫa-mu-um
ka-lu-šu i-te-bi-ir
Dūr^{ki}-Ia-ás-[m]a-aḫ-^{d}Addu
ù ša-ap-li-iš-ma i-re-ú

Translation: The sheep of the Ḫaneans and the *muškēnum*[96] of the bank of the Euphrates have traversed the wadies. Eleven shepherds, in the service of Šamaš-mušalim and Yamaḫamean Ḫaneans, all of them have crossed. They are pasturing at Dūr-Yasmaḫ-Addu and southward.[97]

There is the possibility that Šamaš-mušalim was the chief shepherd in charge of the other eleven herdsmen mentioned here. However, if this was the case, it is surprising that the author of the letter used the term *nāqidū* instead of *kaparrum*,

"under-shepherd",[98] as was done in *ARM* I 118:8 and V 71:6,14.[99]

The other text dealing with the use of tribal shepherds by royal officials is *ARM* V 15:7-20. This letter was written by Išhi-Addu, the king of Qatna, to Yasmaḫ-Addu, the Assyrian viceroy at Mari. It supplies us with a good example of the type of cooperative agreements which could be made by allied states during this period. There is also evidence here which demonstrates the role played by the *sugāgū* as administrative tools of the Mari government.

immerāti^{ḫa}-ka ú-ḫa-na[100]
aš-šum {iš-tu} bi-ru-ni-im-ma
immerātim^{ḫá}ša it-ti immerāti^{ḫá}-ka
li-ri-ú
ri-tim ma-di-iš ma-d[a]-at
awīli^{meš} su-qá-qì-ka
tú-ur-da-a[m-m]a
lu-wa-e-er-šu-nu-š[i-i]m-ma
ù immerāti^{ḫá}-ka
a-na qa-ti-šu-nu
lu-up-qí-id-ma
ù immerāti^{ḫá}-ia
it-ti immerāti^{ḫá}-ka
pu-ḫu-ur[101] li-ri-ú

Translation: I will quarter your sheep since they are truly in need. The sheep, which are with your sheep can (then) graze. The pasturage is quite abundant (here). Send me your *sugāgū* so that I can give them instructions and (then) entrust your sheep to their hands. Thus my sheep will be gathered with your sheep to graze.

The specification of *sugāgū* as the men to be in charge of the proposed flock transfer may shed some light on this tribal official's abilities as an organizer of tribal manpower. In addition to simply being instructed on the manner in which these sheep were to be moved, they also would have been charged with providing safe conduct through tribal territory which would have to be traversed and over which the individual *sugāgum* had jurisdiction. Thus, they must have exercised extensive influence over the various nomadic groups which they represented.[102]

Raiding

One final category of economic activity engaged in by the pastoral nomads of the Mari kingdom to obtain food and manufactured goods from the sedentary community was raiding.[103] The origins of this practice go back to the need for constant regimentation of defenses against predators by the pastoral nomadic peoples. This tended to develop within them an inherent militaristic quality. They would have developed eventually a skilled and well-equipped mobile military force as just another tool for the survival of the herding group.[104] Still another result of this training would have been their achievement of military superiority over their settled neighbors. The villages would then have come to be regarded as easy targets for the infrequent raiding activities of the pastoral nomads.[105]

Part of the economic necessity for raiding by the migratory peoples springs from the fact that the nomads are much less able to do without the manufactured and edible products of the urban centers than is the sedentary population for nomadic trade goods and raw materials. In order to mine this supplementary resource, when the settled community is reluctant or unwilling to deal with the pastoral nomads on a plane equitable to both, the herders may be forced to take what they wish or depart the area.[106] In addition, the environmental exigencies with which the pastoralists have to contend (such as disease, famine, drought, and predators) often reduce the number of animals in their herds. When this becomes too severe or the opportunity is too inviting, they raid other nomadic pastoral groups as well as village herds in order to recoup their losses and rebuild their personal prestige among the members of their tribal group.[107]

Raiding was also an important economic activity engaged in by the pastoral nomadic tribes of the Mari region. Evidence from the cuneiform letters shows that these excursions were at times primarily designed to augment the herds of the raiders. Thus in *ARM* VI 57:4'-7'[108] Merḫum passed on the report of one of his operatives to his superior, Baḫdi-Lim.

[um-ma š] u-[m]a[109] 30 awīlū^{meš} Su-tu-ú
[ša immerāti^{ḫá}]-šu-nu ú-[š]a-am-qí-tu
[a-na ša-ḫa-ṭì-im] uk-t[a]-ṣí-[r]a-[a]m

[ù i-na-an-na pa-ḫa]-r[u]-ma i-pa-ḫu-ur

Translation: He spoke in this manner, "30 Suteans, who had allowed their sheep to perish, have prepared for a raid and have now assembled en masse."

Apparently, the author of this letter placed the blame for the raid by the Suteans on that tribal group's poor herding practices.

Another mention of sheep raiding by a company of pastoral nomads is found in *Benj.* 988:c. In this instance, the Yaminites involved seemed to be having no success with their venture at all. Each attempt at larceny was foiled by the forces of the government. Zimri-Lim even boasted that although they had made three separate raids and had managed to abscond with some sheep each time, they were relieved almost immediately of their booty by the police forces. As a result, (15) [*ù w*]*a-ar-ku-um ú-ul i-da(sic)-ru-ma a-na ši-ta-aḫ-ḫu-t*[*im*] *qa-tam ú-ul i-pa-ra-s*[*u*], "no one who had taken part in the raids derived any benefit from them."

A somewhat more lucrative encounter for the pastoral nomads is described in *ARM* IV 80:1-5. The raid outlined here, which was staged by Ḫaneans, was against the livestock of Šubat-Enlil. In this particular case, even the royal oxen and sheep were taken by the nomads. The reason given for this bit of pillage was provided in a very succinct statement: (line 4), *ṭe-em awīl Ḫa-na meš iš-nu-ú-ma*, "The decision of the Ḫaneans has been changed." It would appear that some sort of understanding had been made between the Ḫaneans and the city of Šubat-Enlil,[110] but now the nomads had for reasons of their own chosen to disregard it.

The migration routes of tribal groups often brought them within close proximity of villages and their flocks. As a result, they took advantage of this opportunity to raid the towns' outlying areas and then moved on their way. *ARM* I 83:31-39 discusses how at times the tribal migratory groups[111] would join together after the time of the harvest in traveling to summer pasture. Along the migration route, from time to time, they would stop at regular staging areas and send out raiding parties.

a-na a-aḫ ^{nār}Purattim
ur-ra-du-nim
ù i-nu-ma i-na pu-ru-sà-tim
immerāti^{ḫá}-šu-nu i-ša-aq-qú-ú
i-nu-mi-šu ši-iḫ-ṭà-am rabām
iš-ša-ḫi-tú

Translation: They will come down to the bank of the Euphrates and when they have watered their sheep in the streams, they will then launch a great raid.

This type of great raid by the combined man power of the tribal clans may be the circumstance presented in *ARM* V 23:8-21. Tarim-Šakim, a high government official, reported to Yasmaḫ-Addu at Mari about the progress of the Sutean migrants and the raiding they had engaged in along the way.

ù 2 li-im ^{awīl}Su-[tu-um]
[a-n]a šu-ku-un[112] pu-[uḫ-ri-im][113]
ip-ḫu-ru-ma [a-na na-we-e-em]
ša ma-a-at Qa-ta-[nim^{ki}]
ša-ḫa-ṭe$_4$-em
it-ta-al-ku
ù la-ma an-ni-tim-ma
1 šu-ši ^{awīl}Su-tu-um ki-ir-rum
ša-ni-t[um a-n]a Ta-ad-mé-er^{ki}
ù Na-ša-la-a^{ki}[114]
ša-ḫa-ṭim il-[l]i-ku-ma
re-qú-su-nu-ma i-tu-ru-nim
ù 1 awīlam i-na Su-te-i Ta-ad-[mé-ra-yi^{ki}]
i-du-ku

Translation: . . . and 2000 Suteans have assembled into a combined striking force. They have gone into the steppe pasturelands[115] of the land of Qatanum to raid. At the same time another group of 60 Suteans went to raid near Tadmer and Našala. They returned empty handed, however, one man among the Suteans of Tadmer was killed by them.

It may, perhaps, be wondered whether the government authorities really had such remarkable success at defeating the raiding nomadic groups every time out. There seems to be a better than even chance that at least in a few of these cases the bureau-

crats involved in writing the reports minimized their losses. This may have been to gain favor with the king or to just keep their jobs.

At any rate, raiding was an economic fact of life for both the pastoral nomads and their victims in the Mari region. It brought in a certain amount of additional capital, replaced losses in the pastoralists herds, and served to expend the surplus tensions built up among the nomads during their long periods of migratory life by providing them with an action oriented activity.

Tribal Fluidity and Demographics

The frequent dispersal of tribal personnel, based either upon the economic factors of herding or upon the need to obtain additional goods and capital for the members of the migratory group, is a prime factor in the development of the characteristically fluid nature of the pastoral nomadic tribes.[116] The continual reshuffling of personnel lends a degree of instability to the social organization of the nomadic group. Because of this, many facets of their social organization center around the relationships between the groupings of large and small sections of the pastoral nomadic community.[117]

Integrated or mixed tribal communities. The large number of designated tribal divisions (*gāyûm*)[118] in the Mari texts points up the amount of fragmentation which their ecological situation and occupation demanded. The extent to which this disintegration into tribal fragments can go is illustrated by the case of the 'Anaza tribe, which resides in areas from the Arabian Peninsula through most of the countries of the Fertile Crescent. It is said to consist of 20,000 tents, which are then divided into an immense number of conflicting subtribes.[119]

Beyond this simple division into subgroups, there was also a continual sloughing off of personnel from the various tribal organizations in the texts. Men or even whole families would move out of one area and into that of another tribal group, or they might become unattached from their tribal affiliate for some reason. This may have been the result of recent seasonal or military service which kept them for a time while the rest of their migratory section traveled to another part of the

country. Thus, they would then attach themselves to whatever tribe was accessible or would have them.[120] As a result, name changes, name mixtures, and geographical incongruities with tribal groups occupying areas completely outside their normal territories are frequently evident in the Mari material.

One of the most obvious of these illustrations of tribal fluidity is cited in *Benj.* 989:c where mention is made of the *Ḫa-na-a DUMU.MEŠ-Ia-mi-in*, "Ḫanean Yaminites." Here, the most likely explanation is that the Ḫaneans in question had simply moved into a traditionally designated Yaminite area and the government official writing to Zimri-Lim at Mari about them was using either an affiliation that they had adopted or which he had invented to distinguish these Ḫaneans from other groups of the same tribe.[121]

In another letter it might be construed that one tribal section had become associated with an entirely different pastoral organization based upon geographical proximity. *Benj.* 992:b provides a report to Zimri-Lim that:

šа-ni-tam aš-šum DUMU.MEŠ-Ia-am-ma-ḫa-ma-wi^{ki}
ša be-lí iš-pu-ra-am iš-tu ūmin^{mi-im}
ša be-lí i-na na-we-e DUMU.MEŠ-Ia[-mi-in]
im-ḫa-ṣu it-ta-[al-k]u-nim
ma-am-ma i-na ḫa-al-ṣ[i]-ia
ú-ul i-ba-aš-ši
ḫa-al-ṣu-um ša-lim

Translation: Secondly, in regard to the Yammaḫameans about which my lord has written me, since the time when my lord attacked the encampments of the Yaminites, they (the Yammaḫameans) have departed. There are none in my district. The district is doing well.

It would again appear that a tribal group unrelated to the other (the Yammaḫameans being a subtribe of the Ḫaneans[122]) had been grazing their flocks and living within the territory of that other tribe (the Yaminites). However, the answer to this particular situation probably lies in the tendency of both tribal and urban communities to give the territory where a particular tribal group resides the name of that tribe.[123] Other migratory groups may come to live in these areas and some of their members may even cross over and join the company of the

local tribal congregation. But, quite often they will retain their basic individuality despite any name change which may be applied to or by them.[124]

The use of particular tribal names may in fact eventually take on a social implication defining status or basic identity.[125] For instance, among the Pathan groups of Afghanistan and western Pakistan, there are social conventions which prevent and even discourage the incorporation of new members. These social institutions are based upon family and group economics since they practice ultimogeniture and the sons therefore do not leave their fathers' house until they are well over 30 years of age. The resulting surplus of males within the individual migratory groups necessitates that no new members be added.[126]

On the other hand, in the same general area live the Baluch pastoral groupings. Their chiefs tend to compete among themselves to attract the greatest number of new members of their sections as possible in order to increase their individual prestige and tax base. Added to this is the fact that in their family structure they encourage the young male to marry early and leave their fathers as soon as possible. Thus, they could always use another herder to help with the flocks. The natural result of these two differing social priorities is a constant flow of displaced (due to war, accident, crime or disaffection[127]) members of the Pathans into the Baluch clans. Social pressure is then applied on them to adopt Baluch characteristics and to abandon their ties to their former Pathan tribes. Eventually, only slaves and lower class menials continue to identify themselves as still being Pathan tribalists.[128]

Nomadic pastoralist groups also may develop new or integrated characters as a result of the partial or complete sedentarization of a portion of their members. As has been discussed in a previous chapter,[129] the process toward settlement by pastoral nomads is often the result of success or failure in coping with the vagaries of herding economics. Bad management or bad luck may lead to impoverishment just as the opposite could develop into immense wealth. In both cases, each an extreme, the eventual result could be absorption by the sedentary community.[130] At any rate, the final result leaves at least

a portion of the tribal group in a different ecologic and economic niche than that of the rest of the tribe.[131]

This brand of "mixed community" also is in evidence as part of the economic social situation during the Mari period. *ARM* VIII 11, which has been dealt with in a previous context,[132] distinguishes between the members of the clan *(bītum)* of Awin which led a sedentary existence, *DUMU.MEŠ-A-wi-in wa-aš-bu-ut Ap-pa-an*[ki], and those who had chosen to remain in the encampments of the pastoral nomads, *DUMU.MEŠ-A-wi-in ḫi-ib-ru-um ša na-wi-im.*[133] Such diversification of tribal occupation and membership may have been quite common. However, the extant material gives us only a few tantalizing glimpses at what may have been the norm rather than the exception.

alānum. Some intimation of this type of social arrangement may be found in the usage and meaning of the term *alānum* in the Mari texts. There has been a good deal of speculation on this word and its implications for sedentarization of the nomadic groups. The definitions to be found in the literature usually center on these specifications: "any place in which a tribe or part of a tribe settles permanently or temporarily, either in a collection of tents and mud huts or a larger village-like settlement."[134] J.-R. Kupper pictured the *alānum* as semipermanent installations, which served as a base where women and children could be quartered while the men went on raids and to which they could return after the seasonal migration.[135] J. Gibson spoke of them in similar terms but added the stipulation that they were likely to be located in the vicinity of cities and thus could serve as way stations for the nomadic pastoral community between journeys.[136] So it would appear that, like *nawûm,*[137] the meaning to be applied to *alānum* often depends upon the context in which it appears.

The description implicit in the texts for *alānum* is quite often one of a nomadic settlement set within the close environs of a city or town. *ARM* III 16:5-6 pinpoints them in this manner: . . . *a-la-ni ša DUMU.MEŠ-Ia-mi-na ša i-ta-at Ter-qa*[ki] . . . , "the Yaminite villages which are in the environs of Terqa." While not speaking specifically of the *alānum, ARM* II 137:26-29 does mention that Yaminites had been hemmed into the territorial limits of the city of Tuttul by the local

ḫazannum.[138] Two of his rival officials, Abum-EL and Yasmaḫ-Addu,[139] make this accusation concerning Lanasum, the *ḫazannum* of Tuttul:

26 le-em-nu-um ù a-ia-bu-um[
[DU]MU.MEŠ-Ia-mi-na^{ki} ka-la-[šu-nu]
ù i-ta-at a-lim Tu-ut-tu-[ul^{ki}]
i-sa-aḫ-ḫu-ur . . . .

Translation: [. . . .] is an evil-doer and an enemy [ ]. All of the Yaminites and the environs of the city of Tuttul he has hemmed in.

Presumably, the Yaminites referred to here had villages or dwellings of some kind near Tuttul, which they used upon occasion but certainly not year round.

ARM II 48:8-9 is a report by Baḫdi-Lim, the prefect of Mari and its district, that *Ḫanū*^{meš} *iš-tu na-wi-im ki-šu-dam-ma/ù i-na li-ib-bi a-la-ni-ma wa-aš-bu*, "the Ḫaneans have arrived from the pastureland encampments and are dwelling in the villages." It is very likely that these villages were fairly close to Mari since Baḫdi-Lim repeatedly had sent messengers to the Yaminites to assemble and there does not seem to be any great time lag on his receiving reports from them on their missions.

An example of the *alānum* of the pastoral nomadic tribes being associated with both cities and pastoral encampments appears in *ARM* III 12:16-26.

ša-ni-tam pa-na-nu-[u]m la-[m]a be-lí
a-na harrānim i-la-ku DUMU.MEŠ-[I]a-mi-na iš-ti-na-a
sà-ar-ra-ru iš-tu e-le-nu-um
a-na a-la-ni-e-šu-nu i-la-ku-nim-ma
ù i-[t]u-ur-ru
i-na-an-na iš-[t]u ša be-lí a-na harrānim ú-še-ši-ru
ù ši-ip-ṭà-am dan-na-ti[m] iš-ku-na-an-ni-ši-im
uz!-na-am[140] ú-[t]e-e[r]-ma
ki-ma pa-[n]a-nu-um ma-[a]m-ma-an i-[n]a sà-ar-ra-ri
[i]š-[t]u e[-l]e-nu-um a-na a-la-ni-e-šu
ú-ul il-l[a-kam]

Translation: On another matter, not long again, before my lord went on campaign, the Yaminites, as one man, were

> in revolt. They had gone to their villages in the Upper Country and (there) they had returned. Now, since my lord went on campaign and laid strict orders upon us, I have from time to time heard that as previously, no one from among the rebels, no one from the Upper Country will go to their towns (which were near the cities).

The implication here is that the Yaminites had established villages near Terqa, as well as in the Upper Country. This gave them the necessary shelter they needed when in the vicinity of the settled community as well as in their major grazing area. In addition, the staging area in the Upper Country also served as a refuge for them whenever there might be a threat of their being drafted to go on campaign. They would then remain there until that unwelcome possibility was no longer imminent.[141]

Another quality of the nature of the *alānum* is detailed in *ARM* II 33:11'-19'. In this letter Ibal-pī-El writes to Zimri-Lim that he had sent 50 troops with orders to Sadunlaba and Ibal-Addu with the idea in mind of preventing those *alānum* which were hostile to the city of Ašnakkum from uniting against it. Following this action, he then determined that he personally would have to conduct a survey in order to *da-ḫa-at a-la-ni-e/* [*ša it-*] *ti-šu na-ak-ru a-ša-al*, "inform myself of those villages which were hostile." From this context it is evident that the villages which were threatening Ašnakkum must have been fairly close to that city or there would not have been so much urgency about dispatching the 50 soldiers to defend it and its region. However, the *alānum* which Ibal-pī-El was going to personally inspect were probably at some distance from the city of Ašnakkum and had only been supplying recruits to the hostile groups.

kaprātum. There is also another term used in the Mari documents to designate living and working areas utilized by the nomadic and sedentary tribal groups. This label, which is somewhat analogous to *alānum*, is *kaprātum*. A. Marzal describes them as "hamlets" or small groups of buildings, always located within the territorial control of a town. He explains that it was the king who distributed these holdings at his own discretion and thus they were at times to be considered as political

prizes.[142] An obvious example of this partisan apportioning of *kaprātum* appears in *Benj*. 984:b.

. . . . šum-ma ni-ṭe$_4$-il be-[lí-ia]
10' Ḫa-na^{meš} a-nu-um-mi-iš a-na a-aḫ Purat[tim]
li-ir-dam-ma i-na ka-ap-ra-at DUMU.MEŠ-Ia-mi-na
1 ka-ap-ra-am li-id-di-in-šu-nu-ši-im

Translation: . . . . If it is the wish of my lord, now allow the Ḫaneans to go down to the bank of the Euphrates and give them one village from among the Yaminite villages.[143]

Apparently, at one time all the villages in this area had belonged to the Yaminites and so, like we today refer to an old house in our neighborhood as "so-and-so's" house, even though they may have moved away long ago, they were still referred to as such despite the fact that at least one was now being transferred to the custody of the Ḫaneans. This may reflect changing political fortunes or priorities of the Yaminites.

Still, there are also examples of the reaffirmation of a particular group's right to use the *kaprātum*. Just such an arrangement is confirmed in *ARMT* XIII 144:26-29.[144]

26 qa-[tam pa-]ni-tam ša i-nu-ma Ia-aḫ-du-u[n-Li-im]
a-bi-ka ma-a-at Ia-ap-tu-ri-i[m]
a-lam Ta-al-ḫa-ya-am[145] ù-ka-ap-ra-ni-šu
a-na Tur-Si-im-a-al nu-ut-te-[e]-er

Translation: In the same manner as in the time of Yaḫdun-Lim, your father, the land of Yapturim, the city of Talḫayam, and its villages we have returned to the Sim'alites.

By this action, Yawi-ila displayed the good intentions of the regime of Zimri-Lim and perhaps also paid back a political debt to the Sim'alites for their support of Zimri-Lim's accession to the throne at Mari.[146] It seems that during the previous few years the Sim'alites had been denied their former rights to these properties listed above.

The fact that the *kaprātum* were considered as part of the royal domain is exemplified in a letter written to Zimri-Lim by Baḫdi-Lim *ARM* VI 58:20-21. In the course of his report, he passed on the information of a possible Sutean raid which had been transmitted to him by his subordinate, Merḫum. He then noted that he had made adequate preparation for it.

20 a-na Za-bi-lim Ma-ši-im ù k[a]-ap-ra-tim
[š]a ḫa-al-ṣí-ia ú-ba-ar-ri[147]

Translation: I warned Zabilum, Mašum, and the villages of my district.

Thus, the economic importance of these villages is shown by the fact that a government official thought it worth warning them of the raid in just the same manner as he warned the larger population centers in the district.

As a result of the evidence provided by instances of tribal fluidity (based upon labor demands and herding economics) and the integration of the tribal community into both nomadic and sedentary ways of life, it seems safe to conclude that the tribes mentioned in the Mari archive cannot be categorized in any sort of strict manner. Sedentarization, as well as retribalization (i.e., the conscious return of peasant elements into the nomadic pastoral groups),[148] must have been fairly common occurrences. It may have even become a necessity at times to keep a balance of the general population in order to promote the economic welfare of both segments of the Mari society.[149]

There must have developed a closeness, and not just a geographic one, between the pastoral nomadic groups in the Mari kingdom and the village communities. Of course, economic and social differences did cause a certain amount of friction between them. Still, interaction between them played a significant role in shaping their society. The activities of the tribal groups and the local villages often have been overlooked by both ancient and modern historians. However, the case of the symbiotic community in the Mari kingdom demonstrates that their activities can be just as important to the understanding of their historical period as those of the kings and government officials who ruled them.

NOTES

CHAPTER III

[1]Flannery, K. V., "The Ecology of Early Food Production in Mesopotamia," *Science* 147 (1965), 1255, describes this specialization and redistribution of economic subareas as the best means of adapting to any given ecologic region.

[2]Spooner, B., *The Cultural Ecology of Pastoral Nomads* Philippines, 1973), 25, places most nomadic populations into the second of his list of progressions, "horticulturalists and pastoralists with a ranked society." See also J. Henninger, "La société bedouine ancienne" in *L'antica società beduina*, ed. F. Gabrieli (Rome, 1959), 70, for another view of this evolutionary process.

[3]Spooner, B., "The Status of Nomadism as a Cultural Phenomenon in the Middle East" in *Perspectives on Nomadism*, eds. W. Irons and N. Dyson-Hudson (Leiden, 1972), 126-27, notes that in modern Iran the "peasants and nomads proclaim competing ideologies, but form one cultural system." Cf. also the discussion in W. W. Swidler, "Adaptive Processes Regulating Nomad-Sedentary Interaction in the Middle East" in *The Desert and the Sown*, ed. C. Nelson (Berkeley, Calif., 1973), 23-24.

[4]Bacon, E. E., "Types of Pastoral Nomadism in Central and Southwest Asia," *SWJA* 10 (1954), 47. One step in this process probably involved the use of seasonal camps in grazing areas. K. V. Flannery, "Food Production," 1255 and J. Oates, "The Background and Development of Early Farming Communities in Mesopotamia and the Zagros," *Proceedings of the Prehistoric Society* 39 (1973), 164, discuss early evidence of this type of "herding village" at the site of Ali kosh ca. 6000 B.C. Oates also suggests in "Prehistoric Settlement Patterns in Mesopotamia" in *Man, Settlement and Urbanism*, eds. P. J. Ucko, R. Tringham, and G. W. Dimbleby (Herefordshire, Eng., 1972), 301-2, that at about this same time there were probably groups of nomadic herdsmen contemporary with and in some sort of economic relationship with the settled communities of the area.

[5]Hole, F., Flannery, K. V., and Neeley, J. A., *Prehistory and Human Ecology of the Deh Luran Plain* (Ann Arbor, 1969), 368-69. Note also the figures (13 fold) given on population increases in this period (5000-4500 B.C.) in T. C. Young, Jr., "Population Densities and Early Mesopotamian Urbanism" in *Man, Settlement, and Urbanism*, 831.

[6]Rowton, M. B., "Autonomy and Nomadism in Western Asia," *Or.* 42 (1973), 249, points out that "full exploitation of the environment's economic potential was possible only where a concerted effort on the part of nomad and farmer took the place of their traditional rivalry. Hence a built-in tendency toward symbiosis is profoundly characteristic of nomadism in Western Asia." Cf. also W. Goldschmidt, "Independence as an Element in

Pastoral Social Systems," *AQ* 44 (1971), 137, for a discussion of the initiation, without coercive means or by subordinating efforts, of collaborative arrangements.

[7]Adams, R. M., "The Study of Ancient Mesopotamian Settlement Patterns and the Problem of Urban Origins," *Sumer* 25 (1969), 119-20. He makes the statement that both the sedentary and nomadic elements are "participants in a continuing process of interaction that shapes the societies of herdsmen and farmer alike." G. E. Mendenhall, "Social Organization in Early Israel" in *The Mighty Acts of God*, eds. F. M. Cross, W. E. Lomke, and P. D. Miller, Jr. (New York, 1976), 137, posits that for the beduin culture to survive some type of symbiotic arrangements with the "more productive villages and towns" must be made.

[8]Salzman, P. C., "Political Organization Among Nomadic Peoples," *Proceedings of the American Philosophical Society* 111 (1967), 119. There is no evidence of an established market place in this period of Mesopotamian history. K. Polanyi, "Marketless Trading in Hammurabi's Time" in *Trade and Market in the Early Empires*, eds. K. Polanyi, C. M. Arensberg, and H. W. Pearson (Glencoe, Ill., 1957), 20-22, terms the type of exchange methods in the Old Babylonian period as "dispositional," trading methods. In this system, goods were transferred according to laws and customs of "equivalency." Cf. also A. L. Oppenheim's study of this question in "A Bird's-Eye View of Mesopotamian Economic History" in *Trade and Market in the Early Empires*, 30-32.

[9]Rowton, M. B., "Urban Autonomy in a Nomadic Environment," *JNES* 32 (1973), 202-3.

[10]Ibid., 203. He compares this to a feudal chiefdom, which lacks the nomadic element, and the tribal chiefdom, which lacks the nontribal component in the population.

[11]Rowton, M. B., "Autonomy and Nomadism in Western Asia," 249. L. S. Leshnik, "Pastoral Nomadism in the Archaeology of India and Pakistan," *World Archaeology* 4 (1972), 150-51, also speaks of a similar situation in which the peripheral areas of agricultural land touch on the grazing zone of the pasturalists. This contributed to the initiation of close contacts and associations formed between the two groups.

[12]Rowton, M. B., "Enclosed Nomadism," *JESHO* 17 (1974), 17. Thus, in the texts it was the *merḫum* of the district of Sagarātum or of the "Upper Country" who reported to the king or governor about the *nawûm* and the activities of the tribal groups.

[13]Ibid., 28. B. F. Batto, *Studies on Women at Mari* (Baltimore, 1974), 137, remarks on this in the Mari kingdom and suggests that Mari diplomacy, as a result of the constant association between tribe, town, and state, had more affinity to the Amorite culture than it did to that of southern Mesopotamia, which was more urban oriented.

[14]Ibid., 30.

[15]Bacon, E. E., "Types of Pastoral Nomadism in Central and Southwest Asia," 52, posits that this communion between pastoral groups and the village population is much more common than the more publicized acts of hostility. To be sure, it is incorrect to make arbitrary statements (such as that in W. Dostal, "The Evolution of Bedouin Life" in *L'antica società beduina*, 23) that the relationship between the sedentary and nomadic groups are always antagonistic. It seems extremely unlikely that they would have established only the minimal number of economic contacts and otherwise maintained complete isolation from each other.

[16]"External nomads" are best exemplified by the camel nomads of the Arabian desert. However, as I have noted previously, the camel was not domesticated or even mentioned in the time of the Mari texts.

[17]The textual material which will be presented from Mari appears to show that the tribes adapted to this "enclosed" situation and established at least limited bonds of trust and goodwill with the urban culture. S. N. Kramer, *Sumerian Mythology* (New York, 1961), 98-101, "The Marriage of Martu," provides early evidence of propagandistic literature in favor of contact between cityman and nomad. This legend details how the "barbarian" (nomad) god, Martu, marries the daughter of a townsman and thereby legitimizes contact between the two peoples. In the next chapter in Kramer's book (pp. 101-3), "Inanna Prefers the Farmer," it appears that there are also instances of hostility between the two groups in these epic tales. Here, farmer and pastoralist compete for Inanna and when she chooses the farmer it appears there will be a fight. However, in the end the farmer god, Enkindu, salves the shepherd god's (Damuzi) hurt by offering him gifts. The lesson here seems to be that peaceful coexistence is possible.

[18]Barth, F., *A Tribe of the Khamseh Confederacy: The Basseri of South Persia* (Oslo, 1961), 104-5, describes this practice by the wealthy nomads of Persia, who first turn a portion of their flocks into a more stable form of wealth, namely landed property. They will then let it out to villagers on contract, which returns a portion of the harvest to the landlord. See also G. R. Fazel, "The Encapsulation of Nomadic Societies in Iran" in *The Desert and the Sown*, ed. C. Nelson (Berkeley, Calif., 1973), 139.

[19]Spooner, B., *Cultural Ecology*, 4. Cf. also the discussion by W. Swidler, "Adaptive Processes Regulating the Formation of Flocks and Camps Among the Brahui of Baluchistan" in *Perspectives on Nomadism*, eds. W. Irons and N. Dyson-Hudson (Leiden, 1973), 23, which traces a progression of nomadic adaptation based upon the roles which agricultural villages, market towns, and cities play in the social framework of which the nomad is a part.

[20]See the effect on migration patterns of the Baluch-speaking tribes, the Yarahmadzai and Gamshadzai, based on taking advantage of both the best pasture available and the date harvest as outlined in P. C. Salzman, "Multi-Resource

Nomadism in Iranian Baluchistan" in *Perspectives on Nomadism*, eds. W. Irons and N. Dyson-Hudson (Leiden, 1972), 63-66.

[21]Amiran, D. H. K. and Ben-Arieh, Y., "Sedentarization of Beduin in Israel," *IEJ* 13 (1963), 167.

[22]Leshnik, L. S., "Pastoral Nomadism in the Archaeology of India and Pakistan," *World Archaeology* 4/2 (1972), 151.

[23]Dossin, G., "Les bedouins," 50.

[24]For an example of this, see L. S. Leshnik, "Pastoral Nomadism," 151-52.

[25]*Benj.* 985:a.

[26]For suggestions on the reconstruction of this text, see W. von Soden, "Neue Bände der *Archives royales de Mari*," *Or.* 22 (1953), 209 and H. Klengel, "Benjaminiten und Hanäer," *Wissenschaftliche Zeitschrift der Humboldt-Universität zu Berlin* 8 (1958/59), 215. They both read line 7 as *eqel aššat [U]š?-šu-ul-tu*, field of the women of Uššultu."

[27]Cf. Chapter II, p. 47 for translation of the relevant lines (26-28, 36-37, and 41-43).

[28]Luke, J. T., "Observations on *ARMT* XIII 39," *JCS* 24 (1971), 20-23.

[29]Certainly, as J. Van Seters, *Abraham in History and Tradition* (New Haven, Conn., 1975), 15, notes, the simple practicing of agriculture by pastoral groups does not signal any great move on their part to become sedentarized. There was a certain amount of sloughing off of members of the tribal community but this was based on a variety of economic and social reasons. Cf. F. Barth, "Capital, Investment and the Social Structure of a Nomadic Group in South Persia" in *Capital, Saving and Credit in Peasant Societies*, eds. R. Firth and B. S. Yamey (London, 1963), 78-79 and T. R. Stauffer, "The Economics of Nomadism in Iran," *MEJ* 19 (1965), 294.

[30]Birot, M., "Les lettres de Iasîm-Sumu," *Syria* 41 (1964), 51, gives the translation for *wuššurum* as "affranchir" or "céder" or "libérer" based on context. M. B. Rowton, in a private communication, writes me that Luke may have misunderstood the context here. He states that *wuššurum* "normally denotes the act of releasing (in the sense of allocating) crown land to deserving individuals. Hence the land mentioned probably represents Jaminite fields confiscated by the palace after the defeat of the Jaminites."

[31]Luke, J. T., "*ARMT* XIII 39," 22-23, describes *mānaḫtu* as a term which appears no where else in the Mari letters and has the meaning here of "the cost of labor, seed, and equipment expended in planting and harvesting the crop." Citing the Old Babylonian law code of Hammurabi (G. R. Driver and J. C. Miles, *The Babylonian Laws*, I [Oxford, 1960], 142-43, 169) he shows that the term *mānaḫtu* in this period also held the

roviso that the payment for the above investment was to be repaid to the investor before the division of shares. However, ny failure on the part of the investor to provide all that as promised in the contract called for the forfeiture of the ebt owed to that investor. It was exactly this provision hich Iasîm-Sumû was warning the king about when the order to release" the plows had been sent to him.

32 Ibid., 23.

33 Rowton, M. B., "Enclosed Nomadism," 20-21. H. Charles, *ribus moutonnières du moyen Euphrates* (Damascus, 1939), 149, escribes this same phenomenon as a "double morphologie" in espect to this study of the 'Agêdat.

34 Gellner, E., "Introduction: Approaches to Nomadism" in *he Desert and the Sown*, 3-6, points out in his discussion of he relevance of the segementary model of internal tribal organization that examples of cooperation between segments of tribal group do exist. They may be for defense purposes as ell as such mutually beneficial activities as the maintenance f a hydraulic system or the careful preservation of pasturelands. The principle of coercion and organization in these ases need not be strong leaders or the sanctions of political uthorities. They may depend simply on the obligations defined y the tribal group in its concept of the relation of the segents and herding units to the total society.

35 See Patai, R., "The Middle East as a Culture Area," *iddle Eastern Journal* 6 (1952), 6, for this sort of dual tribl character among the Kurds, and W. A. Mitchell, "Movement and astoral Nomadism: a Tentative Model," *Rocky Mountain Social cience Journal* 8 (1971), for a somewhat similar situation mong the Chaamba Berazga nomads of Northwest Central Sahara.

36 Rowton, M. B., "Enlcosed Nomadism," 20, has also suggested a parallel to this textual situation in *ARM* VI 42. In his document there is also mention of a portion of the *Jasma*(?) lan's flocks grazing in the *nawûm*. He takes this reading as n indication that another part of this clan may have been living elsewhere, i.e., as sedentary villagers.

37 Malamat, A., "Mari and the Bible," 145, says that the hirteen men here were all clan heads of Awin. The *ḫibrum* f which they were representatives was "a separate union of amilies closely linked together within the larger unit of the lan or tribe--thus the term was used specifically to indicate n association of wandering families which had drawn into loser union as a result of their nomadic status."

38 Muntingh, L. M., "Amorite Married and Family Life According to the Mari Texts," *Journal of Northwest Semitic Languages* (1974), 58, translates *naḫālum* as "to inherit or apportion" nd describes its use in a legal transaction here as evidence f a land transfer procedure within the family (tribal) group nd outside the normal sales procedure practice. J. Klima, La vie sociale et économique à Mari" in *La civilisation de Mari* Paris, 1967), 46, also sees it as an attempt by the clan to et around laws preventing a family from relinquishing its land

and compares it to the Ugaritic formula *eqlat nahāli*. H. W. F Saggs, "Review: J. Bottéro, *Archives royales de Mari* VII and G. Boyer, *Archives royales de Mari* VIII," *JSS* 5 (1960), 414-15 compare it to Hebrew *nḫl* which is used in a similar sense in Num 34:17,18 and Josh 19:49. He translates *naḫālum* "to grant by dividing off."

[39]Cf. Falkenstein, A., "Review: *ARM* VII and VIII," *Bi.Or* 17 (1960), 178 and Saggs, H. W. F., *JSS* 5, 414, for a discussion of this translation and the significance of the ritual meal.

[40]See Chapter II, p.52, and the full treatment of this presented in P. E. L. Smith, and T. C. Young, "The Evolution of Early Agriculture and Culture in Greater Mesopotamia: a Trial Model" in *Population Growth: Anthropological Implications*, ed B. Spooner (Cambridge, Mass., 1972), 23, on the topographical necessity for this grazing practice in Northern Mesopotamia.

[41]Evidence of this is to be found in Syria (L. E. Sweet, *Tell Toqaan: a Syrian Village* [Ann Arbor, 1960], 99), India (L. S. Leshnik, "Pastoral Nomadism," 151) and in Baluchistan and South East Turkey (W. Swidler, "Adaptive," 24-25).

[42]Cf. Bates, D. G., "Differential Access to Pasture in a Nomadic Society: The Yoruk of Southeastern Turkey" in *Perspectives on Nomadism*, eds. W. Irons and N. Dyson-Hudson (Leiden, 1972), 49, for instances of formal contracts being made between the Yoruk tribesmen of Southeastern Turkey and the villagers in that region for access to the village fields for grazing.

[43]For *lētum*, "cheek, side, bank", see *CAD* "L", p. 151, paragraph 2' and W. von Soden, *AHw*, p. 546.

[44]MacDonald, J., "The Identification of *Bazaḫātu* in the Mari Letters," *RA* 69 (1975), 142, defines these men as "troubl shooters," who had the responsibility of keeping order in their district. This apparently also included, according to him, the containment of the cattle which were grazing on the banks of the Ḫabur river.

[45]On the obscure term, *LÚ.DIDLI*, see M. Birot, *ARMT* XIV (Paris, 1974), 222.

[46]See the same sort of activity in *ARMT* XIV 24:9-4', wher a *rabi Amurru* was also charged with recruiting men to rebuild a fallen rampart.

[47]Leshnik, L. S., "Pastoral Nomadism," 151 and J. T. Luke *Pastoralism and Politics*, 75-76.

[48]Coon, C. S., *Caravan: The Story of the Middle East* (New York, 1958), 171. He describes them as specialized grour which are mutually dependent upon the others. This division of labor thus allows for the best possible use of the resource of the area.

[49]Cohen, Y. A., "Marriage and the Family" in *Man in*

Adaptation: The Institutional Framework, 28, points to climate, pasture, and the water supply among others as factors requiring adjustment of household organization.

[50]Pastner, S., "Ideological Aspects of Nomad-Sedentary Contact: A Case from Southern Baluchistan," *AQ* 44 (1971), 175, mentions one case among the Makran nomads in which the flocks were left with a portion of the herding group while the remainder of the male members engaged in seasonal occupations, including caravaneering, shepherding, and participation in local harvests.

[51]Cf. F. Barth, "Pathan Identity and its Maintenance" in *Ethnic Groups and Boundaries*, ed. F. Barth (Boston, 1969), 124-25 for occurrences of this among the Pathan tribes of Afghanistan and western Pakistan.

[52]See especially *ARMT* XIII 39 and XIV 80.

[53]Gottwald, N. K., "Were the Early Israelites Pastoral Nomads?" in *Rhetorical Criticism*, ed. M. Kessler (Pittsburgh, 1974), 230, suggests this was the origin of traveling "guilds" of craftsmen who serviced large communities.

[54]Birot, M., "Iasim-Sumu," 36, suggests that it was the power of the government which was the major factor in the appearance of nomadic personnel participating in nonpastoral activities. Cf. M. B. Rowton, "Dimorphic Structure and the Tribal Elite," 241, for another view of this.

[55]Sasson, J., *The Military Establishment at Mari* (Rome, 1969), 46, translates this as "deserter" and makes the comment that these men, who had left the hire of Mari's enemies, were probably chagrined at being asked to pluck sheep.

[56]Cf. *CAD* "A", II, 510. This term also appears in *ARM* IV 36:34, VII 191:6' and 117:3.

[57]See *CAD* "B", 97-98 and its appearances in *ARM* II 140:5, 10, 13 and V 67:20.

[58]Although there was no actual tribal group mentioned in this text, the use of the tribal official, the *sugāgum*, in the attempt to get the remainder of the workers to come is clear evidence that tribal members were involved.

[59]Finet, A., "Une affaire de disette dans un district du royaume de Mari," *RA* 53 (1959), 59. A similar case is described in M. Lambert, "L'infiltration nomade dans l'empire d'Ur III," *RA* 54 (1960), 44. In this text a group of Amorite nomads also term the proferred hiring price as insufficient or unacceptable.

[60]Rowton, M. B., "Dimorphic Structure and the Tribal Elite," *Studia Instituti Anthropos* 28 (1976), 241, suggests that the tribesmen could not be forced by the government to work in the corvée and thus had to be hired. This, he says, created a labor shortage in the kingdom with the tribesmen having the upperhand as far as choosing where and when they wished to work.

[61]This text first appeared as Dossin's *Benj.* 989:a.

[62]Moran, W. L., "Review: M. Weippert, *Die Landnahme der israelitischen Stämme in der neueren wissenschaftlichen Diskussion*," *CBQ* 30 (1968), 645, rightly criticises Weippert (cf. English version--*The Settlement of the Israelite Tribes i Palestine*, 120-21) for describing this resentment to forced labor as a part of the "nomadic ideal." Moran considers it to be simply the general human reaction of the *sugāgum*, who felt he was being put upon, rather than a part of the nomadic characteristic which caused him to reply in this manner.

[63]A detailed examination of this tribal official will appear in the next chapter in respect to his dealings as an intermediary between tribe and state. D. O. Edzard, "Altbabylonisch *nawûm*," *ZA* 53 (1959), 168-73, provides a short summary of his functions in the Mari texts.

[64]Finet, A., "Une affaire de disette," 65, sees this letter as a plea to the king by Kibri-Dagan, who feels the insolent reply to be a personal affront aimed at him.

[65]Cf. *Benj.* 986:a and b where the Yaminites ally themselv with the kings of Zalmaqum.

[66]The usual method of enlisting was based upon the *tēbibtum*, "census." This process will be discussed in Chapter IV. Note, however, *ARMT* XIV 80 in which men are chosen from villages as part of an arrangement made by their villages to obtain the use of a team of oxen.

[67]Sasson, J., *Military Establishment*, 34.

[68]Jean, C. F., "Arišen dans les lettres de Mari," *Semitic* 1 (1948), 21, B.5990.

[69]J.-R. Kupper's original interpretation of this text (*Le nomades*, 15), which held that these Ḫaneans were caravaneers has been disputed by S. Smith, "Yarim-Lim of Yamḫad." *RSO* 32 (1957), 168-69 and by J. T. Luke, *Pastoralism and Politics*, 16 M. B. Rowton has written me that he tends to agree with Kupper original idea. He feels that the Ḫaneans would not have lacke for wool and thus would not have to depend upon the government for supplies of this commodity.

[70]Still another text (published by M. Birot, "Nouvelles épigraphiques au palais de Mari [salle 115]," *Syria* 50 [1973], 6) mentions Ḫaneans as part of a garrison in the northern regi near Subartu. M. B. Rowton, "Dimorphic Structure and the Trib Elite," 242, takes this as evidence that Ḫaneans were often pa of the regularly maintained army corps.

[71]This man also appears in other texts as a commander (*AR* II 25:7') and as a *sugāgum* (*ARM* IX 70).

[72]Held, M. "Philological Notes on the Mari Covenant Rituals," *BASOR* 200 (1970), 34, n.17, describes *iagatum* as a West Semitic stratum word and compares it to Hebrew *yāgôn*.

[73]Falkenstein, A., "Review: *ARM* IV, V, VI," *Bi.Or.* 13 (1956), 31, restores line 11 based on this line and adds that lines 13-14 thereby provide further emphasis.

[74]For this N-stem form see *CAD* "A", I, 45-46, *abâtum*. It also appears in *ARM* I 28:6; 63:8 and IV 37:9.

[75]This military elite is described by J. Sasson, *Military Establishment*, 18-19, as a "privileged" group, who devoted much of their time to the protection of the king. Cf. *ARM* II 23:11'; V 49:13 and 70:25-29.

[76]See T. Asad, "The Bedouin as a Military Force: Notes on Some Aspects of Power Relations between Nomads and Sedentaries in Historical Perspective" in *The Desert and the Sown*, 65-66, for the effects on pastoralists who joined the early Islamic conquest.

[77]Rowton, M. B., "Tribal Elite," 241, posits that the reluctance to comply with conscription orders may have been based upon the degree of autonomy retained by the Ḫaneans. Thus their military activities were not always those sanctioned by the king and they did not always participate in government campaigns.

[78]Soden, W. F. von, "Zu den politischen Korrespondenzen des Archives von Mari," *Or.* 21 (1952), 83, notes the distributive connotation of the tan-stem used here.

[79]The restoration of Z[I.MU]NU$_x$ (*issimanum*, "provisions") in line 15 is based on a communication I received from M. B. Rowton. For this word, see *CAD* "I", 202, paragraph c'.

[80]See p. 111 for a discussion of the proximity of these villages to the enlistment point.

[81]*ipallaḫma* is a scribal error. The context calls for *ipallaḫuma* with the subjunctive ending.

[82]Cf. *ARM* VIII 11 for this type of tribal status split. Rowton, "Autonomy," 255, sees this distinction also in the specification required of the two groups: one (*naqdū*) is "destitute" and the other from well-to-do families--*damqūtum*.

[83]Evans, G., "An Old Babylonian Soldier: Notes on the Archive of Ubarrum," *JCS* 14 (1960), 25, n.11, suggests that this latter group of men were hostages. This is possible in light of the usual desertion rate of tribal soldiers; but, here I think the distinction is purely a social one based on an even-handed policy toward all types of nomadic people by the regime of Šamši-Addu.

[84]According to H. Lewy, "The Historical Background of the Correspondence of Baḫdi-Lim," *Or.* 25 (1956), 345-46, Karana was at that time under seige and Yasim-El was dispatched to relieve its garrison.

[85]Anbar-Bernstein, M., "La région au sud du district de

Mari," *Israel Oriental Studies* 5 (1975), 14, notes that this same Suḫean commander, Yaqim-Lim, is also mentioned in *ARM* II 30 in the context where he is again defending the northern dis trict from enemy incursion.

[86]Sasson, J., *Military Establishment*, 16, says that the title *ālik pan* was one given as a sign of special favor.

[87]Dossin, G., "*Adaššum* and *Kirḫum* dans des textes de Mari *RA* 66 (1972), 117, Tx. A.826:18-20.

[88]Noth, M., "Remarks on the Sixth Volume of the Mari Texts," *JSS* 1 (1956), 331, remarks that the horse mentioned here was one among the other precious objects which the carava was transporting. It was not a draft animal during this perio and was rare enough to be given as gifts to kings (Cf. *ARM* V 20).

[89]See MacDonald, J., "The Role of the *Ṣuḫārū* in the Mari Correspondence," *JAOS* 96 (1976), 62, for this interpretation o the military role of the *ṣuḫārū* here at Mari and in the Old Testament (cf. *na'ar* I Kgs 18:43, II Kgs 6:15 and I Sam 25: 18ff.). See also A. Finet, "Le *ṣuḫārum* à Mari," *RAI* 18 (1972) 70, for a discussion of their role in this text as minor functionaries.

[90]Gottwald, N. K., "Israelites," 230.

[91]Luke, J. T., *Pastoralism and Politics*, 101, n.114.

[92]These are seen to be important economic factors among the Marri Baluch (R. N. Pehrson, *The Social Organization of the Marri Baluch*, ed. F. Barth [Chicago, 1966], 7). Cf. also L. E. Sweet, *Tell Ṭoqaan*, 98, for this process of hiring shepherds to help with village flocks and herds.

[93]Finkelstein, J. J., "An Old Babylonian Herding Contract and Genesis 31:38ff.," *JAOS* 88 (1968), 32. The parallel text he cites is an Old Babylonian tablet of Samsu-iluna-*YBC* 5944. Cf. also Postgate, J. N., "Some Old Babylonian Shepherds and Their Flocks (with a contribution by S. Payne)," *JSS* 20 (1975) 2-5, for a detailed examination of herding contracts and their stipulations, which are usually based upon losses and growth percentage.

[94]*ARM* II 45:7'-11' may also involve the use of hired shepherds but the text is broken and there is no mention of how the royal cattle will actually be driven to the pasturage area of the king.

[95]Cf. M. B. Rowton, "Enclosed Nomadism," 26, for a discussion of this joint migratory plan as evidence of integratio of nomad and state within the symbiotic community.

[96]Speiser, E. A., "The *muškēnum*," 338, portrays these men as "fief-holders charged with the care of the lands of the crown." Apparently, this also extended to the care of the roy al flocks.

[97]M. B. Rowton has pointed out to me that the verb here is *re'ûm*, "to pasture." Cf. W. von Soden, *AHw*, b, 978.

[98]For the use of the term *kaparrum* elsewhere, see *TCL* XI 162 as cited by J. N. Postgate, "Shepherds," 10.

[99]Unfortunately, there is no mention of nomadic tribal members serving as the shepherds and under-shepherds in these two texts. However, the possibility that they are in evidence here is a good one.

[100]Bottéro, J. and Finet, A., *Archives royales de Mari,XV: Repértpoire analytique des tomes I à V* (Paris, 1954), 204, suggest that the denominative or *ḫanû* is like that used in tablet XIII of the series *Har.ra=hubullu* published by A. L. Oppenheim and L. F. Hartman in *JNES* 4 (1945), 161, line 73: *imeru ḫa-nu-ú*, "fat sheep."

[101]Soden, W. F. von, "Neue Bande," 207, points out that this stative form also appears in *ARM* II 39:54 and is to be translated, "meine Schafe sollen mit deinen Schafen gemeinsam weiden."

[102]A more extensive discussion of the role of the *sugāgum* will appear in Chapter IV. For other intimations about the use of the *sugāgū* in *ARM* V 15, see F. Pintore, "Review: J. Sasson, *The Military Establishment at Mari*," *Oriens Antiquus* 8 (1969), 255, who sees the *sugāgū* as a regular overseer of transhumant activity. (Cf. also J.-R. Kupper, *Les nomades*, 17-18).

[103]An attendant activity, tribute gathering for the "protection" against raiding by the tribes, will be discussed in the next chapter in the section on tribal leaders.

[104]Irons, W. G., "Livestock Raiding among Pastoralists: an Adaptive Interpretation," *Papers of the Michigan Academy of Science, Arts and Letters* 50 (1965), 397.

[105]Asad, T., "Military Force," 71 and S. H. Lees and D. G. Bates, "The Origins of Specialized Nomadic Pastoralism: a Systematic Model," *American Antiquity* 39 (1974), 191.

[106]Spooner, B., *Cultural Ecology*, 18.

[107]Gottwald, N. K., "Israelites," 227. W. G. Irons, "Raiding," 393, adds that the dispersing of animals among a larger number of people, through raiding, rather than allowing them to be clumped in huge herds by the very rich diminished those natural hazards as well as evening out social organizations.

[108]This same situation is reiterated in *ARM* VI 58:15-18.

[109]This restoration is based on A. Falkenstein, "Review: ARM IV, V, VI," 31. He points to *ARM* I 118:19' as another example of the use of the verb *ušamqitū*.

[110]Agreements such as this were fairly common in the history of intercourse between tribe and village. For this see L. Sweet, *Tell Ṭoqaan*, 191, where *xuwa* tribute was paid by the Syrian villages in exchange for protection against raiders. Cf also L. Sweet, "Camel Pastoralism in North Arabia and the Minimal Camping Unit" in *Man, Culture, and Animals*, eds. A. Leeds and A. P. Vayda (Washington, D.C., 1965), 137 and N. K. Gottwald, "Israelites," 227, for similar arrangements.

[111]Luke, J. T., *Pastoralism and Politics*, 117-18, identifies them as Suteans.

[112]Soden, W. F. von, "Neue Bande," 207, is basically unsure what to do with this form since he says that the D-stem of *šakānum* does not appear in Old Babylonian contexts except in the specialized meaning of "to install the *šaknu*." J. Bottero and A. Finet, *ARMT* XV, 260, cites this explanation by von Soden but cannot come up with an explanation for its usage here either.

[113]Sasson, J., *The Military Establishment at Mari*, 60, n.70, describes *pi/uḫrum* as a technical appellative, meaning that "joining together of two independent corps." He cites *ARM* II 75:6 as well as G. Dossin, "Signaux lumineux au pays de Mari," *RA* 35 (1938), 181-82.

[114]Luke, J. T., *Pastoralism and Politics*, 115, uses this description of tribal movement to chart the major areas used by the Suteans in an east to west progression--from Tadmor (200 km. west and slightly north of Mari) to Qatna (west north west of Mari, ca. 360 km.) and finally to Nasala (southwest of Tadmor ca. 100 km. on the route from Tadmor to Damascus). Cf. also F. Tocci, *La Siria nell'età di Mari* (Rome, 1960), 94-95 and G. Dossin, "Le royaume de Qatna au XVIIIe siècle avant notre ère d'après les 'Archives royales de Mari'," *Bulletin de l'accadémie royale d'archéologie de Belgique* 5/XL (1954), 423, for this same type of geographic charting.

[115]*Benj.* 988:a speaks of 300 Yaminites going out to raid the *nawûm*, but in this case the raid was to be staged in an area on the banks of the Euphrates. J. T. Luke, *Pastoralism and Politics*, 134-35, n.71, points out that in most cases the raiding was not designed to overwhelm towns and cities, but rather they were planned as hit and run strikes on the pasturing zones around the urban centers.

[116]Adams, R. M., "The Study of Ancient Mesopotamian Settlement Patterns and the Problem of Urban Origins," *Sumer* 25 (1969), 121, points out that ". . . fluidity and an apparent lack of structure in intergroup relations offer adaptive advantages that should not be ignored, principally, flexibility in pursuing alternative subsistence modes under adverse conditions, or in securing contingent support from a variety of related groups in different circumstances . . . ."

[117]Spooner, B., "Towards a Generative Model of Nomadism," *AQ* 44 (1971), 203. He states that this is the lowest level of social organization in the tribal society. Political

organization and authority roles are also initiated at this level.

[118]Cf. M. Birot, "Textes économiques de Mari, III," *RA* 49 (1955), 15-18, Text AB, in which thirteen separate *gāyûm* sections of the Ḫanean tribe are listed. M. B. Rowton, "Dimorphic Structure and the Parasocial Element," *JNES* 36 (1977), 189, points to the fact that *gāyûm* is never used in respect to the Jaminites. He suggests the explanation that they "were still in the process of tribal reintegration and did not yet have full tribal structure."

[119]Awad, M., "Settlement of Nomadic and Semi-Nomadic Tribal Groups in the Middle East," *International Labour Review* 79 (1959), 27.

[120]Aharoni, Y., *The Land of the Bible, a Historical Geography* (Philadelphia, 1962), 221-27, documents the evidence of fluidity among the early tribes of Israel, based upon the genealogical lists in the Old Testament. Cf. also M. Noth, *The Old Testament World* (Philadelphia, 1962), 66-75, for a similar discussion of the movement of tribal clans into new geographic areas and their assimilation into the clans of those regions.

[121]For similar conclusions, see J. T. Luke, *Pastoralism and Politics*, 152-55. H. Klengel, "Benjaminiten und Hanäer," 212, has suggested that the usage here actually designates those "Benjaminites settled or living in Ḫana." Either way, the process would be the same. It is unlikely, as M. Weippert, *Settlement*, 115-16, n.59, suggests, that the use of the name Ḫanean here is a simple denominative for "nomads."

[122]Luke, J. T., *Pastoralism and Politics*, 150-51, correctly bases this identification on *ARM* V 81:5-13, which speaks of the Ḫaneans of Yamaḫamum.

[123]Leemans, W. F., "The Contribution of the Nomads to the Babylonian Population," *JESHO* 1 (1957-58), 139.

[124]Thompson, T. L., *The Historicity of the Patriarchal Narratives* (*BZAW* 133) (Berlin, 1974), 64.

[125]Rowton, M. B., "Dimorphic Structure and the Problem of the 'Apirû-'Ibrîm," *JNES* 35 (1976), 15, notes that among the Papi, a Lur tribe, the use of the general term "Lur" connoted only the average tribesmen, not the elite. However, among the Muntafiq Arabs, when speaking of the "Muntafiq," were referring only to the tribal elite.

[126]Barth, F., "Pathan Identity," 124-26.

[127]Among this gathering of displaced or tribeless persons, may be included that group known as the *Ḫabirū* in the Mari letters. Seemingly, these rootless people, for one reason or another, gravitated out of organized tribal groupings and tended to become mercenaries or raiders. A further discussion of these persons will come in Chapter IV.

[128]Barth, F., "Pathan Identity," 124-25.

[129]See Chapter I, pp. 20-21 above.

[130]Rowton, M. B., "'Apirû-'Ibrîm," 14. Note this process among the Basseri in F. Barth, "Nomadism in the Mountain and Plateau Areas of South West Asia" in *The Problems of the Arid Zone* (UNESCO, Arid Zone Research XVIII, 1962), 350, and in W. G. Irons, "Variation in Economic Organization: a Comparison of the Pastoral Yomut and the Basseri" in *Perspectives on Nomadism*, eds. W. G. Irons and N. Dyson-Hudson (Leiden, 1972), 102.

[131]Barth, F., "Ecologic Relationships of Ethnic Groups in Swat, North Pakistan," *American Anthropologist* 58 (1956), 1088, divides these niches into "natural areas" in which that of the transhumant Kohistanis is subdivided as far as the agriculturalist Pathans are concerned and these subdivisions are further cross-cut by the migratory requirements of the pastoral nomads of the area, the Gujars.

[132]See above p. 90.

[133]Malamat, A., "Mari and the Bible," 145-46, points out that this shows that the process of settlement was also indulged in by subtribal as well as tribal groupings. He compares this dual natured clan to the Kenites of the Old Testament, part of which were farmers (I Sam 30:29) and part of which were nomads (Judg 4:11, 17 and 5:24).

[134]Edzard, D. O., "Altbabylonisch *nawûm*," 71. For a similar statement, see H. Klengel, "Halbnomaden am mittleren Euphrat," *Das Altertum* 5 (1959), 198 and A. Marzal. *The Organization of the Mari State* (University of Chicago, Ph.D. dissertation, 1969,) 92-93. L. Matouš, "Einige Bemerkungen zum Beduinenproblem in alten Mesopotamien," *Archiv Orientální* 26 (1958), 633, put forth that it was related in meaning to Hebrew *'ohēl*, but this has been discounted on the grounds that it is too limited a term to encompass the Akkadian connotation.

[135]Kupper, J.-R., *Les nomades*, 13. Cf. also P. Fronzaroli, "L'ordinamento gentilizio semitico e i testi di Mari," *Archivio Glottologico Italiano* 45 (1960), 43-45.

[136]Gibson, J. C. L., "Light from Mari on the Patriarchs," *JSS* 7 (1962), 58.

[137]For discussion of this term, see pp. 59-63 above.

[138]Marzal, A., *The Organization of the Mari State*, 14-16, sorts out the various administrators mentioned in this text and their bureaucratic reasons for feuding. They all seem to be ganging up on Lanasûm, the *ḫazanum* of Tuttul, and he is here trying to vindicate himself. The fact that Zimri-Lim would have to remove him personally indicates that his office of local city administrator was one made and taken away by royal decree.

[139]Rowton, M. B., "Urban Autonomy," 213, points out that Jasmaḫ-Addu was a Jaminite "king" (cf. G. Dossin, "Les archives

épistolaires du palais de Mari," *Syria* 19 [1938], 112) in the settlement of Jariḫ, which was not far from Tuttul and was probably the tribal center of the Jaminites of Jariḫu. As a result, he would have been closely involved in the affairs of Tuttul and the affects the administrators there would have on his tribe.

140 Soden, W. F. von, "Zu den politischen Korrespondenzen des Archives von Mari," *Or.* 21 (1952), 84, gives this restoration and the translation "ich brachte das Ohr züruck; i.e., ich hörte wieder hin."

141 See Marzal, A., "The Provincial Governor at Mari: His Title and Appointment," *JNES* 30 (1971), 192, for a somewhat different interpretation. He adds that the *šipṭum* order gave Kibri-Dagan the troops necessary to prevent the Yaminites from returning to their villages near Terqa and causing trouble while the king was on campaign.

142 Marzal, A., *The Organization of the Mari State*, 106-10. M. Noth, *Die Ursprünge des alten Israel im Lichte neur Quellen* (Koln and Opladen, 1961), 16 ff. and n.22, took a more limited view of them saying that they were "apparently really a complex of storehouses . . . such as itinerant shepherds are in the habit of having . . . to store and secure the produce of their work in the fields." Cf. also M. Weippert, *Settlement*, 119-20.

143 There is a restatement and confirmation of this transaction in *Benj.* 984:c.

144 Finet, A., "Iawi-ilâ, roi de Talḫayûm," *Syria* 41 (1964), 134 and 140, describes this particular endowment as a sign of favor shown by a suzerain to his vassal.

145 Rowton, M. B., "Urban Autonomy," 212, takes Talḫajum to be the center of the dimorphic chiefdom in the district of Idamaraṣ, which had been controlled by the Sim'alite tribe and was now being returned to them.

146 For another example of Sim'alites supporting the government of Zimri-Lim, see *Benj.*991:b,c.

147 Oppenheim, A. L., "The archives of the Palace of Mari, II," *JNES* 13 (1954), 148, notes that the nuance for *burrûm* here is more nearly "to warn" than "to announce." Cf. *ARM* VI 34:5 for a similar usage.

148 Awad, M., "Settlement," 48, states that the reasons for this action range from protection to prestige.

149 Gottwald, N. K., "Israelites," 241.

CHAPTER IV

THE RELATIONS BETWEEN TRIBE AND STATE

Beyond the realm of day to day contacts between tribal and nontribal elements within the dimorphic society, there existed in the Mari kingdom an interplay of physical and social actions which affected the culture as a whole. These were generated by the presence of an expanding, diversified urban authority, based at Mari, which controlled the majority of the area occupied by the pastoral nomadic groups of the region. The basic reason for the existence of the Mari cuneiform documents is this government complex. It was the members of the bureaucracy who wrote the letters, made the decisions, and to a large extent formed history's opinion of them and their subject population. This final segment of my study will treat both the productive and counterproductive aspects of the relationship between tribe and state in the Mari kingdom.

Political Influences on Pastoral Nomadic Groups

In order to depict effectively the total environmental experience of the pastoral nomads mentioned in the Mari documents, it now becomes necessary to detail the role played by a third (the other two being ecologic and economic) factor which influenced their occupational existence. This was the political character of their society.[1] Like the other two, it also influenced the pastoralist's regulation and maintenance of a workable balance between the animal and human population. Both the tribal and individual migratory groups were faced at times with political obstacles or aids, such as those involving the use of croplands or the establishment of ties with the village farming communities. Both of these could affect the social as well as the physical character of the people involved.[2]

Nomadic pastoral groups have to be able to perceive the character of the urban authority and come to terms with it. Their alliances and political decisions in this regard often hinge on the effective strength of the urban government in relation to the tribes and on the state's ability to police its holdings.[3] Like every force of their environment faced by the

nomadic pastoralists, the realities of existence within the confines of a political kingdom had to be met imaginatively and with a willingness to adapt to changing circumstances.

In a dimorphic society, the key to a political balance between tribe and village and tribe and state lies in the economic framework of the society. There are countering factors of capital and investment on both sides which contribute to political fluctuation or stability.[4] The pastoralists, because of the fast return upon their capital investment, receive a high rate of return which is constant and self-perpetuating. This, of course, would be cut back by ecologic controls. Still they generally maintain at least a small measure of an advantage over the agricultural sector.[5] On the other hand, to the agriculturalists and the urban community in general, time is a large factor in getting a practical return on their investment. Thus, it becomes essential for them to control the land in order to achieve economic success and stability.[6]

One way for the state to accomplish this goal is for it either to exploit or eliminate portions of the local tribal elite. This gives them greater control over the population and also prevents, to some extent, local revolts and unrest.[7] Complete elimination of the tribal elite is usually employed when the costs of maintaining and controlling them become more than it is worthwhile or convenient to bear any longer.[8]

These strivings for control of political and economic supremacy are among the reasons for some of the first mentions of the tribal groups in the Mari letters and inscriptions. As has been noted above, there were several shifts of power in this area between the time the Lim-dynasty was established at Mari by Yaḫdun-Lim and the time when Ḫammurabi of Babylon conquered that small kingdom and dethroned Zimri-Lim. Between the two Lim dynasts there was an Assyrian interregnum headed by Šamši-Addu and his two sons, Išme-Dagan and Yasmaḫ-Addu. Much of what occurred during the period when these two political regimes alternately held control hinged upon the cooperation or hostility of the tribal groups.

Autonomous dimorphic chiefdoms. M. B. Rowton has described the demographic situation extent in the Mari area as one in which a number of pastoral enclaves existed as separate entities

These enclaves of pastoral nomadic population were located within the regions of the sedentary community, but at the same time operated as autonomous polities and were actually dimorphic chiefdoms.[10] A tribal group or a tribal confederation was based in each of these with a particular town serving as the tribal center. This group would have had its own local elite headed by a tribal chief.[11] Because they considered themselves autonomous, these chiefdoms lacked the desire and the institutions that would have bound them to the larger society in the Mari kingdom.[12]

Since each pastoral enclave was autonomous, their only joint action was in the prevention of encroachment of any larger organization, such as that represented by the emerging state at Mari. Their mutual defense league became an historical reality with the discovery of the foundation inscription of Yaḫdun-Lim.[13] In this recounting of royal accomplishments, a number of Yaminite pastoral enclaves[14] are said to have attempted to defend their right to political autonomy. They had joined together to combat the new political machine which had been forged by Yaḫdun-Lim at Mari. The outcome was of course in the Mari monarch's favor since the inscription was written by his scribes and not those of the Yaminites. Thus we find recorded in column III, lines 4-21:

^{m}La-ú-um šar Sa-ma-nim^{ki}
ù ma-at Up-ra-bi-im[15]
^{m}Ba-aḫ-lu-ku-li-im šar Tu-tu-ul^{ki}
ù ma-at Am-na-ni-im[16]
^{m}A-ia-lum šar A-ba-at-tim^{ki}
ù ma-at Ra-ab-bi-im
šarru an-nu-tu-um
i-ki-ru-šu-ma
a-na ti-lu-ti-šu-nu
ṣa-ab Su-mu-E-bu-uḫ
ša ma-at Ia-am-ḫa-ad^{ki}
il-li-ka-am-ma
i-na a-li-im Sa-ma-nim^{ki}
um-ma-at DUMU-mi-im
iš-ti-ni-iš ip-ḫu-ru-šum-ma
i-na ka-ak-ki-im da-an-nim

3 šarrî an-nu-ti-im
ša DUMU-mi-im ik-mi

Translation: La'um, king of Samānum and the land of the Uprabum, Baḫlukulim, king of Tuttul and the land of the Amnanum, Aiālum, king of Abattum and the land of the Rabbium, these kings attacked him (Yaḫdun-Lim) and to aid them (also) came the army of Sumu-Ebuḫ of the land of Yamḫad. At the town, Samānum, the troops of the Yaminites assembled to him (Sumu-Ebuḫ)[17] as a single entity and in a mighty battle these three kings of the Yaminites he (Yaḫdun-Lim) put in chains.[18]

Still another example of Yahdun-Lim's dealings with the pastoral elite and the forces of dimorphic chiefdoms is presented in his "disc-inscription,"[19] column I, lines 15-20:

7 šarrāni^{meš}
ab-bu-ú Ḫa-na
ša uq-ta-ab-bi-lu-nim
ak-mi-šu-nu-ti
ma-at-šú-nu
a-na i-di-ia ú-te-er

Translation: Seven kings, "fathers" of the Ḫaneans, who fought against me, I treated them as prisoners and turned their land to my side.

J. T. Luke has noted[20] that the Ḫanean kings mentioned her were never again alluded to after the time of Yaḫdun-Lim and that the kings of Mari adopted the title "King of the Ḫaneans and Akkadians."[21] This was in contrast to the kings of the Yaminites who appear several times during the reigns of other kings.[22] Luke believes that this shows that the Mari government had "only limited success in preventing external alliance by tribal groups."[23] It should be pointed out, however, that this theory does not take into consideration the possibility that these *šarrū*, "kings," or *abbū*, "fathers," were chosen from the tribal population. They could have been chiefs of an integrated tribal society which had ties as well as members in both the nomadic and sedentary communities.

Changes in the tribal elite. Aside from the fact that the urban authorities were never completely successful in curtailin

all of the activities of the tribal leaders, the appearance or nonappearance of these leaders was most likely based upon economic and social developments. It may have been that as a portion of the urban culture was incorporated or assimilated into the culture of the tribal units, the tribes lost the need to select men to hold the post of *šarrum*.[24]

In any case, no matter how strong or weak the central government's claims to sovereignty, the very fact that a claim is made provides the means for manipulation within the local political machinery by those tribal leaders who are elevated to heightened status by the state. They can actually use the urban authority's ambitions for their own benefit in order to obtain a position of even greater power in their limited zones of influence.[25]

Political Contact Points Between Tribe and State

An increase in the intimacy of relations between the sedentary society and the pastoral nomadic tribal groups tends to increase dramatically the amount of political stratification in the tribes.[26] The use by the central government of local tribal leaders as a conduit between the tribe and state allows these leaders to exercise greater influence over their individual tribal groups. Since it is more efficient for the government to deal with small, hand-picked numbers of individuals, many of the former chiefs and subleaders may be relegated to inferior positions in the tribes.[27] Their demotion may also be based on the government's attempts to drive a wedge between the tribe and the tribal elite. By doing this the state could eliminate possible rivals and local power bases.[28]

Eventually, the most important function these designated local officials would perform would be to serve as mediators between the tribal population, and the village and urban communities. F. Barth has stated that this "touches on a very fundamental problem in the organization of 'plural' societies." What he has in mind is a society composed of ethnically distinct groups. Each maintains close and constant interchanges on certain matters, while remaining unconnected in other aspects of their social and economic life. The tribal chiefs, who also served the central government, could thus form the link

which would allow for communication and the resolution of differences between the segments of the society.[29]

The artificially heightened tribal elite can even manipulate communications at times, changing the value and form of information. This gives them the capability to define any given situation for the various groups involved.[30] In addition, since by its nature the government bureaucracy is a fluid aggregation, the only way for its members to keep continuity with the local population is for each administrator to seek to perpetuate the good relations established by his predecessor with the tribal chiefs.[31]

merḫum. Before discussing the tribal chiefs (*sugāgū*) of the Mari texts, however, it is necessary to examine that portion of the government hierarchy which dealt directly with the concerns of pastoral nomadic groups. The one official who had the greatest degree of responsibility for tribal activities and movements as they affected the affairs of the kingdom was the *merḫum*. There does not seem to have been too many of these appointed administrators. A. Marzal identifies only four--assigned to Tuttul, Idamaraṣ, Zalmaqum, and Šubat-Šamaš.[32]

Quite often the *merḫum* was said to be dealing with problems or the well-being of the *nawûm*.[33] As a result of this, it would appear that his primary concern was with the nomadic division of the tribal groups.[34] One text which illustrates some of the duties of the *merḫum* is *ARMT* XIV 86:17-27.

ša-ni-tam awīlū^{meš} ša a-na sa-ag-bi[35]
^{m}I-ba-al-pi-Èl me-er-ḫu-um
e-li na-we-e-em ša be-lí-ia
iš-ku-nu $^{\text{awīl.meš}}$Up-ra-pa-a-yi^{ki}
i-mu-ru-ma immerāti^{ḫá}-šu-nu
im-ḫa-ṣú te$_4$-ma-am an-ne-em
i-na a-ḫi-ti-ia-ma eš$_{15}$-me-e-ma
a-na be-lí-ia áš-tap-ra-am
ù awīlē^{meš} ša ba-za-ḫa-tim
a-na eqel 2-àm bi-ri
a-na šêpim na-ka-si-im aš-pu-ur-ma

Translation: On another matter, the men whom Ibal-pī-El, the *merḫum*, has appointed as guards over the pasturage encampment of my lord, saw the Uprapeans driving away their

flocks. This information, I heard from my retainers, and I have written to my lord. Also I have sent the men of the *bazaḫātum*[36] for a distance of two double miles to block (the Uprapeans') passage.

There are several conclusions to be drawn from this report. First, the *merḫum* held prime responsibility for the doings of his section of the *nawûm*. Second, he could delegate some of his authority to various levels of the district's police forces which were available to him (*sagbū* and *bazaḫātum*) in order to insure that there was a minimum of illegal activity carried out by the nomadic pastoral groups. In this instance, the Uprapeans had apparently decided to leave the confines of the government supervised pasturage area and Ibal-pī-El was attempting to counter their move by putting into operation a network of resistance to stop them.

In another letter, *ARMT* XIV 121:39-47, the governor of Sagarātum, Yaqim-Addu, found it necessary to ask the king to instruct the *merḫum* of his district to summon the *muškēnū* from the *nawûm*. They were being ingathered because of the imminent approach of a large enemy force (lines 24-28).

^{awīl}m[u-uš-ke-nu-um n]a-wa-am i-na-aṭ-ṭà-a[l-ma]
XX[XXX u]m-ma šu-nu-ma <ú>-ul nu-X[
[n]a-wa-a-a[m]qa!-ṣú-[u]m ma!-li ù ni-t[i?
   am-mi-nim]?
a-na dan-na-tim tu-še-ri-ba-an-ni-[t]i
[an-ni-tam ^{awīl}mu-u]š-ke-nu-u[m XXX]
[XXXXXX]na [XXXXXX]
^{awīl}me-er-ḫe-em li-wa-er-ma
[na-w]a-a-am ša qa-ṣi-im a-na ṣe-e[r]
[. . .]-ia li-ik-m[i-s]u

Translation: The [*muškēnū*] have their eyes fixed upon (their) flocks . . . . Thus they spoke: "We are [n]ot . . . . the [st]eppe[37] is (still) full of flocks and so [why] would you have us enter into the fortified place?" [This] (is what) the [*muš*]*kēn*[*um* said?] . . . .the *merḫum* should be ordered to have them assemble the flock(s) of the steppe at [. . .].

Despite the *muškēnum's* professed reluctance to leave this

pastureland, they actually were interested in taking advantage of the situation of unrest created by the invasion. In another text, they did just that while a group of *ḫabirū*-marauders were raiding their area.[38]

As is evident in this above text, the *merḫum* was also involved in organizing and carrying out defense plans. The information on local situations which they were able to obtain and pass along must also have been very important to the defense strategists. A text published by G. Dossin[39] demonstrates this conclusively. This letter was written by Ḫami-ištamar, the governor of the province between the Baliḫ and Euphrates rivers, to Zimri-Lim. He reported that two officials from the upper Euphrates country had come to him with information concerning the activities of Carchemish and Zalmaqum. These two men, Kiḫilum, a *merḫum*,[40] and Amirum, a *šapiṭum*, were then sent on to the king with their news.

In an extremely broken document[41] a *merḫum* was called in for a conference to help plan the defense of Ašnakkum against the *ḫabirū*. In this case, as in the text just mentioned above, it is likely that the intimate knowledge these administrators would have acquired from dealing with the population groups in their districts would have been invaluable to the government in times of internal conflict and invasion. It is possible that the *merḫum*[42] employed spies and informants from among the pastoral nomads in order to keep abreast of the present situation.[43]

Members of the pastoral nomadic tribes were probably hired quite often for the jobs handed out by the *merḫum*.[44] In *ARMT* XIV 80:4-20 a *merḫum* had a key role in the enrollment of Ḫaneans from their villages in exchange for the use of a team of oxen. It was the completion of this task and his departure which was then used as a lever to influence the compliance of the conscripted men (lines 11-20).

. . . um-ma a-na-ku-ma
^{awīl}mer-er-ḫu-um it-ta-la-ak
at-tu-nu a-na mi-nim wa-aš-ba-tu-nu
i-na u_4-mi-šu-ma ^{awīl}Ḫa-na^{meš}
ka-la-šu ú-še-sú-ú
as-sú-ur-ri ^{awīl}su-ga-gu^{meš}

te-qí-tam i-ra-aš-šu-ú um-ma-a-mi
^{awīl}Ḫa-na^{meš} i-na a-la-ni$^{\text{ki.ḫá}}$ sà-pi-iḫ
1 awīlum i-na $^{\langle\text{awil}\rangle}$Ḫa-na^{meš} i-na ḫa-al-ṣi-im
ú-ul i-ba-aš-ši

Translation: Thus I said: "The *merḫum* has (already) gone. Why are you now waiting?" On that day, all of the Ḫaneans were enrolled. Heaven forbid that the *sugāgū* will (attempt to) make the excuse that, "The Ḫaneans are scattered from the villages (with) not one among the Ḫaneans (still) existing in the district."

This text demonstrates the degree of authority invested in the actions of the *merḫum* and also gives us a definitive example of the governmental chain of command. In respect to tribal affairs, the line of communication was drawn from the *merḫum* through the *sugāgū* and down to the individual tribal member.[45] This channeling of instructions and the mediation of conflicts through an administrative hierarchy allowed vested interests and varied social units to become more equalized. Further, it also promoted better communication between the members of the bureaucracy, the tribes, and the government itself.[46]

sugāgūm. The powers invested in this second rank of government officials, the *sugāgū*, were actually only extensions of the power of the urban authority itself. As F. Barth has demonstrated in his study on the Basseri, "the power of the chief is based mainly on sources outside the tribal system, and does not arise in or become delegated from the scattered nomadic camps."[47] The very institutionalization of permanently established leadership roles within the dimorphic society can be traced directly to the amount and constancy of interaction between nomadic tribes and the sedentary population.[48]

Once a permanent relationship is established between the two communities, there tends to be a grasping after power and influence by both parties. The government authorities which wish to increase their rule over the nomadic tribal groups find it more convenient to deal exclusively with a single tribal leader rather than with a group of elders. Thus they appoint their "own" man and grant him extraordinary powers.[49] However, this leader is seldom blind to the opportunity provided by this commission, both for himself and for his tribesmen.

As a result, he usually moves to make his superiors in the government and the pastoral groups he represents feel dependent upon him as their servant and contact point.[50]

His role as a mediator provides the tribal group he represents with some degree of autonomy as a result of their working within the system of the authority structure of the sedentary culture. The buffer, which the mediation provides, eliminates many of the clashes between tribe and state which would otherwise occur because of differing social traditions and practices.[51]

In the Mari texts, the *sugāgum*, while not a hereditary "chief," probably served the needs of both the nomadic and the sedentary tribesmen.[52] He operated in various capacities, including bureaucratic, judicial, and military roles. His responsibilities also covered the recruitment among the tribal peoples of men to engage in various work projects and to serve in the armed forces.[53]

The selection process of the *sugāgum* apparently was based primarily upon the payment of bribes to the government. A clear example of this policy for obtaining the office appears in *ARM* V 24:5-24.[54] In this case, Tarīm-Šakim, a functionary in the administration of Yasmaḫ-Addu (the Assyrian viceroy at Mari), reported on the negotiations being carried out subsequent to the death of a *sugāgum*.

^{m}Ba-aq-qum awīl Ti-iz-ra-aḫ^{ki}
a-na ši-im-tim
it-ta-la-ak
ù awīlū^{meš} māru^{meš} Ti-iz-ra-aḫ^{ki}
i[l]-li-ku-ni-im-ma
um-ma-a-mi Ka-a-li-Ìl-ma
a-na ša-pí-ru-ti-ni[55]
Tr. šu-ku-un
Rev. ù 1 manâm kaspam
a-na é-kál-lim qa-ba-šu
id-di-in
i-na-an-na a-nu-um-ma
^{m}Ka-a-li-Ìl-ma
a-na ṣe-er be-lí-ia
aṭ-ṭà-a[r-d]a-aš-šu

be-lí a-na su-qá-[q]ù-tim
[ša] Ti-iz-ra-aḫ^{ki}
[li]-iš-[ku]-un-[š]u-ma
[1] manâm kaspam a-ša-ri-[iš]
[li-im]-ḫu-ru-[š]u

Translation: Baqqum, the man of Tizraḫ, has died. The men of Tizraḫ came to me and spoke in the following manner: "Appoint Kali-Ilima as our *šāpirum!*" He has already promised a mina of silver to the palace as payment. Now I am sending Kali-Ilima to my lord (so that) my lord may [appoint] him as *sugāgum* of Tizraḫ (and) [accept] there (in Mari) the mina of silver from him.

A somewhat similar situation is presented in a badly damaged text, *ARM* I 119:5-22. Here, Yatarum, the *sugāgum* of Ia-il, had died and now five men of that town had come to Yasmaḫ-Addu with an apparent request that they have some say in the selection of his successor. Thus, the mention of silver and 500 sheep may have been their bargaining point in this supplication. The large sum which they were willing to pay may reflect the degree to which the town and countryside was interested in getting the man they wanted into the office of *sugāgum*. This may also have been based upon a particular tribal leader's ability (through charismatic qualities, wealth, or some other means)[56] to organize a campaign to promote his interests.

ARMT VII 311:12-21[57] also adds some insight on the selection process, both as it had become under the influence of the central authority and as it had previously been during times of more evident tribal independence.

^{m}I-zi-sà-ri-e
^{m}Ia-im-si-Èl
^{m}Mu-ut-ra-me-e
^{awīl}šibūt^{meš} Sa-ga-ra-tim^{ki}
ša a-na su-qá-qù-tim il-li-k[u]
kasap su-qá-qù-ti-šu-nu
is!-ni-qú
ši-im qí-[š]a-t[i-šu-nu]
a-na be-lí-ia a-na-[ku]
lu-ud-di-in

Translation: Izi-sarê, Yāmsi-El, and Mut-ramê,[58] the elders of Sagarātum, who have come to (receive) the *sugāgum*-offices, have paid the silver for their *sugāgu*-ships. The sum total of their gifts to my lord I shall give.

The scene presented here had the *šībūtum* come to buy the office of *sugāgum* for themselves from the government. H. Klengel has posited that this may have been a shadow of the previous practice in which it was a prerequisite for the prospective *sugāgum* to have first served as a *šibûm*.[59] Indeed, this "moving-up" process probably went back to a time when men of higher position were chosen by a tribal council.[60]

There is also something to be seen in this text in respect to the nature of the integrated tribal community. A. Marzal indicated that these *šībūtum* were probably members of the city population but at the same time still retained their tribal status. They had attained their positions as "city-elders" of Sagarātum while fulfilling, at least nominally, a similar function for the migratory tribal unit.[61] At any rate, their affiliation with the urban setting probably made them more attractive to the government as *sugāgū* since they would be able to see both the sedentary and the nomadic pastoral tribal perspective.

ARM IX 70 and 169 apparently also serve as corroborating evidence of the payment of bribes to obtain the *sugāgu*-ship. However, they actually provide us with another aspect of the duties of the *sugāgū* as well as some of their privileges. The general concensus on these two texts is that they portray two Ḫanean *sugāgū* paying large numbers of sheep (200 and 250 respectively) to the government center at Terqa for their positions.[62] G. Evans adds the theory that the payment mentioned here was made in each case by an incumbent to the office, who had to pay additional bribes in order to retain his position.[63] M. Birot cites *ARM* IX 248:13'-15' as further proof that Baḫdi-Addu, the *sugāgum* mentioned in *ARM* IX 70, was at least scheduled to have made a payment.[64]

However, an examination of the two texts does not necessarily demand this payment-scheme explanation. In both tablets the allusions of payment for the office are somewhat ambiguous.

ARM IX 70:1-5 reads:

2 ME UDU[ḫá]
ša su-qá-qù-ut
Ba-aḫ-di-[il]Addu
awīl Ia$_{8}$-ba-si-im[k][[i]?]
i-na Ter-qa[[ki]]

Translation: Two hundred sheep for the *sugāgu*-ship, Baḫdi-Addu a man of the Yabasum; in Terqa . . . .

ARM IX 169:1-5 goes as follows:

2 ME 50 UDU[ḫá]
ša su-qá-qù-ut
Mi-il-ki-[il]Addu
mār Ḫa-li-ḫa-du-un
ša a?-n[a? š]u?-du-nu

Translation: Two hundred-fifty sheep for the office of *sugāgum* held by Milki-Addu, son of Ḫaliḫadun, which are to be given? for? . . .

It may be possible to conclude, based on the evidence in these texts, that the amounts mentioned were not payments for an administrative office. Rather, what appears here may have been a sort of scribal shorthand employed to signify the number of sheep which were to be retained by the *sugāgum* from those collected in taxes as his remuneration for services rendered to the state. Thus, these office holders would have been allowed to skim off a particular number of sheep before remitting the remainder to the Mari government.[65]

By allowing this practice to serve as a sort of salary (perhaps based upon a percentage)[66] for working with the bureaucracy, both the *sugāgum* and the government would have been able to profit. The urban authority would, as a result of this arrangement, have been able to obtain the services of natural leaders from the tribal society and along with them the general cooperation of the tribes they represented. In addition, the powers of the office would have been an enticement to the most opportunistic men available in the tribes, along with their group of retainers.

ARMT XIV 46:6-25 provides us with both the general qualifications demanded by the government of Mari as well as the

evident pressures placed upon the *sugāgū*. In this document Yaqim-Addu, the governor of Sagarātum, reported to Zimri-Lim about the *sugāgum* in his district.

. . . A-ḫa-am-nu-t[a] ki-a-am
iq-bi um-ma-a-mi s[u-g]a-gu-ut
Dūr^{ki}-Ia-aḫ-du-Li-im {X}
ú-ul e-ep-pé-{X}-eš$_{15}$
du-pu-ra-ku[67] ša ša-ka-nim li-[i]š-ku-nu
i-na-an-na aš-šum ṭe$_4$-mi-i[m]
ša a-na ṣe-er be-lí-ia
aš-pu-ra-a[m]
^{m}Ma-aš-ḫu-um ^{awīl}laputtum
a-bu-ul-la-tim ka-li[68]
ù A-ḫa-am-nu-ta i-na Ma-r[i]^{ki}-ma
a-lum Dūr^{ki}-Ia-aḫ-du-Li-im [n]a-di
i-na-an-na ^{m}{X}A-ḫa-am-nu-ta
be-lí li-pa-aḫ-ḫi-id-ma
a-na Dūr^{ki}-Ia-aḫ-du-Li-im
li-it-ta-al-kam šum-ma A-ḫa-am-nu-[t]a
la i-ma-ga-ar 1 awīlam ták-lam
ša Dūr^{ki}-Ia-aḫ-du-Li-im ú-ša-al-la-mu
be-lí li-wa-e-ra-aš-šu-ma
li-iṭ-ru-da-aš-šu

Translation: . . . Aḫamnûta spoke to me in this manner: "The office of *sugāgum* of Dūr-Yaḫdun-Lim I cannot exercise, (thus) I have removed (i.e., resigned).[69] (Therefore) one (who has the right to be named) should be named." Now, concerning the report which I have sent to my lord, Mašḫum, the *laputtûm*, has been held at the gate and Aḫamnûta (is) in Mari (and) the city of Dūr-Yaḫdun-Lim is neglected. Now, my lord should instruct Aḫamnûta that he should go to Dūr-Yaḫdun-Lim. If Aḫamnûta does not consent to this, my lord should designate and have sent to me a trustworthy man, who can administer Dūr-Yaḫdun-Lim.

Despite the evident failure of Aḫamnûta to measure up to the pressures of his office, his example must have been the exception. It seems unlikely that anyone would have given up this most lucrative position easily. In fact, in the remainder of the instances in which the job changed hands, it occurred

upon the death of the previous office-holder.[70] As has been noted above, the large sums paid to obtain the office of *sugāgum* also point to the fact that it was worth a great deal to the official.[71] At the very least, it paid enough to allow him to provide a stipend to his body of retainers and prevent him from having to "moon-light" as a leader or instigator of raiding parties.[72]

The *sugāgū* were under a great deal of pressure from the urban authorities to see that royal orders were carried out in a swift and orderly manner. This was augmented by the individual official's desire to make himself look good and thereby increase his influence and power in his district. In *ARM* II 92: 14-28 is found an example of the type of commands passed through the *sugāgum* to the tribal groups. In it Kibri-Dagan reported that he had personally assembled the various *sugāgū* and told them that the Yaminites were not to be allowed to depart for the Upper Country pasturelands. In the face of this command, the *sugāgū* were to see that order was maintained in the Yaminite villages.

Very likely, this command to keep them in their villages was based on at least two factors. First, the Yaminites were probably needed to serve in the armed forces[73] in the near future and, second, any movement of the tribal groups within the kingdom entailed at least some disruption of the degree of control the government exercised over them.[74] Given the chance to move with or without permission, the nomadic groups would have had the opportunity to engage in raiding or some other rebellious activities.[75]

At the end of text *ARM* II 92, the district governor reenforced his orders by issuing this direct threat:

. . . ma-an-nu-um at-ta
ša 1 awīlum i-na a-li-ka e-li-iš
it-ta-al-la-ku-ma
a-na ṣe-ri-ia la te-re-de-[e]-šu
[pí]-qa-at ú-ul ta-ba-lu-u[ṭ]

Translation: . . ."Whoever among you who does not seize any man from your villages who leaves for the Upper Country and does not bring him to me, most assuredly, you shall not (be allowed to) live!"[76]

On other occasions, the *sugāgū* were included in a sort of comprehensive formula along with the *laputtū*[77] and the *bazaḫātum* when general orders were handed down. Thus, in *ARM* II 103:10-16 Yaqim-Addu told Zimri-Lim that he had placed his instructions concerning the apprehension of some escaped artisans of Sumuditana in stern terms to this triad of officials. *ARMT* XIV 75:7-14 also follows this pattern of communication of orders.

a-na awīlē^{meš} ša ba-za-ḫa-tim ù a-li-ša-am
a-na ^{awīl}su-ga-gi^{meš} ù ^{awīl}lapputtū^{meš}
dan-na-tim aš-ku-un um-ma a-na-ku-ma
^{awīl}Ia-am-ḫa-de-em^{ki} ù Za-al-ma-[q]a-ia-am^{ki}
ša ki-ma e-li-iš i-la-ku
[š]a? [t]up-pí be-l[í-i]a
[XXXXXX] awīlē^{m}[^{eš}]
[šu-nu-ti ar-ḫi-i]š ta-ra-ni-iš-šu<-nu-ti>

Translation: To the *bazaḫātum*[78] and town by town to the *sugāgū* and the *laputtū*, I sent stern orders. I spoke in these terms: "(All) the Yamḫadeans and the Zalmaqueans[79], who have gone up (north?), according to the tablet of [my l]ord [. . . .] (these) men, [they are rapidly] to be returned to me."

In this instance, the three district officials were given the responsibility to prevent unauthorized movement and desertion of soldiers. The fact that the government relied upon this village-by-village surveillance system was held over the heads of members of the army as a deterrent to their desertion.[80]

One other similar triumvirate of officials named as receiving orders simultaneously in the texts was that of the *sugāgū*, *laputtū*, and *šībūtum*. In the two cases where this list appears, however, the matters seem to be of a more mundane nature than the searching out of escaped criminals and enemy troops. *ARMT* XIV 65:6 simply states that they were assembled together by Yaqim-Addu to hear the king's instructions, to deliberate on them and presumably to carry them out in their zones of control. Similarly, in *ARMT* XIV 64:3-14, this same governor of Sagarātum called them together and this time had them swear an oath to carry out their duty of supplying replacements for Zimri-Lim's ally, Ḫammurabi of Babylon.

However, some members of the district leadership could not always be relied upon to perform as ordered. This may have been due to tribal pressures placed upon them or even a lack of real influence over the groups which they were appointed to represent. There is also the possibility that some of the leaders were either powerful enough or far enough away from direct government control to disregard the royal commands. Whatever the reason, Yaqim-Addu pointed out in *ARMT* XIV 64: 10-14 that:

aš-šum ṣa-bi-im Am-na-na-i^{ki}[81]
ša Sa-ḫ̮-ri-i^{ki}
ub-bu-bi-im a-na ^{awīl}su-ga-gi-[š]u-[n]u
ḫamši-šu a[š-p]u-ur-ma
ú-u[l il-l]i-ku-nim

Translation: On the subject of the Amnanean soldiers of Saḫ̮ri's[82] census, I have written [their] *sugāgum* 5 times, but they have not come.

As might be expected from an official of this type, the prime concerns of the *sugāgū* were with tribal relations and population control. In the above text, a *sugāgum* was responsible for the implementation of the *tēbibtum*, "census."[83] In fact, their aid was at times enlisted for this process when efforts of the regularly appointed census takers (*ebbū*)[84] failed to get the job done. For example, in *ARM* III 20 Kibri-Dagan reported that although he had appointed three census takers for his district, three of the Yaminite villages had not consented to send their men to be inscribed by these men. The sequel to this circumstance was then detailed in *ARM* III 21:5-11. This letter, sent by Kibri-Dagan as well, noted that the task was finally accomplished by using *sugāgū*[85] as census takers.

aš-šum ṣa-bi-im ša a-la-ni ša DUMU.MEŠ-Ia-mi-na
ub-bu-bi-im
awīlū^{meš} su-qá-qù-šu-nu
[i]l-li-ku-nim
awīli^{meš} eb-bi-šu-nu
aš-ku-un-ma
ṣa-ba-am iš-ṭú-ru-nim-ma

Translation: Concerning the taking of the census of the troops

of the cities of the Yaminites, their *sugāgū* have come. I appointed their census takers (and) they inscribed the troops.

There is some ambiguity in the text which allows the supposition that the *sugāgū* were not actually serving personally as *ebbū*. Still, the fact remains that their presence and consultation were definite factors in getting the Yaminites to comply with the census procedure.[86] It may have simply been that the tribesmen were afraid of the government *ebbū*, who would not have been as understanding of irregularities in the counting. *ARM* I 6 also provides another angle on the complexities of dealing with the tribes in respect to this touchy issue of census taking. Lines 6-12 outline Yasmaḫ-Addu's assessment of the potentially volatile situation inherent in the projected *tēbibtum* of the Yaminites.

aš-šum DUMU.MEŠ-Ia-mi-in ub-bu-bi-im
ta-aš-pu-ra-am DUMU.MEŠ-Ia-mi-in
a-na ub-bu-bi-im ú-ul i-re-id-du-ú
tu-ba-ab-šu-nu-ti-ma a-ḫu-šu-nu awīlū^{meš} Ra-ab-ba-ia
ša i-na e-bi-ir-tim i-na ma-a-at Ia-am-ḫa-ad^{ki}
wa-aš-bu i-še-em-mu-ú-ma i-ma-ra-sú-nu-ši-im-ma
a-na ma-ṭi-šu-nu ú-ul i-tu-úr-ru-nim[87]

Translation: You have written to me, (Šamši-Addu) concerning the censusing of the Yaminites: "The Yaminites have not come for the censusing." If you census them, their brothers, the Rabbeans, who are dwelling in the land of Yamḫad will hear about it and will be angry with them and they will not return to their own land.

There were apparently some unstated causes for rivalry or manipulation of the arrangements between the segments of the tribal units which led to this circumstance. Šamši-Addu's decision on how to resolve the problem without antagonizing either group was then given in lines 13-21:

mi-im-ma la tu-ub-ba-ab-šu-nu-ti
ši-pí-iṭ-ka-a-ma du-ni-in-šu-nu-ši-im
ši-ip-ṭà-am ki-a-am i-ki-in-šu-nu-ši-im
um-ma-mi šarrum ḫarranam i-la-ak ka-lu-ma
a-di ṣi-iḫ-ri-im li-ig-da-mi-ir

su-ga-gu-um ša ṣa-bu-šu la gu!-mu-ru-ma
1 [awī]lam i-iz-zi-bu a-sa-ak šarrim i-ku-ul
ki-a-am ši-ip-ṭà-am i-ki-in-šu-nu-ši-im
mi-im-ma la tu-ub-ba-a[b-š]u-nu-ti

Translation: (Therefore,) under no circumstances, shall you census them. (Rather,) give them a strong talking to as follows: "The king is going on campaign. Let every man, including boys, assemble. The *sugāgum*, who does not assemble his (allotment of) troops, who allows even a single man to remain behind, will be in violation of the interdict of the king." Give them this ultimatum, but whatever you do, do not cens[us th]em!

The solution to waive the institution of the *tēbibtum* for the Yaminites in order to prevent trouble with the indignant Rabbeans was a master stroke of diplomacy by Šamši-Addu. By doing this and instructing the *sugāgū* to assemble the men needed, he allowed both sides to save face. The Yaminites could then make their own count (according to their ability and desire to supply soldiers) and provide the state with the requested troops without having their own manpower supply endangered.[88] The government authority was saved from any official embarrassment or sign of weakness towards the tribes by placing the responsibility for the successful completion of recruitment upon the shoulders of their appointed tribal leader, the *sugāgum*. Thus the positive relations established with the tribal groups by the central government were preserved and a convenient scapegoat was available in case the quota of men needed for the king's campaign was not met.[89]

The texts in which the *sugāgum* serves as a legal and administrative representative for the tribal groups point up his role as a mediator. *ARM* IV 16:10'-13' demonstrates the peacemaker role which they were required to perform at times. Here, Yasmaḫ-Addu described to his father, Šamši-Addu, the measures he took in the face of a famine in the region of Suḫum.[90]

ù a-nu-um-ma áš-ta-pa-ar
su-qá-qù ša Su-ḫi-im i-pa-ḫu-ru
ši-ip-ṭà-am[91] a-na-di-šu-nu-ši-im
ù li-ib-ba-šu-nu ú-na-aḫ

Translation: And this I announced: "The *sugāgū* of the Suḫeans are to assemble (and) a strict order I will give them," and (thereby) appease their hearts.

Apparently, some concession was to be made to the *sugāgū* to prevent the Suḫeans from rebelling. It is probable that food and other goods were to be sent to them.[92]

The fact that the *sugāgū* had great influence over their tribal groups and could organize aggressive actions comes to light in the contents of *ARM* II 53:13-32. In this letter, Yasmaḫ-Addu, an administrator under Zimri-Lim, relayed the demands of the Yaminites' *sugāgū*. They wished to regain a number of villages belonging to them which had apparently fallen into the hands of a certain Laḫun-Dagan. He must have been allied or on agreeable terms with Zimri-Lim since his boats were to ferry the party of Yasmaḫ-Addu across the Euphrates (line 7). In order to strengthen their plea, they engaged Ṣûrâ-Ḫammû, a Yaminite leader of some stature,[93] and Yarim-Lim, a client of Zimri-Lim,[94] to present their case to Yasmaḫ-Addu and to the king. The threat of violence to get their ends was very implicit in their message.

[šu]m-ma La-ḫu-un-^{il}Da-gan
[la i]-il-la-ak ú-lu ne-da-ak-šu
ú-lu šu-ma i-na ^{iṣ}kussê-šu
nu-ṭa-ap-pa-ar-šu[95]. . . .

Translation: If Laḫun-Dagan does not depart, we will either kill him (Zimri-Lim) or we will set him down from his throne.

The seriousness to which Yasmaḫ-Addu took this threat is to be seen in the fact that in lines 29-31 he recommended to the king that he grant all that they desired.

There were purely legal matters which were dealt with at least in part by the *sugāgum*. *ARM* VIII 6:12'-14' listed Abdu-Dagan, the *sugāgum* of Bit Ḫuqqum, as a witness-guarantor of a contract involving a field.[96] Similarly, in *ARM* VIII 100:20 a *sugāgum* named Kali-Addu was included in a list of many other men in the text who were serving as witnesses to a legal transaction. In still another case, *ARM* VI 40:5-12, the *sugāgum* certified the appointment of a certain Yasarti-El of Ḫišamta

into the *biḫrum* class of the army. This action was challenged, however, by Yasīm-Sumu, a functionary of the urban community, who may have felt that some of his powers of appointment were being usurped. He charged that the man was listed as being a slave of the palace and therefore not eligible to be appointed to this special class of warriors.[97] The challenge may also demonstrate a certain amount of the prejudice which may have been felt by the urbanite officials for their tribal counterparts.[98]

One of the poignant episodes in the texts which deals with the position of the tribal peoples in the Mari kingdom and the role which their leaders played is presented in *ARMT* XIV 8:5-13. It appears from this letter that during the reign of Zimri-Lim even the religious practices of the tribal population were strictly controlled. The *sugāgū* were forced to come to the district governor of Sagarātum to obtain permission from the king so that their icons of the gods could be released to them for the festivals in the villages. Previous to this time all of the sacred statues had been stored in the fortress cities of the kingdom in order to prevent the pastoralists from rallying around them or using them to curse the government. It must have been very demoralizing to the tribes to have to ask permission from the government officials[99] to worship their ancestral gods.

$^{\text{awīl.meš}}$su-ga-gu ša ḫ[a-a]l-ṣí-im
aš-šum ilāni^{meš} ša i-na S[a]-ga-ra-tim^{ki}
ù Dūr^{ki}-Ia-aḫ-du-Li-im
ka-lu-ú i-na a-wa-[tim]
ki-a-am iṣ-ba-tu-ni-i[n]-n[i$_5$]
Tr um-ma-a-mi nīq[ētum^{ḫá}-ma]
ilāni^{meš} wa-aš-še-e[r-ma][100]
i-na bītāti^{ḫá}-[š]u-[n]u
Rev. nīqētim^{ḫ}[^{á} l]i-i[q]-q[ú-š]u-nu-ši-im

Translation: The *sugāgū* of the d[ist]rict have questioned me concerning the gods, which are collected in Sagarātum and Dūr-Yaḫdun-Lim, in these terms: "Relea[se] the sac[rificial] gods so that sacrifices can be [offer]ed to them in [their] temples."

Aside from basic tribal affairs, the *sugāgū* were also at

times involved in military activities. As has been noted, they aided in the assembling of military personnel.[101] They also were required occasionally to help winnow out those of the recruits who may have had loyalty problems, specifically the deserters from the armed forces. In *ARM* I 13 some men had fled from the army at Qatanum and their commander, Samidaḫum, had ordered their tribal leaders, the *sugāgū*, to enchain them and return them to him. However, Šamši-Addu countermanded this order with one of his own which directed that the deserters were to be accepted freely back into the army.[102] Whatever the reason may be, Šamši-Addu had again managed to read correctly the feelings of the tribesmen who had been conscripted. He saw that the best way to insure fewer problems with conscriptment and desertion of the troops was to provide a sign of magnanimity toward those who had deserted.[103]

ARM II 18:4-14 also placed the *sugāgum* in a position of responsibility in respect to the disposition of deportees (probably resulting from military activities). A certain man had been deported to Mari but had then fled that city. Now, a *sugāgum* reported to Išme-Dagan, the elder son of Šamši-Addu:

> ^{awīl}na-si-ḫu ša a-na Ma-[r]i^{ki}
> na-ás-ḫu iḫ-ta-li-iq
> a-ḫ[a]-šu an-na-nu-um
> a-na pu-ḫa-ti-šu a-na [M]a-ri^{k}[^{i}] [. . .

Translation: The deportee, who had been deported to Mari, has fled. His brother is here (now) as his replacement at Mari . . . .

It may be that the man was a deserter or a hostage and as such his brother was held legally responsible when he fled from Mari.

More explicitly to do with the military aspect of the *sugāgū*'s role are *ARM* II 118 and *ARMT* XIII 33. In these two documents, Baḫdi-Addu, a *sugāgum* in *ARM* IX 70, was said to be in command of some Ḫanean troops. Similar evidence of the *sugāgum*'s military involvement is provided in *ARM* IV 74. In this text were listed a number of troops and their leaders who were to be supplied with a garment. Among them were the *sugāgū* and the sons of the *sugāgū*.[104] A parallel situation, where it is possible to make an identification based upon grouping, is

found in *ARMT* VII 215:33-36. Again the *sugāgū* were listed, along with 33 other men who were involved with the military.[105]

There were times, of course, when the *sugāgū* chose the wrong master to serve or, as in *ARM* V 2, were involved in a minor revolt. Most likely, the result outlined in this letter was the same as occurred in the majority of cases when a rebellion was instigated. Yasmaḫ-Addu cryptically reported to his brother, Išme-Dagan, that he had suppressed the revolt and ^{awīl}*su-qá-qù*^{meš} [*ka-lu-šu-nu*]/(5) *di-ku* . . . . ,"[all of their] *sugāgū* are dead . . . . ," along with the "ring leaders" (*awīlū*^{meš} *qa-da-tu*[*m*][106]).

The *sugāgū* are mentioned in the Mari texts as having several functions and duties. However, their prime role in the bureaucracy was as the representative of their tribal group and as the mediator between that unit and the authorities of the state. His power may have been increased by his recognition by the bureaucracy, but it must have still been necessary for him to satisfy the needs of the tribe in order to continue to exercise real influence with its members. The use of picked leadership by the government could eventually aid in consolidating the tribal population into the greater society.[107] However, to create a more viable working arrangement some degree of balance between the two forces would have been necessary. Otherwise, when one or the other had gained a monopoly of power and could dictate the terms of the interchange of dealings between them, then the power of the mediator would have been lessened and eventually destroyed.[108]

šībūtum. There was one final group of individuals who exercised some power over the activities of the Mari pastoral nomadic groups as well as the segments of the tribal groups who had settled in the towns. These were the *šībūtum*, "elders." It is quite easily determined on the basis of the texts that these men were involved with both the nomadic and sedentary units of the tribes in the Mari kingdom.[109] In respect to their mention as representatives of the pastoral groups, the texts are at times not very explicit, only intimating that they spoke for a particular traveling group of people. Thus, in *ARM* II 83:18-19 Kibri-Dagan wrote to Zimri-Lim that the *šībūtum* of the Yaminites had failed to assemble (presumably after being

ordered to do so) and in *ARM* III 65:5-9 news of the journeying of 10 *šībūtum* of the Ḫaneans to the king was forwarded to the monarch by Yaqim-Addu. The main reason for presuming that these men were supposed to be representing migratory groups lies in the negative argument that they are not expressly associated with a town or village as is the case with other *šībūtum*.[110]

The majority of cases in which the *šībūtum* were mentioned do place them with a particular urban site. They were either categorized by town or district. So, for example, *ARMT* VII 311: 12-21 provides a mention of three elders who were said to be from Sagarātum. Five *šībūtum* from the town of Kurgiš were said to have arrived at Sagarātum in *ARMT* XIV 114:8-10. Likewise, *ARMT* XIV 104:11-12 even had the elders of the beseiged city of Raṣama dealing in the negotiations with Atamrum, the leader of the enemy forces.

The cuneiform texts also have the *šībūtum* serving as representatives among the village population. *ARMT* XIV 121:28-30 noted that the *šībūtum* had failed to enter Sagarātum from their villages when summoned to do so by Yaqim-Addu. Interestingly enough, these same, often recalcitrant individuals were mentioned in *ARMT* XIV 55:17-23 (in a broken context) as serving the government when called upon to do so.

. . . . La-na-su-PI-um
a-na Bu-nu-ma-^{d}Addu ki-a-am iq-bi
um-ma-a-mi i-nu-ma be-lí a-na Ia-am-ḫa-ad
i-lu-ú aš-šum nīqim a-na li-ib-bi
a-lim^{ki} a-na e-re-bi-im iṣ-ṣ[a]-b[a-a]t-ma
[l]a-ma ^{awīl}šibūt^{meš} a-lim^{k}[^{i} XXX] 50 ṣa-bu-um
it-ti-ka i-ru-bu [XXXX]

Translation: . . . Lanasûm spoke to Bunuma-Addu (the king of Niḫriya) in these terms: "When my lord goes up to Yamḫad, he shall take charge of the matter of the sacrifice in (any)[111] village (which) he may enter. Before the elders of the town . . . 50 soldiers will enter with you . . . .

Whether the *šībūtum* mentioned here actually wished to cooperate with the king's planned pilgrimage may not have made much difference. The 50 soldiers which were to accompany the messenger were most likely instructed to keep order while Zimri-Lim was in the town and of course to insure the cooperation of the local

officials.

The most probable conclusion to be drawn concerning the *šībūtum* is that they were originally an integral part of the pastoral nomadic tribal group's organization as a planning body and decision maker on patterns of movement and other aspects of herding.[112] However, when segments of the migratory tribal groups took up residence in the towns and villages, the elders among them were retained as an advisory body.[113] At any rate, their retention by both segments of the tribal community highlights the closeness with which tradition, if not tangible links, held the integrated tribal society together.

A. Marzal has suggested that there may have been for a time two sets of elders, one with the nomadic groups and one serving the sedentary members in the municipalities. Eventually, they could have merged and perhaps a single individual become strong enough to proclaim himself *šarrum*.[114] This may actually have been the sequence of events during the period after the fall of the Ur III dynasty and before Yaḫdun-Lim's rise to power.[115] However, once the rise of the national state of Mari managed to eclipse the power of the dimorphic chiefdoms,[116] these individual petty kings would have had to consolidate (as they did to fight Yaḫdun-Lim[117]) or relinquish their powers. Thus, I think that under the Mari kings the *šībūtum* served both segments of the tribes, and the practice of having a set of elders for the pastoralists and the town dwellers may have been reinstituted.

As can be seen in many of the texts which have been dealt with so far, the pastoral nomadic tribal community did not always submit itself passively to government control. Indeed, Zimri-Lim was forced to make alliances and spend several of the early years of his reign pacifying the various rebellious elements in his kingdom.[118] However, since it was seasonally necessary for the tribes to migrate through areas that were administered by the Mari government, they had to adapt themselves to the situation. This adaptation might have involved reducing the size of the migratory unit so that it could remain as inconspicuous as possible. However, a course of action such as this would have left them without the necessary means to produce a strong political organization when it might prove

expedient. The Mari government could then have taken advantage of their weakness by fabricating a branch of the bureaucracy (consisting of the *merḫum* and *sugāgū*) especially designed to keep them in line with government policy.[119]

Any dealings between the tribal leaders which may have occurred, unless they affected the welfare of the state, would not have appeared in the Mari letters and so cannot be proven to have occurred. However, it is possible to argue that the Mari tribal leadership communicated fairly frequently with each other. This is based upon the fact that an exchange of information would have been necessary for them to be able to make decisions on basic animal management and family dealings.[120]

Tribal Reactions to the Central Urban Authority

The use of manipulative or forceful means by the government in order to exploit or control the tribal groups in their region can also lead to conflicts between the tribe and state. The tensions which are generated by these methods[121] may also be heightened by feelings of resentment among the tribesmen against infringements on their freedom of movement and choice. These tensions may manifest themselves in acts of sabotage, raiding, smuggling, occasional open warfare, and a good deal of mutual suspicion.[122]

Staged acts of defiance. The correspondence from the Mari archive provides ample evidence of these anti-government reactions by the tribal groups. For instance, *ARM* VI 30 and *ARMT* XIV 121 both speak of the desertion of tribal troop contingents. *ARM* II 48 describes how the Ḫaneans refused to even assemble from their villages for conscription. And, finally, *ARM* III 38 actually contains the insolent reply of the Yaminite *sugāgum*, who flatly refused to comply with Kibri-Dagan's request for corvée laborers. All of these and more[123] were probably based, at least in part, upon the tribal members' reluctance to become completely subservient components in the urban social system. From their point of view, it was apparently necessary that service to the state also serve the needs of the tribal community as much as possible in order for lasting peaceful arrangements to be established.[124]

One of the most common means employed by the pastoral

nomadic tribesmen to escape the influences placed upon them by the government is to simply migrate elsewhere. This is facilitated by the basic occupational requirement of herdsmen to move their flocks periodically to new pastures. The central authority, of course, recognizes the need for such movement by the pastoralists, but they wish as a rule to channel it within the defined boundaries of their recognized sphere of influence. Thus, in the letters from the Mari officials, the attempts by the herders to migrate to seasonal pasturelands and the actions of the government to stall or circumvent unauthorized movement are well documented.

In *ARM* II 102:5-27 just such a move as described above was put into motion. The *bazaḫātum* were instructed to seize anyone who left for the Upper Country, despite the fact that grazing areas around Sagarātum had given out. Similarly, in *ARM* II 92:16-28 the *sugāgū* were warned to prevent their tribal groups from departing for this same Upper Country.[125]

ARMT XIV 86 provides a couple of examples of "anti-social" activity by pastoral people and the government's reaction to them. The first action which proved unacceptable to the urban authorities was discovered by a traveling mission of royal messengers.

. . . . Ku-sa-an mār ši-i[p-ri-i]m
awīl Kar-k[a-m]i-iš^{ki} ^{d}Ša[maš-re]-di
ù 1 ^{awīl}tap-pu-šu ša be-lí-ia
iš-tu Kar-[k]a-m[i]-iš^{ki} a-na ṣe-er
be-lí-ia i-la-ku-nim 4 $^{awīl.meš}$Up-ra-pi-a-yu^{ki}
i-na ḫu-mu-ṣi-im[126] ša 1 a-ia-lim
[iš]-ḫi{-X}-ṭú-šu-nu-ti-ma
^{d}Šamaš-re-di ù ^{awīl}tap-pa-šu
i-du-ku ù awīl Kar-ka-mi-iš^{ki} ú-ṣé-e-em

Translation: .. . . , Kasan, a mess[enger] of Karkemish, Ša[maš-re]di and his companion, who are (subjects) of my lord, were in the process of going from Karkemish to my lord. Four Uprapeans, who were skinning a stag, attacked them (and) Šamaš-redi and his companion were killed (but) the man of Karkemish escaped.

These messengers of the king were probably killed by the Uprapeans in order to either cover up their poaching or prevent

the travellers from taking their food. It may be that the penalty for killing animals without permission was sufficiently strict to warrant these murders. To be sure, the Uprapeans were not interested in leaving any witnesses to their action.

The second part of the letter again has the Uprapeans involved in illegal activities.[127] These tribesmen had been discovered driving away their flocks and presumably were on their way to an area outside the jurisdiction of the government.[128] Thus, the *bazaḫātum* were dispatched to block their passage.

"Withdrawal" and "retribalization." Such movement out of the political control of the urban authority by a segment of the population has been described by G. Mendenhall,[129] and more recently by his student J. T. Luke,[130] as "withdrawal." This sort of practice would have allowed both the sedentarized and near-sedentarized elements of the tribal population to exit themselves from a too oppressive situation in the same manner as the nomadic members had done. However, Mendenhall and Luke qualified their definition saying that this movement did not include physical and geographic withdrawal, as has been described above by the tribal groups. They applied it primarily as an explanation for the origins of the *ḫabirū* (the unaffiliated segment of the population) and their activities. I feel this limits the possibilities inherent in this idea. It would apply to compensatory migration patterns[131] and temporary withdrawal to escape unwelcome demands or requirements placed upon the tribes by the state.[132]

N. Gottwald styled this refusal to be drawn into permanent social context a reaction to an infringement of traditional values. The subsequent return to the migratory groups by the settled tribal members he terms "re-tribalization."[133] In fact, just such a decision to turn away from a single social viewpoint may also have been part of the impetus toward pastoral nomadic specialization in the first place. At any rate, the tensions and conflicts which resulted in withdrawal or some other act of noncompliance simply points up the need for balance which must be maintained for the symbiotic interrelationship between nomad and sedentary to remain viable.[134]

ḫabirū

Aside from the instances of seasonal or compensatory migration and rebellion by the tribal groups, there was also an individual reaction which produced a separate segment of the population. These people had totally severed their individual ties with both the tribal and urban communities. They were identified in the texts as the *ḫabirū*.[135] They were outcasts from both segments of the social and economic life in the Mari region. In order to survive in any numbers, they had to combine forces and form a sort of population splinter group. This eventually became a minor force in the area and a source of concern for the security officers of the kingdom of Mari. M. Rowton, because of their nebulous backgrounds and their ill-defined placement in the society of the times, took their name, *ḫabirū*, to be a "social ethnonym"--that is, a designation for a group which is primarily based on social rather then ethnic characteristics.[136] They took their label from their anti-social society rather than from the groups which fostered them. If they had a dual name, such as Yamutbalian-*ḫabirū*,[137] the latter name would have had precedence in the minds of the other segments of society.

This population element, because of its aggressive nature and activities, was confined to the upper regions of the Ḫabur valley. This was a self-imposed restriction of movement, based primarily on the fact that there were too few of them to force their way into the more populous areas of the kingdom. Furthermore, the rough terrain and scrub forest, which still adequately covered the hills, at that time, served as an attractive "hide-out" for the marauding bands. This area could be easily defended against any group of government forces which was foolish enough to follow them there.[138] The only documented large scale movements out of their bases were occasioned by their employment as mercenaries by the various rival factions in the northern Mesopotamian area.

The Mari correspondence documents several of the activities of the *ḫabirū*. Simple raiding by this group in the region of Idamaraṣ was almost continuous. *Ḫabirū* 28:39-44 depicts them in an act which was fairly common among the regular tribal groups, carrying off sheep.[139]

u_4-um tup-pí an-ni-im a-na ṣe-er be-lí-ia u-ša-bi-lu
a-na-ku a-na Lu-ḫa-ia^{ki} at-ta-la-ak
a-na pa-ni Za-al-ma-qí-im awīlū.meš Ta-al-ḫa-iú^{ki}
ù ḫa-bi-ru Lu-ḫa-ia^{ki} iš-ḫi-tú
5 ME immerātu^{ḫá} ù 10 awīli^{meš} lu-ú ša i-du-ku
lu-ú ša il-qú-ú an-ni-im it-ba-lu [

Translation: The day I sent this tablet to my lord, I went to Luḫaia. Before (this) the Zalmaqeans of Talḫaia and the *ḫabirū* had raided Luḫaia. They either killed or carried off 500 sheep and 10 men. This is what they took [. . . .].

The raid described in this text is not an example of a pastoral group's attempt to augment or replace its herds. In this case the *ḫabirū* were merely interested in collecting spoils, perhaps as wages for helping the Zalmaqeans storm the town.

It appears that in most cases the *ḫabirū* were in the hire of someone else.[140] Thus, in *Ḫabirū* 19[141] and 26 individual band leaders were named and presumably were for hire to the highest bidder along with their followers. In text 26 there is even the note that these *ḫabirū* forces planned a raid at the very gates of the city of Ašnakkum. The number of men necessary to stage such a daring raid would have had to be fairly large, and therefore, they were most likely assembled as a mercenary force. They actually represented a large number of smaller raiding bands.[142]

The most blatant use of the *ḫabirū* as mercenary soldiers is presented in *ARM* II 131:10-15. The situation was described by Mašum, one of several men designated as functionaries of the palace and as such an integral member of the bureaucracy. He informed Yasmaḫ-Addu of a belligerent move by one of the rival kings in the vicinity of Mari.[143]

. . . Ia-pa-ḫa-^{il}Addu
a-lam Za-al-lu-ul^{ki} i-na a-aḫ ^{nār}Purattim
e-bé-re-tam an-ni-tam i-pu-uš
ù qa-du-um 2 li-im ṣa-bi-im ḫa-bi-ru
ša ma-a-tim i-na li-ib-bi a-lim ša-a-ti
wa-ši-ib . . . .

Translation: . . . Yapaḫ-Addu has established a camp[144] (at) Zallul on the bank on this side of the Euphrates[145]

> and with him are 2,000 *ḫabirū* soldiers of the land. They are residing in the midst of this camp.

Perhaps the main point to be made from this text, aside from the obvious fact that the *ḫabirū* were serving as mercenaries, is that they were designated as being *ša mātim*, "of the land."[146] This highlights the fact that no clear tribal distinctions were ordinarily made in respect to the *ḫabirū*. This was probably because they themselves did not acknowledge any previous affiliations. They were a diverse collection of the flotsam and jetsam of their society. Only their own needs and those of their employers were important to them.

Surely, every society has some group which approximates these individuals in some particulars. The very rigidity which is necessary for a distinct cultural unit to become recognizable as such also serves to alienate those elements who cannot or do not wish to cope with it. Thus, the movements of the Mari pastoral nomadic peoples into closer ties with the urban authority and its culture must have had an effect on all segments of the tribal and urban community. As has been noted, certain groups will tend to slough off from the migratory unit. Some will eventually either join the village population or re-emerge in another tribal group. Some, however, like the *ḫabirū*, will join groups of social dropouts, who choose to go their own way for a period of time or permanently.

To summarize this portion of the study of the pastoral nomadic tribes of the Mari kingdom it need only be reemphasized that they existed as part of a dimorphic society. Because their settlements and grazing areas were enclosed within the environs of the Mari state, the tribes had to integrate their culture with that of the urban community. This was manifested in the close ties between the nomadic and sedentary segments of the tribal population and between the tribes and the urban culture. There were, of course, instances of friction and distrust. These, however, were often based upon the conflicting interests inherent in their differing economies and occupational patterns. Both the tribal and sedentary societies of the Mari kingdom were complex and multi-leveled. Still, it was possible, with the intervention of mediators and a fairly consistent administration, for the groups to cooperate in the

common exploitation of their region.

NOTES

CHAPTER IV

[1]See F. Barth, "A General Perspective on Nomad-Sedentary Relations in the Middle East" in *The Desert and the Sown*, ed. C. Nelson (Berkeley, Calif., 1973), 11, for this sort of analysis of the effects of political factors on the Basseri tribesmen of southern Persia.

[2]Cf. S. L. Pastner, "Ideological Aspects of Nomad-Sedentary Contact: a Case from Southern Baluchistan," *AQ* 44 (1971), 179.

[3]Bates, D. G., "The Role of the State in Peasant-Nomad Mutualism," *AQ* 44 (1971), 117. See also D. H. K. Amiran, "Effects of Climatic Change in an Arid Environment on Land Use Patterns" in *Changes of Climate*, (UNESCO, Arid Zone Research XX) (Belgium, 1963), 440, for statements about weak governments and the "suitability" of a clash between farmer and nomad and nomad and central power bases. J.-R. Kupper, "Le rôle des nomades dans l'histoire de la Mesopotamie ancienne," *JESHO* 2 (1959), 122-26, draws similar conclusions, saying that the nomadic groups tend to have a freer rein when there is no strong government to deter their actions.

[4]Rowton, M. B., "Autonomy and Nomadism in Western Asia," *Or*. 42 (1973), 248-49, notes that civilizations in western Asia tend to oscillate between urban and pastoral control when no effective balance was struck between tribe and state. This is one explanation given for the Amorite dynasties which assumed control of many of the major cities, including Babylon, after the fall of the Ur III dynasty. Cf. A. Haldar, *Who Were the Amorites?* (Leiden, 1971), 51-66, 82 and G. Buccellati, *The Amorites of the Ur III Period* (Naples, 1966), 328-30, for discussion of this political oscillation and the role of the Amorite tribes.

[5]Barth, F., "General Perspective," 19. N. Dyson-Hudson, "The Study of Nomads" in *Perspectives on Nomadism*, eds. W. G. Irons and N. Dyson-Hudson (Leiden, 1972), 24, provides a list of the significant factors involved in herding with a discussion of their importance to the individual migratory group.

[6]Ibid., 19-20. See also D. G. Bates, "Differential Access to Pasture in a Nomadic Society: The Yoruk of Southeastern Turkey" in *Perspectives on Nomadism*, eds. W. Irons and N. Dyson-Hudson (1972), 59.

[7]Rowton, M. B., "Dimorphic Structure and the Tribal Elite," *Studia Instituti Anthropos* 28 (1976), 248-49. He cites A. Bausani, *The Persians From the Earliest Days to the Twentieth Century* (London, 1971), 143, which notes that tribal chiefs "were considered to be *hākim* (governors), that is, officers of the state appointed and dismissed at the will of the *shāh*"

during the Safavid period.

[8]Barth, F., "General Perspective," 19-20. Cf. also M. B. Rowton, "Enclosed Nomadism," *JESHO* 17 (1974), 23, n.1 and "Dimorphic Structure and the Tribal Elite," 249, for a discussion of some possible reasons for the elimination of the "kings" among the Mari tribal groups.

[9]Rowton, M. B., "Enclosed Nomadism," 17.

[10]Rowton, M. B., "Urban Autonomy in a Nomadic Environment," *JNES* 32 (1973), 203, describes these as including nomads as well as sedentary and nontribal population elements.

[11]Ibid. Rowton also notes in "Dimorphic Structure and the Tribal Elite," 240, that in western Asia the ". . . tribes which formed part of established territorial states have tended to reaffirm and strengthen their autonomy whenever the power of the central government weakened. In doing so the more powerful tribal confederacies would begin to function as incipient autonomous states within the sovereign state." He goes on, on p. 246, to suggest that in the "Upper Country" region, some of the urban dynasts were tribesmen although their tribal affiliation was not mentioned in the texts when it was not politically important or the tribe had "disintegrated", thereby leaving only its name to the region. However, since this process of tribal disintegration was a very slow procedure and ties to the tribes often remained strong for many years, the kings in these regions retained affiliations which were often only marks of ancestry. Still, tribal structure and forms might also be perpetuated in these regions. For instance, in *ARM* X 33:23-29, the dynasts of Idamaraṣ included in an executive meeting a discussion of the effects on kinship ties implicit in some projected marriage arrangements.

[12]Cohen, Y., "Adaptation and Evolution: An Introduction" in *Man in Adaptation: The Institutional Framework*, ed. Y. Cohen (Chicago, 1971), 16, describes this as a common arrangement among stateless societies. He then goes on to suggest that the chiefdom represented a transitional stage between stateless and state oriented societies.

[13]Dossin, G., "L'inscription de foundation de Iaḫdun-Lim, roi de Mari," *Syria* 32 (1955), 1-28. G. Mendenhall, "Social Organization in Early Israel" in *The Mighty Acts of God*, eds. F. M. Cross, W. E. Lemke, and P. D. Miller, Jr. (New York, 1976) 141, points out that "the traditional village self-sufficiency simply cannot cope with organized force of foreign origin and therefore must form larger social units willy-nilly."

[14]Rowton, M. B., "Urban Autonomy," 214; A. Malamat, "Campaigns to the Mediterranean by Iaḫdunlim and other Early Mesopotamian Rulers," *Studies in Honor of Benno Landsberger on his 75th Birthday* (*AS* 16) (Chicago, 1965), 370, also makes the point that these three chieftains most likely took advantage of Yaḫdun-lim's campaigns to the Mediterranean in order to stage their revolt.

[15]Buccellati, G., *Cities and Nations of Ancient Syria*

(Rome, 1967), 140, states that the use of the titular here in conjunction with the names of three known pastoral nomadic tribes (Uprabum, Amnanum, and Rabbum) points to a situation in which the rule of the king over the nomadic population was "kept distinguished" from his overlordship to the urban community. This does not seem to take into account, however, that both elements would have been fighting here against the forces of Yaḫdun-Lim and that these cities may have all served as tribal centers or autonomous dimorphic chiefdoms. They had at that time become large enough to compete (at least as a combined confederacy) with the city states of the Mari kingdom.

[16]Cf. J. J. Finkelstein, "The Genealogy of the Ḫammurapi Dynasty," *JCS* 20 (1966), 101-2, for a history of this tribe and the Yaḫruru along with the tracing of ties between them and the Ḫammurabi dynasty and later with the region around Sippar in the latter half of the Old Babylonian period.

[17]The text is ambiguous. Either they (a) assembled to him (i.e., Sumu-Ebuḫ) or (b) assembled against him (i.e., Yaḫdun-Lim). This second translation is employed by A. L. Oppenheim in "The Dedication of the Shamash Temple of Yaḫdun-Lim" in J. B. Pritchard, *Ancient Near Eastern Texts Relating to the Old Testament*, 3rd edition, with Supplement (Princeton, N.J., 1969), 556.

[18]Similarly, later in this same inscription (col. III, lines 28-30 and col. IV, lines 1-2), Yaḫdun-Lim described how he destroyed the Ḫanean city of Ḫamân and captured its king, Kaṣūri-ḫala.

[19]Thureau-Dangin, F., "Iaḫdun-Lim, roi de Ḫana," *RA* 33 (1936), 51. J.-R. Kupper has recently republished this inscription in "L'inscription du 'Disque' de Yaḫdun-Lim," *Kramer Anniversary Volume* (*AOAT* 25) (Germany, 1976), 299-303.

[20]Luke, J. T., *Pastoralism and Politics in the Mari Period: a Re-examination of the Character and Political Significance of the Major West Semitic Groups on the Middle Euphrates, ca. 1828-1758 B.C.* (University of Michigan Ph.D. dissertation, 1965), 165-66.

[21]Cf. *ARM* VI 76:20. M. B. Rowton, "Dimorphic Structure and the Tribal Elite," 241, posits that Zimri-Lim was listed as king of the Ḫaneans first and only secondly as king of the Akkadians because the Ḫaneans had at that time fully accepted the king of Mari as their paramount chief. In addition, the Ḫanean element of the population was larger and more important than the Akkadian.

[22]See *ARM* II 36:11-12; III 10:4'-5' and G. Dossin, "Les noms d'années et d'éponymes dans les 'Archives de Mari'" in *Studia Mariana*, ed. A. Parrot (Leiden, 1950), 55, #6: *šanat Zi-im-ri-li-im da-am-da-am ša DUMU.MEŠ-Ia-mi-na i-na Sa-ga-ra-tim*^{ki} *i-du-ku ù šarrani*^{meš}*-šu-nu i-du-ku*, "The year when Zimri-Lim inflicted a defeat of the Yaminites at Sagarātum and killed their kings." M. B. Rowton, "Dimorphic Structure and the Tribal Elite," 241, compares the more modern case of the Abdali (later Durranī) tribe in Afghanistan which, like the Ḫaneans,

was an ally of the state while another large tribal group, the Ghilzai, remained, like the Yaminites, hostile to the government. This latter group continued to cause problems which threatened to destroy the cohesion of the state.

[23] Luke, J. T., *Pastoralism and Politics*, 166.

[24] Rowton, M. B., "Dimorphic Structure and the Tribal Elite," 241, suggests that one mark of the Ḫaneans' integration (but *not* subjection) into the Mari society was that they "fully accepted the kings of Mari as their paramount chief."

[25] Bates, D. G., "The Role of the State," 117. Cf. also C. S. Coon, *Caravan: The Story of the Middle East* (New York, 1958), 262-68, for the variation of the power based between Islamic tribes and nations.

[26] Irons, W. G., "Variation in Political Stratification among the Yomut Turkmen," *AQ* 44 (1971), 155 and B. Spooner, *The Cultural Ecology of Pastoral Nomads* (Philippines, 1973), 34-35, note that the chiefdomship will develop in the nomadic pastoral group only where there is a need for a high degree of control or mobilization of men or resources or when relations develop with neighbors or a central government. This latter reason requires the creation of a high-status, plenipotentiary representative to mediate between them.

[27] Awad, M., "Living Conditions of Nomadic, Semi-Nomadic and Settled Tribal Groups" in *Readings in Arab Middle Eastern Societies and Cultures*, ed. A. M. Lutfiyya (The Hague, 1970) 141.

[28] Rowton, M. B., "Dimorphic Structure and the Tribal Elite," 248-49. He cites *ARM* III 70:4'-11' and *Benj.* 988:b: 35-40 to demonstrate the lowering of the role of the kings to a status of unimportance as vassals or as generalized (scapegoat) enemies of the state.

[29] Barth, F., *A Tribe of the Kamseh Confederacy: The Basseri Nomads of South Persia* (Oslo, 1961), 77. See also D. G. Bates, "Differential Access," 59, for some of the factors balanced by the mediation which prevent detrimental occurrences from happening to both eco-systems.

[30] Ahmed, A. G. M., "Tribal and Sedentary Elites: a Bridge Between Two Communities" in *The Desert and the Sown*, ed. C. Nelson (1973), 90-93, describes these actions by the elite group among the Rufā'a al-Hai nomads of the region along the banks of the Blue Nile.

[31] Barth, F., "Nomadism in the Mountain and Plateau Areas of South West Asia" in *The Problems of the Arid Zone* (UNESCO, Arid Zone Research XVIII) (1962), 349.

[32] Marzal, A., *The Organization of the Mari State* (University of Chicago Ph.D. dissertation, 1969), 65. He opts for the theory that they may have been confined to districts in the Upper Country. See in this regard *ARM* I 62.

[33]Dossin, G., "Le *madārum* dans les 'Archives royales de Mari,'" *RAI* 18 (1972), 56, suggests that the term *merḫum* (corresponding to Hebrew *mir'ah*, "pasturage"), provides an etymological clue to the function of this official. He served as both an overseer and also a check on the movements of the tribes and their flocks in the grazing areas.

[34]See M. B. Rowton, "Urban Autonomy," 213, who makes this distinction and posits that the *ḫazannum* official was in charge of the urban community. I presume that this would have also included the tribal settlers in these towns.

[35]Cf. W. von Soden, *AHw*, 1002, for a listing of the instances where these special agents were used. See also *ARM* II 98:4'-10' where they were apparently employed by a *sugāgum*. M. Anbar, "'Les *sakbû* et les *bazaḫātum* à Mari'--une mise au point," *UF* 7 (1975), 592, also lists their duties in the Mari region.

[36]Cf. J. MacDonald, "The Identification of *Bazaḫātu* in the Mari Letters," *RA* 69 (1975), 142-45, for a discussion of these officers as both a police force and as "trouble shooters" for the local administrators.

[37]Note here that *nawûm* is used specifically for "flocks" and/or "migratory group" with another word used to designate the steppe (*kaṣû*). For other uses of *kaṣû* in the Mari correspondence, see *ARM* VI 57:12; V 81:25, 36:32, 33:9 and II 120:20, 23.

[38]Bottéro, J., *Le problème des Ḫabiru à la 4e recontre assyriologique internationale* (Paris, 1954), 22, Tx. A 807, #27.

[39]Dossin, G., "Les archives épistolaires du palais de Mari," *Syria* 19 (1938), 111-12.

[40]Marzal, A., "The Provincial Governor at Mari: His Title and Appointment," *JNES* 30 (1971), 198-99, has a discussion of this text and the view that since the *merḫum* was mentioned first, he had some kind of authority over the *šapiṭūtum*. Note also in *ARM* I 62:5'-14' that Ḫabduna-Dagan was appointed as a *merḫum* after previously serving as a *šapiṭum*.

[41]Bottéro, J., *Ḫabiru* 21-22, Tx. A 633, #26:20-30.

[42]Marzal, A., *The Organization of the Mari State*, 63-64, has the argument that *LÚ me-er-ḫu-ú* (line 26) is to be read as a singular (contra J. Bottéro, *Ḫabiru*, 22). He cites *ARM* IX 257:12' where the same expression is used to refer to one person --*I-ba-al-Ìl me-er-ḫu-ú*. Marzal also conjectures that it is this same Ibal-El who is spoken of here in this text.

[43]Cf. *ARMT* XIV 84:4'-15' in which Yaqim-Addu, the governor of Sagarātum, used spies (*misulātam*) to check on the plans of the Yaminites and to plant false information with the beggars who were being used by the Yaminites as spies.

[44]See above pp. 85-101 for other instances of the

employment of pastoralists in nontribal and nonpastoral activities.

[45]Cf. W. G. Irons, "Variation in Political Stratification," 151, for a similar system in which the Persian government appointed from the sedentary population an official named the *sarkardeh*. This man then dealt through the tribal chiefs, known as *saqlau*, in order to get the government business carried out.

[46]Barth, F., *Basseri*, 79. See also G. R. Fazel, "The encapsulation of Nomadic Societies in Iran" in *The Desert and the Sown*, ed. C. Nelson (1973), 136, for this practice by the Iranian government in its use of the *kadkhodas*, "section chiefs," of the Boyr Ahmed tribes. Still another instance is found during the Safavid period (1500-1700) in Persia. A. Bausani, *The Persians from the Earliest Days to the Twentieth Century* (London, 1971), 143, notes that at this time the chiefs of the nomadic tribes were appointed as government officials by the *shāh*.

[47]Ibid., 129. W. Goldschmidt, "Independence as an Element in Pastoral Social Systems," *AQ* 44 (1971), 138-39, describes a similar situation among the Marri Baluch, whose nomadic segments avoid authority roles and strive as much as possible to do " . . . without the intervention of the sedentary officials."

[48]Spooner, B., *Cultural Ecology*, 34. M. B. Rowton, "Dimorphic Structure and the Tribal Elite," 249, explains that it is quite normal for a tribe in an "enclosed nomadic" situation to include full-time nomads as well as a "semi-sedentary tribal elite, composed of landowners, military commanders, officials, and even urban dynasts."

[49]Awad, M., "Living Conditions," 141.

[50]Marx, E., *Bedouin of the Negev* (Manchester, 1967), 45-46. He goes on to qualify this as being especially important to landless tribes who have to hire some of their members out to aid the tribe. The chief would be in a position to see that jobs were given to them by the government and local towns. See also W. G. Irons, "Variation in Political Stratification," 155.

[51]Gilbert, A. S., "Modern Nomads and Prehistoric Pastoralists: The Limits of Analogy," *JANES* 7 (1975), 68-69.

[52]Malamat, A., "Aspects of Tribal Societies in Mari and Israel" in *La civilisation de Mari* (*RAI* 15) (Paris, 1967), 133. See also on this M. B. Rowton, "Enclosed Nomadism," 23, n.1.

[53]Sasson, J., *Northernmost Syria: a Survey of its Institutions Before the Fall of Mari (ca. 1757 B.C.)* (Brandeis University Ph.D. dissertation, 1966), 55-56, has a full discussion of these duties. M. B. Rowton, "Dimorphic Structure and the Tribal Elite," 244-45, also details his functions for the state and for the tribal groups.

[54]For a similar view, see G. Evans, "The Incidence of Labour-Service at Mari," *RA* 57 (1963), 67, n.3.

[55]Weippert, M., *The Settlement of the Israelite Tribes in Palestine* (Naperville, Ill., 1971), 126, n.81, states that the *šāpirūtum* and *sugāgūtum* were used interchangeably for the same office. J. T. Luke, *Pastoralism and Politics*, 90, notes that the abstract noun is quite rare and cites *ARM* II 68:6 where he takes it to refer to a military office. G. Mendenhall, "The Census Lists of Numbers 1 and 26," *JBL* 77 (1957), 55, n.18, uses the equation of *sugāgum* with *šāpirum* to delineate the official position of the Biblical *sōfer* in Judges 5 where it is evident that the man in question had nothing to do with writing. It may indeed be that the two terms are different names for the same functionary. However, it is also possible that *šāpirūtum* belongs to a different category and the central government simply chose to incorporate this office into another, similar office, the *sugāgūtum*.

[56]Spooner, B., *Cultural Ecology*, 34. M. B. Rowton, "Dimorphic Structure and the Tribal Elite," 244, cites *ARMT* VII 140:18' as proof that this office of *sugāgum* was not confined to just a few influential tribesmen, since in this text there is mention of 40 *sugāgū*. He also notes *ARMT* VII 311:12-21, which lists several *sugāgū* in one town. Perhaps, they represented different tribal subgroups in that town.

[57]Published in J. Bottéro, "Lettres de la salle 110 du palais de Mari," *RA* 52 (1958), 164-66.

[58]Cf. J. Sasson, "The *ENGAR/ikkarum* at Mari," *AOAT* 25 (1976), 404, for other mentions of this man. He apparently served in several capacities, including *ENGAR/ikkarum* (a type of farm bureau officer) in *ARM* VIII 67:4-5, *sugāgum* in VII 198, a person in control of a *babtum* group of 17 persons in VII 180: iv:30, and he is listed as a financial contributor to an upcoming military expedition in IX 258:ii:14. Sasson suggests that he was one among a fairly large group of "all-purpose bureaucrats" of a second or third echelon in the Mari administration.

[59]Klengel, H., "Zu den *šībūtum* in altbabylonischer Zeit," *Or.* 29 (1960), 367.

[60]See, for instance, E. A. Speiser, "Background and Function of the Biblical *nāśī'*," *CBQ* 25 (1963), 113-14. He suggests that the *nāśī'* in Num 1:16 and Exod 34:31 most likely obtained their position as a result of an election by the appropriate tribal council.

[61]Marzal, A., *The Organization of the Mari State*, 128-29.

[62]Luke, J. T., *Pastoralism and Politics*, 160. Cf. also J. Sasson, *The Military Establishment at Mari* (Rome, 1969), 57, n.46 and M. Birot, *ARMT* IX, 296. M. B. Rowton, "Dimorphic Structure and the Tribal Elite," 244, takes this position.

[63]Evans, G., "Labour-Service," 67, n.3.

[64]Birot, M., *ARMT* IX, 298. He suggests that Baḫdi-Addu was listed in with a group owing tax arrears as a reminder to

him of the payment (now overdue) which he was to make for his *sugāgu*-ships in *ARM* IX 70. However, in most cases (*ARM* I 119, V 24, and VII 311) payment was made before the office was bestowed. In *ARM* IX 248 he probably had just gotten behind in his payment of collected taxes. This does not mean that he was still paying for his office with periodic bribes. It only shows that he was either a slow administrator or a slightly untrustworthy one.

[65]Tax collection activities by the *sugāgū* were documented in *ARMT* VII 140:18' and IX 248:13'-15'. Cf. also G. R. Fazel, "Encapsulation," 133-35 for this sort of skimming by tribal leaders in Southwest Iran.

[66]Sasson, J., *The Military Establishment at Mari*, 13, is correct in suggesting that the 10 shekels paid to the *sugāgum* in *ARM* VII 215:3-14 was only a symbolic salary, since it was obviously not enough to satisfy the needs of the tribal leader.

[67]Cf. W. von Soden, *AHw*, 177, for *ṭaparu*, "sich entfernen." See also *ARM* I 73:24 for the imperative *du-up-pé-er*.

[68]For *abullātum kalûm*, see *CAD* "A," 86/f. "to confine to the city." Note also *ARM* I 76:9, III 37:23, and VI 42:9. In this text, Mašum, the *lapputtûm*, was probably assigned to Dūr-Yaḫdun-Lim in order to provide that town with some of the administrative services which Aḫamnûta was either incapable or unwilling to perform. The fact that this was an unsatisfactory arrangement is to be seen in Yaqim-Addu's statement that this city was being neglected. Very likely, the tribal members of its population did not wish to be administered by a nontribal official.

[69]This idiom, in this context, demands a translation of "to resign" rather than "to be removed from office" (as it is in *ARM* V 37:9 and II 137:34). This is because later in the text Aḫamnûta was to be given the option to return to his office. Surely such an option would not have been made by the Mari government to this *sugāgum* if it had been responsible for his removal. At least one would expect some mention in the text of this previous action by either Yaqim-Addu or Aḫamnûta.

[70]See *ARM* I 119 and V 24.

[71]Fazel, G. R., "Encapsulation," 135, relates how the tribal leaders were coaxed into serving the state by having their power base affirmed and by granting them a substantial portion of the taxes collected by them.

[72]Cf. W. Irons, "Livestock Raiding among Pastoralists: an Adaptive Interpretation," *Papers of the Michigan Academy of Sciences, Arts, and Letters* 50 (1965), 407-8, for an outline of this process as it applied to the Persian tribal leader, the *saqlau*, and the necessity for its existence in order to maintain economic stability among the tribal units. An article by myself and D. W. Young will appear in *Or.* 46 (1977), dealing with the parallel situation between the role of the *saqlau* and the *sugāgum*, "The *raison d'être* of the *sugāgum* at Mari."

[73]See C. F. Jean, "L'armée du royaume de Mari," *RA* 42 (1948), 147, for the use of tribal troops in the Mari army.

[74]Weippert, M., *The Settlement of the Israelite Tribes in Palestine*, 114 and J. T. Luke, *Pastoralism and Politics*, 257-58.

[75]Cf. *ARM* III 16:3-24 especially for the type of situation they may have feared, in which men left the villages but at the same time left their wives or "lovers" behind to serve as spies. Thus, when they came back at night to see the women, they could collect the information which would have allowed them to raid the area with impunity.

[76]*ARMT* XIV 80:4-20 also takes this no nonsense tact, but it does not contain an explicit death threat.

[77]The *laputtûm* officials seem to have been tied to the village population in a parallel relationship to the ties the *sugāgum* had with the tribal people. In *ARM* II 103, both were said to be spoken to "town by town." J. Sasson, *Military Establishment*, 15, notes that beside the responsibility to watch for escaped people in their area, the *laputtûm* also delivered weapons (*ARM* VI 69) and carried messages of military importance (*ARM* VI 57:9).

[78]MacDonald, J., "*Bazaḫātu*," 143, takes their role in this text to prove their powers to arrest as special police agents.

[79]Cf. *Benj*. 986:a for another case where the Zalmaqeans were a threat to Zimri-Lim's kingdom.

[80]Note also this system employed against foreign armies in G. Dossin, "*Adaššum* et *Kirḫum* dans des textes de Mari," *RA* 66 (1972), 118, Tx. A2801:32-36. In this instance the responsibility for capturing Ešnunnan soldiers was placed upon the *sugāgū* and *laputtū*.

[81]The tribal jealousies which can split subgroups is quite evident in this text where a Yaminite subtribe boycotted a conscription to serve under Ḫammurabi. The confusing nature of this action is the result of the fact, pointed out by J. J. Finkelstein, "The Genealogy of the Ḫammurapi Dynasty," 102, that that king probably belonged in direct descent to members of the Amnanum, who had settled in the Sippar region during Ur III. The explanation may lie in an old tribal split which alienated the various groupings and eventually became a permanent source of emnity between them.

[82]Bottéro, J. and Finet, A., *ARMT* XV, 133, locates this town in the district of Sagarātum. It also appears in *ARM* III 68.

[83]Speiser, E. A., "Census and Ritual Expiation in Mari and Israel," *BASOR* 149 (1958), 19, notes that the several forms of this process, including counting for military as well as legal purposes, was secular in character. On p. 25 he goes on to qualify this, saying that the fear of being enrolled was so

great that the *tēbibtum* took its name from the incidental process of ritual "purification," which is its original meaning. This is in contradiction to J.-R. Kupper, *Les nomades en Mésopotamie au temps des rois de Mari* (Paris, 1957), 22-29, which viewed this as "une cérémonie purificatoire."

[84]For the deputizing of these members of the bureaucracy, see *ARM* III 19:14 and III 21:10. See also A. Finet, "Une affaire de disette dans un district du royaume de Mari," *RA* 53 (1959), 59, lines 33-48.

[85]See H. Klengel, "Halbnomaden am mittleren Euphrat," *Das Altertum* 5 (1959), 203 and "Benjaminiten und Hanäer," *WZH* 8 (1958/59), 218, for discussion of this "commissioner" role of the *sugāgum*.

In *ARM* IV 7 Yasmaḫ-Addu was instructed by Šamši-Addu to go to the *nawûm* and meet with the *sugāgū* of the banks of the Euphrates in regard to his taking a *tēbibtum* of that region.

[87]In G. Dossin, "Iamḫad et Qatanum," *RA* 36 (1939), 47, line 12 appears the exact same phrase, used in respect to some Rabbeans who had come to graze their sheep in the vicinity of Mari and now refused to return to their regular pasturelands in northern Mesopotamia.

[88]Rowton, M. B., "Urban Autonomy," 214, points to this text to prove that during the reign of Šamši-Addu the Yaminites enjoyed a larger degree of autonomy than was the case under Zimri-Lim. He says that this is to be seen in their being allowed here to escape the census.

[89]Amiran, D. H. K., "Nomadic and Beduin Population in the Census Returns of Mandatory Palestine," *IEJ* 13 (1963), 247-48, provides documentation of another instance when government officials had to rely on estimations of the available man power as a result of tribal opposition to the census.

[90]Anbar, M., "La région au sud du district de Mari," *Israel Oriental Studies* 5 (1975), 13-14, places Suḫum in the region north of Yabliya, in the frontier zone of the kingdom, in the environs of Ḫit.

[91]Marzal, A., *The Organization of the Mari State*, 52, defines this type of order as "an enjoining command, an authoritative decree or edict given by the highest authority; it affects the army, has religious connotations and implies a threat."

[92]A similar emergency grain shipment may be the subject of *ARM* IV 64:2'-5'. In this broken text, all the wheat of Kumulḫim was to be sent to Šubat-Enlil.

[93]Cf. J. T. Luke, *Pastoralism and Politics*, 221-22, for a description of the activities of this man and his possible status among the Yaminites.

[94]Sasson, J., "*ENGAR/ikkarum* at Mari," 407, points out that Yarim-Lim is also named in *ARM* II 93 by Kibri-Dagan as a man of

Yaḫrur, a town near Ekallatum. The town probably took its name from the Yaminite subtribe which established it.

[95]For this restoration, see W. von Soden, "Neue Bande der *Archives Royales de Mari*," *Or.* 22 (1953), 198. In this context, *CAD* "D," *duppuru* (2al'), p. 187 reads *nu-da-ap-pa-ar-šu* as "we shall remove him from office (i.e., his throne)."

[96]Marzal, A., "The Provincial Governor at Mari," 201, points to the mention in this text of the governor, *ša-pí-ṭú-u[m]*, the *sugāgum*, and a divine penalty clause, *ašnakkum*, as proof of the special circumstances of this transaction. However, the use of both urban and tribal officials may indicate that the contract involved a member of an integrated tribal group as is the case in *ARM* VIII 11.

[97]Sasson, J., *Military Establishment*, 22, says that the challenge came because "only a free man, *awīlum*, was considered worthy of entering the military" and Yasarti-El was said to be listed as a *warad ekallim*, "slave of the palace." However, in *ARMT* XIV 121:9 some Ḫanean troops who had been sent (but had subsequently deserted) to help with the defense of the district of Sagarātum were described as *wardi*[meš] *ekallim*. Thus, it can be seen that although these men might not be allowed to join the elite *biḫrum* class of warriors, they were certainly included in the body of the army. M. B. Rowton, "Dimorphic Structure and the Tribal Elite," 242, n.88, hazards the guess that this man had been included in the appointments to the *be'rum* corps because the *sugāgum* was having trouble filling his quota of "volunteers."

[98]A similar disagreement over the appointment of a tribal member to a royal office, *madārum*, is depicted in a text published by G. Dossin, "Le *madārum* dans les 'Archives royales de Mari,'" *RAI* 18 (1972), 61, Tx. A. 3821:11-13. In this text a certain Saḫbarum is derided as being the *mār ha-ba-[tim]*, "son of a raider." Dossin equates this with "bedouin." The post of *madārum* had duties ranging from provincial governor to ruler of a vassal town. One other text in this article, A. 2741:9-14, mentions that a *madārum* was appointed to sit on the throne of Eshnunna after the death of its king. This was done in order to curry favor with Ḫammurabi of Babylon according to Dossin. It is said that the *sugāgū* of that area had petitioned that this appointment be made swiftly in order that civil control be maintained and the tribal elements remain quiet.

[99]See *ARM* II 37:6-14. In this letter it is noted that the government official, Ibal-El the *merḫum*, substituted a donkey foal as the sacrificial animal to conclude a treaty between the Ḫaneans and Idamaraṣ. These two parties had originally planned to sacrifice a puppy and a goat. (Cf. M. Held, "Philological Notes on the Mari Covenant Rituals," *BASOR* 200 [1970], 40, for a discussion of this text.) The action of ignoring the tribal customs with respect to sacrificial animals was probably an attempt by the government of Mari to show that it was the perogative of the central authority to make treaties among its subjects and that these people would have to bow to the urban religion in this matter. *ARM* VIII 11 also provides one more note of a duality of religions in the Mari kingdom.

However, in this case from the reign of Šamši-Addu, the tribal religion was given its due along with that of the Assyrian overlords. To conclude the deeding of land in this document, the "herbs" of both Šamši-Addu and of Awin the Rabbean were symbolically eaten. Again the difference in emphasis in dealing with the tribal groups is to be seen in this contrast between Zimri-Lim's and Šamši-Addu's actions.

[100] This is an Assyrianism. The Old Babylonian form would be *wuššerma*.

[101] *ARM* I 6 and III 6.

[102] See A. Marzal, "The Provincial Governor at Mari," 190, for this intervention on the part of the king. Note also *ARM* I 128:5-11 for *sugāgū* being consulted in regard to Ḫanean deserters.

[103] Yaqim-Addu may have had this case in mind when in *ARMT* XIV 82:5-22 he advised Zimri-Lim to allow Ḫanean deserters to go in order to appease the remainder of the Ḫanean troops who had assembled for a campaign against Eshnunna.

[104] *ARM* VI 67:10-14 also mentions the giving of a garment to a *sugāgum*, Innaḫan (see him also in *ARMT* VII 215:3). In this particular text he was said to go at the head of the Ḫaneans and thus the *mardatum UŠ* garment was given to him as a cloak of military rank and royal favor.

[105] Sasson, J., *Military Establishment*, 11, suggests that the order of appearance of these men in this "payroll" text reflected their military rank. Thus, the *sugāgum* was, according to this theory, second only to the *Gal a-mu-ri-im*.

[106] Oppenheim, A. L., "The Archives of the Palace of Mari, II," *JNES* 13 (1954), 144, notes that the use of *qaqqadum* in this connotation is rare in Old Babylonian texts.

[107] Salzman, P. C., "Political Organization Among Nomadic Peoples," *PAPS* 111/2 (1967), 129, states that this sort of happening occurred among several tribes, including the Tuareg and Fulani. See also M. B. Rowton, "Dimorphic Structure and the Tribal Elite," 248-49.

[108] Irons, W. G., "Variation in Political Stratification," 156.

[109] For a listing of the functions performed by the *šibūtum* for the tribes and the government, see A. Marzal, *The Organization of the Mari State*, 141 and H. Klengel, "Zu den *šibūtum* in altbabylonischer Zeit," *Or.* 29 (1960), 357-75.

[110] This may also be true of those *šibūtum* listed along with *sugāgū* and *laputtū* in *ARMT* XIV 64 and 65. Each of these officials would probably have represented a different segment of the population. In the villages, the *laputtū* served the regular sedentary community while the *šibūtum* served the tribal members of the village population.

[111]D. W. Young has suggested this possible translation to me and indeed it does seem to fit the situation presented here. Certainly, when the king traveled within his kingdom or to the lands of vassals or allies, it would have been his perogative to officiate at local religious ceremonies. Furthermore, it would have been a mark of his control over all aspects of the lives of his subjects to do this. The fact that Zimri-Lim made fairly frequent trips up to Yamḫad is seen in his year-names. S. Smith, "Yarim-Lim of Yamḫad," *RSO* 32 (1957), 162, notes that two of these formulae are named for such trips (numbers 20 and 32 in G. Dossin, "Les noms d'années et d'éponymes dans les 'Archives de Mari'," *Studia Mariana*, ed. A. Parrot [Leiden, 1950], 57, 60) and in the first of these he is said to have dedicated a statue to the weather god of Aleppo. J. M. Munn-Rankin, "Diplomacy in Western Asia in the Early Second Millennium B.C.," *Iraq* 18 (1956), 69-70, 78-79, notes the close relations which existed between Zimri-Lim and Yamḫad. It served as his refuge during the Assyrian interregnum and he married the daughter of Yarim-Lim its king. However, relations deteriorated after the death of that king because Yamḫad chose not to come to the aid of Zimri-Lim when Ḫammurabi of Babylon decided to extend his kingdom northward and swallowed up the Mari kingdom. The fact that fifty soldiers were assigned to go to the village with the king in this text may reflect this changing political situation.

[112]Cf. F. Barth, *Basseri*, 26, and W. W. Swidler, "Some Demographic Factors Regulating the Formation of Flocks and Camps Among the Brahui of Baluchistan" in *Perspectives on Nomadism*, eds. W. Irons and N. Dyson-Hudson (1973), 73, for these camp-oriented functions of the tribal "elders."

[113]Luke, J. T., *Pastoralism and Politics*, 90, qualifies this statement by saying that little is known about the *šibūtum*'s activities because most of them were intratribal in nature and thus of little interest to the government authorities. This could explain a part of their obscure nature, but certainly not all. Still, there are many more texts to be published and perhaps some of them will fill in some of the blank spaces in our understanding of them.

[114]Marzal, A., *The Organization of the Mari State*, 131.

[115]See M. B. Rowton, "Autonomy and Nomadism in Western Asia," *Or.* 42 (1973), 256, for mention of tribal elite residing in the city of Eshnunna in a text published by I. J. Gelb, "An Old Babylonian List of Amorites," *JAOS* 88 (1968), 39-46, Tx. TA 1930.

[116]See M. B. Rowton, "Urban Autonomy," 202, and my discussion above pp. 133-35.

[117]See above, pp. 133-34.

[118]See in G. Dossin, "Les archives épistolaires," 117-18, lines 24-27, for Itur-Asdu's famous letter to Zimri-Lim assessing the political situation of this period: "There is no king who is powerful all by himself. Ten or fifteen kings follow

Ḫammurabi of Babylon; as many follow Rim-Sin of Larsa; as many follow Ibal-pi-El of Eshnunna; as many follow Amut-pi-El of Qatna (and) twenty kings follow Yarim-Lim, the king of Yamḫad." Cf. also *Benj.* 986:a, 987:b, 990:b, and 991:a for the rebellion of the Yaminites and the alliances they made with the king of Zalmaqum. They also chronicle the opportunism of some groups, such as those headed by Qarni-Lim and Bina-Ištar, who were willing to let the two opposing groups fight it out before joining the winner's side.

[119] Cf. F. Barth, "Ecologic Relationships of Ethnic Groups in Swat, North Pakistan," *AA* 58 (1956), 1087-88, for a similar development among the Pathans. Note also M. B. Rowton's discussion of "divide and rule tactics" by the Mari government against the Yaminite kings in "Dimorphic Structure and the Tribal Elite," 248.

[120] J. T. Luke, *Pastoralism and Politics*, 80, provides this assessment of the textual material. Note also above, pp. 52-54, which discusses the importance of an information exchange mechanism among the migratory units of a given region.

[121] Cf. D. G. Bates, "The Role of the State in Peasant-Nomad Mutualism," *AQ* 44 (1971), 117-18, for some of the methods employed by the Ottomans to control the tribal groups. They were based usually on the principle of the shifting of support from one group to another in order to insure that no one tribe could build a strong local power base.

[122] Cf. F. Barth, "Nomadism in the Mountain and Plateau," 341. He states that many conflicts " . . . tend to develop between tribal values and loyalties, and the demands of the bureaucratic State administrations."

[123] In this regard see *ARM* II 30, 33, 53. Note in addition, that in *ARM* II 80:6-8 Zakīra-Ḫammu reported to Zimri-Lim that, in an act of unexplained vandalism, some passing Ḫaneans had sunk the ferry used to transport grain across the river.

[124] Barth, F., "General Perspective," 18. M. B. Rowton, "Dimorphic Structure and the Tribal Elite," 241, points out that the signs of integration by the Mari tribal groups are not found in acts of subjection to the state, but rather in their willingness (at least on the part of the Ḫaneans) to take part in wars and labor activities.

[125] For other instances in which the Yaminites actually did go to the Upper Country and as a result served as an embarrassment, if not a clear danger, to the Mari authorities, see *ARM* III 12 and *Benj.* 985:b.

[126] For this D-stem infinitive form, see *CAD* "H," 60, which translates it "to skin."

[127] See above, pp. 136-37, for this text.

[128] *ARM* V 27 may also describe such a move. In this letter the Yaminites managed to cross over to the Mt. Bisir region before Tarim-Šakim was able to.

[129]Mendenhall, G. E., "The Hebrew Conquest of Palestine," *BA* 25 (1962), 66-86. His most recent statement on this appears in "Social Organization in Early Israel" in *The Mighty Acts of God*, ed. F. Cross, W. E. Lemke, and P. D. Miller, Jr. (New York, 1976), 132-51.

[130]Luke, J. T., *Pastoralism and Politics*, 35-38, 272-75.

[131]I am defining compensitory migration as that movement by the herding unit which is based upon physical, social, or political influences. This may range from migration due to the exhaustion of grazing to unscheduled movement in order to evade conscriptment into the armed forces.

[132]See *ARM* III 12 and V 27 for this type of withdrawal.

[133]Gottwald, N. K., "Domain Assumptions and Societal Models in the Study of Pre-Monarchic Israel," *SVT* 28 (1975), 98-99.

[134]Rowton, M. B., "Dimorphic Structure and the Parasocial Element," *JNES* 36 (1977), 189, points out that some segments of the Mari population were made up of elements still in the process of retribalization. As such, they were considered tribal rabble by more stable groups in the area.

[135]These unattached people are also mentioned in the El Amarna texts in much the same sort of context--usually as mercenaries or members of raiding bands. For a presentation of the literature on the *ḫabirū*, see M. Gray, "The Ḫabiru-Hebrew Problem in the Light of the Source Material Available at Present." *HUCA* 29 (1958), 135-202 and most recently M. B. Rowton, "Dimorphic Structure and the Problem of the 'Apirû-'Ibrîm," *JNES* 35 (1976), 13-20.

[136]Rowton, M. B., "'Apirû-'Ibrîm," 15. He uses the example of the name "Turk," which was almost universally applied with a social connotation until a rise of nationalism in Anatolia returned its ethnic meaning.

[137]*Ḫabiru*, 19, Tx. A 2939, #19:11-14.

[138]Rowton, M. B., "The Topological Factor in the Ḫabiru Problem," *Studies Landsberger* (*AS* 16) (Chicago, 1967), 384.

[139]See *Benj*. 988:c and *ARM* VI 57:4'-17' and VI 58:5-21. See also W. Irons, "Livestock Raiding Among Pastoralists," 393-414.

[140]This may also be due to the fact that these were the most significant and dangerous bands with which the government would have to deal. Those smaller raiding parties who may have occasionally preyed upon village and tribe probably were overlooked in the district reports when they were overshadowed by the activities of the larger groups.

[141]This text pinpoints actual tribal members, Yamutbalians, who had become *ḫabiru*. *Ḫabiru*, #33:14, although fragmentary,

also seems to name a Suḫean as a *ḫabirum*. J. T. Luke, *Pastoralism and Politics*, 275, argues that no Yaminites were named as being *ḫabiru* because of the strong control Zimri-Lim had over them. This, however, seems to override the basis of "withdrawal" since it was supposedly the process of movement outside of political control, but not necessarily into banditry or eternal conflict. Compromise might be possible in some cases which allowed a return of the tribal members or estranged urbanites to the kingdom's control.

[142]Izinabû had only thirty men in his command. It is to be assumed that several groups such as his were combined to make a raid against Ašnakkum possible. It was certainly a serious threat since the *merḫum* had been asked to enlist what aid he could against them.

[143]See A. Finet, "Iawi-ilâ, roi de Talḫayum," *Syria* 41 (1964), 140-41, for the background to this situation of open hostility.

[144]This *alum* was probably not a new city, built just for this purpose. Rather, the site of Zallul was at a strategic point on the river and thus served as a natural point for Yapaḫ-Addu to attempt to defend. He set up camp in the environs of this city.

[145]Lewey, H., "Šubat-Šamaš and Tuttul," *Or*. 27 (1958), 3, n.1, argues (contra J.-R. Kupper, *Les nomades*, 252, n.1) that the fortified camp of the enemy was on the same side of the river as the defending forces. They were separated by 30 *iku* of disputed territory.

[146]Compare this designation with the general term *ṣa-ab ma-a-tim*, "soldiers of the land," in *ARM* I 42:37-38.

CONCLUSION

This study's primary aim has been to bring about a better understanding of the tribal peoples mentioned in the texts from the Mari archive. The approach I have used has been an interdisciplinary one--employing anthropological, topographic and demographic materials as tools with which to draw analogies on the material in the ancient texts. I have attempted to provide a clearer picture of the pastoral nomadic and sedentary groups among the Mari tribes by emphasizing their social, economic, and political environment.

The examination of the texts in conjunction with the anthropological studies of modern and near-modern tribal groups has shown that the Mari tribes formed a portion of what can be termed a "dimorphic society." They lived within the general confines of the Mari government's influence and much of their herding activity was predicated on their relations with the village communities of the region and with the officials of the central authority. This study has pointed out that such central aspects of tribal existence as seasonal migration, grazing rights, social and political organization were affected by their interaction with the urban culture based at Mari.

The fact that nomadic pastoralism was recognized as a specialized occupation among the tribal groups of the Mari kingdom provides a key to the position of these groups in the overall culture. For at least a portion of the tribal population, herding was their chosen field of endeavor, not just the first of a chain of occupations they would hold on their way toward civilization. There was no continuous or preordained process whereby the pastoral nomads reached sedentarization or retribalization. There were influxes of new peoples into the Mari region from time to time (and consequent name changes for the land and the people), but the texts show that nomadic pastoralism remained a viable economic alternative to a fully agricultural or urban life for the tribal population.

It would, in fact, be a mistake to attempt to classify one particular tribal group in the Mari texts as completely nomadic or completely sedentary in this period before the domestication

of the camel. The differences in character, position, and membership of the various Mari tribal peoples were due in the main to the individual adaptations made by them to the more dominant urban culture with which they were obliged to deal. In addition, the pressures and dangers of living in a marginal physical environment played a determining role in the decisions made by the migratory groups and their individual members.

It has been my intention in using analogous material from studies of more recent pastoral nomadic groups to provide the historian of the Mari period with an additional means to advance his research. I believe that judicious utilization of this data can (and has in this study) help define the role and importance of these previously obscure tribal groups. They formed a fairly large portion of the population of ancient northern Mesopotamia and thus cannot be glossed over or ignored.

By presenting information on the basic aspects of herding and their affects on the groups which practice them, one comes to see them as producers and participants in the economy of their region. In the same manner, when it can be shown that the political organization of a tribal group can be drastically changed by its relations with a central authority, then the parallel evidence from these ancient texts is provided with a sense of familiarity, thereby making them more intelligible to the researcher and student.

Certainly, this study has not been able to answer every question about the pastoral nomadic tribes of the Mari kingdom. Many subjects are simply not mentioned in the texts so far published. Such topics as basic animal husbandry, intratribal communication and decision making, tribal cult and legend, and the full implications of the interchanges between the individual migratory units and the local villages are either imperfectly mentioned or ignored in the letters. Additional study of these subjects must await the publication of future volumes of texts.

Among the other studies which deserve further examination when more data becomes available are the effects of tribal fluidity and the aspects of tribal territorial rights. In addition, I feel that the rules of the *rabi Amurru* and the *sugāgum* deserve further amplification. The nonpastoral

activities performed by the tribal members for the government may also yield interesting results in respect to their affect on sedentarization and acculturation of the tribalists.

The interdisciplinary method employed in this study has given it an advantage over previous studies which chose to merely chronicle the texts or discuss them from a single view point. The approach used here has tried to present both the urban and nomadic side of what is discussed in the documents. In addition, there has been a conscious effort to provide economic and social influences on the activities of the government and its subjects. I feel that this interdisciplinary approach is necessary for a complete understanding of the historical and anthropological aspects of this period. It provides a means of facilitating research and determining, as nearly as possible, the background in which ancient events were documented.

INDEX OF MARI TEXTS CITED*

28: 39-44(pp. 159-160)
33: 14(p. 177, n.141)

Birot, M., "Textes économiques de Mari, III," *RA* 4 (1955), 15-31, Tx *AB*(p. 127, n.118)
"Nouvelles épigraphiques au palais de Mari (salle 115)," *Syria* 50 (1973), 6(p. 122, n.70)

Bottero, J. "Lettres de la salle 100 du palais de Mari," *RA* 52 (1958), 164-6(p. 169, n.57)

Dossin, G. "Signaux lumineau au pays de Mari," *RA* 35 (1938), 181-182(p. 126, n.113)
"Les archives épistolaires de palais de Mari," *Syria* 19 (1938), 111(p. 80, n.107); 111-112(p. 138; 167, n.39; 167, n.39); 117-118: 24-27(p. 175, n.118); 124(p. 74, n.46; p. 75, n.61); 112(pp. 128-129, n.139)
"Iamḫad et Qatanum," *RA* 36 (1939), 47: 12 (p. 172, n.87); 49: 3-5(p. 63; p. 80, n.106)
"Les noms d'années et d'éponymes dans les 'Archives de Mari," *Studia Mariana*, ed. A. Parrot. Leiden, 1950, 55, #6(p. 165, n.22); 57, #20(p. 175, n.111); 60, #32(p. 175, n.111)
"L'inscription de Foundation de Iaḫdun-Lim, roi de Mari," *Syria* 32 (1955), col III, ll 4-21(pp. 133-134); col III, ll 28-30(p. 165, n.18); col IV ll 1-2(p. 165, n.18)
"Adassum et *Kirḫum* dans des textes de Mari," *RA* 66 (1972), 117, Tx 826: 18-20(p. 124,

n.87); 118, Tx 2801: 14-19(p. <u>65</u>; p. 81, n.118); 32-36(p. 171, n.80)

"Le *madārum* dans les 'Archives royales de Mari'," *RAI* 18 (1972), 61, Tx A 2741: 9-14 (p. 173, n.98); A 3821: 11-13(p. 173, n.98)

Finet, A., "Une affaire de disette dans un district du royaume de Mari," *RA* 53 (1959), 59(p. 94; p. 121, n.59); 33-48(p. 172, n.84)

Jean, C. F. "Arišen dans les lettres de Mari," *Semitica* 1 (1948), 21 Tx 5990(p. 122, n.68); <u>10-14</u>(p. 96)

Thureau-Dangin, F., "Iaḫdun-Lim, roi de Ḫana," *RA* 33 (1936), col I, ll <u>15-20</u>(p. 134)

*Underlining indicates transliteration and translation of the text or a portion of the text appear on the designated pages.

BIBLIOGRAPHY

BOOKS

Adams, R. M. *Land Behind Baghdad.* Chicago, 1965.

Aharoni, Y. *The Land of the Bible, A Historical Geography.* Philadelphia, 1962.

Albright, W. F. *The Biblical Period from Abraham to Ezra.* New York, 1963.

________. *Yahweh and the Gods of Canaan.* Garden City, N.Y., 1969.

Ashkenazi, T. *Tribus semi-nomades de la Palestine de nord.* Paris, 1938.

Barth, F. *A Tribe of the Khamseh Confederacy: The Basseri Nomads of South Persia.* Oslo, 1961.

________. *Models of Social Organization.* Royal Anthropological Institute of Great Britain & Ireland, Occasional Papers 23, 1966.

________. *Ethnic Groups and Boundaries.* Boston, 1969.

Batto, B. F. *Studies on Women at Mari.* Baltimore, 1974.

Bausani, A. *The Persians from the Earliest Days to the Twentieth Century.* London, 1971.

Birot, M. (ed.) *Archives royales de Mari, IX: Textes administratifs de la salle 5.* Musée de Louvre, Department des Antiquités Orientales, Textes Cunéiformes, XXX. Paris, 1960.

_________. *Archives royales de Mari, IX: Textes administratifs de la salle 5 du palais.* Paris, 1960.

_________. *Archives royales de Mari, XII: Textes de la salle 5 du palais (2e partie).* Paris, 1964.

_________. *Archives royales de Mari, XIV: Lettres de Yaqim-Addu Gouverneur de Sagarātum.* Paris, 1974.

Bohannan, P. *Social Anthropology.* New York, 1963.

Bottéro, J. *Le problème des Ḫabiru à la 4e recontre assyriologique internationale.* Paris, 1954.

__________ and Finet, A. *Archives royales de Mari, XV: Répertoire analytique des tomes I à V.* Paris, 1954.

__________. (ed.) *Archives royales de Mari, VII: Textes administratifs de la salle 110.* Musée du Louvre, Department

des Antiquités Orientales, Textes Cunéiformes, XXVIII. Paris, 1956.

________. *Archives royales de Mari, VII: Textes économiques et administratifs.* Paris, 1957.

Boyer, G. (ed.) *Archives royales de Mari, VIII: Textes juridiques et administratifs.* Musée du Louvre, Department des Antiquités Orientales, Textes Cunéiformes, XXIX. Paris, 1957.

________. *Archives royales de Mari, VIII: Textes juridiques.* Paris, 1958.

Braidwood, R. J. and Howe, B. *Prehistoric Investigations in Iraqi Kurdistan.* Studies in Ancient Oriental Civilizations, 31. Chicago, 1960.

Braudel, F. *The Mediterranean and the Mediterranean World in the Age of Philip II,* Vol. 1. New York, 1972.

Brinkman, J. A. *A Political History of Post-Kassite Babylonia, 1158-722 B.C.* Analecta Orientalia, 43. Rome, 1968.

Buccellati, G. *The Amorites of the Ur III Period.* Naples, 1966.

________. *Cities and Nations of Ancient Syria.* Rome, 1967.

Burke, M. L. *Archives royales de Mari, XI: Textes administratifs de la salle 111 du palais.* Paris, 1963.

Butzer, K. W. *Environment and Archeology.* Chicago, 1971.

Charles, H. *Tribus moutonnières de moyen Euphrates.* Documents d'études orientales de l'institut Francais, VIII. Damascus, 1939.

Chelhood, J. *Introduction à la sociologie de l'Islam.* Paris, 1958.

Coon, C. S. *Caravan: The Story of the Middle East.* New York, 1958.

Dossin, G. (ed.) *Archives royales de Mari, I: Lettres.* Musée du Louvre, Department des Antiquités Orientales, Textes Cunéiformes, XXII. Paris, 1946.

________. *Archives royales de Mari, I: Correspondance de Šamši-Addu.* Paris, 1950.

________. (ed.) *Archives royales de Mari, IV: Lettres.* Musée du Louvre, Department des Antiquités Orientales, Textes Cunéiformes, XXV. Paris, 1951.

________. *Archives royales de Mari, IV: Correspondance du Šamši-Addu.* Paris, 1951.

________. (ed.) *Archives royales de Mari, V: Lettres.* Musée du Louvre, Department des Antiquités Orientales, Textes Cunéiformes, XXVI. Paris, 1951.

________. *Archives royales de Mari, V: Correspondance de Yasmaḫ-Addu.* Paris, 1952.

________, Bottéro, J., Birot, M., Burke, M. L., Kupper, J.-R., and Finet, A. *Archives royales de Mari, XIII: Textes divers.* Paris, 1964.

Driver, B. R. and Miles, J. C. *The Babylonian Laws,* Vol. 1. Oxford, 1960.

Dussaud, R. *La pénétration des Arabes en Syrie avant l'Islam.* Paris, 1955.

Dyson- Hudson, N. *Karimojong Politics.* Oxford, 1971.

Edzard, D. O. *Die "Zweite Zwischenzeit" Babyloniens.* Wiesbaden, 1957.

Forde, D. *Habitat, Economy, and Society.* New York, 1934.

Gelb, I. J. *Hurrians and Subarians.* Studies in Ancient Oriental Civilization, 22. Chicago, 1944.

Goldschmidt, W. *Comparative Functionalism: an Essay in Anthropological Theory.* Berkeley, Calif., 1966.

Haldar, A. *Who Were the Amorites?* Leiden, 1971.

Hole, F., Flannery, K. V., and Neely, J. A. *Prehistory and Human Ecology of the Deh Luran Plain.* Ann Arbor, 1969.

Huffmon, H. B. *Amorite Personal Names in the Mari Texts.* Baltimore, 1965.

Jean, C. F. (ed.) *Archives royales de Mari, II: Lettres.* Musée du Louvre, Department des Antiquités Orientales, Textes Cunéiformes, XXIII. Paris, 1948.

________. *Archives royales de Mari, II: Lettres diverses.* Paris, 1950.

Johnson, D. L. *The Nature of Nomadism.* Department of Geography Research Paper, 118. University of Chicago, 1969.

Klengel, H. *Geschichtes Syriens im 2. Jahrtausend v.u.Z., Teil 1-Nordsyien.* Berlin, 1965.

Kramer, S. N. *Sumerian Mythology.* New York, 1961.

Kupper, J.-R. (ed.) *Archives royales de Mari, III: Lettres.* Musée du Louvre, Department des Antiquités Orientales, Textes Cunéiformes, XXIV. Paris, 1948.

________. *Archives royales de Mari, III: Correspondance de Kibri-Dagan.* Paris, 1950.

________. (ed.) *Archives royales de Mari, VI: Lettres*. Musée du Louvre, Department des Antiquités Orientales, Textes Cunéiformes, XXVII. Paris, 1953.

________. *Archives royales de Mari, VI: Correspondance de Baḫdi-Lim*. Paris, 1954.

________. *Les nomades en Mésopotamie au temps des rois de Mari*. Paris, 1957.

Lambton, A. K. S. *Landlord and Peasant in Persia*. London, 1953

Larsen, M. T. *The Old Assyrian City State and its Colonies*. Copenhagen, 1976.

Leemans, W. F. *The Old Babylonian Merchant, His Business and His Social Position*. Leiden, 1950.

________. *Foreign Trade in the Old Babylonian Period*. Leiden, 1960.

London Meteorological Office. *Tables of Temperature, Relative Humidity, and Precipitation for the World*. London, 1966.

Luke, J. T. *Pastoralism and Politics in the Mari Period: a Re-examination of the Character and Political Significance of the Major West Semitic Tribal Groups on the Middle Euphrates, ca. 1828-1758 B.C.* University of Michigan Ph.D. dissertation, 1965.

Mair, L. *Primitive Government*. New York, 1964.

________. *Anthropology and Social Change*. London, 1969.

Marx, E. *Bedouin of the Negev*. Manchester, 1967.

Marzal, A. *The Organization of the Mari State*. University of Chicago, Ph.D. Dissertation, 1969.

Mellaart, J. *The Neolithic of the Near East*. New York, 1975.

Monteil, V. *Les tribus du Fars et la sédentarisation des nomades*. Paris, 1966.

Moscati, S. *The Semites in Ancient History*, Cardiff, 1959.

Musil, A. *The Manners and Customs of the Rwala Bedouin*. New York, 1928.

Noth, M. *Die Ursprünge des alten Israel im Lichte neur Quellen*. Köln and Opladen, 1961.

Oberling, P. *The Qashqā'i Nomads of Fars*. The Hague, 1970.

O'Callaghan, R. T. *Aram Naharaim*. Rome, 1948.

Oppenheim, M. P. von. *Die Beduinen*, I. Leipzig, 1939.

Orlin, L. L. *Assyrian Colonies in Cappadocia*. The Hague, 1970.

Parrot, A. *Mari: capitale fabuleuse.* Paris, 1974.

Pehrson, R. N. *The Social Organization of the Marri Baluch,* ed. F. Barth. Chicago, 1966.

Pritchard, J. B. *Ancient Near Eastern Texts Relating to the Old Testament.* (3rd edition with Supplement). Princeton, N.J., 1969.

Sasson, J. *Northernmost Syria: a Survey of its Institutions Before the Fall of Mari (ca. 1757 B.C.).* Brandeis University Ph.D. dissertation, 1966.

________. *The Military Establishment at Mari.* Rome, 1969.

Schmidt-Nielsen, K. *Desert Animals: Physiological Problems of Heat and Water.* Oxford, 1964.

Spooner, B. *The Cultural Ecology of Pastoral Nomads.* Addison-Wesley Module in Anthropology, 45. Philippines, 1973.

Sweet, L. E. *Tell Ṭoqaan: a Syrian Village.* Ann Arbor, 1960.

Thompson, T. L. *The Historicity of the Patriarchal Narratives.* BZAW 133. Berlin, 1974.

Tocci, F. M. *La Siria nell 'età di Mari.* Rome, 1960.

Van Seters, J. *Abraham in History and Tradition.* New Haven, Conn., 1975.

Weippert, M. *The Settlement of the Israelite Tribes in Palestine.* Naperville, Ill., 1971.

Wirth, E. *Syrien: eine Geographische Landeskunde.* Darmstadt, 1971.

Zeuner, F. E. *A History of Domesticated Animals.* New York, 1963.

ARTICLES

Adams, R. M., "Factors Influencing the Rise of Civilization in the Alluvium: Illustrated by Mesopotamia" in *City Invincible, a Symposium on Urbanization and Cultural Development in the Ancient Near East*, eds. C. H. Kraeling and R. M. Adams. Chicago, 1958, 24-34.

________, "Agriculture and Urban Life in Early Southwestern Iran," *Science* 136 (1962), 109-22.

________, "The Study of Ancient Mesopotamian Settlement Patterns and the Problem of Urban Origins," *Sumer* 25 (1969), 111-23.

Aharoni, Y., "Nothing Early and Nothing Late: Re-writing Israel's Conquest," *BA* 39, (1976), 55-76.

Ahmed, A. G. M., "Tribal and Sedentary Elites: A Bridge Between Two Communities" in *The Desert and the Sown: Nomads in the Wider Society*, ed. C. Nelson. Berkeley, Calif., 1973, 75-96.

Albright, W. F., "The Land of Damascus Between 1850 and 1750 B.C.," *BASOR* 83 (1941), 30-36.

________, "Abram the Hebrew, a New Archaeological Interpretation," *BASOR* 163 (1961), 36-54.

Amiran, D. H. K., "Effects of Climatic Change in an Arid Environment on Land Use Patterns" in *Changes of Climate*. UNESCO, Arid Zone Research, XX. Belgium, 1963, 439-42.

________, "Nomadic and Beduin Population in the Census Returns of Mandatory Palestine," *IEJ* 13 (1963), 247-52.

________, and Ben-Arieh, Y., "Sedentarization of Beduin in Israel," *IEJ* 13 (1963), 161-81.

Anbar, M., "La région au sud du district de Mari," *Israel Oriental Studies* 5 (1975), 1-17.

________, "Les *sakbû* et les *bazaḫātum* à Mari--une mise au point," *UF* 7 (1975), 592.

Asad, T., "The Beduin as a Military Force: Notes on Some Aspects of Power Relations Between Nomads and Sedentaries in Historical Perspective" in *The Desert and The Sown*, ed. C. Nelson, 1973, 61-73.

Askenazi, T., "La tribus arabe: ses elements," *Anthropos* 41-44 (1946-49), 657-72.

Awad, M., "Settlement of Nomadic and Semi-Nomadic Tribal Groups in the Middle East," *ILR* 79 (1959), 25-56.

________, "Living Conditions of Nomadic, Semi-Nomadic, and Settled Tribal Groups" in *Readings in Arab Middle Eastern Societies and Cultures*, ed. A. M. Lutfiyya, The Hague, 1970, 135-48.

Bacon, E. E., "Types of Pastoral Nomadism in Central and Southwest Asia," *SWJA* 10 (1954), 44-68.

Barth, F., "Ecologic Relationships of Ethnic Groups in Swat, North Pakistan," *AA* 58 (1956), 1079-89.

________, "Land Use Patterns of Migratory Tribes of South Persia," *Norsk Geografik Tidsskrit*, 17 (1960), 1-11.

________, "Nomadism in the Mountain and Plateau Areas of South West Asia" in *The Problems of the Arid Zone*. UNESCO, Arid Zone Research, XVIII. 1962, 341-55.

________, "Capital, Investment and the Social Structure of a Nomadic Group in South Persia" in *Capital, Saving and Credit in Peasant Societies*, eds. R. Firth and B. S. Yamey. London, 1963, 69-81.

________, "On the Study of Social Change," *AA* 69 (1967), 661-69.

________, "Pathan Identity and its Maintenance," in *Ethnic Groups and Boundaries*, ed. F. Barth. Boston, 1969, 117-34.

________, "A General Perspective on Nomad-Sedentary Relations in the Middle East" in *The Desert and the Sown*, ed. C. Nelson. Berkeley, Calif., 1973, 11-21.

Bates, D. G., "The Role of the State in Peasant-Nomad Mutualism," *AQ* 44 (1971), 109-31.

________, "Differential Access to Pasture in a Nomadic Society: The Yoruk of Southeastern Turkey" in *Perspectives on Nomadism*, eds. W. Irons and N. Dyson-Hudson. Leiden, 1972, 48-59.

Berger, R. and Protsch, R., "The Domestication of Plants and Animals in Europe and the Near East," *Or.* (1973), 214-27.

Berque, J., "Introduction to Nomads and Nomadism in the Arid Zone," *ISSJ* 11 (1959), 481-98.

Birot, M., "Textes économiques de Mari, III," *RA* 49 (1955), 15-31.

________, "Le sens de *NÍG.DU* dans les textes de Mari et de Chagar-Bazar," *RA* 52 (1958), 177-82.

________, "Les lettres de Iasîm-Sumu," *Syria* 41 (1964), 25-66.

________, "Simaḫlânê, roi de Kurda," *RA* 66 (1972), 131-39.

________, "Nouvelles épigraphiques au palais de Mari (salle 115)," *Syria* 50 (1973), 1-11.

Bökönyi, S., "Zoological Evidence for Seasonal or Permanent Occupation of Prehistoric Settlements" in *Man, Settlement, and Urbanism*, eds. P. J. Ucko, R. Tringham and G. W. Dimbleby. Herefordshire, Eng., 1972, 121-26.

Bottéro, J., "Lettres de la salle 110 du palais de Mari," *RA* 52 (1958), 163-76.

Braidwood, R. J. and Howe, B., "Southwestern Asia Beyond the Lands of the Mediterranean Littoral" in *Courses Toward Urban Life*, ed. R. J. Braidwood and G. R. Willey. Chicago, 1962, 132-46.

Braidwood, R. J., "Summary of Prehistoric Investigations in Kurdistan in Relation to Climate Change" in *Changes of Climate*. UNESCO, Arid Zone Research, XX. Belgium, 1963, 251-54.

Burke, M. L., "Lettres de Numušda-Naḫrari et de trois autres correspondants à Idiniatum," *Syria* 41 (1964), 67-103.

Butzer, K. W., "Physical Conditions in Eastern Europe, Western Asia, and Egypt before the Period of Agricultural and Urban Settlement," *CAH*², I/1. Cambridge, 1970, 35-69.

Cahen, C., "Quelques mots sur les hilaliens et le nomadisme," *JESHO* 11 (1968), 130-33.

Cohen, Y. A. "Adaptation and Evolution: an Introduction" in *Man in Adaptation: The Institutional Framework*, ed. Y. A. Cohen. Chicago, 1971, 1-22.

________, "Marriage and the Family" in *Man in Adaptation: The Institutional Framework*, ed. Y. A. Cohen. Chicago, 1971, 23-30.

Crown, A. D., "Climatic Change, Ecology, and Migration," *Australian Journal of Biblical Archaeology* 1/4 (1968-71), 3-22.

________, "Some Factors Relating to Settlement and Urbanization in Ancient Canaan in the Second and First Millenium B.C.," *Abr-Nahrain* 11 (1971), 22-41.

________, "Toward a Reconstruction of the Climate of Palestine 8000 B.C. - 0 B.C.," *JNES* 31 (1972), 312-30.

Delcor, M., "Quelques cas de survivances du vocabulaire nomade en Hebreu Biblique," *VT* 25 (1975), 307-22.

Dossin, G., "Signaux lumineux au pays de Mari, *RA* 35 (1938), 174-86.

________, "Les archives épistolaires du palais de Mari," *Syria* 19 (1938), 105-26.

________, "Les archives économiques du palais de Mari," *Syria* 20 (1939), 97-113.

________, "Benjaminites dans les textes de Mari," *Mélanges syriens offerts à M. René Dussaud, II*. Paris, 1939, 981-96.

________, "Iamḫad et Qatanum," *RA* 36 (1939), 46-54.

________, "Une révélation du dieu Dagan à Terga," *RA* 42 (1948), 125-34.

________, "Le noms d'années et d'éponymes dans les 'Archives de Mari'," *Studia Mariana*, ed. A. Parrot. Leiden, 1950, 51-61.

________, "Le royaume de Qatma au XVIIIe siècle avant notre ère d'apres les 'Archives royales de Mari'," *BARB* 5 (1954), 417-25.

________, "L'inscription de foundation de Yaḫdun-Lim, roi de Mari," *Syria* 32 (1955), 1-28.

________,"A propos du nom des Benjaminites dans les 'Archives royales de Mari'," *RA* 52 (1958), 60-62.

________, "L'ordalie à Mari," *Comptes rendus des séances de l'académie des inscriptions et belles-lettres, 1958*, 387-92.

________, "Les bedouins dans les textes de Mari" in *L'antica società beduina*, ed. F. Gabrieli. Rome, 1959, 35-61.

________, "Un projet de stèle de victoire de Zimri-Lim," *Syria* 48 (1971), 2-6.

________, "*Adaššum* et *Kirḫum* dans des textes de Mari," *RA* 66 (1972), 111-30.

________, "Le *madārum* dans les 'Archives royales de Mari'," *RAI* 18 (1972), 53-63.

Dostal, W., "The Evolution of Bedouin Life" in *L'antica società beduina*, ed. F. Gabrieli. Rome, 1959, 11-34.

Downs, J. F., "Domestication: an Examination of the Changing Social Relationships Between Man and Animals," *Kroeber Anthropological Society Papers* 22 (1960), 18-67.

Drew, I. M., Perkins, D., and Daly, P., "Prehistoric Domestication of Animals: Effects on Bone Structure," *Science* 171 (1971), 280-82.

Dyson-Hudson, N., "The Study of Nomads" in *Perspectives on Nomadism*, eds. W. Irons and N. Dyson-Hudson. Leiden, 1972, 2-27.

________, "Pastoralism: Self-Image and Behavioral Reality," in *Perspectives on Nomadism*, eds. W. Irons and N. Dyson-Hudson. Leiden, 1972, 30-47.

Easton, D., "Political Anthropology," *Biennial Review of Anthropology*. Stanford University, 1959, 237ff.

Ecsedy, I., "Tribe versus Empire, Tribe versus Society in the Period of the Turks," *Ethnographia* 86 (1975), 91-103.

Edzard, D. O., "Altbabylonisch *nawûm*," *ZA* 53 (1959), 168-73.

Ellis, M. de J., "Taxation in Ancient Mesopotamia: The History of the Term *miksu*," *JCS* 26 (1974), 211-50.

Engberg, R. M., "Tombs of the Early Second Millenium from Baghuz on the Middle Euphrates," *BASOR* 87 (1942), 17-23.

Evans, G., "An Old Babylonian Soldier: Notes on the Archive of Ubarrum," *JCS* 14 (1960), 34-42.

________, "A note upon *ARM* I 20:4'-15'," *RA* 56 (1962), 211-12.

________, "The Incidence of Labour-Service at Mari," *RA* 57 (1963), 65-78.

Falkner, M., "Studien zur Geographie des alten Mesopotamien," *AFO* 18 (1957), 1-37.

Fazel, G. R., "The Encapsulation of Nomadic Societies in Iran" in *The Desert and the Sown*, ed. C. Nelson. Berkeley, Calif., 1973, 129-42.

Finet, A., "L'expression *reš warḫim* dans les lettres de Mari," *Bi.Or.* 10 (1953), 85-88.

________, "Une affaire de disette dans un district du royaume du Mari," *RA* 53 (1959), 57-69.

________, "Iawi-ilâ, roi de Talḫayûm," *Syria* 41 (1964), 117-42.

________, "Le *ṣuḫārum* à Mari," *RAI* 18 (1972), 65-72.

Finkelstein, J. J., "The Genealogy of the Hammurapi Dynasty," *JCS* 20 (1966), 95-118.

________, "An Old Babylonian Herding Contract and Genesis 31: 38f.," *JOAS* 88 (1968), 30-36.

Fisher, L. R., "Abraham and His Priest-King," *JBL* 81 (1962), 264-70.

Flannery, K. V., "The Ecology of Early Food Production in Mesopotamia," *Science* 147 (1965), 1247-56.

________, "Origins and Ecological Effects of Early Domestication in Iran and the Near East" in *The Domestication of Plants and Animals*, eds. P. J. Ucko and G. W. Dimbleby. Chicago, 1969, 73-100.

Frick, F. S., "The Rechabites Reconsidered," *JBL* 90 (1971), 279-87.

Fronzaroli, P., "*su-ga-gu-um* Sceicco," *La Parola del passato* 14 (1959), 189-93.

________, "L'ordinamento gentilizio semitico e i testi di Mari," *Archivio Glottologico Italiano* 45 (1960), 43-45, 127-49.

Gelb, I. J., "The Early History of the West Semitic Peoples," *JCS* 15 (1961), 27-47.

________, "WA=aw, iw, uw in Cuneiform writing," *JNES* 20 (1961), 194-96.

________, "An Old Babylonian List of Amorites," *JAOS* 88 (1968), 39-46.

________, "Prisoners of War in Early Mesopotamia," *JNES* 32 (1973), 70-98.

Gellner, E., "Introduction: Approaches to Nomadism" in *The Desert and the Sown*, ed. C. Nelson. Berkeley, Calif., 1973, 1-9.

Gibson, J. C. L., "Life and Society at Mari and in Old Israel," *Transactions of the Glasgow University Oriental Society* 18 (1959-60), 15-29.

________, "Observations on Some Important Ethnic Terms in the Pentateuch," *JNES* 20 (1961), 217-38.

________, "Light from Mari on the Patriarchs," *JSS* 7 (1962), 44-62.

Gilbert, A. S., "Modern Nomads and Prehistoric Pastoralists: The Limits of Analogy," *JANES* 7 (1975), 53-71.

Goldschmidt, W., "Theory and Strategy in the Study of Cultural Adaptability," *AA* 67 (1965), 402-7.

________, "The Dynamic Adaptation of Sebei Law" in *Man in Adaptation: The Institutional Framework*, ed. Y. A. Cohen. Chicago, 1971, 119-27.

________, "Independence as an Element in Pastoral Social Systems," *AQ* 44 (1971), 132-42.

Gottwald, N. K., "Were the Early Israelites Pastoral Nomads?" in *Rhetorical Criticism: Essays in Honor of J. Muilenberg*, eds. J. Jackson and M. Kessler. Pittsburgh, 1974, 223-55.

________, "Domain Assumptions and Societal Models in the Study of Pre-Monarchic Israel," *SVT* 28 (1975), 89-100.

Gray, M. P. "The Habiru-Hebrew Problem in the Light of the Source Material Available at Present," *HUCA* 29 (1958), 135-202.

Grintz, J. M., "On the Original Home of the Semites," *JNES* 21 (1962), 186-206.

Hallo, W., "The Road to Emar," *JCS* 18 (1964), 57-88.

Harlan, J. R., "A Wild Wheat Harvest in Turkey," *Archaeology* 20 (1967), 197-201.

Helbaek, H., "Ecological Effects of Irrigation in Ancient Mesopotamia," *Iraq* 22 (1960), 186-96.

________, "Plant Collecting, Dry-Farming, and Irrigation Agriculture in Prehistoric Deh Luran" in *Prehistory and Human*

Ecology of the Deh Luran Plain, eds. T. Hole, K. V. Flannery, and J. A. Neeley. Ann Arbor, 1969, 383-426.

Held, M., "Philological Notes on the Mari Covenant Rituals," *BASOR* 200 (1970), 32-40.

Henniger, J., "La société bédouine ancienne" in *L'antica società beduina*, ed. F. Gabrieli. Rome, 1959, 69-93.

Herre, W., "The Science and History of Domestic Animals" in *Science in Archaeology*, eds. D. Brothwell and E. Higgs. London, 1969, 257-72.

Huffmon, H. B., "Prophecy in the Mari Letters," *BA* 31 (1968), 101-24.

Irons, W. G., "Livestock Raiding Among Pastoralists: an Adaptive Interpretation," *Papers of the Michigan Academy of Science, Arts, and Letters* 50 (1965), 393-414.

________, "Variation in Political Stratification Among the Yomut Turkmen," *AQ* 44 (1971), 143-56.

________, "Variation in Economic Organization: a Comparison of the Pastoral Yomut and the Basseri" in *Perspectives on Nomadism*, eds. W. G. Irons and N. Dyson-Hudson. Leiden, 1972, 88-104.

Jacobsen, T., "The Reign of Ibbī-Suen," *JCS* 7 (1953), 36-47.

________, "Early Political Development in Mesopotamia," *ZA* 52 (1957), 91-140.

________, and Adams, R. M., "Salt and Silt in Ancient Mesopotamian Agriculture," *Science* 128 (1958), 1251-58.

Jean, C. F., "Excerpta de la correspondance de Mari, IV," *RA* 36 (1939), 62-69.

________, "Lettres de Mari: transcription et traduction," *JCS* 1 (1947), 149-63.

________, "Arišen dans les lettres de Mari," *Semitica* 1 (1948), 17-24.

________, "Lettres de Mari, IV, transcrites et tradiutes," *RA* 42 (1948), 53-78.

________, L'armée du royaume de Mari," *RA* 42 (1948), 135-48.

Kirkbride, A. S., "Changes in Tribal Life in Trans-Jordan," *Man* 23 (1945), 40-41.

Klengel, H., "Benjaminiten und Hanäer," *WZHB* 8 (1958/59), 211-27.

________, "Halbnomaden am mittleren Euphrat," *Das Altertum* 5 (1959), 195-205.

________, "Zu den *šībūtum* in altbabylonischer Zeit," *Or.* 29 (1960), 357-75.

________, "Zu einigen Problemen des altvorderasiatischen Nomadentums," *Ar.Or.* 30 (1962), 585-96.

Klíma, J., "La vie sociale et économique à Mari," *La civilisation de Mari. RAI* 15. Paris, 1967, 39-50.

Krader, L., "The Ecology of Nomadic Pastoralism," *ISSJ* 11 (1959), 499-510.

Kupper, J.-R., "Une gouvernement provincial dans le royaume de Mari," *RA* 41 (1947), 149-83.

________, "Baḫdi-Lim, prefet du palais de Mari," *BARB* 40 (1954), 572-87.

________, "Le rôle des nomades dans l'histoire de la Mésopotamie ancienne," *JESHO* 2 (1959), 113-27.

________, "Sutéens et Ḫapiru," *RA* 55 (1961), 197-200.

________, "Correspondance de Kibri-Dagan," *Syria* 41 (1964), 105-16.

________, "L'opinion publique à Mari," *RA* 58 (1964), 79-82.

________, "Northern Mesopotamia and Syria," *CAH*[2], Vol.II/1. Cambridge, 1973, 1-41.

________, "L'inscription du 'Disque' de Yaḫdun-Lim," *Kramer Anniversary Volume. AOAT* 25. Germany, 1976, 299-304.

Laessøe, J., "IM 62100: A Letter from Tell Shemshara," *Studies in Honor of Benno Landsberger on his 75th Birthday. AS* 16. Chicago, 1965, 189-96.

Lambert, M., "L'infiltration nomade dans l'empire d'Ur III," *RA* 54 (1960), 44.

Landsberger, B., "Remarks on the Archive of the Soldier Ubarum," *JCS* 9 (1955), 121-32.

Leemans, W. F., "The Contribution of the Nomads to the Babylonian Population," *JESHO* 1 (1957-58), 138-45.

________, "Old Babylonian Letters and Economic History," *JESHO* 11 (1968), 171-226.

Lees, S. H. and Bates, D. G., "The Origins of Specialized Nomadic Pastoralism: a Systematic Model," *American Antiquity* 39 (1974), 187-93.

Leshnik, L. S., "Pastoral Nomadism in the Archaeology of India and Pakistan," *World Archaeology* 4 (1972), 150-66.

Levine, R. A., "The Internalization of Political Values in Stateless Societies" in *Man in Adaptation: The Institutional Framework*, ed. Y. A. Cohen. Chicago, 1971, 288-98.

Lewy, H., "The Historical Background of the Correspondence of Baḫdi-Lim," *Or.* 25 (1956), 324-52.

________, "Šubat-Šamaš and Tuttul," *Or.* 27 (1958), 1-18.

Lewy, J., "Old Assyrian Caravan Roads in the Valley of the Habur and the Euphrates and in Northern Syria," *Or.* 21 (1952), 293-306, 393-425.

________, "Studies in Historic Geography of the Ancient Near East," *Or.* 21 (1952), 1-12, 266-92, 394-495.

________, " Amurritica," *HUCA* 32 (1961), 31-74.

Liverani, M., "The Amorites" in *Peoples of Old Testament Times*, ed. D. J. Wiseman. Oxford, 1973, 100-33.

Luke, J. T., "Observations on *ARMT* XIII 39," *JCS* 24 (1971), 20-23.

MacDonald, J., "The Identification of *Bazaḫātu* in the Mari Letters," *RA* 69 (1975), 137-45.

________, "The Role and Status of the *Ṣuḫārū* in the Mari Correspondence," *JAOS* 96 (1976), 57-68.

Mahhouk, A., "Recent Agricultural Development and Bedouin Settlement in Syria," *MEJ* 10 (1956), 167-76.

Malamat, A., "Mari and the Bible," *JAOS* 82 (1962), 143-50.

________, "Campaigns to the Mediterranean by Yaḫdunlim and other Early Mesopotamian Rulers," *Studies Landsberger*. *AS* 16. Chicago, 1965.

________, "Aspects of Tribal Societies in Mari and Israel," *La civilization de Mari*. *RAI* 15. Paris, 1967, 129-38.

________, "King Lists of the Old Babylonian Period and Biblical Genealogies," *JAOS* 88 (1968), 163-73.

Mallowan, M., "Development of Cities," *CAH*[2], Vol.I/1 Cambridge, 1971, 325-462.

Marzal, A., "The Provincial Governor at Mari: His Title and Appointment," *JNES* 30 (1971), 186-217.

________, "Two Officials Assisting the Provincial Governor at Mari," *Or.* 41 (1972), 359-77.

Matouš, L., "Einige Bemerkungen zum Beduinenproblem in alten Mesopotamien," *Ar.Or.* 26 (1958), 631-35.

Matthews, V. H. and Young D. W., "The *raison d'être* of the *sugāgum* at Mari," *Or.* 46 (1977), 122-26.

Mellaart, J., "The Earliest Settlements in Western Asia," *CAH*[2], Vol.I/1 Cambridge, 1971, 248-303.

Mendenhall, G. E., "Puppy and Lettuce in Northwest Semitic Covenant Making," *BASOR* 133 (1954), 26-30.

________, "The Census Lists of Numbers 1 and 26," *JBL* 77 (1957), 52-66.

________, "The Hebrew Conquest of Palestine," *BA* 25 (1962), 66-86.

________, "Social Organization in Early Israel" in *The Mighty Acts of God*, eds. F. M. Cross, W. E. Lemke, and P. M. Miller, Jr. New York, 1976, 132-51.

________, "Migration Theories vs. Culture Changes as an Explanation for Early Israel," *SBL Seminar Papers*. Missoula, Montana, 1976, 135-43.

Mitchell, W. A., "Movement and Pastoral Nomadism: a Tentative Model," *Rocky Mountain Social Science Journal* 8 (1971), 63-72.

Mohammed, A., "The Nomadic and the Sedentary: Polar Complementaries--Not Polar Opposites" in *The Desert and the Sown*, ed. C. Nelson. Berkeley, Calif., 1973, 97-112.

Moran, W. L., "Mari Notes on the Execration Texts," *Or*. 26 (1957), 339-45.

Moscati, S., "The 'Aramaean Aḫlamū'," *JSS* 4 (1959), 303-7.

Munn-Rankin, J. M., "Diplomacy in Western Asia in the Early Second Millennium B.C.," *Iraq* 18 (1956), 68-110.

Muntingh, L. M., "Amorite Married and Family Life According to the Mari Texts," *Journal of Northwest Semitic Languages* 3 (1974), 50-70.

Nakata, I., "Annu in the Mari Texts: a God or Goddess?" *JANES* 5 (1973), 299-307.

Noth, M., "Remarks on the Sixth Volume of the Mari Texts," *JSS* 1 (1956), 322-33.

Oates, J., "Prehistoric Settlement Patterns in Mesopotamia" in *Man, Settlement and Urbanism*, eds. P. J. Ucko, R. Tringham, and G. W. Dimbleby. Herefordshire, Eng., 1972, 121-26.

________, "The Background and Development of Early Farming Communities in Mesopotamia and the Zagros," *PPS* 39 (1973), 147-81.

Oppenheim, A. L. and Hartman, L. F., "The Domestic Animals of Ancient Mesopotamia According to the XIIIth Tablet of the Series *ḪAR.ra=ḫubullû*," *JNES* 4 (1945), 152-75.

Oppenheim, A. L., "A Bird's-Eye View of Mesopotamian Economic History" in *Trade and Market in the Early Empires*, eds. K. Polanyi, C. M. Arensberg, and H. W. Pearson. Glencoe, Ill., 1957, 27-37.

Pastner, S. L., "Camels, Sheep, and Nomad Social Organization: a Comment on Rubel's Model," *Man* 6 (1971), 285-88.

________, "Ideological Aspects of Nomad-Sedentary Contact: a Case from Southern Baluchistan," *AQ* 44 (1971), 173-84.

Patai, R., "Nomadism: Middle Eastern and Central Asian," *SWJA* (1951), 401-14.

________, "The Middle East as a Culture Area," *MEJ* 6 (1952), 1-21.

Perkins, D., "The Beginnings of Animal Domestication in the Near East," *AJA* 77 (1973), 279-82.

Perrot, J., "Palestine-Syria-Cilicia" in *Courses Toward Urban Life*, eds. R. J. Braidwood and G. R. Willey. Chicago, 1962, 147-64.

Polanyi, K., "Marketless Trading in Hammurabi's Time" in *Trade and Market in the Early Empires*, eds. K. Polanyi, C. M. Arensberg, and H. W. Pearson. Glencoe, Ill., 1957, 12-26.

Posener, G., Bottéro, J., and Kenyon, K. M., "Syria and Palestine c. 2160-1780 B.C.," *CAH*^{2}, Vol.I/2. Cambridge, 1971, 532-94.

Postgate, J. N., "Some Old Babylonian Shepherds and Their Flocks (with a contribution by S. Payne)," *JSS* 20 (1975), 1-21.

Reed, C. A., "A Review of the Archeological Evidence on Animal Domestication in the Prehistoric Near East" in *Prehistoric Investigations in Iraqi Kurdistan*, eds. R. J. Braidwood and B. Howe. Chicago, 1960, 119-45.

________, "The Pattern of Animal Domestication in the Prehistoric Near East" in *The Domestication of Plants and Animals*, eds. P. J. Ucko and G. W. Dimbleby. Chicago, 1969, 361-80.

Rochefort, R., "Les effets du milieu sur les communautés humaines des régions arides; adaptation de ces communautés aux conditions locales du milieu" in *Human and Animal Ecology*. UNESCO, Arid Zone Research, VIII. Paris, 1957, 11-42.

Römer, W. *Fraunenbriefe über Religion, Politik, und Privatleben in Mari. AOAT* 12, 1971.

Rowley, H. H., "Recent Discovery and the Patriarchal Age," *BJRL* 32 (1949-50), 44-79.

Rowton, M. B., "The Topological Factor in the Ḫapiru Problem," *Studies Landsberger. AS* 16. Chicago, 1967, 375-87.

________, "The Physical Environment and the Problem of the Nomads" in *La Civilisation de Mari. RAI* 15. Paris, 1967, 109-22.

________, "The Woodlands of Ancient Western Asia," *JNES* 26 (1967), 261-77.

________, "The Role of the Watercourses in the Growth of Mesopotamian Civilization" in *lišan mithurti: Festschrift Wolfram F. von Soden*. *AOAT* 1. Berlin, 1969, 307-16.

________, "The Abu Amurrim," *Iraq* 31 (1969), 68-73.

________, "Urban Autonomy in the Nomadic Environment," *JNES* 32 (1973), 201-15.

________, "Autonomy and Nomadism in Western Asia," *Or.* 42 (1973), 247-58.

________, "Enclosed Nomadism," *JESHO* 17 (1974), 1-30.

________, "Dimorphic Structure and the Problem of the 'Apirû-'Ibrîm," *JNES* 35 (1976), 13-20.

________, "Dimorphic Structure and Topology," *OA* 15 (1976), 17-31.

________, "Dimorphic Structure and the Tribal Elite," *Studia Instituti Anthropos* 28 (1976), 219-57.

________, "Dimorphic Structure and the Parasocial Element," *JNES* 36 (1977), 181-98.

Rubel, P. G., "Herd Composition and Social Structure: On Building Models of Nomadic Pastoral Societies," *Man* 4 (1969), 268-73.

Ryder, M. L., "Changes in the Fleece of Sheep Following Domestication (with a note on the coat of cattle)" in *The Domestication of Plants and Animals*, eds. P. J. Ucko and G. W. Dimbleby. London, 1969, 495-521.

Salzman, P.C., "Political Organization Among Nomadic Peoples," *PAPS* 111 (1967), 115-31.

________, "Introduction to Comparative Studies of Nomadism and Pastoralism," *AQ* 44 (1971), 104-8.

________, "Movement and Resource Extraction Among Pastoral Nomads: The Case of the Shah Nawazi Baluch," *AQ* 44 (1971), 185-97.

________, "Multi-Resource Nomadism in Iranian Baluchistan" in *Perspectives on Nomadism*, eds. W. G. Irons and N. Dyson-Hudson. Leiden, 1972, 60-68.

Sasson, J., "Mari Notes," *RA* 65 (1971), 172.

________, "Biographical Notices on Some Royal Ladies from Mari," *JCS* 25 (1973), 59-78.

________, "The *ENGAR/ikkarum* at Mari," *Kramer Anniversary Volume*. *AOAT* 25. Germany, 1976, 401-10.

Smith, P. E. L., "Land-Use, Settlement Patterns, and Subsistence Agriculture: a Demographic Perspective" in *Man, Settlement, and Urbanism*, eds. P. J. Ucko, R. Tringham, and G. W. Dimbleby. Herefordshire, Eng., 1972, 121-26.

________, and Young, T. C., Jr., "The Evolution of Early Agriculture and Culture in Greater Mesopotamia: A Trial Model" in *Population Growth: Anthropologic Implications*, ed. B. Spooner. Cambridge, Mass., 1972, 1-59.

Smith, S., "Yarim-Lim of Yamḫad," *RSO* 32 (1957), 155-84.

Speiser, E. A., "The *muškēnûm*," *Or.* 27 (1958), 19-28.

________, "Census and Ritual Expiation in Mari and Israel," *BASOR* 149 (1958), 17-25.

________, "'People' and 'Nation' of Israel," *JBL* 79 (1960), 157-63.

________, "Background and Function of the Biblical *nāśīʾ*," *CBQ* 25 (1963), 111-17.

________, "Amorites and Canaanites" in *At the Dawn of Civilization: The World History of the Jewish People, I*, ed., E. A. Speiser. New Brunswick, N.J., 1964, 162-69.

________, "The Patriarchs and Their Social Background" in *Patriarchs: The World History of the Jewish People, II*, ed. B. Mazar. New Brunswick, N.J., 1970, 160-68.

Spooner, B., "Towards a Generative Model of Nomadism," *AQ* 44 (1971), 198-210.

________, "The Status of Nomadism as a Cultural Phenomenon in the Middle East" in *Perspectives on Nomadism*, eds. W. G. Irons and N. Dyson-Hudson. Leiden, 1972, 122-31.

Stauffer, T. R., "The Economics of Nomadism in Iran," *MEJ* 19 (1965), 284-302.

Stenning, D. J., "Transhumance, Migratory Drift, Migration: Patterns of Pastoral Fulani Nomadism," *JRAI* 87 (1958), 57-74.

Sweet, L. E., "Camel Pastoralism in North Arabia and the Minimal Camping Unit" in *Man, Culture, and Animals*, eds. A. Leeds and A. P. Vayda. Washington, D.C., 1965, 129-52.

Swidler, N., "The Development of the Kalat Khanate" in *Perspectives on Nomadism*, eds. W. G. Irons and N. Dyson-Hudson. Leiden, 1972, 115-21.

Swidler, W. W., "Some Demographic Factors Regulating the Formation of Flocks and Camps Among the Brahui of Baluchistan" in *Perspectives on Nomadism*, eds. W. G. Irons and N. Dyson-Hudson. Leiden, 1972, 69-75.

________, "Adaptive Processes Regulating Nomad-Sedentary Interaction in the Middle East" in *The Desert and the Sown*, ed. C. Nelson. Berkeley, Calif., 1973, 23-41.

Tadmor, H., "Historical Implications of the Correct Rendering of Akkadian *dâku*," *JNES* 17 (1958), 129-41.

Thureau-Dangin, F., "Iaḫdun-Lim, roi de Ḫana," *RA* 33 (1936), 49-54.

Vaux, R. de, "Les patriarches hebreux et l'histoire," *RB* 72 (1965), 5-28.

Wilcke, C. von, "Zur Geschichte der Amurriter in der Ur-III Zeit," *WO* 5 (1969-70), 1-31.

Wilson, H. C., "An Inquiry into the Nature of Plains Indian Cultural Development," *AA* 65 (1963), 355-69.

Whyte, R. O., "Evolution of Land Use in South-Western Asia" in *A History of Land Use in Arid Regions*. UNESCO, Arid Zone Research XVII, ed. L. D. Stamp. Paris, 1961, 57-118.

Wright, H. E., "Climate and Prehistoric Man in the Eastern Mediterranean" in *Prehistoric Investigations in Iraqi Kurdistan*, eds. R. J. Braidwood and B. Howe. Chicago, 1960, 71-97.

Yeivin, S., "The Age of the Patriarchs," *RSO* 38 (1963), 277-301.

Young, T. C., Jr., "Population Densities and Early Mesopotamian Urbanism" in *Man, Settlement, and Urbanism*, eds. P. J. Ucko, R. Tringham, and G. W. Dimbleby. Herefordshire, Eng., 1972, 827-42.

REVIEWS

Aro, J., "Review: G. Boyer. *Archives royales de Mari, VIII: Textes juridiques et administratifs,*" *OLZ* 55 (1960), 260-62.

Falkenstein, A., "Review: *Archives royales de Mari,* I, II, III," *Bi.Or.* 11 (1954), 112-17.

________, "Review: *Archives royales de Mari,* IV, V, VI," *Bi.Or.* 13 (1956), 26-32.

________, "Review: *Archives royales de Mari,* VII, VIII," *Bi.Or.* 17 (1960), 175-79.

________, "Review: *Archives royales de Mari,* IX," *Bi.Or.* 20 (1963), 165-67.

Garelli, P., "Review: J.-R. Kupper. *Les nomades en Mésopotamie au temps des rois de Mari,*" *RA* 52 (1958), 39-42.

Gelb, I. J., "The Early History of the West Semitic Peoples," *JCS* 15 (1961), 27-47.

Goetze, A., "Review: J.-R. Kupper. *Les nomades en Mésopotamie au temps des rois de Mari,*" *JSS* 4 (1959), 142-47.

Hirsch, H., "Review: M. Birot. *Archives royales de Mari,IX,*" *ZA* 56 (1964), 282-84.

Leemans, W. F., "The Contribution of the Nomads to the Babylonian Population," *JESHO* 1 (1957-58), 138-45.

________, "Old Babylonian Letters and Economic History," *JESHO* 11 (1968), 171-226.

Moran, W. L., "Review: M. Weippert. *Die Landnahme der israelitischen Stämme in der neueren wissenschaftlichen Diskussion,*" *CBQ* 30 (1968), 644-45.

Noth, M., "Remarks on the Sixth Volume of the Mari Texts," *JSS* 1 (1956), 322-33.

Oppenheim, A. L., "The Archives of the Palace of Mari, (A Review of *ARM* I, II, III)," *JNES* 11 (1952), 129-39.

________, "The Archives of the Palace of Mari, II," *JNES* 13 (1954), 141-48.

Pintore, F., "Review: J. Sasson. *The Military Establishment at Mari,*" *OA* 8 (1969), 254-55.

Saggs, H. W. F., "Review: J. Bottéro. *ARMT* VII and G. Boyer. *ARM* VIII," *JSS* 5 (1960), 411-17.

Soden, W. F. von, "Zu den politschen Korrespondenzen des Archives von Mari," *Or.* 21 (1952), 75-86.

________, "Neue Bande der *Archives royales de Mari,*" *Or.* 22 (1953), 193-209.

________, "Review: *Archives royales de Mari,* VI, XV, VIII," *Or.* 28 (1959), 314-17.

Wiseman, D. J., "Review: G. Buccellati. *The Amorites of the Ur III Period,*" *JSS* 16 (1971), 86-88.

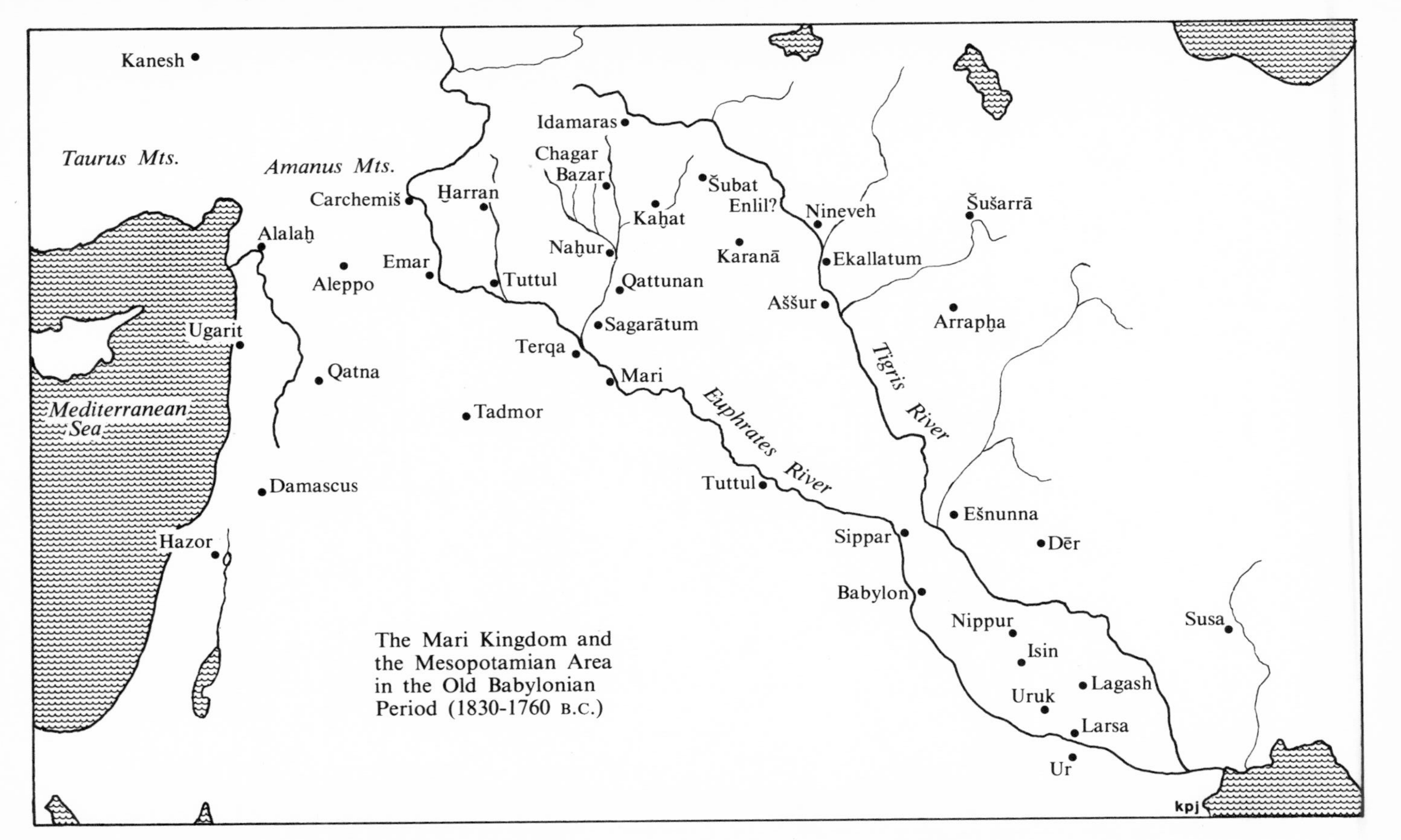

The Mari Kingdom and the Mesopotamian Area in the Old Babylonian Period (1830-1760 B.C.)

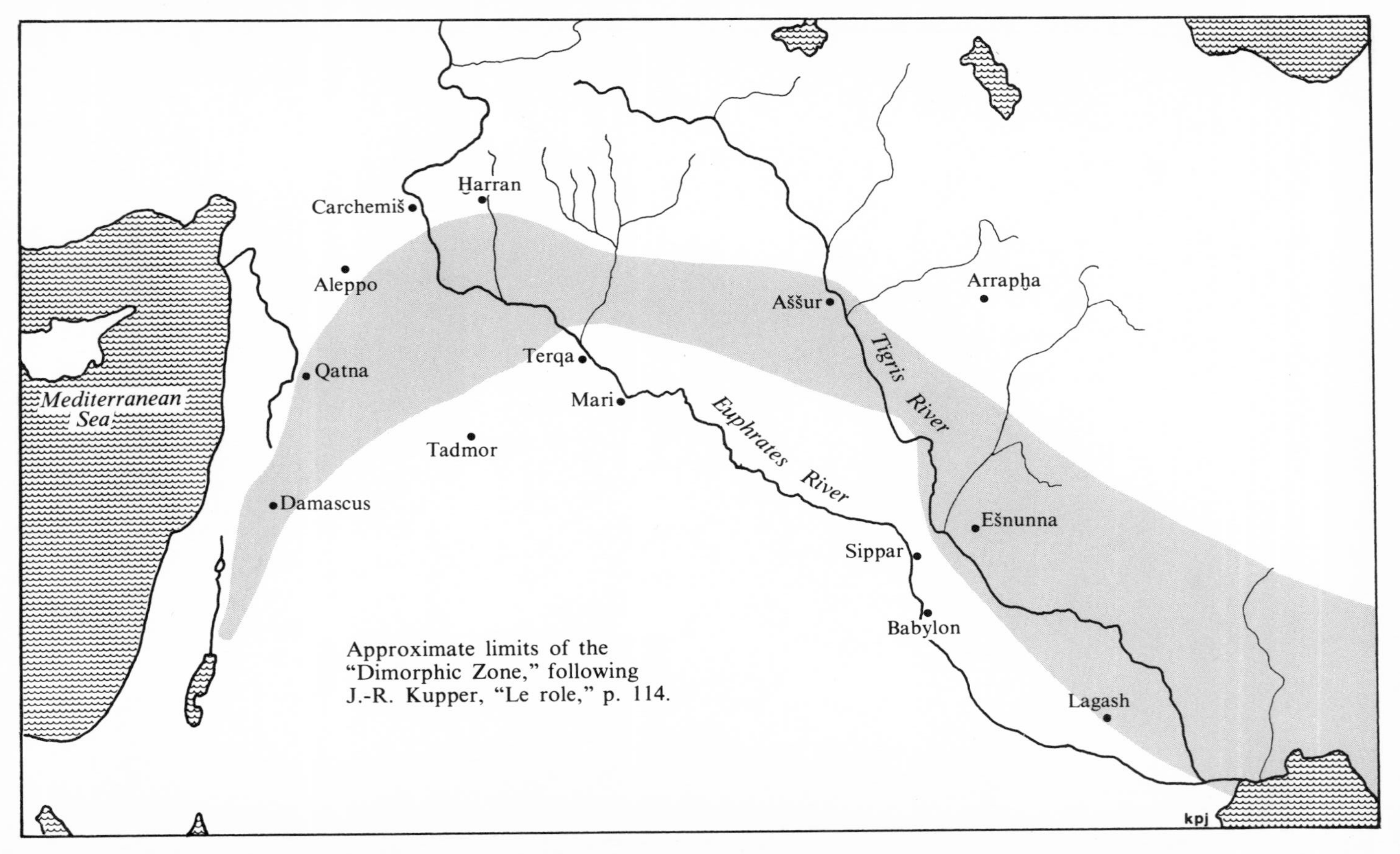

Approximate limits of the "Dimorphic Zone," following J.-R. Kupper, "Le role," p. 114.

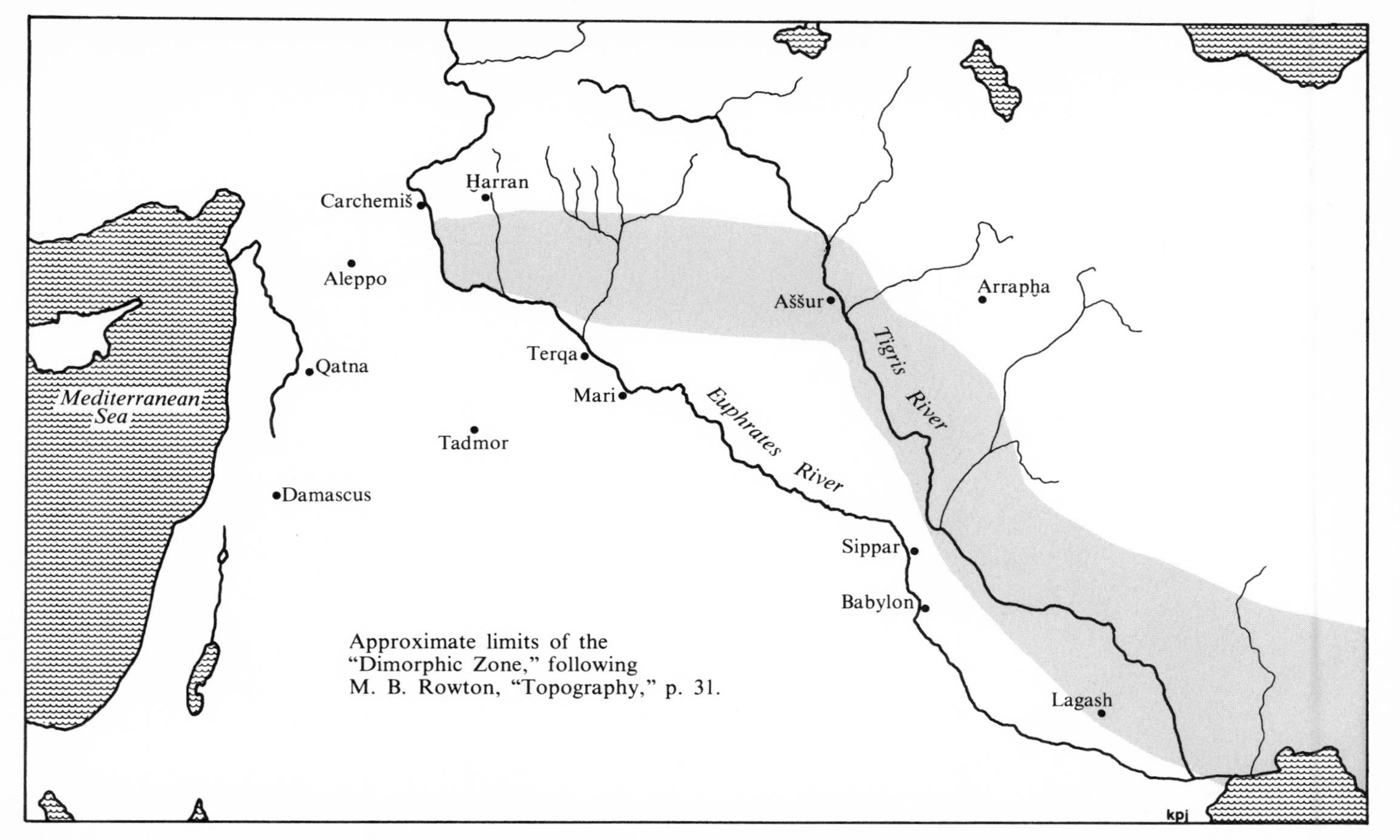

Approximate limits of the "Dimorphic Zone," following M. B. Rowton, "Topography," p. 31.